THINKING AHEAD

Pirelli: 150 Years of Industry, Innovation and Culture

edited by Fondazione Pirelli

FONDAZIONE PIRELLI

Marsilio

pirellibuildsthefuture

Do not rest on steps already taken, [...]
wander along other paths, set out again
walking to search again.

Bruce Chatwin

The restlessness to research,
the sting of doubt, the wish
for dialogue, the critical spirit, measure
in judging, the philological scruple,
the sense of the complexity of things.

Norberto Bobbio

CONTENTS

P.006   Marco Tronchetti Provera
Choosing Innovation

P.008   Maria Cristina Messa
**Knowledge
Is Progress**

P.012   Ferruccio Resta
**Competitive
Technologies**

P.016   Guido Saracco
**The Research
Community**

P.020   Antonio Calabrò
**The Clear Night
of Science**

VISIONS

P.034   Ian McEwan
Pay Attention

P.039   Sir Geoff Mulgan
**Digital Nomads
of New Works**

P.045   David Weinberger
Technology's Future

IDENTITY

P.052   Ernesto Ferrero
Portrait of a Pioneer

P.067   Giuseppe Lupo
**The Industrial Elegance
of Rubber**

P.080   *The Origins of a Long History
of Innovation*

P.091   Monica Maggioni
**Restarting
in the Aftermath
of the World Wars**

P.110   *New Challenges
and Major Opportunities*

P.115   Claudio Colombo
**The Strain of
Manufacturing Growth**

P.128   *Transformations of the Country
from after the Second World War
to the 1980s*

P.139   Bruno Arpaia
**Changing Pace between
Power and Control**

P.154   *Hi-Tech Lab Challenges and
Development of New Products*

P.156   Maurizio Boiocchi
Felicitous Patents

P.162   Enrico Albizzati
**The Fascination
of Photonics**

P.167   Pierangelo Misani
**Digital Technologies
for Development**

P.176   *The 'Beautiful Factory'
Where Music and Work Mingle*

P.178   Renzo Piano
A Human–Scale Project

P.186   Salvatore Accardo
**Production Rhythm
for String Orchestra**

TRANSFORMATIONS

P.194 Juan Carlos De Martin
**The Human Governance
of Machines**

P.201 Ermete Realacci
Father Enzo Fortunato
**Corporate Values
for Sustainability**

P.207 Paola Dubini
**Industrial Sites
as Cultural Heritage**

P.278 Fondazione Pirelli
**Showcasing
the Work, between
Memory and Future**

P.282 **Illustrated Chronology
1872–2022**

P.298 Authors' Biographies

P.304 Bibliography

P.306 Index of Names

RESEARCH

P.224 Carlo Furgeri Gilbert
**The Amazing Face
of Raw Materials
and High–Tech
Simulators**

Choosing Innovation

A company is a living and growing being, and over time has to steer a course towards innovation with the understanding of playing an active role in the process of change in the widest meaning of the term. This involves taking responsibility for its products and production processes, for its corporate finances in relation to the real economy, and for its services and goods. Organisational issues, industrial relations, corporate governance, marketing strategies and communication must also be taken into account. Thus, the protagonists of this innovation are the people who are part of the company as a community and naturally, also its *stakeholders*. A thought beyond the customary schemes, like navigating the high seas—the most exciting voyage possible—of economic and social transformation. Leverage is made on fundamental values to create further economic value while following the synergies that are developed between productivity, competitiveness, and environmental and social sustainability.

Over the course of its history, Pirelli has always known how to connect memory to innovation. Its story spans three centuries—the 1800s of the Second Industrial Revolution, the 1900s with its crises and economic boom centred on manufacturing and mass consumption, and then the controversial 2000s with its radical digital technologies—and always inspired by the powerful idea that growth is based in robust roots seen in the quality of products offered to the market and in advanced industrial processes. Furthermore, quality is attained only if far-sightedness and decisive support is given to scientific research and technology, to people and the environment, and in improving the workplace in the sense of liveability and safety.

In short, the history of Pirelli is founded on the acknowledgement of an open and inclusive corporate culture that can create genuine synergies between the humanities and scientific field.

There are many possible examples such as the research conducted by Giulio Natta in the Pirelli laboratories prior to being awarded the Nobel Prize in 1963 for Chemistry, the collaboration with great writers for the *Rivista Pirelli* and today's in-house magazine *World*, the company's financial reports, the projects by the Fondazione Pirelli, and the close relationships with Italian and international universities for the development of ever-more advanced products and processes. We must also consider the attention given towards aesthetics seen in the photography of the Pirelli Calendar, the contribution of contemporary artists in the HangarBicocca, our commitment to the design of the ideal working space by renowned architects such as Vittorio Gregotti, Renzo Piano, and Gio Ponti, and the customary attention paid towards corporate welfare.

For us, all this has a very specific definition: 'Industrial Humanism'.

We have always been guided by a fundamental idea which, in the last years of the 1900s took form in an advertising slogan that rapidly proved to be a great success: 'Power is nothing without control'. The immediate reference was the performance of a new series of tyres, but the real significance was much more profound.

Indeed, our corporate culture is made by the awareness of having to manage the fine blend between resourcefulness and safety, experimentation and social responsibility, extreme speed and governability of on-going processes, the pleasure of technological and sporting challenges and a sense of social relations. Indeed, the individual's desire for victory or success is inextricably bound to team effort, while economic growth to our customary care and attention towards the community. These are not simple relations in the dynamic and sometimes contradictory unfolding of history, but they must be in some way identified. They are also very topical at a time like the present, when environmental and social crises, pandemics and dramatic shifts in geopolitical equilibrium and economic relations are deeply wounding Europe and aggravating its

by

Marco Tronchetti Provera

-

**EXECUTIVE VICE CHAIRMAN,
CHIEF EXECUTIVE OFFICER OF PIRELLI AND
CHAIRMAN OF FONDAZIONE PIRELLI**

fragility and uncertainty. From this point of view, we need to endure in searching for a new balance, not only with a profound passion for the evolution of technology, but also with an ethical choice based on the construction of better relations among political and economic cultures in the various areas of the world, strengthening of dialogue albeit in times of burning conflicts and sharp contradictions. The positive relationship between 'power' and 'control' can be the cornerstone for a healthier social capital to be invested in a more sustainable environmental and social development.

Through the contributions of leading figures from the worlds of science, research, history, and literature, these pages will primarily give a contemporary vision of many aspects of industry such as technologies, machinery, productive and organisational assets, materials, and human skills. Indeed, our factories are places in which science and knowledge are given much space and we have an open and responsible approach towards change and an awareness of the opportunities as well as the economic and above all human costs that all this entails.

In the various volumes curated and published by the Fondazione Pirelli over the years, we addressed issues of work, sport, communication and the relationship between artistic creativity and manufacturing. Now our focus is on the long voyage between the birth of a company, its current status, and the future that we are building today.

Innovation, conceived as an identifying mark, is already evident in Giovanni Battista Pirelli's vision that pushed him—at twenty-three years of age and after graduating from Politecnico di Milano—to travel to the main European industrialised nations and find his passion in a hitherto unknown field in Italy: the world of rubber.

The company originated from that choice to be first off the starting blocks with an original and entrepreneurial approach in a new sector in which everything had to be learnt, invented, and experimented. It all started with a small factory in Via Ponte Seveso where French technology was used initially but soon new in-house processes were developed and adopted. It was a short and rapid progression to start producing belts, valves, tubes, sheathed—and later waterproof—cables, swimming caps, and from the start of the 1900s, tyres. Everything made from rubber.

From 1907 the Paris-Peking motor race (won by Itala with Pirelli tyres with 20 days advantage over the nearest competitors) opened a new season initially with competitive automobile races, following racing events for motorbikes and then bicycles. Prototypes were experimented and tested on the road and the results from these events were used to develop new technologies. Indeed, innovation involved constructing and testing in extreme competitive conditions and then applying these results to products destined for the general market. The racing track was our vast, open-air laboratory and it is still like this today as we keep pace with the frenetic evolution of science and technology, of consumption and customs.

History tells the tale of factories expanding throughout the world, of cables to transmit energy and telecommunications signals, of tyres with ever-superior performance, and in the last few years of the 1900s, of the extraordinary advances made in the photonics sector.

In our factories, investment is made on robots and innovative machinery for mixing, made possible due to our cutting-edge research into new materials, nanotechnologies, and cutting-edge choices in chemistry and physics.

Today Pirelli is synonymous with digital industry, artificial intelligence, open innovation, and data-driven production and commercial processes. We support award-winning research on sustainability and *smart mobility* and tyres that—in the high-tech and greater added value ranges—are already being marketed to meet the challenges of electric cars and self-driving cars with the help of our *cyber tyre*. In the world in movement, it is of primary importance to continue focusing on Pirelli 'power' and 'control'.

Knowledge Is Progress

by
Maria Cristina Messa

–

**MINISTER FOR
UNIVERSITIES
AND RESEARCH**

9 —

'Without knowledge there is no progress'. Over time this statement has been transformed into a truism, an obvious assertion upon which we do not dwell because we consider it a fact and to which, as a corollary, we attach another expression: 'More knowledge equals more progress'.

Yet things are not quite like that.

Science is a non-linear process with which relationships between concrete phenomena and past knowledge are hypothesised and verified, so its relationship with development cannot be based on some form of direct consequentiality.

It is necessary, therefore, for a new knowledge to be developed on a continuous basis, as any result that has any scientific validity requires consolidated knowledge in order to be used and to be a factor of progress, but it also requires new skills to be developed, jointly with appropriate technologies and reactive environments. Last, but not least, it is necessary for all this to be rendered accessible and transferable from the scientific communities to young people, businesses and society, so that, in addition to the birth of new knowledge being propagated and triggered, it can also have repercussions on the territory, such as creating and doing business, developing innovation, improving the quality of life of people and the environment.

The important thing is that society—much larger than the communities of professionals alone—believes in Science and invests resources, energies and ideas, even when faced with the possible risks of failure. Drawing strength from the awareness that Science can be trusted. Not because it is perfect, immune from mistakes: scientific conquests are not at all imperishable, immaculate, nor are they the fruit of linearity. After all, they are only true until they are shown to be false. But Science can be trusted simply because it remains the only key we have to being the protagonists of the world in which we live, to be able to understand, interpret, modify and orient it, hopefully always aiming at the best.

In the history of humanity, Science, through its multiple variations and manifestations—from art to technology—, has always been alongside people and freed them. It has been a kind of extending prosthesis that has increased the possibilities of action and reaction, favouring the evolution of the species and the transformation of the environment.

Today, despite some oversights on the part of the pseudo-sciences, it is unthinkable to imagine ourselves far removed or excluded from Science and from technology. Ours is a society immersed in techno-science.

This paradigm shift, amplified by globalisation, has raised the bar of competition in every sector—from research to production systems—and has radically modified the terms of the debate between countries, between businesses, but also between the research groups themselves.

One of the effects, perhaps the most significant in the scientific world, is the need, in order to compete, to have recourse to highly trained researchers, to major research infrastructures, to the capacity for aggregation, as well as to make most of the scientific results accessible and applicable, to invest in the specialisation and verticalisation of knowledge. On the other hand, for the production world this means overcoming production fragmentation, seeking specialisation, shifting competitiveness from labour costs to investments in radical, as well as incremental innovation, and to the strategic decision to raise the quality of products.

In order to be the protagonists of this changed perspective, and not prey to it, it is necessary to render the relations more fluid and structured between those who develop knowledge and those who use it to make or transform products.

To be aware, then, that the speed of technological progress imposes the transcending of the confines between scientific disciplines and shifts the attention from the discovery in itself to its applications and the multidisciplinary skills that its management requires. For this reason, in recent years themes such as enabling technologies, the expression of advanced knowledge with high innovative potential, the green economy, digitisation, artificial intelligence, biomaterials and precision medicine have made the need even clearer to bring the concepts of 'science' and 'technology' into the more general one of 'knowledge', which includes 'know-how', 'savoir faire' and 'knowing how to get things done'.

Knowledge society, the one that will ferry us into the near future, like the major transformations in scientific thought and technological innovation, rests on a unitary vision that sweeps away every disciplinary boundary. Moreover, the protagonists of scientific revolutions themselves are distinguished by being animated by great curiosity, by passions and interests that go way beyond the paradigms and limits of a single specific disciplinary field.

This unitary and anthropocentric vision of knowledge is particularly familiar to us Italians. It has its roots in the Renaissance, a season when the idea of a person free from fears and constraints, someone courageous, dignified, intellectually autonomous, open to change, to the new, to beauty, thirsty for knowledge, attracted by technology, animated by profound religious, ethical and political passions, was established and disseminated for the first time.

During that particular season, thanks to the original combination between expectations and possibilities, ambitions and knowledge, the distance between knowledge and its applications, between creativity and technology, was set to zero. The workshop became the place for meeting and exploration, for production guided by knowledge and oriented towards the search for beauty and harmony. This interaction made awareness and *savoir faire* grow, favouring the advancing of the frontiers of knowledge, from technology to the arts. Furthermore, it enabled what we today define as 'pervasive innovative capacity', that is, the introduction and adoption of radical and incremental innovation, in other words,

At the basis of every innovation and knowledge there is always a meeting, an exchange

original cultural, technological, artistic and scientific paradigms destined to change the lives of individuals and communities for the better, to be expressed in all fields. After many centuries, the need is arising again to recover those same synergies and virtuous interactions, also in order to emerge from the impasse of a crisis that has immobilised this country for years and that the recent pandemic has made even more burdensome.

We are aware of the impossibility of maintaining positions of reference on the markets without investing in quality advanced services or of remaining competitive, intervening only on the costs of production, remaining 'small enterprises', delocalising, reorganising salaries and employment, or having recourse to the usual tax incentives.

This can no longer be done.

The speed of change is so fast that the life cycle of technologies, processes and products is significantly reduced. The rapid production and marketing of vaccines to combat the SARS-CoV-2 pandemic has broken down the last resistances associated with the time variable. Consequently, the centre of gravity of the value chain and competitiveness has shifted onto the quality and quantity of knowledge developed, adopted and speedily introduced into the production circuits, that is, onto people's capacity to imagine, anticipate, orient and govern ideas, processes and technologies.

After all, this is what the great pioneers of industrialisation have known how to do. It is what, amongst other things, Giovanni Battista Pirelli did at the end of the nineteenth century when he built the plant for the production of rubber items in Milan and launched the company's first tyre for velocipedes, the synthesis of a number of innovations both in the preparation of materials and in the construction of tyres.

Today, the challenge of reindustrialisation, even in the more traditional sectors, those considered mature and more exposed to competition from the emerging countries, can only be met if we are capable of focusing on products and services with high added value, on advanced technologies, on the digitisation of processes and, above all, on people, on their capacity to continually acquire specific and transversal skills and abilities.

It is necessary for training, research and production to know how to value and encourage the interaction between forms of knowledge, whatever their extraction and nature may be, because at the basis of every innovation and knowledge there is always a meeting, an exchange.

In addition to extensive, transversal, flexible skills, the new challenges also require the creation of proactive contexts, generating organisational, process and product innovation.

One topical and critical theme is deciding where to position yourself with respect to the major changes under way: that is, whether to be a 'colony country', forced to buy and import advanced technologies and products that are necessary for development, or to be a 'champion country', capable of governing transformations and new enabling technologies, of making the processes, products and services in all the economic sectors highly competitive and high-quality.

The ecosystems of innovation are one of the most advanced responses in order to become national and international points of reference in those sectors with a greater potential for growth and technological discontinuity, sort of intelligent meta-workshops, distributed, diversified, focused on the interdependence of the actors—public and private, scientific and productive—, driven by goals oriented towards incremental innovation and by the capacity to cooperate and compete (*coo-pete*) in different market areas or even in the same market.

During its one hundred and fifty years of history, Pirelli has associated continuous innovation as its identifying feature, becoming a reference point on a global scale.

It has done so by collaborating and investing in research and in young people. Trusting their ideas, encouraging their projects.

Our hope is that this strategy will endure and lead to new, more important successes, for the company and for the country.

Competitive Technologies

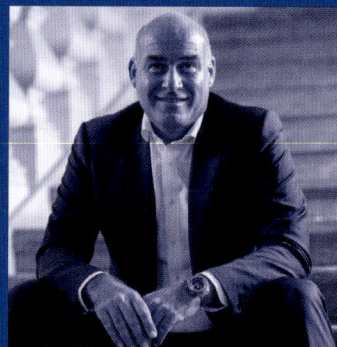

by
Ferruccio Resta
-
**RECTOR OF THE
POLITECNICO DI MILANO**

'Change is the only certainty in manufacturing and the fast forward button is permanently engaged', wrote Gillian Darley in her investigation of the topic of the factory. This definition seems to represent Pirelli very well. Not only because of the easy metaphor of the motor car, but also of that drive for innovation that has distinguished it over time: an industry capable of renewing itself, where change means research and ability to interpret the major trends in technological development. One aspect that it has in common with the university and that has not yet exhausted its propulsive power.

It is no coincidence that the destiny of Pirelli and that of the Politecnico di Milano are doubly connected. In 1872 Giovanni Battista Pirelli, a brilliant graduate of the then Regio Istituto Tecnico Superiore, embarked upon what was an unprecedented initiative in Italy: the rubber industry. This was a successful insight that made ground within a sector that was not particularly well developed at the time. It was the idea for a start-up—as we would say today— which came about following a trip abroad. 'In the Brain of a Romantic Student, the Project for a New Industry' was the title of an article in the *Rivista Pirelli* in 1949.

The history of the founder of what today is a player established on the main markets of the world is the dream that can be glimpsed in the ambition of so many students, male and female, talented researchers who liven up the classrooms of our university: an open mind, a cosmopolitan mentality, but a Milanese heart. This is still Pirelli today, in the relationship that it has kept alive with the Politecnico di Milano. These are the features of an identity that has remained faithful to itself and to its roots, and that shares part of its DNA with the Politecnico: the capacity to anticipate the times, its international dimension, its feet well planted in the territory.

Pirelli is in fact one of the great symbols of Milan. A hard-working, open city that, of that second industrial revolution in which Giovanni Battista Pirelli took his first steps, still today, in the age of industry 4.0, retains the desire to experiment that makes the modern factory a major laboratory. A test location not only for technological discoveries, but also for those values that reflect the social and economic changes, accompanying the innovation of product and process with new meanings.

The very concept of the factory has changed drastically with time and in its more recent definition contains various meanings within itself. Factory 4.0 is the speed of digital, the impact of new technologies on the environment, the training of people. It is the acquiring of new skills, the supply of new services, cultural transmission. Models that are increasingly focused on knowledge. The factory therefore becomes a place of knowledge in addition to being a place of know-how. The contemporary version of the factory is more similar to that of a science park, in which ideas as well as products are developed and where a cleaner, quieter, and safer production regains its place within urban fabrics, to be integrated with the social functions of cities. It is the affirmation of a modern conception of industry, no longer understood as a necessarily peripheral element, incompatible with the rhythms of modern life, or as a place to be hidden. On the contrary, it is a place to be shown and experienced.

In recent years Pirelli, which, unlike other industrial players exposed to the dynamics of globalisation, has never abandoned its native city, has been the protagonist of an important process of urban regeneration in the Bicocca district, produced by the synergy between innovation and research, between creativity and culture, between public and private. A model that has inspired the Politecnico di Milano, which in the zone of the Bovisa is giving shape to a genuine district of innovation, bringing the city closer to the experience of major metropolises such as Paris or Barcelona. A space shared between university and business, a science and technology park based on the cooperation between production and research within an ecosystem of innovation that draws energy from a continuous process of contamination. The university thus becomes a laboratory open to the exchange of ideas, a space for the many Pirellis, for the many young firms capable of anticipating major themes, of understanding the potential of high-impact technologies—from quantum to hydrogen, from nanotechnologies to space—of predicting developments, from the more futuristic—from bioplastics to the 3D printing of foodstuffs—of developing a critical approach to technological progress. In short, a major centre of technology foresight that shares indications and sustainable choices with greater impact for society and the environment.

In this way, the university takes its place not only as a point of conjunction on specific themes, but also as the proponent of a long-range vision focusing on precise aspects within a multidisciplinary perspective approach. One representative example is precisely that of mobility, which is dear to Pirelli, with which the Politecnico can number various collaborations, ranging from innovative materials to the intelligent tyre, arriving at a new driving simulator; a joint centre on the mobility of the future, a meeting place for the most striking technological trends, ranging from big data to artificial intelligence, to new materials, to sustainability, to the impact on the environment and on services.

These are aspects that, not by chance, place the theme of mobility and transport at the centre of our National Recovery and Resilience Plan, and also at the point of convergence for the other five missions of the programme: digital, because mobility will be

The university becomes a laboratory open to the exchange of ideas, a space for the many Pirellis capable of anticipating major themes

increasingly interconnected and intelligent; the green revolution, because mobility will not exist unless it is in a sustainable form; education and research, because new training paths will be developed in these spheres that are capable of meeting complex challenges; inclusion and cohesion, because it is the physical networks and digital infrastructures that define the relationship and the interaction between people and entire territories; and last but not least, health, since new transport systems, sensor-fitted and intelligent, will make the difference in terms of safety and the safeguarding of human lives.

I am thinking, therefore, of sensor-fitted infrastructures, enabling the use of predictive maintenance techniques, of a widespread electric mobility network, of connected low-impact vehicles. I am thinking of autonomous mobility and the use of artificial intelligence systems, of the enormous potential existing in the management of data and personalised services. Finally, I am thinking of the development of the regulatory system, of precise new behavioural models and public policies. There is no doubt, in fact, that the future of our cities and our economy will depend on mobility.

Having said that, the factory of the future, like the university of the future and many key sectors of economic development, will be a node within complex situations, at the centre of networks made of skills, tools, relationships and opportunities. Not coincidentally, I consider the management of complexity to be the central issue of contemporary society. It will therefore be necessary to know how to tackle non-linear situations that today already suggest a multiform approach, which in turn means we cannot avoid a careful reflection on the dualism between specialisation and systemic vision; between local and global; between tradition and the need for innovation.

And so it is a good idea to ask ourselves what the future concept of the factory will be. I would define it through a series of adjectives. The first is *attentive*, an industry capable, that is, of keeping the person at the centre of their own actions and of valuing their creative intelligence. Then I would add *committed* in maintaining the worker's quality of life at a high level, as this is their primary resource and the source of any real change. It will

therefore be *educational*, called upon to transmit ethical values and knowledge in paths of continuous growth. It will be *sustainable*, ready to launch new regenerative business models, both for individual products and for production systems designed to be reused and upgraded. It will be *hyperconnected* and *personalised*, far removed from the standardisation of serial production: a radical transition in a market that will increasingly demand products and solutions modelled according to the needs of the individual and of the moment. Finally, it will be *reliable*, capable, that is, of reacting to and withstanding global risks, and *resilient*, meaning flexible but not unstable.

For this reason it will be necessary, at all levels within the business, to introduce and publicise a new conception of the factory based on the management of complexity and on the 'culture of change'. That same work of transformation that Pirelli set under way after the Second World War and that still exists today. A genuine propensity for transformation, which is the cornerstone of this century. After all, economic and social sciences teach us that, at the moment when the culture of change pervades an organisation, various aspects of life—of individuals, of businesses, of factories, of society—become functional elements. This change must be anticipated, planned and placed within a system. The university can and must take responsibility for meeting this need, helping the economic players and political decision-makers understand the transformations under way, supporting the sharing of experiences that embrace the entire country system. A real paradigm shift that is based not so much on the initiative of the individual as on a wide-ranging, modern, youthful and competitive project. A vision that is able to set the conditions for a sustainable development and for the growth of the new generations.

The Research Community

by
Guido Saracco
-
**RECTOR OF THE
POLITECNICO DI TORINO**

The construction of a community, defined by Adriano Olivetti as the only way to overcome the separation between production and culture and increase the quality of life and work, both inside and outside the company, is a goal that has significantly permeated not only industrial, but also academic culture, in Piedmont and Italy. A community that, within the company, was made up of workers, engineers, architects, but also of artists, writers, poets and draftsmen, who worked together in close contact and who were guaranteed common environments and social services including residential housing, medical practices, kindergartens, cafeterias, libraries and free cinemas. A community that, outside the company, also took on the form of a fluid and intelligent system in which shareholders, public bodies, businesses and universities worked in synergy to 'build' a territory, a human, social, cultural and economic landscape. So it is that idea of community of Adriano Olivetti, the illustrious graduate of the Politecnico di Torino, which is echoed today in the concept of 'making a system', of the increasingly clear importance for a company, whether large or small, to open up and establish a dialogue with its territory, or, with the parties, whether institutional and not, that make up its social fabric. To grow and innovate, of course, but above all to have a positive effect on the present, to truly be an engine of development and wellbeing. To be a community company. Such a concept is perhaps misused, abstract, utopian, but in my view it is good today more than ever. We have lived, and are still living, within a historical event that marks *de facto* a watershed for us and for the world we live in, after which many things will change. A change that will have an impact on a systemic, global level, and that we cannot allow ourselves to suffer, as a small link in that same system. The paradigm shift that awaits us, and that we are already experiencing, must be accompanied, and if possible ridden, by making the principles of antifragility our own, which is perhaps the best and most effective response we can give to the terrible 'Black Swan' event that has struck us with the pandemic, which has exacerbated the already tragic economic crisis that we were undergoing is to agree to change and evolve, emerging from the crisis stronger than before.

What does all this mean for Turin and for Piedmont? It means beginning to think in an increasingly collaborative way. And it is here that the ability of businesses and universities—two important engines of innovation—to reinforce their dialogue, to make it systematic and able over time to generate a decisive impact on the territory and society, comes into play. The Politecnico di Torino has already been investing in this dialogue for years, through the construction and its inner consolidation of a genuine 'ecosystem of innovation' that values the development of expertise and research, to sharing and implementing them, with the development of innovative goods and services for and with companies. An ecosystem such as to guarantee a complete coverage of the chain of Technological Transfer, bringing together the supply of innovation, the companies involved in it, the potential demand and the actors in the financial sector, so as to encourage the creation of a market to speed up both the development and the adoption of new technologies. This is a path that the Politecnico has embarked upon in the past, with major Italian firms such as Pirelli, and that will continue to travel along in the near future, attempting to grasp as well as possible the major opportunities offered by the PNRR [The Italian National Plan for Recovery and Resilience]—a full-blown antifragile last-gasp lunge by Europe, unthinkable without the pandemic—the resources of which will be invested in strengthening its institutional action but also in research and development projects in close collaboration with businesses to support the processes of digitisation, ecological transition, sustainable mobility, social inclusion and health.

Europe is asking for this in a loud voice.

Also, the path towards antifragility, though complex, has already permeated the entire Piedmontese territory. The acknowledgement that Turin had become an industrial area of crisis two years ago led the main social actors— entrepreneurial associations, trade unions, universities, foundations and government bodies—to join together in a shared development project, being fully aware of having to change, as individual institutions, and at the same time of having to promote team work and common intentions. This is the so-called *coopetition*: an alliance between the main actors of economic and social development to be more effective, sustainable and competitive.

In the Turinese territory, we are collaborating with all the institutions in order to establish genuine 'communities of knowledge and innovation', providing training services— professional, academic and continuous—as well as research—interdisciplinary and functional to production chains—technological transfer and other services; for example, the development of start-ups with the purpose to support and attract SMEs and have them cooperate with large enterprises—automobile, aerospace, IT, food and more—and finally, creating new jobs for skilled workers all the way up to middle managers.

This, together with relaunching the entire country potentials through the funds of the PNRR, can enable us to truly reverse the trend and make us stronger than before.

The Pirelli group has always been a player in this tough game. For more than sixty years, Pirelli has been a significant industrial resource for the whole of Piedmont and a privileged interlocutor for the Politecnico di Torino. A few years ago there was the important project that saw the Politecnico itself in the front line—alongside the local institutions—in research and development associated

The focus on the cross—fertilization of know—how, both based on technologies and humanities, is a challenge

with the plan of relaunching Pirelli's industrial foothold in Settimo Torinese. This plan envisaged the creation of a new and more competitive industrial pole for the production of tyres for cars and heavy vehicles focusing on the use of innovative technologies. Among these, the new generation MIRS™, or the substantial evolution of the robotic process of production of tyres guaranteeing the quality and uniformity of the product, the Cyber Tyre, the future 'intelligent' tyre fitted with sensors capable of transmitting useful information for driving and controlling the vehicle, and TSM, a new process for mixing materials with high levels of quality and reliability. From this important collaboration a very profitable dialogue begun between Pirelli and the research facilities at the Politecnico, in particular the Cyber Tyre centre at the Cittadella Politecnica, created precisely within the scope of this relaunching plan to further develop production processes and more advanced products based on the outcome of Pirelli's technology.

In recent years, this cooperation generated a considerable number of dissertations and PhDs on these specific sectors as well as development projects that are still ongoing.

These are all actions that strengthen the collaboration between Pirelli and the Politecnico and that open up to positive scenarios for the future.

We need to work in synergy on four key elements: competitiveness, technology, quality and sustainability. These are the only principles that can guarantee to keep a strong industrial presence in Piedmont and in Italy, in this age of major changes.

Yet there is another important aspect that makes the relationship between the Politecnico di Torino and the Pirelli group special and that consolidates our dialogue, both present and future.

This has to do with a common sensitivity, insight and something that, again and with surprising consistency, strongly evokes the concepts of collaboration, community and cooperation to devise and develop new technology, yet this time not among universities, businesses and institutions, but by putting together different know-how and disciplines that through cross-contamination provide the stock of responses that we will all will resort to in interpreting both our present and future.

The focus on the cross-fertilization of know-how, both based on technologies and humanities, is a challenge that the Politecnico has taken up stronger than ever, since we believe that there is no equally good option od for the future other than that of creating and training a new concept of engineer-humanist, who will be capable of interpreting reality with broader scope and more in depth. This is a challenge that Pirelli itself has always proven to have close to its heart since the aftermath of the Second World War, when Pirelli welcomed into its community engineer-poet Leonardo Sinisgalli, the father founder—together with the Pirelli management—of the *Rivista Pirelli*, a shining example of an endeavour that addressed with great foresight to the cross-fertilization among different disciplines, with poets and writers such as Raffaello Baldini, Eugenio Montale, Salvatore Quasimodo, Giuseppe Ungaretti and Orio Vergani together with scientists and engineers such as Giuseppe Ambrosini, Giovanni Canestrini and Guido Cesura seated around a table to discuss science and technology.

This is an experience that Pirelli, with the work of its Foundation, continues to value, together with many other actions that place the promotion of scientific and humanistic culture at the heart and in the forefront of the company.

Within this frame of cooperation, it is not by coincidence that the Politecnico di Torino planned the Biennale Tecnologica, a major cultural event on these topics. We believe that events such as the Biennale Tecnologica are bound to develop further in the coming years, since we believe that openness to all forms of knowledge is the primary goal that a university and a company that look to the future must steadfastly pursue if they wish to evolve and drive change, to build a new, more inclusive and democratic social paradigm.

The Clear Night of Science

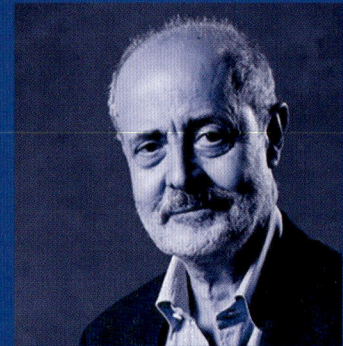

by Antonio Calabrò

-

**SENIOR VICE PRESIDENT
INSTITUTIONAL AFFAIRS
AND CULTURE OF PIRELLI
AND DIRECTOR OF
FONDAZIONE PIRELLI**

'How is the night?'
'Clear'.
These are the last lines of *Life of Galileo* by Bertolt Brecht; the scientist has just accepted to subject himself to the impositions of the Doctors of the Church by abjuring his discoveries regarding the motion of the Earth around the Sun, thus impoverishing the power of scientific proof over theological credence. Because of his fear, he subjects himself to the harshness of power, but he does not give up. He continues to study the movement of the celestial bodies and the laws of physics and of astronomy, because he always finds strength in science. The extraordinary beauty of research, of discovery and of knowledge; a truth to be verified, discussed and in any case, to be put to the test.
A departure to be experienced.
A sky still to be gazed at.
'How is the night?'
'Clear'.
Despite everything.
Life of Galileo debuted at the Piccolo Teatro in Milan on 22 April 1963 and was directed by Giorgio Strehler. The role of the protagonist was played by Tino Buazzelli, who gave one of the most intense and effective interpretations in the history of theatre. Reference is still made to that edition by Strehler in the meetings with students for 'Teatro Scienza', an initiative organised by the Piccolo Teatro together with the Politecnico di Milano, the Statale and Bicocca universities in Milan and the Silvio Tronchetti Provera and Umberto Veronesi Foundations. Condensed and captured within the dialogue and in the scenes with its lacerating, intense drama charged with hope, is a sense of profundity and human experience towards scientific and moral questions which have constantly accompanied the history of progress, of development, and the construction of a better civilisation.

The night is also clear in the hard times of today, with a dramatic war in Ukraine in the heart of Europe and through the winds of 'cold war' blowing on geopolitical balance as well as despite health crises and technological fragility, coupled with extraordinary opportunities for economic development yet untenable social disparity, admirable scientific progresses and escalating economic disequilibria. Luminous yet uncertain times in which we could abandon ourselves to the temptation of poetry, to bewilderment (*Only this is what we can tell you today, / that which we are not, that which we do not want*[1]). Alternatively, we could entrust ourselves to the possibilities offered by scientific advances in general, for health and for raising the quality of life and the betterment of working conditions as well as the hard and yet essential effort to redesign a new world order. Walking through crises while avoiding the shadows of the 'fatal escape into magical thinking' that scorns knowledge and scientific competency and is sadly widespread in our country as confirmed by the latest Censis Report on the dangers of 'cultural regression'.[2] It is comforting to see the emergence of new opportunities to face the challenges of managing complexity as documented by the most recent research of Giorgio Parisi, recently awarded the Nobel Prize for Physics. Despite everything, including the very crisis generated by the idea of progress, our voyage is reaching the end of the night and the first glimpse of dawn is already visible. Indeed, just as Galileo taught us. There are special places in which all these contrasting cultural and social conditions meet, intersect and evolve. These are productive structures; industrial plants; in short, factories.
The factory, a truly ancient word and recently at the centre of public debate in a period of re-found Italian and European 'industrial pride'. From the second half of the 1700s and the entire 1800s, the factory became the symbol of modernity, of the new dimension of

production and consumption, and of the unsettling economic and social transformation. During the long and controversial 1900s, they were protagonists of the political and economic panorama of a century dominated by the automobile and mass transportation, of chemistry and telecommunications, of consumption and the transformation of lifestyles, of conflict and widespread wellbeing.

Even now, while the scientific and technological innovations, digital economy and artificial intelligence are creating crises for the traditional productive organisations by upsetting the customary professional structures and favouring the primacy of 'services' and the so-called 'tertiary' sector, factories or neo-factories still play a pivotal role in the economic panorama. It is precisely in the factory that the evolution of science and technology, work and life, research and production, economic needs and social values, innovation and environmental protection are all condensed. Competition, and environmental and social sustainability.[3]

At the start of the new millennium, factories seemed to have disappeared from the scenario, despite being present in wide territories but marginalised from any role in 'progress'. Today, they have returned, with new organisations and new values.

Factories. That is to say machine civilisation and 'industrial humanism'.[4] A special place to experiment and construct new productive and cultural syntheses. A place in which awareness of the relationships between industry and culture grows, proving the inescapable relationship between the factory and culture.

Indeed, enterprise and culture do not belong to different universes but are part of the same one. Doing business—and even more so industrial business—means investing and working on changes in the market, in consumption, and in production technologies and this requires a focus on research and innovation to be able to follow technical and social transformations. Innovation—the key word—is laden with cultural and symbolic significance and encompasses everything: technologies, materials, new products and the relative innovative production processes, industrial relations between the various actors in the corporate and work scenarios, corporate governance, marketing, and communication languages. What is this if not a wider culture incorporating science, economics and the humanities, or in short, a corporate culture? In other words, we have to progress from a traditional vision of 'business and culture' to a more powerful vision charged with profound values: 'business is culture'.[5]

So, let us return to the factory but now exercising our memory. Reading once again those pages of the *Pirelli Magazine* in which Leonardo Sinisgalli[6]—engineer and poet—talks of the creative and almost sacred dimension of industrial production: 'As I stepped into the factory hatless, it was like entering a basilica and I observed the movements of the workers and the machinery as if witnessing some form of rite'. Yes, a veritable ritual or:

Peculiar rite of childbirth akin to the multiplication of the fish, an egg hatched under the mother hen, the explosive blossoming of an apple tree, preparing bread dough in an old kneading trough. Under these industrial roofs, men and machines busy themselves in their tasks that always have something miraculous: Metamorphosis! The starting line is confusion, and the finishing line is order; we start from a caterpillar and end with a butterfly. Materials are elaborated, masticated, pulled, moistened, strengthened, shaped, sewn and then, an object is created.

It was spring 1949 when Sinisgalli talked of the *L'operaio e la macchina*. He had just recently returned to Milan after a tormented back and forth between his hometown of Montemurro in the rough Lucanian hills and the capitals of industrialised Italy; Ivrea in the years of Adriano Olivetti and Milan with Pirelli were key players in building creative and industrious connections between manufacturing, finance, science, and publishing. Vittorio Sereni was in charge of corporate communication and of the *Pirelli Magazine* and had already started to create his dense web of interconnections between technology and literature.

A story of machines:

The machine has an incalculable reserve of seeds. It can throw out a sphere, or a tyre in a few seconds or in a few minutes. It can squeeze or compress a wire of a tube for hundreds of hours without stopping. There is undoubtedly something monstrous in all this, but beyond these detractions, there is also something marvellous. I would say that these marvels are even the foundations or the origin of an incredible physiology. Machines cannot make mistakes, they cannot permit themselves any false move, they cannot reflect; they produce prearranged shapes and objects, perfect forms and perfect objects that are the same and rather like a multiple birth.

Sinisgalli was a sophisticated technician who knew how to plan, construct and manage the inner workings

Indeed, enterprise and culture do not belong to different universes but are part of the same one

of machines. As an expert engineer, he developed applications; as a man of letters, he wrote down his stories:

It is clear—due to the absence of reflection or indecision and the irrevocable nature of each gesture—that we consider machines as being lesser organisms. They work with closed eyes; they do not hear nor see. When opening their eyes they become intelligent but only for a moment, when they realise that the human watching over them is momentarily absent. That instant, when the human's eyes are closed or hands idle, could be disastrous but the machines are unfailing in their panting, breathing, snoring or purring away; they are happy with their masters. There is no difference between a worker nearby the machines, or an assistant, a nurse or an obstetrician attending a woman in childbirth. The machines are constantly in labour, in a perpetual state of feverishness. The worker can never abandon them, even when muttering drowsily.

Awareness and Safety; Technique and Competence. Sinisgalli insists:

There are machines and machines. Electrical machines for example, or those thermal ones to generate electricity do not need to be powered, they need only heat or water. The vast family of machine tools like lathes, drills, milling cutters,

It is most opportune to refer to Sinisgalli and the *Pirelli Magazine* in a publication that strives to reconstruct the story of the first 150 years of activity of one of the leading Italian multinationals through the comparison of different voices, opinions and testimonials. The period from the 1950s to the early 1970s more than any other was when the dynamics of Italy and Europe's economic and social history were constructed on foundations of extraordinary growth that brought together industrial productivity and wellbeing, competitiveness and welfare, improvement in the quality of work and the level of earnings, greater consumerism and more modern customs. In brief, a market economy and democracy.

In that period, Italy was an excellent paradigm of growth and to such an extent that the economic boom was labelled 'miraculous' with dynamics that in little over a decade took Italy from being a provincial and agricultural country with marginal economic influence to one of the most industrialised countries in the globe. The Pirelli Skyscraper designed by Gio Ponti inaugurated in spring 1960 was to become one of the main symbols of this boom.[7]

This mass industrialisation had some extraordinarily powerful motors. First of all, the political choice of Europe to opt for a common market. Secondly, the intelligent use of funds made available by the Marshall Plan, also aimed

'As I stepped into the factory hatless, it was like entering a basilica'

however, need a constant presence and uninterrupted assistance and the worker is confined to a very small space. At the Bicocca—or at least in various units—the work of the machines is a complementary process. There is none of the nerve-racking frenzy of certain workshops where automatism reigns supreme.

The conclusion is clear: from 'machine civilisation' to industrial humanism:

The individual at Bicocca loses neither capacity nor renounces any innate genius. Indeed, one can measure and recognise this capacity in the object (either the product or goods). The individual is helped by the docile machine.

These exemplary words can also be applied to the evolutionary process of machines from an era of data driven production to Artificial Intelligence. In any case, no matter how sophisticated and advanced the productive structure, 'the docile machine helps'. To quote a famous phrase by Adriano Olivetti, 'it is a factory made for Man, not Man for the factory'.

at stimulating the process of industrialisation, and then the low salaries or at least until the early 1960s. There was also an uncommon capacity of drawing together industrial mass production with high-quality products and above all, by distinguishing these products with special attention to their beauty and design.

Everything was feasible, even public investments for large-scale infrastructure projects. The choices made by IRI, ENI and later ENEL, following nationalisation of the electricity generating industry in 1963, were to focus on core industries and on energy. The growth of a creative, fast-moving, determined and somewhat daring entrepreneurial sector was also important. There was the social dynamism of generations ready to wager on a better future for themselves and for their children. The fast-growing cities from the 'industrial triangle' of Turin-Milan-Genoa to the territories of Bergamo and Brescia and later a headlong urbanisation towards the North-East and then down to Emilia. Obviously, this was not without great personal and social cost, just see the film *Rocco and His Brothers* by Luchino Visconti of 1960 for a dramatic testimony of the Milan hinterland which was probably the most welcoming and integrated of these new urban areas. Progress was made in the scientific and technological sectors as seen by the Nobel Prize for Chemistry assigned in 1963 to Giulio Natta following his research work in the Pirelli laboratories in Montecatini. Civil society also was eager for transformation on political, economic and cultural planes. A complex, contrasted and contradictory process. Following the Treaty of Rome, in January 1958 the six founding countries of Europe launched the European Common Market (ECM) to foster economic and commercial exchange which was a fundamental step forward from the birth of the European Coal and Steel Community (ECSC) in 1951. This was created to eliminate any possible future conflict caused by sourcing raw materials as had happened previously and to favour trade and exchange based on cohesive and common policies. Over time, everyone would continue on the same road up to the birth of the euro in 1999, and the more recent EU policies to counteract pandemics and recession.

And now, after the breakout of the war in Ukraine, to build a strong autonomy for Europe on the major pillars of foreign and defense policy, energy, scientific and technological research. All this to ensure security and strengthen the values of democracy.

Again, in the early years of the 1960s the world was witnessing a more relaxed climate between the USA and the USSR while Pope John XXIII issued the encyclical *Pacem in Terris* in April 1963, an epochal invitation for peaceful cohabitation, the regeneration of public spirit, and of family and personal values. In 1963, Italy witnessed its first Centre-left government headed by Aldo Moro. The members of the Government were exponents from the Christian Democrats, Italian Socialist Party in its first government role, the social Democrats and the Republican Party. Moro launched an ambitious programme of reforms which, however, was soon hindered by powerful conservative currents.

Following the boom, the economy slowed down while salaries and social unrest increased, only to escalate in the late 1960s and continue for the entire 1970s. Social innovation, however, continued to progress; the television soon became the protagonist of a rapid and extraordinary mass transformation in languages, customs, expectations, consumption, and habits. The cultural sector now archived the neorealist movement and new innovative currents emerged; the birth of Gruppo 63 in the literary field, with Alberto Arbasino, Nanni Balestrini, Umberto Eco, Angelo Guglielmi, Edoardo Sanguineti; the cinema successes of 'Italian-style comedy', with ironic and scathing series of portraits of Italian society; musical triumphs of rock and international appreciation for Italian designers, like Franco Albini, Achille Castiglioni, Vico Magistretti, Enzo Mari, Alessandro Mendini, Bruno Munari, Gio Ponti, Ettore Sottsass.

Italy was a fast- and forward-moving country. Its growth was uneven between the industrialised North and the South which was unable to close the historical gap and bore the burden of mass immigration of the more enterprising sectors of the younger generations towards factories in the Lombardy and Piedmont regions. But in any case, progress was made. Living conditions improved. The political response to these problems which tended to worsen due to the absence of any long-term solutions was that of momentary compromise and then deferments. Italy stepped into the grim years of the 'years of lead' characterised by terrorism and social division then it entered more cheerful periods reaching the excessive and almost impertinent 1980s. The early 1990s saw a period of crisis and then a recovery was made under the banner of Europe with the birth of the euro. Now we have reached today's hard-won and hurried times, a complicated, injured and hopeful contemporaneity held hostage between pandemic, dramatic environmental issues, social clash and flashes of war that, until very recently, we did not think we could see. Considering all this, is Italy still a country connotated by innovation? Yes, if we consider this with a critical spirit, and especially when considering its industrial sector. The stories and the points of view gathered in these pages offer a significant testimony of the powerful characteristics found not only in key events in the history of Pirelli but also in the exemplary progress made by many other enterprises. The sign of a true and veritable 'polytechnic culture' which—precisely through the industrial experience—is the ability to bring together humanistic know-how and scientific expertise, the quality of products, industrial processes and a profound leaning towards beauty, towards creative scientific research and scrupulous attention for technological precision. Attention towards the individual and a passion for transformation, for challenges, and for new dimensions of doing and living. In short, innovation and a sense of responsibility.

In 1839 Carlo Cattaneo founded a magazine in Milan called *Il Politecnico*. An enthusiastic lover of culture and science, Cattaneo was a paradigm of the Lombardy culture of transformation, vestiges of which can still be felt today. Edited as a 'monthly repertory of applied studies of prosperity and social culture', *Il Politecnico* was also a magazine published in Milan from 1945 to 1947 as an initiative of Elio Vittorini, one of the most prolific cultural promotors of the 1900s engaged not for a 'consolatory' culture but one capable of 'protecting from suffering' and able to stimulate and interpret political, social and cultural changes.[8] The two university institutions with an international outlook in Milan are both 'Politecnici' or polytechnics and are focused on bringing together engineering and philosophy, skills of 'knowing how to' and 'why to do', values of sense and of constructive ability. The 'polytechnic culture' is a dimension of Italian excellence and is an original outlook on the world. A legacy of Humanism and the Renaissance. The fallout of Galileo's critical intelligence and the later Neapolitan and Lombard Illuminists, Liberal Federalism, Positivism and the intelligent and productive application of new electric and electronic technologies. Today's industrialisation which has kept pace with the changes of the 1900s and of the new millennium took Italy to second place in European manufacturing power after Germany (and first position in many sectors) by creating leverage on quality

A 'polytechnic culture', precisely through the industrial experience, is the ability to bring together humanistic know—how and scientific expertise, the quality of products, industrial processes and a profound leaning towards beauty manufacturing to guide the economy through the dry period of the COVID-19 pandemic and the consequential recession that followed[9] which we hope will also withstand the upheavals and risks of recession and even stagflation as a consequence of the war in Ukraine and the conflict between the USA and EU. Polytechnic culture and industrial humanism will hopefully endure. And everything will be done to continue writing, even so, and *Thinking Ahead*.

It is useful to read once again two of the many possible testimonials to comprehend the extraordinary tension which characterised a corporate culture with a dense network of industrial values and other more wide-reaching civil ones.

The first is that of Adriano Olivetti, delivered in the midst of the economic boom at the end of the 1950s:

The factory cannot only look at the profit index. It has to distribute wealth, culture, services, democracy... I imagine a factory for Man, not Man for the factory... Sometimes when I work until late and see the lights of the workers doing a double shift—office workers and engineers—I feel the urge to go to greet them as a mark of gratitude.[10]

The second is by Leopoldo Pirelli and taken from *The Ten Rules of the Entrepreneur*, written in autumn 1986 and delivered during a ceremony of the College of Engineers in Milan:

Our credibility, our authority—and I would also add, our legitimisation in the eyes of public opinion—are directly related to the role that we play by participating to overcome economic and social disequilibria in the countries in which we operate: the company is evermore considered as representing a meeting place between values oriented towards maximum technical and economic progress and the human values for the improvement of working conditions and life in general.[11]

In both these testimonies there is a fundamental idea that the company is seen as a complex, difficult and hard-to-conquer community but also a place where conflicts are lived and mediated. An extraordinary living organism oriented towards the market. A dynamic, flexible, and variable creature in which ideas and passions, experiences and projects, diverse skills and technical competencies converge and amalgamate into a highly original mix to favour the coexistence of an awareness of the past with an ambitious vision of the future.

Indeed, in the company, it is the people and the wealth of their differences that is the driving force for production and transformation. The responsibilities of the entrepreneur, shareholders and managers of the governing group are condensed in the capacity to make essential decisions for the growth of the company while taking into consideration relations with the various interlocutors.

Many years after these innovative judgements by Adriano Olivetti and Leopoldo Pirelli, economic theory would start to speak of stakeholder values, to be considered together with and in perhaps even before shareholder values which is the economic value (profits and stock exchange listing) for shareholders. But it is precisely through this minority vision founded on profound roots, the entrepreneurial experience of enlightened entrepreneurs between the nineteenth and twentieth centuries, and the finest Italian economic culture[12] that today—with the dissemination of values regarding environmental systems and social sustainability and corporate ethics—the Italian economy and in particular its industry can hold up to the challenges of an epochal 'changing paradigm' for production, consumption, lifestyles and can contribute to construct a 'circular economy' headed towards the future.

This change in paradigm has not only technological connotations, but as Pope Francis reminds us, embodies something more anthropological by directly addressing the responsibility of the individual, as a conscious subject in the construction of positive change, and of a socially and ethically acceptable metamorphosis. It also generates a profound cultural change in economic science: Jean-Paul Fitoussi, Joseph Stiglitz and Martine Durand[13] wrote *Measuring What Counts* after examining the inadequacies of GDP (gross domestic product) as a key indicator in economic processes (a quantitative measure) and proposed new instruments capable of evaluating various sectors such as public policies of costs and investments, indicators for the level of well-being, the development of human capabilities, access to health care and education and so forth. Instruments such as the Equitable and Sustainable Well-Being (BES) index elaborated by ISTAT (Italian Statistics Agency) are already being adopted in Italy as a reference index for the annual budgetary legislation, and this is an ongoing process still to be perfected.

Travelling alongside quality is entrepreneurial innovation which has a strong social connotation in Italy not only in large-sized enterprises and indeed, the dense network of small- and medium-sized enterprises is very aware of this issue.

Productivity and solidarity travel side-by-side towards a meaningful horizon for future generations. Also, EU indications for the Recovery Plan lead in this same direction by designating investment in a *green* and *digital* economy, and in research and education for the 'Next Generation'.

The historical outlook that we have described is founded on one definition: that of a 'progressive' company, stressing the adjective used by Giovanni Battista Pirelli in a speech in 1880. 'Progressive' and thus engaged in interpreting, implementing, and relaunching progress. Therefore, a company strong in avant-garde technology for all its rubber-based products but also attentive to 'the hand of the individual'. Open to innovation in the widest acceptation of the term (products and production, materials, corporate organisation, social involvement) and bolstered by the awareness of being caught between conflict and concordance, of being a motor for construction of a shared history characterised by improved economic, cultural, and social equilibria.

Historical wisdom yet also contemporary with profound roots embedded in the best traditions of ancient thought.

'Every single thing is troubled, more than what Man can possibly say; the eye is never sated by seeing, and the ear is never tired of hearing' are the words that we read in Qohelet 1.8[14], a fundamental volume for those who want to settle accounts with history and the cyclic changes that have accompanied it. An 'eye never sated by seeing', despite the temptations of the 'whirlpool', of 'emptiness' and the 'sapping words' that afflict the biblical author[15], is an extraordinary definition of the desire of discovery, of scientific curiosity, of technological passion, or an innovative and characteristic earnestness. The company is seen not as a machine to generate profit (however indispensable) but more as a subject of change, and its very culture and ethics defines its values, conditions, horizons and it dictates its projects and behaviours. Precisely, Innovation.

In the company, it is the people and the wealth of their differences that is the driving force for production and transformation

'Now, let's look inside, and we'll understand something' was the favourite phrase of the engineer Luigi Emanueli, considered the father of modern electric technology, and the driving force during the first half of the 1900s of many technological transformations in the cables and tyres produced by Pirelli. His approach was to look inside the machine or study its products to understand every detail of the logics and rules of its functioning. Construct, disassemble, and reconstruct. 'Look inside' with the approach of a scientist and the ability of a mechanic. There is profound significance in those words that has always animated the entire Italian industry in its finest moments of growth and in the construction of a competitive market. A commitment to do, and to do well. Creative intelligence and a preoccupation for betterment; a sense of equilibrium and of beauty.

A definition of excellence is perhaps maintaining technical and productive competitiveness with European or international companies, perhaps more robust for various reasons: size, financial support, availability of raw materials, public support for industry and scientific research, and for their technological applications.

In short, the Italian industry continues to grow through a widespread appreciation for creativity, flexibility, and quality and Pirelli is an exemplary paradigm and true testimony to the civilisation of innovation and work.

Everything started on 28 January 1872 in the studio of the notary Stefano Allocchio in Milan. This was when the limited partnership company G. B. Pirelli & C. was created. The entrepreneur was Giovanni Battista Pirelli, recently graduated from the Politecnico di Milano and who had just completed a long training tour of the most industrialised countries in Europe where his attention was drawn to a material not yet present in Italy: rubber or caoutchouc. This was the seed of the company: an innovative idea that then grew into tubes, valves, belts, sheathed cables, and then later raincoats, swimming caps, toys... and then from the early 1900s, also tyres. Everything made of rubber; everything started in a little industrial factory in Via Ponte Seveso, a few workers and leading-edge machinery. Then it grew, first in Italy and then rapidly to the rest of the world. Innovation was seen from two perspectives: in the products and in the choice of targeting highly selective and difficult international markets: cables transmit communication signals and energy, tyres for the most gruelling sporting competitions, starting with the victory of the Peking to Paris motor race of 1907, and for everyday yet sophisticated objects.

The entire 1900s followed this pattern, with great attention to quality and efficiency of the productive plants which were now developed in an international network, from Italy to Germany, Great Britain to Romania, Brazil and Argentina to the United States and Mexico, Russia and China, Turkey and Indonesia (to list only some of the countries were the company is still present today). Today's headlines talk of innovative and digital factories that are attentive towards environmental and social issues, renewable energy, and safety and always with an underlying idea of the 'beautiful factory', well-designed, luminous, transparent, and safe in which the quality of the workplace and the quality of the products advance hand in hand. The factory in Settimo Torinese with the 'Spina' designed by Renzo Piano to unite two production plants and housing offices, service areas and research laboratories in a park with four hundred cherry trees is a fine example of the paradigm adopted also in other Pirelli plants in the world.

There is a chapter dedicated to documenting the close relations between Research & Development and industrial production. Then we have innovation in the photonics sector (some pages dedicated to the historical reconstruction and direct testimony of this process). Our work in fibre-optic cables—in collaboration also with Italian and international universities—led to a series of discoveries and patents in the 1990s. In the early years of this millennium, when Pirelli became the majority shareholder in Telecom (now privatised for many years), the company adopted an avant-garde strategy in the telecommunications sector: priority was given to contents and data, the development of international alliances in Europe and South America, integration between investments in networks and services to be offered on the market. The fundamental idea was to focus on Telecom as a large Italian company with a strong presence in a global and expanding market and to create leverage on those innovative capacities which over time had been consolidated in Telecom and Pirelli research centres (a

written at this moment and demand from economic and corporate cultures a profound commitment for analysis and proposals for new economic and social equilibria. Markets, welfare and democracy are all under tension and therefore science and knowledge are necessary for this new dimension of responsibility.

To better understand, we can take a step backwards to the early 1990s, the years when the new Pirelli communication strategy was planned, and the powerfully evocative slogan was first used: 'Power is nothing without control'.

Indeed, it was precisely the active and responsible relationship between power and control that interpreted the sign of the times and attributed to this symbolic phrase a dimension that went far beyond a merely brilliant publicity campaign.

Today's headlines talk of innovative and digital factories that are attentive towards environmental and social issues

more precise reconstruction can be found in the pages of *Pirelli. Innovazione e passione* by Carlo Bellavite Pellegrini, with a wide range of documents and original testimonials).[16] A series of external interferences in the company and political pressures on its corporate strategies hindered this process. Italy lost the lead of a company with a wide range of international prospects and a primary role in the telecommunication sector. Exiting from Telecom, Pirelli reorganised its strategies and focused on its historical core business of tyres, investing all its innovative and productive capacities in this sector. The historical and contemporary relations with the racing world are also a precious testimony. Indeed, competitive events from rallying to Formula 1 offer extraordinary opportunities to evaluate and design new products. The racing and practice tracks are open-air laboratories, tangible workbenches to test new products and designs in extreme conditions. The results of this are seen in the production of a high range of products for the market. This virtuous circle of relations between racing track and road reinforced the competitive side of Pirelli and defined the horizons for future development.

Indeed, innovation is an all-round phenomenon, especially now when we enter a scenario with new challenges. The electric car and mobility in the smart city; digital factories, robots in the context of a data driven factory, hi-tech simulators, nanotechnologies, cyber tyres, AI applied to research, production, and consumption. These chapters tell of a history which is being lived and

In the last decade of the 1990s, paradigms for the interpretation and management of international processes following the collapse of the Berlin Wall, the implosion of the Soviet Union and the end of the so-called 'bipolar equilibrium' that had defined global governance up until the end of the 1980s rapidly changed. Liberal democracy and the market economy triumphed. In economics, processes of globalisation and transformations took hold and were accentuated through internet and the ever-more intense use of network-based processes. The world was suddenly interconnected, the perception of time and space changed radically, and even relations between social and economic subjects were transformed.

The war cry was 'Less State, more market' but also less politics and more economics was heard, while the role of the economy was accentuated through the weight of finance and particularly in the privileged sector of speculative finance towards which politics and governments worldwide seem to have renounced any guiding responsibility, control or sanctions for abuse or irregularity. Everything seemed to be changing, in the wake of the extraordinary acceleration of progress, technology, and the accumulation of wealth and to such a degree as to overshadow political, economic and social disequilibria which will soon emerge to settle the outstanding accounts.

And thus, we have power but not control. This is a lesson that should not be forgotten.

The dialectics on these two dimensions was dealt with

in many of the more critical reflections of the twentieth century and their echoes were still heard in the early years of the current century and with consequences on the analysis and opinions in the political, economic, and scientific spheres and their technological connotations, from the spin-off from physics and the innumerable applications of IT, and other fundamental cultural structures.

Even in the current period of great transition, these dialectics are still to be reinterpreted with an attentive eye towards persistence and metamorphosis. Control is needed to have power.

In times of crisis one can find recourse in the classics. A possible reference to leaf through is *Dialectic of Englightenment* by Max Horkheimer and Theodor W. Adorno[17], with its constant search for a synthesis between Greek wisdom and contemporary knowledge, between the significance of sacred in the Bible and the scientific and philosophical curiosity between 'Jerusalem and Athens'.[18] One figure to focus our attention on is Ulysses, the archetype of man who totally embodies the worries of travel and research, and who knows well the fragility of existence and the strength of will. A hero of interrogatives, of critical intelligence, and of the challenges of the future, which is a very topical issue today. Indeed, Ulysses and his journey are used by *Dialectic of Englightenment* for another observation: the awareness of limits and how this should be kept present every time when faced with the beguiling force of power.

In brief: during his journey of discovery, Ulysses takes on the challenges of progress—new opportunities for existence, reaching the limits of the magical and immortality—and witnesses its crisis at the same time. The nomadic Ulysses is seen as a man of research and science in the poetical works of Homer. He is curious, investigative, and always ready to restart; like all of us, Ulysses too is a contemporary being.

Then we return to Galileo, from where we started and to his idea of the scientific process of 'try and try again', adding data, verifying knowledge with new experimentation, constructing consensus and always open to more pertinent questions; always alternating between the power of discovery and verifying its validity. Thus, we see that science is like a journey; a tale to be told. According to Walter Benjamin[19] and the suggestive poetry of Bruce Chatwin: 'Wander along other roads, start out once more to continue seeking'.[20]

These aphorisms are still valid today, in times of the diffusion of Artificial Intelligence and the profound and ever more accelerated transformation of mechanisms of production, exchange, and consumption that require the definition of new codes that Luciano Floridi—a philosopher attentive to the ethics of information—names 'Onlife'. He demands the 'government of the Infosphere'[21] to construct horizons of common sense and legal norms for urban systems from smart cities[22], for productive activities burdened with destructive pressures, for new opportunities of employment and for economic relations defined according to the values of social and environmental

sustainability. A culture of *green* and *blue* was the effective synthesis of Salvatore Veca[25] who, in the Milan hinterland dense in social, cultural and scientific history and values of solidarity, identified the national and international paradigms of possible development on how to use technologies to save both cities and citizens from ancient and new inequalities, from all types of disparities be they digital, generational, of gender or culture.

'The technological leap needs a new digital conscience', insists Mauro Magatti, sociologist from the Università Cattolica di Milano and one of the most attentive theoreticians in the moral and social implications of the ongoing changing 'economic paradigms'. 'The web cannot be at chaotic jungle where the rule of the strongest reigns supreme. Therefore, it is urgent to reinforce the institutional infrastructure—made of national and supra national limits—to contrast the evident disequilibria of power that are evident today and to favour the multiple potentialities that are now opening up thanks to the web'.[24] With the approval of the Digital Service Act, Europe has already defined a series of informed choices in this respect. Due to its complex scientific, economic, and social culture and for a capacity to interpret 'the anthropocentric, trustworthy and sustainable dimensions' of Artificial Intelligence, Italy can represent an ideal reference in this process.[25] However, there are still many roads to be followed.

What we need is to return to the times of the *magister*, suggests Natalino Irti,[26] the wise jurist who uses the suggestive force of etymology: *magister* comes from *magis* which means 'he or she who knows' and 'beyond' and denotes a quantitative superiority which is different from *plus* which expresses only quantity. Therefore, we need *magisters* capable of disseminating knowledge, of transmitting love for science, to teach how to research, investigate, and to tell. A contemporary, profound and diffuse knowledge base. Multidisciplinary, and to use once more a word that appears often in these pages, 'polytechnic'.

In this corporate world, the time of transversal skills has come. From neuroscientists and cyberphilosophers to elaborate algorithms indispensable for industrial transformation and of services is provided by the choice of master programmes organised by the Universities of Brescia and Trento and the Vienna Polytechnic and the Centro Casa Severino (developing on the legacy of the late philosopher Emanuele Severino), working on bioethics, information technology, law and neurosciences. Also, the Polytechnics of Milan and Turin organise training activities of this type. The reference horizons can be traced back to indications in a very topical book, *The New Rules of Robotics. Defending Human Expertise in the Age of Artificial Intelligence* by Frank Pasquale, professor at the Brooklyn Law School. Working on 'enhanced intelligence' Pasquale states that to define its values, potentialities, limits, and consequently its rules means to take advantage of the positive possibilities and circumscribe the negative effects.[27]

The word polytechnic appears again when dealing with the corporate sector, to their organisational systems and industrial relations with unions and other social actors. And especially in politics for all that regards investment on public funded research and fiscal stimuli for private and applied research, for education and welfare mechanisms destined to reduce or minimise the negative social effects of technical and economic transformation.

Here is another key issue: the construction of a close relationship between different generations, between the eagerness for research and change, the innovative force of the younger generations and the deep and consolidated knowledge base and experience of older generations. This is one step ahead for the new digital culture; dialectics and dialogue to be initiated in schools, in the workplace, and as a constant practice through lifelong learning. Again, to return to the classics, Ulysses both teaches and learns from Telemachus. Then Aeneas—a landmark figure for western culture—escapes from the Trojan War; he carries his elderly father Anchises on his shoulders and leads his son Ascanius by the hand and together they set out in their quest for salvation. Three generations caught between their memories and the future, between the responsibility of being a father and the loving and grateful attentiveness

their technological consequences, and with the threats of 'technological domination'. This highlights the sadly unexpressed possibility of comprehension and therefore the governability of complex contemporary phenomena. This could not be more opportune when taking on the challenges of Artificial Intelligence discussed previously and the concern for the self-sufficiency of machine learning with the advances of uncontrollable algorithms. But at the end of the day, we see that even for Heidegger, there is still hope. Digital, environmental and social transition therefore necessitates greater commitment to research, study, and comprehension due also to the reinforcement of that 'polytechnic culture' that we have spoken of previously and that has a solid role to play as able to bring together humanities and scientific competencies and generate far-sighted stimuli for the critical thoughts of 'engineers-philosophers'.

Therefore, scientific and technological transformation requires greater awareness of the fundamental criteria involved in the process of *trial and errors*, following the lessons of Karl Popper.[30] A complex growth in parallel with Artificial Intelligence and data analysis instruments reduce

Polytechnic culture and industrial humanism will hopefully endure. And everything will be done to continue *Thinking Ahead*

of being a son, roots deeply set in tradition while the gaze is looking to the future to a new start for both life and for history. 'To have been is a condition to be',[28] said Fernand Braudel, one of the leading historians of the twentieth century.

History, and innovation, and opportunities, and shadows. Now we come to our final reflection. Starting from the rather severe words of Heidegger:

What is truly worrying is not that the world is transforming into an absolute dominion of technology. What is much more worrying is that Mankind is not at all prepared for this radical shift. It is much more worrying that we're still not able to achieve, through meditative thinking, and reflection, an adequate comparison with what is really taking place during our era.[29]

These words by one of the most controversial philosophers of the twentieth century, were recently remembered by Umberto Galimberti in *Dialogo sul lavoro e la felicità*. They insist on the requirement and potential for critical thought when faced with scientific innovation and

the times of the trials and thus open new opportunities for targeted and prompt investigations.

Thus, power expresses itself, by asking for control. It is therefore imperative to construct a positive social capital (companies as responsible actors operating between competitiveness and social inclusion, are the fundamental protagonists). Cultural and moral maps have to be rewritten to navigate the oceans of contemporary transition and attempt to make sense of the crises, the fractures, the wars.

The horizon that is needed is a human scale economy in which the generation of economic value is founded on social, civil, and human values and of a better and more balanced re-composition of globalisation of a re-globalisation, in a multipolar world in which work is being done to de-escalate conflicts and intensify, despite any tension, possibilities for dialogue, confrontation, exchange and collaboration.

Therefore, we need the 'meditative thinking' of Heidegger.[31] We have to regain that basic trust that inspires science. Despite everything, and to cite Popper once again, it is 'the seduction of the future' that makes us live.

NOTES

1 E. Montale, *Non chiederci la parola*, in *Ossi di seppia*, Turin, 1925.

2 Censis, *Rapporto sulla situazione sociale del Paese 2021*, Milan, 2021.

3 A. Ross, *The Industries of the Future*, New York, 2016; M. Bentivogli, *Contrordine compagni. Manuale di resistenza alla tecnofobia per la riscossa del lavoro e dell'Italia*, Milan, 2019.

4 *Umanesimo industriale. Antologia di pensieri, parole, immagini e innovazioni*, edited by Fondazione Pirelli, Milan, 2019.

5 N. Beccalli Falco, A. Calabrò, *Il riscatto. L'Italia e l'industria internazionale*, Milan, 2012.

6 L. Sinisgalli, 'L'operaio e la macchina', in *Pirelli. Rivista d'informazione e di tecnica*, II, 2, 1949, p. 27.

7 *Skyscraper Stories*, Venice, 2020.

8 E. Vittorini, *Il Politecnico*, Turin, 1975.

9 M. Fortis, 'Il rimbalzo post pandemia dell'economia italiana è figlio anche di Industria 4.0', in *Il Sole 24 Ore*, 8 December 2021.

10 A. Olivetti, *Città dell'Uomo*, Milan, 1960.

11 *Leopoldo Pirelli. Valori e passioni di un uomo di impresa*, Milan, 2012.

12 And here are some fundamental references: Antonio Genovesi and 'civil economy', the teachings of Carlo Cattaneo, liberalism with evident social influences of Piero Sraffa and Luigi Einaudi and the original interpretation of Keynes by Franco Modigliani, Nobel Prize winner for economics in 1985, and Federico Caffè, Claudio Napoleoni, Giorgio Fuà, Siro Lombardini, Paolo Sylos Labini and so on.

13 J.-P. Fitoussi, J. Stiglitz, M. Durand, *Measuring What Counts for Economic and Social Performance*, Paris, 2018.

14 G. Ceronetti, *Qohélet o l'Ecclesiaste*, Turin, 1970, 1.8.

15 G. Ravasi, *Qohelet*, Rome, 2012.

16 C. Bellavite Pellegrini, *Pirelli. Innovazione e passione, 1872-2017*, Bologna, 2017.

17 M. Horkheimer, T.W. Adorno, *Dialectic of Enlightenment*, London, 1973.

18 M. Bonazzi, 'Ulisse, l'esiliato che porta alla Bibbia', in *La Lettura*, literary supplement of *Corriere della Sera*, 19 December 2021.

19 W. Benjamin, *Selected Writings*, 4 vols., Harvard University Press, 1996–2003.

20 B. Chatwin, *In Patagonia*, Milan, 1982. Translation by Paolo Maria Noseda for this volume.

21 L. Floridi, *Pensare l'infosfera. La filosofia come design concettuale*, Milan, 2020.

22 C. Ratti, *Smart city, smart citizen*, Milan, 2013.

23 S. Veca, 'Idee da cambiare', in *Città*, November 2021.

24 M. Magatti, 'Salto tecnologico e nuova coscienza digitale', in *Corriere della Sera*, 23 July 2021.

25 G. Finocchiaro, L. Floridi, O. Pollicino, 'Intelligenza artificiale e norme', in *Il Sole 24 Ore*, 7 December 2021.

26 N. Irti, 'L'università vive nella continuità maestri-allievi', in *Il Sole 24 Ore*, 12 December 2021.

27 F. Pasquale, *Le nuove leggi della robotica. Difendere la competenza umana nell'era dell'intelligenza artificiale*, Milan, 2021.

28 F. Braudel, *Il Mediterraneo. Lo spazio, la storia, gli uomini, le tradizioni*, Milan, 1987. Translation by Paolo Maria Noseda for this volume.

29 In P. Iacci with U. Galimberti, *Dialogo sul lavoro e la felicità*, Milan, 2021.

30 K. R. Popper, *Conjectures and refutations: the growth of scientific knowledge*, New York, 1962.

31 M. Heidegger, *Saggi e discorsi*, Milan, 1954. Translation by Paolo Maria Noseda for this volume.

VISI

Changes and transformations will
concern all spheres, cultural, working
and technological. Aspects on which
to reflect, guided by visions of the world
that will come.

ONS

Ian McEwan

-

WRITER

PAY ATTENTION

Science and literature move, with various instruments, following the same principle: the beauty of observation. They investigate the mysteries of the world and the human spirit. They unveil aspects of nature and reveal hidden emotions. And they attempt, each in their own way, to clarify how a different political, social and cultural equilibrium can be built and therefore described. The important thing is to associate the memory with the challenges of innovation. And to insist on the responsibilities of scientists and technologists for a quality development and people of letters for the representation of a better future.

think of science and literature as forms of investigation. Their ways of knowing the world are profoundly different, but they share common ground in the beautiful clarifying call to *pay attention*. As we look with amazement and horror at the climate catastrophe we may be walking towards, we will need the strengths of these two great endeavours to guide us if we are to make it through.

When we wonder about the future, it is worth taking time to reflect on the past. In contemplating the beautiful revolutionary act that science represents, it is useful to call on the resources of literature. Therefore, let the imagination fly back 2367 years, to a pristine lagoon on the Mediterranean island of Lesbos, where a man in his late thirties stands on the shore staring into the shallows at the teeming animal and plant life there. For the next two years, he will study it and record his observations and will found a subject that will come to be known as biology.

The revolutionary moment will not be in the correctness of his conclusions, because he will be wrong about much. The leap in consciousness lies in the decision of this man, whose name is Aristotle, not only to *exist* in the natural world, like everyone around him, but to pay attention and question it, observe it over time as dispassionately as he can, discover life-cycles, structures, processes, to reason about probable causes and to set down his thoughts, with drawings and tables, so that others might read and add to them and challenge them.

As for the beauty, it is in the impulse to curiosity, to which he wishes to bring organisation and deeper understanding so that his wonder can only increase. As a fellow biologist, Charles Darwin would one day write in the resounding summary at the end of his *Origin of Species*, 'There is grandeur in this view of life.' Living things are made of cells, invisible to the naked eye, which enclose cascades of biochemical reactions as well as the enfolded recipe for their own continuation. It was hard to advance an understanding of nature without a microscope—and for that the world would have to wait for the brilliant technologist and observer, Van Leeuwenhoek in the seventeenth century.

But the night sky, especially the solar system with its regular phases, was simpler than a single cell and could be observed with the naked eye. Here was yet another beautiful and revolutionary development in the history of human understanding. It is simple to state: mathematics can describe and even predict the inanimate physical world. We may take Ptolemy, who was working in the second century AD, as our intellectual hero, the first to fully connect mathematics to astronomy. Ptolemy, and long after him, Galileo, paid attention and discovered that the lifeless world has innate order and symmetry that equations can express. It has chaos and asymmetry too which, it was discovered centuries later, mathematics can also express.

But so far, biology, mathematics and physics cannot take us very far into the human heart, by which we mean the mind. Science has yet to give us a generally acceptable theory or account of the mind. We do not know, or even know if it is possible to know, how the brain gives rise to the mind. Science struggles to understand who we are, either as individuals or as a society. There are many conflicting schools of psychology and sociology. We have no good equations with which we can predict our own future, the one we will make together.

Of all the arts, literature, with its ease of entering other minds, other times, other possibilities, represents our best means of interrogating who and what we are.

When we wonder about the future, it is worth taking time to reflect on the past

If science is the flowering of our ingenuity, then literature is the expression of that ingenuity in constant conflict with our stupidity. Our cleverness—devising machines to do the work of animal muscles by burning coal then oil and gas—eventually got us into trouble. We have known about the problem and what we need to do about it for forty years. Our stupidity—whose components are inertia, greed, denial, short-term thinking—has stood in our way. The rising curve of greenhouse gas emissions has yet to fall.
There is an expanding library of fiction investigating our climate stupidity. The scale of what we confront is vast and complex and interconnected. We face deep alteration to our culture, politics, flora and fauna, our sense of the seasons, the movement of peoples, our rootedness in the world, our feeling for the future. We might face wars for basic resources like water

and even dry land. There is a zeitgeist, a metaphysics embedded in these changes that we have hardly begun to grasp.
It lies beyond the reach of science. The literature that is being produced now by novelists around the world can help us. It is paying attention. The ancient project of knowing ourselves continues.
Science and technology got us into this predicament, and we rely on them to deliver us from it. An afternoon researching on the internet will bring you face to face with a thousand serious and brilliant initiatives. Civilisation urgently needs clean energy. You will read of work on the efficient extraction of hydrogen from water, larger wind turbines, innovative solar, of AI-regulated electricity grids, an iron-air battery, nuclear energy without harmful nuclear waste, of cold fusion, processes for making high-quality food or bricks or cement out of atmospheric carbon dioxide, scores of ways of re-thinking our chemicals-based agriculture, and of the planting of sea grasses and kelp that are vastly more efficient than trees at extracting CO_2. There are countless more projects in progress.
All of them must enter the fight with our stupidity, our innumerable cognitive defects. It is as if we are witnessing a battle between the gods. The difference is that we are those gods. The better angels of our nature will only win if we learn from Aristotle, Ptolemy and our great scientific and literary traditions—and *pay attention*.

Sir Geoff Mulgan

-

**FOUNDER OF NESTA
AND LECTURER AT
UNIVERSITY COLLEGE
LONDON**

DIGITAL NOMADS OF NEW WORKS

Work is at the centre of radical transformations that technological evolution imposes on our way of living. Workplaces and the structure of cities change. Ethical questions are posed that affect rights, needs, expectations. We move according to rules and values associated with sustainability, both environmental and social. And the very conception of time is modified. Knowledge workers ask for spaces, powers, influence and, more than on productivity, they insist on the wellbeing of employees and on the quality of the balance between work and private life. A new equilibrium to be built.

O ur world is shaped in almost every way by innovation and how we work is no exception. The innovation of electricity made it possible to organize factories, and then offices, that were much larger and dispersed than was possible before. The Internet—and Zoom—have shown that hundreds of millions can work from home rather than their offices.

But what will work be like fifty or a hundred years from now? How much will be shaped by technology and how much by other forces, like changing values or the pressures of climate change? Over the last two centuries farming shrank from around half the workforce in many countries to barely 1 or 2 per cent today, while manufacturing first boomed and then shrank too. Equally far-reaching changes could lie ahead as jobs in offices, retail and driving are destroyed thanks to technologies that make it possible for anywhere to be a place for work, learning or healthcare.

Yet futurology has a mixed record at best in making sense of the world of work and has tended to exaggerate the impact of technology alone. For more than half a century, widespread predictions promised the end of work with jobs replaced by robots and no more jobs for life. These predictions have been uniformly wrong— employment rates have risen, not fallen, and average job tenure has, surprisingly, hardly changed since the 1960s. Yet very similar predictions continue to be made.

In retrospect the futurologists massively underestimated the ability of economies to generate new needs and roles (from UX designers to therapists of all kinds), and they misunderstood the huge shift of women into the labour market, which was partly the result of new technologies transforming work in the home.

Not all of the forecasts were wrong. Today's Amazon warehouses with their 'Human Exclusion Zones' do look very like the dystopian forecasts of the past. But now too we may underestimate the continuities. A hundred years ago many people worked in jobs with very similar titles to today—farmers, soldiers, police, teachers, builders, plumbers, retail assistants, priests. So here I suggest a few fields of change that can help us think through what lies ahead—but also what might not change.

Place—Where Will we Work?

Let's start with where we work. The great sociologist Max Weber thought the big trend of industrial revolution had been to separate work and home. Instead of the family farm or workshop we went to work in factories and offices. Now work and home are again being integrated, a trend greatly accelerated by COVID. Jobs as varied as call centre operators and professors can be done from a sitting room. Some jobs will remain undomesticated for a long time: building work, physical care and policing. But even in these cases a larger proportion of the work can be done from a distance. In principle even policing on the beat can be done with a drone.

This shift is likely to have profound implications for how we organize our homes and our cities. Homes will need to be reshaped to create quiet rooms for work and to increase connectivity. Neighbourhoods may be revitalized with more shared working spaces so that people can at least get out of the constraints of a small house or apartment and experience a little conviviality. Perhaps we will even see a return to the days when children returned home for lunch each day.

But the other shift accelerated by the pandemic runs in an opposite direction. The more work becomes detached from places, the easier it becomes for a minority at least to become nomads following the weather or events, spending a few months here and few months there, a nightmare for nation states and tax collectors but not bad for a minority, particularly those without children.

Psychology

Another big change already underway but likely to continue is how we feel about feelings. In the past, work was expected to be hard. It was bound to involve drudgery, repetition and often bullying. Trade unions could mitigate these inequalities but not completely. Now in some sectors employers are much more sensitive, partly because of evidence about the links between moods, character and productivity. Psychometric tests have been widely used for jobs since mid-twentieth century but this century the trend is likely to go much further, with more fine-grained assessments of aptitude and personality, and how teams will fit together. We should expect continuous assessment, using AI to interpret tones of voice and facial expressions. This may usher in even more intrusive control. But there is also a possible upside if collective mental health—the patterns of wellbeing in firms or units, and their shared risks of delusion, depression or compulsive behaviours—come to be seen as problems worthy of attention.

Ethics

The futurologists badly underestimated the effects of changing values and ethics on the workplace. Yet these can have just as much impact as technology and the changes in the next century are likely to be just as dramatic. Dominant concerns now in the workplace include issues of gender equality, sexuality, harassment and transgender rights. What might future equivalents be? It's possible there will be more attention to disability of all kinds, not least because one paradox of the future is that there will probably be many more people living with disabilities than in the past, partly as an effect of the success of medicine and longer lives. Will we frown on micro-aggressions or ill-considered jokes? Will our workplaces become less tolerant, or the frontlines of new culture wars?

Sustainability

The biggest ethical issues of all will concern carbon. The next few decades are likely to bring huge efforts to cut carbon as we belatedly take seriously the threat of climate change, and the flaws of the high-consumption and high-waste shape our economy has taken. Many governments are now committed to net zero, as are companies like Siemens and cities like Copenhagen. This will imply less commuting and travel and probably more jobs in maintenance and re-use rather than production (though barely 1 per cent of clothing is now recycled and the mountains of e-waste grow ever bigger with new generations of I-phones or HDTVs). We may see a continued shift in aesthetics as well as ethics: workplaces with a different view of how to use light (perhaps no electric light in the daytime) or how to use water (no plastic or glass bottles) and a turn away from materials like concrete that bring with them such a large carbon footprint.

However, if we look on a longer time horizon the patterns could be more complex. In the worst scenarios large parts of the world become much less habitable—with the Mediterranean facing summers in high 40° C and much of Australia becoming unbearable, along with huge dislocations, food shortages and migrations. On the other hand, a longer time horizon makes it more likely that the world will have sorted out some of the challenges of energy supply with more viable alternatives—hydrogen, fusion or sources we cannot even imagine right now. It is entirely plausible that the twenty-second century—if we make it that far—could bring energy abundance and a reversal of the trends towards frugality and minimization that may yet characterize the twenty-first century.

Teams
Most work happens in teams. I'm fascinated by the new field of collective intelligence which is becoming much more scientific in understanding what makes some teams work and others not. One of its big messages is the advantage of diversity—diverse groups where everyone gets some chance to speak are often much better at solving problems or generating good ideas than homogenous ones. I expect this knowledge to become much more widespread and with it better understanding of how to achieve synchronization in teams (where people align their thoughts and actions) and synergy (where people take complementary roles). For now most thinking about teams is hunch and anecdote. Over the next few decades it will become a science.

Fun and Creativity
Many forecasters expect rising demand in jobs for problem solving, creativity and communication: precisely the skills that machines are ill-designed for. An optimistic view projects this into the future furthering the shift that has affected elite jobs, startups and parts of the digital economy with a greater emphasis on purpose, fulfilment and fun to attract and motivate the smartest talent. Of course these trends look unlikely to affect other parts of the supply chain—from Amazon warehouses to mobile manufacturers. But this blurring of the boundaries between work and leisure looks set to spread.

Time
One reason is the shifting relationship between time and work. Over the last two centuries there has been a steady decline on average in working hours, partly because of laws and partly because of changing cultures. In the Netherlands for example average working weeks are now down to 29 hours. With this has come an odd shift in

Many forecasters expect rising demand in jobs for problem solving, creativity and communication: precisely the skills that machines are ill-designed for

status with the highest status now likely to work some of the longest hours (alongside the lowest status in jobs like security guards or truck drivers).

The rest of this century is likely to continue these trends, with declining working hours and ever more countries legislating four- or even three-day weeks. At the same time life expectancy is likely to continue rising. Add these together and we'll see billions of hours liberated for new activities, whether engrossed in the equivalents of VR headsets or savouring psychedelic drugs or developing a portfolio of unpaid work—volunteering, music, arts, gardening alongside paid work.

It used to be thought that the end of work would be a liberation. Instead we've learned that work provides more than money: it also provides status, meaning and friends. One striking survey in Canada found that the most satisfying activity for the over-65s was paid work. A society based on leisure turns out, after all, not to be utopia.

Investment and Assets
We've become used to a division between investment and work: with owners of capital separated from providers of labour. But this is neither inevitable nor natural. Knowledge workers may increasingly want a stake in the firms—partnerships and coops—they work for. And, of course, some of the newer economic models—like Uber—link self-employment with platforms. Looking ahead we may see a much more diverse ecology of ownership.

At the same time what is measured in relation to investment is also set to change, as ESG reporting becomes even more mainstream and companies are judged, on stock markets, for how they treat their employees (a topic addressed for the first time on a large scale in the Harvard corporate reporting study in 2021). A parallel trend could influence workplaces: already some lease contracts link payments to metrics on air quality and employee wellbeing, part of a broader shift to linking asset classes to facts in the material world.

Unevenness
These are just a few of the patterns that may lie ahead. But we shouldn't over-generalise. The patterns affecting the highly educated in cities like Milan, London or Shanghai will be very different from those in less favourable parts of the global division of labour, making shoes in Indonesia, textiles in Bangladesh, or suffering the grind of electronics factories in Guangdong. While for the minority work could become richer, freer and more fulfilling, there is fair chance that for the majority work will become more regimented and controlled. Let's hope not—and that the workers of the future have the power, and the confidence, to demand work that enhances life rather than diminishing it.

David Weinberger

-

PHILOSOPHER

TECHNOLOGY'S FUTURE

Technological evolutions prompt us to 'turn the future upside-down', no longer insisting on 'preventive' attitudes but on the drive to open up to continuous 'developing' possibilities. And it is precisely the opportunities offered by Artificial Intelligence that show us original paths. There is a fear that AI, like machine learning, will end up controlling us. But there is also the hope that we will be able to grasp all the opportunities to prosper in terms of wellbeing, quality of life, health and the environment, committing ourselves creatively to possibilities of development going beyond what we imagine today.

Technology has always been about making more things possible: iron ploughs made new tracts capable of being farmed; accurate clocks made ocean navigation far more reliable; the steam engine brought power to where it was needed, rather than having to be located at the source of its energy. But now we are facing two technologies that not only make more possible, but that are changing how we think about possibility itself. And that in turn means these two technologies are changing how we think the world works and how the future happens.

That's a big claim, but the two technologies are truly revolutionary: the Internet and artificial intelligence in the form of machine learning.

On the other hand, focusing on those two in this brief essay requires not paying sufficient attention to other technologies that are changing our world in huge ways. For example, CRISPR's[1] ability to alter DNA as easily as cutting and pasting text holds open the possibility of eliminating many diseases, improving our senses and physical abilities, and extending life itself. The increase in bandwidth is already changing the work-life balance for much of the world. Virtual reality technology lets us overstep geographic boundaries and reality itself. Intelligent automation is going to increase leisure time. Advances in how we generate and store power are letting us do more while adversely affecting our fragile Earth less. The coming extension of our cultures onto other planets will bring home to us the extent to which we are creatures defined by curiosity.

At the same time, we are increasingly aware that each of these advances have their dark sides. CRISPR can destroy ecologies. The increase in working from home may put us into an always-on work mode. Automation will put some people out of work. Virtual reality may blur boundaries that we don't want blurred. Worst of all, perhaps, is that we have already seen that most technology increases our powers disproportionately, thus too often aggravating the old inequities and inequalities that have long beset humanity. This is perhaps the most disappointing aspect of our current technological surge toward wonders.

The Internet and AI are certainly not free of their very dark sides. Indeed, these two technologies are most often discussed these days in terms of their risks. So here I will talk instead about how they have fundamentally changed the way we face the future in what I think is overall a very positive and healthy way.

Reversing the Future

There is a constant thread through the various ways we humans have thought about the future. Whether our culture conceives of the future as cyclical, linear, progressive, destined, or open, at least since Palaeolithic times we have tried to manage the future by anticipating it and preparing for it: we made a stone hatchet because we anticipated a need for it; we learned to save seeds from this year's crop in anticipation of next year's growing season.

We have spent the last two decades on the Internet repeatedly refuting this basic anticipate-and-prepare strategy of all strategies.

For example, in 1908 Henry Ford and a handful of engineers designed a car that anticipated users' needs so perfectly that nineteen years later the company had sold fifteen million Model Ts without making virtually any changes in its design. Ford still stands as a genius of product design because of this. (For the moment we'll ignore his being a Nazi supporter.)

On the Internet, Minimum Viable Products (MVPs) are an example of the exact opposite of Ford's strategy. A business follows the MVP approach by launching

We may be coming to understand that explanations usually vastly over–simplify a world in which literally everything affects everything all at once, all the time

a product with as few features as possible in order to avoid having to try to anticipate what users want and need. Instead, you give users the minimum they need to find your offering valuable, and then you watch what they do with it, and what they say to you and to one another on the Net about what they'd like to see in it. For Dropbox, that meant initially selling an app that did almost nothing but seamlessly put your work into the cloud. Then over the years it added a very full set of features that it had learned their users wanted. For Slack it meant launching a stripped-down messaging app, and then quickly building out the features users demonstrated they want. Minimum anticipation required.

Or consider the rise of online products that provide open development platforms (APIs) to enable people around the world to add features, to alter the interface, or to integrate the product into very specific workflows beyond the powers of anticipation of any product designer. Or the massive computer games industry's

commitment to enabling users to create 'mods'[2] that alter how the game is played or to create their own maps and challenges for other users. Or the rise of Open Source programming that makes a developer's work available for others to re-use, modify, or add to. Or the prevalence of standards for text and graphics that make them reusable by anyone, especially if the item has a Creative Commons license (as over two billion items do) that let copyrighted works be reused without asking permission; open licenses are the basis of much of the Internet's vibrant culture.

The Internet itself is based on this strategy of *unanticipation*—that is, holding back from anticipating. The openness of the Internet's protocols supports not just text documents but interactive video, collaborative music-making, protein folding games, real-time wayfaring, and media as yet to be invented. That unanticipation of how it might be used has enabled the Net to become the most important medium certainly since paper and ink. It is why the Net has

In worrying about the risk of bias we acknowledge that machine learning can be a 'black box': it works by finding what can be overwhelmingly complex patterns among individual pieces of data

transformed industries from movies to medicine to, yes, tire manufacturing.

Taken at its most fundamental, this is a change in our oldest strategies for managing and controlling the future. We have long seen the future as a set of possibilities some of which we welcome and some of which we dread. We know that over time those possibilities will narrow, just as from a Model T driving through a landscape you see more things in the distance than immediately in front of you. The future, we've thought, consists of the winnowing of possibilities, and our job has been to make sure the possibilities we want are the ones that survive to become the present.

Now the Internet is showing us that we can succeed and thrive beyond our prior anticipations not by working to narrow the future but by creating more and more open possibilities, and especially possibilities that create still more possibilities. In effect, our new strategy is to make more and more future.

This has oddly prepared us for AI's transformation in our thinking about how the world goes together to make a future.

AI's Future

Most of the excitement around AI these days is about developments in machine learning. If you ever use mapping applications when driving, check the weather report, or use the type-ahead function of your smartphone's keypad, then you are already using machine learning. But beyond the seemingly daily breakthroughs in new applications of this remarkable technology are the lessons it is implicitly teaching us.

These lessons spring from the same ground as the widely discussed risks of machine learning: the control it gives to governments and large corporations, and its susceptibility to repeating and amplifying the biases represented in the data that it learns from. These are essential risks that need our diligent attention.

At the same time, we take the risk of control seriously because we believe, correctly, that machine learning can give governments and corporations power because as a technology it is so powerful that it's opening up new possibilities. We worry about the risk of bias in part because we know that sometimes machine learning systems can find patterns in data that are too complex for humans to understand, and thus we may not be able to see biases at work in them. Both the risk of being controlled and of bias are made more dangerous by our naive over-confidence in machine learning's outcomes. Yet the implications of these risks may be leading us to a conclusion that will define a new epoch. In worrying about being controlled by machine learning, we accept that machine learning often works well. In worrying about the risk of bias we acknowledge that machine learning can be a 'black box': it works by finding what can be overwhelmingly complex patterns among individual pieces of data. The conclusion we're drawing together may be: machine learning works *because* it is freed from the need to come up with generalizations and principles that we humans can understand. If so, that is because machine learning is, in important ways, a better representation of the overwhelming, irreducible complexity of the world than our brains can manage on their own.

In short, machine learning may be bringing us to accept that the *world* is the black box: too complicated and particular for us to be able to comprehend. But now we have a tool of knowledge that doesn't handle the complexity of the particulars by reducing them to the general rule or law or principle through which we understand them. Machine learning is more respectful of the particulars, finding patterns that shear off fewer particulars. We may be seeing a cultural and epistemic shift toward particulars over universals.

That will happen if we use our dominant technology as the model by which we frame our self-understanding, as we have done historically. And this is where what we've learned from the Internet comes in: the chaotic complexity of the world exposed by machine learning gives us a mental model that explains why the strategy of unanticipation that we learned on the Internet works so well. For thousands of years we've striven to understand the world by simplifying it under rules and generalizations, at the high cost of frequently under- or over-preparing—the price of the old anticipate-and-prepare strategy. We want science to continue to seek fundamental principles and models. But we may be coming to understand that explanations usually vastly over-simplify a world in which literally everything affects everything all at once, all the time.

This is what happens when we spend a generation on a network that is built out of the chaotic connection of individual pieces. This is what happens when we have a revolutionary new technology that is powered by finding intricate connections among particulars. There is tremendous power and risk in this new framework of understanding and experience. But there is also tremendous truth in it as we face a future in which we thrive not by narrowing possibilities but by opening them up beyond our anticipations, imaginations, and dreams.

NOTES

1   CRISPR, acronym of Clustered Regularly Interspaced Short Palindromic Repeats, is a genome modification technology.

2   This is the pratice of 'modding' that was established starting from the 1990s.

The identity of Pirelli and its evolution
in the scientific-technological development
of products and processes, in visual
communication, in the world of racing
and experimentation, of culture and society
from 1872 to 'tomorrow'.

IDEN

TITY

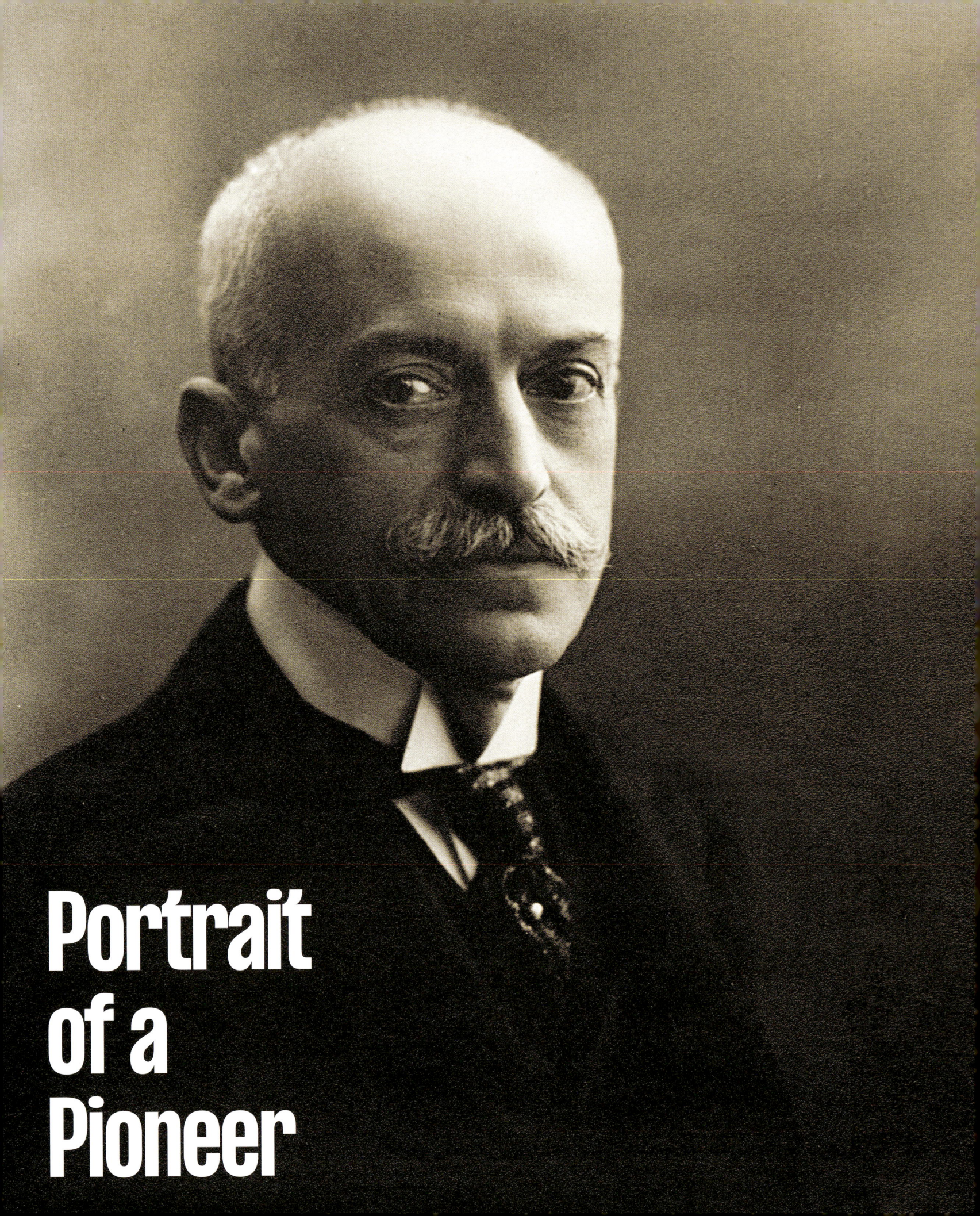

Portrait of a Pioneer

by Ernesto
Ferrero

–

WRITER

What does a particular young boy know or see or want? A boy born in 1848 in Varenna, a village a few miles north of Lecco in the branch of Lake Como made famous in Alessandro Manzoni's novel, *The Betrothed*, on 17 March 1861 upon the Proclamation of the Kingdom of Italy in Turin. His name is Giovanni Battista Pirelli, the eighth of ten children, of which only five survive childhood.

His maternal grandfather, a housepainter, is entered in the General Register Office as 'landowner'; his father Santino, who works as a baker, dies when Giovanni is eight. His mother, Rosa Riva, has to take charge of the onerous task of running the family. In his speech accepting the nomination to senator in 1909, Pirelli recalls a 'very modest home where the only obligations were rectitude and industriousness'; his son Alberto will also speak of 'a modest, but not poor family.'

The boy feels limited by the fake idyllic life on the lake with its still waters and the severe enclosure of the mountains facing it, but he does exceptionally well at school. His teachers say they have never seen such diligence in a student; as if he were driven by a need for knowledge: no need for the thrashings and slaps of a violent education. Studying for him is like fitting out a ship to go far. His mother sends him to school in Como, but is already thinking ahead to Milan.

These are feverish years in Lombardy. After the tensions and repression of the revolts inspired by Giuseppe Mazzini in the early 1850s, the death of Field Marshal Radetzky and a more conciliatory policy (amnesty for many political prisoners and Emperor Franz Joseph's trip to Italy with his wife Elisabeth), open the way for an industrial take-off. In 1857 a government decree launched construction of the Central Station in Milan and an Austrian-Sardinian Treaty provided for connecting the Lombardy and Piedmont railways. Thus, the Milan-Turin line could be opened in 1859. The revision of Empress Maria Theresa's old real estate registry was finished (even though the update was only implemented in 1887). Ambrogio Binda opened a paper mill and Giuseppe Candiani a colourants factory for the works on the Naviglio Pavese (Milan-Pavia canal). Engineer Augusto Stigler came to Milan to produce hydraulic machines and lifts. The tenements in front of the La Scala Theatre were demolished so that the theatre could face Palazzo Marino, Milan's city hall, and a spacious piazza with a statue of Leonardo da Vinci in its centre. A street connecting Piazza della Scala and Piazza del Duomo was planned. Five years later that street would become the Galleria Vittorio Emanuele II.

The war of 1859 lasted only a few weeks—from 27 April to 12 July. After being defeated in Palestro and Magenta, the Austro-Hungarians commanded by Ferenc Gyulai left Milan, Vittorio Emanuele II of Savoy and Napoleon III entered the city. In July, the armistice of Villafranca ceded Lombardy (except for Peschiera and Mantua) to France, which in turn ceded it to the House of Savoy.

Initiatives immediately blossomed: construction and building transformation with 220 projects involving Piazza del Duomo, markets and slaughterhouses. Public gardens in Porta Venezia and the new Fatebenefratelli Hospital in Via San Vittore were opened. Gabrio Casati signed the first organic law on education that called for the establishment of a faculty of Letters and Philosophy (Academy of Science and Letters) and the Regio Istituto Tecnico Superiore, the Royal Superior Technical Institute (the future Polytechnic University), inaugurated in 1863. Francesco Brioschi was headmaster and a future supporter of young Pirelli's initiatives. 1 January 1860 marked the founding of the General Association of Mutual Aid for Milanese workers. In the 1861 census, the Milan population within the circular defensive walls built in the medieval era and during the Spanish domination, was 196,109.

Thus it was not by chance that Giovanni Battista moved to Milan to enrol in the Santa Marta Technical Institute precisely during the year the Kingdom of Italy was proclaimed. The nation born from the adventurous Expedition of the Thousand led by Garibaldi needed to be built practically from scratch. It was a backward agricultural nation with an illiteracy rate touching 75 per cent in the North and almost 95 per cent in the South; France, England and Germany seemed unattainable models. Textile and steel industries and chemistry were in the initial stages and traffic circulation was rudimental. When the first mechanical looms and the Siemens-Martin open-hearth furnaces arrive, the entire Italian mechanical industry, including arsenals and military facilities had less than 20,000 employees.

The investment that the Pirelli widow had made in her son proved to be perfectly right. After graduating from Santa Marta with the highest honours, in 1865, Giovanni Battista enrolled in the Faculty of Physical Sciences at the University of Pavia, attending the preparatory two-year course in mathematical and physical sciences. In 1866–67, the hiatus of the war between Prussia and Austria led to a fervid participation towards the completion of the Risorgimento, the years of the unification of Italy. Giovanni Battista joined the Garibaldi volunteers at 17, fought at Brescia; at 18 he went to Rome to defend Mazzini's dream of a Roman Republic, which shattered in the Battle of Mentana.

He had a photo taken of him, his long rifle by his side, the iconic red scarf around his neck and a uniform with some dignity and elegance. He has a little smile of defiance. After returning to Milan, he enrolled in what was to become 'our Polytechnic' choosing a specialisation in industrial engineering. The founders of the department had created it with the precise intention to train 'a special class of engineers' destined to have a leading role in the new nation's industrial development. Pirelli found there his mechanics professor who had also joined the Garibaldi volunteers: Giuseppe Colombo (1836–1921), a broad-minded man with an extraordinary maieutic talent. Colombo will be decisive for training Pirelli and many other key players of the Milanese business community like the Riva, Salmoiraghi, Saldini and Cabella.

The Polytechnic offered a far-sighted programme aimed, from the beginning, at placing the graduates in the manufacturing process. The team spirit among the students and professors was striking. Pirelli's story is also a wonderful group story, the kind that give the sense of a cohesive community animated by a project and a vision. The polytechnic school implemented a dense network of relations among students, teachers and entrepreneurs. The teaching was not an end in itself; the final aim was having students be a vital part of industry.

Pirelli graduated at the top of his class in 1870, winning one of the two grants set up in memory of the son of an enlightened Milanese aristocrat, Teresa Berra Kramer, whose salon had become a meeting place for many patriots, including Mazzini. The 3,000 liras grant went to the best graduates, so that they could 'complete and perfect their theoretical-practical studies with an educational trip abroad', thus gaining personal experience in highly developed industrial areas.

The young scholar will always be conscious of the decisive relevance that trip had for his education; so much so, in his will he will leave a fellowship to the Polytechnic, for a new graduate to conduct 'studies abroad with the aim of introducing in Italy a new industry or favouring the progress of an industry imperfectly or inadequately implemented'. He intended to return what had been given to him.

The group spirit is also documented in the photo of Pirelli and the other Polytechnic graduates. He is in the centre and already has the air of a leader. He's dressed elegantly, his right hand slipped into his waistcoat, like Napoleon: thick hair parted in the middle, a slim moustache and intense eyes communicating a fever to know and self-confidence. There is nothing provincial about him. He wants to be a protagonist.

He does exceptionally well at school. His teachers say they have never seen such diligence in a student; as if he were driven by a need for knowledge. Studying for him is like fitting out a ship to go far

STORIA DELLE INDUSTRIE PIRELLI
ARCHIVIO STORICO

6   N. *1154*   del Repertorio

COPIA AUTENTICA

dell' Istromento *25 Febbrajo* **1872**

*Convenzione fra il Signor Ingegnere Giovanni
Battista Pirelli per la propria Ditta G. B. Pirelli e C.ᵢ
e il Sig.ʳ Amato Antonio Goulard per la quale
questi viene assunto a Direttore tecnico della
fabrica di Articoli di Gomma elastica nei CC.SS.
di Milano*

a rogito del **D.ʳ STEFANO ALLOCCHIO**

Notajo residente in Milano

Si rilascia al Sig.ʳ Ing.ʳ G. B. Pirelli

From November 1870 to September of the following year, he travelled through Switzerland, Germany, Belgium and France, entirely filling a thick 300-page squared notebook, which miraculously survived the bombings in 1943 and was found in the rubble by a female worker. When he was asked which field of study he intended to deepen, he chose the new industry of elastic rubber called *caoutchouc* (in Italian, *caucciù*). It was the name of the extraordinary new find that promised a notable number of applications but there were no factories producing it in Italy. It was and would become elastic, resistant, waterproof and insulating.

As a student, Pirelli was struck by the story of a French engineer assigned by the Italian Railways to recover the *Affondatore*, the Italian Navy armoured steam ram that, damaged during the battle of Lissa, sank in the bay of Ancona. He remembered that the rubber tubes for the pumps that would lift the hull were lacking. Not to be found in Italy, they had to be imported from France. This story remained in the family memory as a kind of foundation legend.

Machinery wasn't enough; it would be necessary to invest in training the workers

Pirelli's choice to focus on the rubber industry was not initially clear-cut. The young engineer had intended to study the development of the emerging industry, but his mentor Colombo, who knew the manufacturing sector inside out, convinced him to reject the already crowded textiles sector and aim at a fast-developing new sector despite its inherent problems: the pungent, unpleasant smell of *caucciù* and the excessive sensitivity to heat and cold compromising its use. The first solution to the problems had come from the USA when Goodyear patented vulcanisation in 1840, and then other innovations.

Pirelli would have liked to begin his exploratory trip in France, but was put off by the war with the Prussians and the dramatic insurrection of the Paris Commune in 1871. This unexpected event kept him in Switzerland for four months, allowing him to study hydraulic energy systems in depth. He spent another four months in Germany, and then Belgium. He managed to arrive in Paris only in August. As the scholarship funds were finished, he had asked for a money order to be sent from home. Fortunately, it arrived in time, and he cashed it in to pay for the coach.

The diary he kept of his trip is a sort of self-portrait of the artist as a young man. Pirelli took notes on everything with maniacal care and enhanced the information with drawings. Nothing escapes him: pulleys, pinions, turbines, the roofs of the railway stations or the grain market in Munich, sewing machines, wire rope transmissions, tubing and sluice-gates, pig iron foundries, locomotives and wagons. Everything could turn out to be useful. The industrial world was a work in progress that changed every day in the fever of experiments. There are only a few *caucciù* factories; they safeguard their production processes jealously and rebuff the curiosity of visitors. Visiting textile factories was easier, and Pirelli scrupulously took notes on the washing machines and the carding machines that combed, doubled and lengthened the wool. Perhaps in the future it would be useful to know that Mr Oechselin manufactured metal cables and Mr Krunz large 150 hp turbines. Mr Printz produced a million needles per day in eighty operations and compensated the scarcity of manpower by automating his machines. Pirelli kept track of everything with increasing impetus. In Nuremberg, he was very impressed by an immense factory with 3,000 workers who produced railway wagons in a kind of assembly line. In Stuttgart he was amazed to discover that there was a permanent industrial exhibition. However, the euphoria of all this technology did not restrict Pirelli's perspective. Coming from a modest social class led him to carefully consider the human factor. Machinery wasn't enough; it would be necessary to invest in training the workers, teach them to handle the equipment better and contribute to improving it. Technical schools would be necessary: 'The worker is the essential lever for industrial progress'. Education needs to be adapted to the new needs. It was not by chance that the large exhibition in Stuttgart also had an imposing library. In Milan there already existed a Society for Encouragement of Arts and Crafts, why not implement it? Pirelli discovered that in Germany, schooling was compulsory until 14, and included drawing. The teachers were well paid and there were also vocational schools in the evenings. Then, no less important, there were administration, financing, amortisation and economies of scale. Industry was a network with numerous intersections and one needed to know them thoroughly. This multitasking aptitude will deeply mark the course of his entire entrepreneurial activity, where technique, research, finance, organisation, the human factor, civil society and the international horizon will bond together in a virtuous circle.

Of the 138 textile, mechanical, railway and metallurgy companies he visited, only six worked with rubber. Despite good presentation letters, Pirelli had tremendous difficulties in getting through the wall of secrecy protecting that young, rapidly evolving industry, where experience, both positive and negative, dictated any innovation. He did not have to deal only with reticence, but noticed that often he was given deliberately false or imprecise information. Still, he tried to use his personal contacts as best as he could.

So the twenty-two year old engineer who presented himself to the notary Stefano Allocchio on 28 January 1872 to found the first Italian rubber factory was a man who had already acquired consistent know-how and set up significant relations. It was a rather reckless endeavour, as his son Alberto will recall in 1946 when resuming production after the disasters of the war. In 1872, managers, technicians and workers were lacking; workers were more inclined to craftsmanship than disciplined factory work. Investors hesitated in the face of an initiative so loaded with unknowns. There were few people who believed in industrial development and private finance was wary.

The modest capital Pirelli raised with some effort should be considered as 'the manifestation of a group of Lombardy investors' modern viewpoint'. It was 215,000 lire with Limited Partnership set at ten years. The director's monthly salary was 250 lire and 5 per cent of the profits. Among the first subscribers some names

At first, he'd thought of opening a factory in Italy, but all things considered, he decided it was better to become a partner in a thriving business.

The beginnings were problematic. Goulard's technical direction was disappointing, the workers disorganised and the clients perplexed. Comforted by the auditor's appreciation, Pirelli requested increased capital to remediate the initial losses. He moved to a small house next to the factory to keep an eye on everything, took on management of all the functions, doubled his efforts, managed to get out of the shoals and implemented new productions: insulated telegraph wires and electric conductors, manufactured only in England, elastic thread for weaving and, later, bicycle tyres. In three years, sales covered more than half the national consumption of rubber products.

At the 1881 Milan Exhibition, the stand of Giovanni Battista Pirelli, François Casassa & C. booth proudly displayed the sign 'the only Italian *caoutchouc* factory' and a wide selection of elegant raincoats for women. In the background is a photo of the factory built in the open countryside; now 21 Via Fabio Filzi. The Sevesetto, a spillway for the Naviglio canal, runs along the facade

He has five office workers, forty workmen and a steam engine. The first products were tubes, belts, valves and gaskets

stand out: Mrs Berra Kramer, Marquis Ermes Visconti, Knight Commander Francesco Brioschi, Raimondo Visconti, Duke of Modrone, Dr Onorato Zucchi, Professor Colombo, Knight Commander Eugenio Cantoni and Pirelli himself. Quotas ranged from 5,000 to 10,000 lire; Davide Sforni invested the most, 55,000. Pirelli personally procured the necessary machinery in England: purifiers, masticators, mixers and calendaring machines. In Milan, Pirelli has five office workers, forty workmen and a 26 hp steam engine. The first products were tubes, belts, valves and gaskets.

Thanks to the good French contacts he had made, he was able to hire as the first technical director of the new firm, G. B. Pirelli & C., a person he met in Paris, Antoine-Aimé Goulard, experienced in fabricating rubber products. He'd also met another Parisian manufacturer, François Casassa who, six years later, became a partner in the company.

and has a small iron bridge over it. The thick clouds of smoke rising from the single chimney indicate full speed production.

When François Casassa became a partner, the capital rose progressively to 1,100,000 liras, the number of employees increased to 300, sales went from 100,000 to 1,500,000 liras and the average gain was 7,5 per cent. However, the first two engineers, a chemist and an electric engineer, only arrived in 1884. Preparation of the compounds wasn't very different than the unassuming procedures of housewives making risotto. Before lab instruments were available, the rubber's tenacity was tested by biting it. Rubber wasn't skimped on; in fact, too much was used. At the Milan Exposition in 1881, an American technician from Goodyear said the Italian rubber was too good; cheaper rubber could be sold well. Later, there would be well-equipped labs, frantic research and patents, but

Portrait of François Casassa, 1877–1886

The 1,000–ton cable–laying ship constructed in England and named *Città di Milano*, had 3 underwater tanks able to hold 'up to 400 kilometres of submarine cables made of copper, gutta–percha and steel'

an increase in the traditional tensions between the pure technicians and the workers who proudly laid claim to the value of personal experience

Very aware of market demands, Pirelli focused on creating loyalty in the new management and developing it to be up to the challenges. He will be repaid by the professionalism and dedication of a top-class management group of technicians and administrators that accrue decades of loyalty, wisely remunerated and motivated. He will show the same sensitivity towards employees, setting up an emergency fund and a special welfare policy. Equally significant and new was the focus on communication and advertising, considered not less important than production.

The 1880s were marked by a serious economic crisis. The problems of public finance and glamorous bankruptcies of important banks dictated a policy of rigorous and severe saving in Public Finance, and the construction industry crisis forced to introduce the 'politica della lesina', the 'policy of rigorous savings', was compounded by strong social tensions. The first rival companies were set up, launched by ex-collaborators that had learned the trade and struck out on their own, perhaps disloyally. Pirelli suffered but understood and wasn't discouraged. He continued to count on research and quality. He adopted one of Edison's ideas: *Genius is 1 per cent inspiration and 99 per cent perspiration*, in other words, sweat, patience, method and stubbornness.

The national budget recovered only in the last years of the century, and foreign trade increased. Pirelli could reassure his stockholders and greeted with relief the new developments marked by progress in telephony and electrical energy distribution. The Edison Company, born in 1883, implemented the first lighting system for the La Scala. In that same year, a new company, Pirelli & C., a limited joint-stock partnership with a capital of two million lire, took over the liquidated Giovanni Battista Pirelli, François Casassa & C . Pirelli remained the only director.

Even though there were problems, the company did have epic moments. Pirelli took on a challenge that seemed too much for his strength. In 1884–87 the era of underwater telegraph cables began, pioneered by the English. Later, Alberto Pirelli described some of the phases of that industrial and maritime feat: '...lay a continuous cable extending for thousands of kilometres on the sea bottom, as deep as 5 or 6 thousand metres. Grapple it if it broke during the laying and bring it up to the surface or buoy it during rough seas, in order to resume work; organise a naval expedition that would last months, even keeping live animals on board to ensure food.'

The English had connected Italy with its principal islands. Now another 12 underwater cables were needed to complete the Tyrrhenian and Adriatic network. Pirelli assumed the responsibility of signing an agreement with the Italian government; beyond manufacturing the cables, it included a specialised ship for laying them and a 20-year maintenance period.

It was a programme of exceptional technical and financial commitment. The 1,000-ton cable-laying ship constructed in England and named *Città di Milano*, had 3 underwater tanks able to hold 'up to 400 kilometres of submarine cables made of copper, gutta-percha and steel.'

The press followed the feat passionately with patriotic pride, reporting the eulogies of the newly connected cities 'to the Pirelli company, promoter of civilisation.'

The *Città di Milano* would also be used during the 1911–12 Italo-Turkish War to lay new strategic lines, repair cables or cut those of the enemy, navigating as far as the Dardanelles under enemy fire. The success of the Italian cable-laying motivated important contracts with the Spanish government that contracted the Pirelli company to lay the submarine cable between the Balearic Islands and the continent. In only a few years, the Pirelli company laid 1,190 kilometres of cables in Italy, 616 in the Red Sea and 726 in the Spanish seas.

In December 1904, Giovanni Battista Pirelli's two sons, Piero, 23, and Alberto, 22, began to work with him. They were the oldest of the eight children he had with Maria Sormani, whom he married in 1880. Pirelli's sons integrated their studies at the Polytechnic and the Bocconi with experience in the factory under their father's severe supervision. Pirelli applied the same exacting care as with his executives, and it was a real mandate, not just formal. A gesture of faith and motivation that transformed the company summit into a trinity. When he announced the news in a letter to his employees, he underlined the true sense of their entry. The 'cooperation' of the new managers means opening 'a new era of achievements and progressive development', but the objective will only be attained if 'forces of youth' are matched by a 'new diligence and new vigour from each one of you'. Once again, the founder aims at team spirit. Piero was responsible for organisation, production and administration; Alberto managed external relations, where he proved to have diplomatic and political talent. In 1904, he met Edison who showed him one of the first examples of a gramophone. The same year, his father wrote him a significant letter, sending him on a mission to Amazonia (Brazil was the world's biggest market for natural rubber): 'You won't be unpleased by the chance of a bold, high-impact mission worthy of a young man who wants to go a long way.' These sober words reflect an essential style, the knowledge of mankind, the significance of a word with countless innuendos, the elegance of an understatement, the ability to match a wide-ranging vision and the attention to details. Thirty years after his father's travels in northern Europe, Alberto showed the same sharpness in understanding and analysing the complex realities of a savage capitalism.

Pirelli had become a role model, an authoritative charismatic celebrity, who had always wanted to be personally involved in the management of his city, Milan. From 1877 to 1889, he was a member of the City Council and the Chamber of Commerce. He was involved actively in the works of the commission on urban planning, in particular, traffic circulation. On the national level, he fought for a reform of customs duties in order to protect the Pirelli products. Councillor and then president of the bank, Credito italiano, he was able to attend the board meetings of some of the most important industrial companies. He supported the private Bocconi University, was president of Edison and Confindustria, the Italian Industrial Federation. Interested in the world of information, he became one of the principal partners of the newspaper *Corriere della Sera*.

The Pirelli company had solid international prestige. The factories were enlarged and became a little city that exhibited the black plaits of smoke like flying flags. In 1909, a new factory opened in Bicocca on the outskirts of Milan; an excellent area that had the possibility of further development and was part of a vast urban plan providing for transfer of the entire Milanese production. Rubber consumption extended to the newly born automobile industry, sugar and paper factories and the mines. Through constant monitoring of new trends in various world markets, informed by numerous research trips in Europe and the Americas and intelligent diversification, the Pirelli company was able to compete everywhere. It produced underground lead insulated cables for the electricity network, a fast-growing business due to increasing the city lighting systems. At the beginning of the 1900s, Pirelli opened in Spain its first foreign factory, marking the beginning of a gradual internationalisation. The advent of automobiles gave rise to big markets and posed a series of problems that could be resolved only through experience. The interest in 'tyres for automobiles' is documented since 1904–05. Rubberizing was the weak point of the newly born industry and progress was sought through empirical attempts in a climate of secrecy. There was a demand for materials able to resist the stress of greater velocity and substantial weight. So many problems—carcasses exploding, cracks in the tyres, treads breaking and rapid deterioration. It was almost impossible to arrive at one's destination without some kind of breakdown. So many protests and angry debates. It took five years to take off and overcome the obstacles that were much more complex than imagined.

Though Fiat was initially a difficult client to win over, prestigious successes arrived in the field of automobile races. In 1907, an Itala with Pirelli tyres won the Peking-Paris raid with a triumphant parade in the French capitol. Graphically refined posters combining the elegance of Art Déco and the provocations of Futurism exalted Pirelli's racing triumphs. They were the first evidence of a masterly use of publicity that still contributes notably to consecrating the brand. In a 1914 poster by H. L. Roowy (Stanley Charles Roowles), a red racing car with big white tyres, a masked driver looking like Spiderman, races towards a sure victory against a black background.

The logo with the elongated 'P' goes back to those days. In 1958, the poet Vittorio Sereni wrote in the magazine *Rivista Pirelli*: 'The idea of the horizontally lengthened uppercase "P" that covers the other letters like a canopy was originated in New York City one day in 1908'. It was a winning sign even in the crowded American market. It combined a well-controlled momentum to a sense of protection, reliability and grip.

The first trade union agreement was in 1902. Relationships in the company had always been good; it was like a big family and the employees had a sense of belonging. This allowed the company to overcome even the Milanese revolts in 1898. Pirelli knew how to talk with his people; he had grown side by side with them. He was used to handling practical problems without being hindered by ideological concepts or political leanings. Inclined to talking things over, he didn't approve of the authoritative and repressive attitude of the end of the century governments. He had initiated a welfare policy, creating a voluntary fund for aid and pensions well before the institutions. The socialist leaders like Filippo Turati respected him. Turati went to the factory to harangue the workers and Pirelli talked with him. That was the beginning of negotiations that went far into the night. As in the apologue of Menenius Agrippa, for Pirelli a society is 'an intricate totality of delicate organs', not very different from the human machine that requires balance, order, energy and unity of objectives: what we call today, excellent corporate governance.

Through constant monitoring of new trends in various world markets, the Pirelli company was able to compete everywhere

In the early 1900s, Pirelli conquered new markets in Central Europe, supporting the new investments with a shrewd financial policy. The First World War created a dramatic fissure. The Pirelli company was born, grew and became international during decades of peace. Now it had to give up the strongly expanding markets of the Hapsburg and German empires. But even in the turbulent waters of the war, Pirelli acted lucidly, with a foresight

Postcard of the first anniversary of the Società Anonima Cooperativa di Consumo among the employees at the Pirelli factory in Milan, 1901

Stanley Charles Roowy, advertisement for Pirelli tyres, 1914

Domenico Bonamini, view of the Pirelli factory in Milan – Bicocca, 1922

Giovanni Battista Pirelli with his son Piero, 1916

that inspired the post-war moves. He had the breadth of vision of an enlightened statesman.

In a letter to Luigi Einaudi in January 1916, Alberto Pirelli, spokesman for the family preoccupations, manifested the awareness that the post-war period would be even worse than the war years, drugged by the abundance of orders that quadrupled sales, dictating the opening of a new factory in Vercurago. Finding raw materials, thinning out of the workforce called to arms and difficult connections with foreign branches were all problems that could be overcome by facing them with the usual Pirelli pragmatism; the company managed to cover 80 per cent of the Italian Army's needs. However, social tensions, discomfort, contradictions and resentments agitating both the victors and the defeated were another story. There were conflicts between war veterans and the workers movement emboldened by the Russian Revolution, and in general, the total exhaustion after a terrible plague.

In September 1920, the workers occupied the factory, but political and ideological rumblings were kept outside the walls. The tradition of solid relations, negotiating and providing housing for employees carried weight. In his book *Pirelli. Passione e innovazione 1872-2017*, Carlo Bellavite Pellegrini observed that management contrasted the turmoil with articulate responses, not indulging in reactionary or authoritarian temptations.

The post-war period saw a drastic drop in orders, with resulting financial difficulties (the number of employees was halved) that forced Pirelli to reorganise, but the company's reputation was such that notable increases in capital, from 60 to 120 million lire, were underwritten in 1920. Two years later, during the 50th anniversary of its founding, the Pirelli company changed to a new ownership structure based on the holding model, and could exhibit an imposing family tree with a complex ramification starting with the four big Italian factories in Milan, La Spezia, Bicocca and Vercurago. It included participation in numerous Italian companies in textile companies and spinning mills, foreign activities in Spain and Argentina and two plantations in the Far East that stabilised the quantities and prices of the raw materials. The management in which Giovanni Battista had placed his two sons in 1904, enlarged to become a Board of Directors that included, along with the three Pirellis, the experienced and skilled executives Emilio Calcagni, Fabio Palandri and Giuseppe Venosta. Production was concentrated on products with major profitability like tyres, high-voltage cables and, at the end of the twenties, the new telephone industry. Once again, the various corporate structures constructed over the years revealed their functionality: they succeeded in ensuring the necessary financial support while maintaining control for the family and the executives close to it.

The company's 50th anniversary coincided with the rise to power of the Fascist Party. With his keen insight, Giovanni Battista, by character and experience opposed to authoritarian solutions, realised that Fascism would 'freeze' the numerous problems existing instead of trying to resolve them. It would be up to his son Alberto to skilfully play the match with the regime, carrying out institutional roles when requested, but maintaining a distance that removed the danger of unquestioning compromises.

Even in the rapidly growing American financial market the Pirelli company could issue bonds, desirable due to the solidity of a company able to operate in numerous countries with a well-diversified offer of products, so much so, that in 1929, it was the first Italian company listed on Wall Street. That would be how the company was able to go through the Depression without too much harm.

Giovanni Battista Pirelli died on 20 October 1932. I like to think he was an original interpreter of Carlo Cattaneo's polytechnic spirit because of his multiple interests, his curiosity, his planning capacity and his visionary qualities. Not to mention internationality, composed civil militancy, ethical rigour, being anchored to technical methods, science and practicality. His entrepreneurial fever was inscribed in the wider context of an entire cohesive society in an organised fabric of relationships. If he had had the time, he could have also have written about railways, land reclamation, customs duties, commerce, agriculture, finance, public works, and even geography and penitentiary systems, without renouncing literature and history.

Like Cattaneo, he knew that progress is not a linear and progressive course, rather, something exposed to the risk of regressions, delays and falls that require strenuous commitment to individual responsibilities. And like Cattaneo, he wanted to entrust the task of economic modernisation to an active and committed entrepreneurial class able to correct its errors and favour social development.

AN ESSENTIAL BIBLIOGRAPHY

Alberto Pirelli, *La Pirelli. Vita di una azienda industriale*, Milan, 1946, a memoir written by Pirelli's son Alberto.
Giovanni Battista Pirelli, *Viaggio di istruzione all'estero. Diario 1870-1871*, edited by Francesca Polese, Venice, Marsilio, 2003.
Francesca Polese, *Alla ricerca di un'industria nuova. Il viaggio all'estero del giovane Pirelli e le origini di una grande impresa*, Venice, Marsilio, 2004.
Carlo Bellavite Pellegrini, *Pirelli. Innovazione e passione 1872-2017*, Bologna, il Mulino, 2017.

The Industrial Elegance of Rubber

It is 1872 when the young engineer Giovanni Battista Pirelli founds the first Italian factory for the processing of elastic rubber. Thanks to a diversified production, the company also grows rapidly abroad. With the passing of the company's first fifty years of life, Italy is a totally different country compared to the nineteenth-century one in which it had taken its first steps.

by Giuseppe Lupo

-

**WRITER AND UNIVERSITY
LECTURER**

O n 6 August 1866, two weeks after the Battle of Lissa, the ironclad warship of the Italian Navy *Affondatore* was sunk in the Gulf of Ancona in a storm. It was moored in the roadstead to have the damage suffered during the conflict repaired and it took almost a year to raise the hull from the seabed. The difficulties encountered in bringing it to the surface could perhaps have suggested to a young Giovanni Battista Pirelli the idea of producing rubber tubes, which were necessary for that kind of operation. At the origin of the company that would bear his name there was therefore a failure in the Third War of Independence. It was his son Alberto, the second-born, who put forward this suggestion in a book published in Milan in 1946: *La Pirelli. Vita di una azienda industriale.*

At the time to which these facts refer, Giovanni Battista was 18 years old (he was born in Varenna, on Lake Como, in 1848) and it was in the heat of that patriotic fury that he was prompted to participate in Garibaldi's campaigns in Trentino, in 1866 itself, and in Lazio the following year. He was rather short in stature and did not have the imposing physique of a soldier. A photo contained in Alberto's volume depicts him in military uniform, a rifle resting on his right shoulder; he has the gaze of a teenager, serious but not disenchanted. Some time later that young man, who seems like a character from the stories in De Amicis' novel *Cuore*, was to attend the Faculty of Mathematics at the University of Pavia and then transfer to the Regio Istituto Tecnico Superiore in Milan, what is known today as the Politecnico, to graduate in Industrial Engineering under the guidance of Giuseppe Colombo, a key figure in the personal history of Giovanni Battista and the Pirelli company. Colombo, in fact, in 1870, contributed to having him awarded the Kramer Prize, which came with a grant amounting

to 300,000 lire, a significant sum for that period, enabling the new graduate to travel for a long period in Switzerland, France and Germany, in the heart of a continent torn to pieces by the rivalry between Bismarck and Napoleon III, but undoubtedly more advanced than Italy as regards industrial development.

Another photograph contained in Alberto's book depicts his father aged 22: he is sitting at a table in civilian clothing, he has grown a moustache and has the less carefree expression of the Garibaldian volunteer he had previously been. There is also a third photograph, perhaps the most significant of all: Giovanni Battista is at the centre of a group of young engineers—a couple of them sitting with sticks with silver pommels, in poses that are too formal for 20-year olds, all the others standing—and is staring at the black eye of the daguerreotype with the headstrong manner befitting a captain of industry. He appears determined to launch the enterprise he has in mind: the limited partnership company G.B. Pirelli & C., specialising in the production of elastic rubber items. The company was formed in the middle of winter, on 28 January 1872, but it was only seventeen months later, in June of the following year, that it began to produce its first drive belts and, later, raincoats. Giovanni Battista is now 25 years old, he teaches Mechanics at the Società di Incoraggiamento Arti e Mestieri and is considered to be a resourceful and courageous man, a true pioneer in Italy for this kind of production.

The factory was located in open countryside, a few hundred metres outside of Porta Nuova, not far from the point where the most important railway station in Milan was to be built, the future Stazione Centrale. A watercolour by Salvatore Corvaja (which dates back to 1922, but reproduces the original illustration, which has been lost) helps us understand what the factory layout was like by observing it from high up: a building of just 1,000 square metres, with a tall chimney looming over

Inside the electrical
laboratory in the Pirelli
& C. factory in Milan,
after 1884

The first view of the
Pirelli factory in Milan
in a replica by Salvatore
Corvaja from a lost
original, 1922

previous pages
The workers at the exit
of the Pirelli factory
in Via Ponte Seveso
in Milan, 1905,
photo Luca Comerio

*Drawing of the exhibition
of the Pirelli elastic rubber
factory for the 1881 Expo
in Milan*

it and enclosed by a wall surrounded by trees, hedges and lawns, with a gate overlooking a small water course, the Sevesetto. On the pages of *Industriale* magazine of 8 July 1872 it is described as follows: 'it is of an uncommon size and not without that robust elegance of which many foreign establishments are proud'. 'Robust elegance': a summary formula that has the air of an intentional similarity with the models of companies outside of the national territory, to which Pirelli had looked and which it had taken as an example from its beginnings.

To become established in an activity that until that moment was unequalled in Italy, it was necessary to cast the gaze beyond the Alps, in the attempt to learn all possible secrets to make the young factory competitive, organised and technologically avant-garde. It was necessary, in other words, to bridge the gap with Europe and, even if the initial core of employees was rather limited in number—forty blue collars and five white collars—Giovanni Battista immediately wanted to plan in grand style, trusting in the expertise of Antoine-Aimé Goulard, an entrepreneur considered an expert in the production of rubber, whom he had met in Paris during the trip he made thanks to the Kramer Prize. This choice proved to be a mistake. Goulard was not up to the task assigned to him and his name disappeared from the company history. The difficulties encountered in the early phase, however, did not prevent G.B. Pirelli & C. from extending its production range to other items: ropes, washers, valves, carpets, and rubberised fabrics (in 1874), erasers (in 1875), hot water bottles and balls for playing games (in 1877), rubber-coated telegraph wires and undersea electrical cables (in 1879).

Little more than five years had gone by from the birth of the company and it was already possible to glimpse the essential characteristics—the variety of interests, the drive to innovate, research in the chemical field—that would contribute, on one hand, to satisfying the needs of a nation still too young but already ambitious to be a protagonist of European history and, on the other, to winning the trust of the Italian government so as to gradually replace foreign firms in the supply of those products—rubber-coated telegraph wires or undersea electrical cables—intended for civil and military use. 'Our industry is by its nature, and everywhere, progressive', we read in a report drafted by Giovanni Battista in 1880, on the eve of the National Exposition, the major event with which Milan, twenty years after

Unification, confirmed its role as the ethical and economic capital of the country, the 'city that is the most city-like in Italy', as Giovanni Verga wrote. 'Progressive' is a term that perfectly encapsulates the spirit being breathed in the factory in Via Ponte Seveso, and Pirelli certainly could not be missing from the list of exhibitors, yet it was to participate with a modified structured and a new name: Pirelli Casassa & C. There was a change towards the end of the 1870s, when, rather surprisingly, François Casassa moved to Milan; he too, like Goulard, was an expert in the rubber sector and keen to undertake an activity away from France. The presence of this man might have constituted a threat for the future. Casassa, in fact, intended to compete with the Pirelli company, and this was the reason why Giovanni Battista proposed to the shareholders' meeting to welcome him as a partner. In 1877 the birth of Giovanni Battista Pirelli, François Casassa & C. was decided upon and that was the official title with which the company took part in the 1881 Expo, also awarding itself a diploma of honour. The products exhibited were of excellent quality and a certain Mister Fergusson of Goodyear, when visiting the stand, was so impressed by the items that, after finding out the prices, left a note on which he jotted these words: 'Too good, poorer quality will sell as well'.

It was again Alberto who reported this anecdote, and he also made a point of adding the rest of the story. The name Giovanni Battista Pirelli, François Casassa & C. would not have long life. Already in 1883, six years after its incorporation, it had returned to its original wording—Pirelli & C.—with Casassa now occupying the position of technical co-director, at least until his death in 1886. In less than fifteen years, the firm twice intercepted figures of industrialists from across the Alps and on both these occasions Giovanni Battista offered proof that he possessed diplomatic skills, as well as business sense, and that he knew how to manage human relationships, transforming what on the horizon might have appeared as dangers into resources. Understanding where the boundary lies between desire for self-affirmation, anxiety for economic success, and the progress of the country is a crucial matter, especially in the context of the Italy of the late nineteenth century, seeking that entrepreneurial legitimisation in the presence of the European nations that would serve as an engine to drive the entire emerging industrial sector. There is one unmistakable fact: the growth of a single company cannot happen if it leaves aside the principles of modernity, and these are proportionate to the value that is attributed to the organisation and rationalisation of human resources. From this perspective Alberto's book also provides reliable testimony of the managerial mentality that his father transferred into the family business starting from 1880, when he decided to divide production up into three departments, allocating these to the manufacture of technical items (the first), consumer items (the second) and electrical wiring (the third). The two decades that opened with the Expo and concluded with the end of the century were a period of expansion of production. The 'city that was the most city-like in Italy' was racing towards the future with the haste of someone pursuing the models lying beyond the Alps, in France, Germany and England, and technological progress seemed to provide the right opportunities to participate in this endless competition, at the service of mankind and civilisation. The first graduates to emerge from the polytechnics of Milan and Turin began to offer their talents to the factory in Via Ponte Seveso, and Pirelli signed contracts and established alliances, as happened for example with the Edison electrical company, founded by the very same Giuseppe Colombo to whom Giovanni Battista had presented his thesis; so what happened on 26 December 1883 took on a symbolic value, when the theatre season at La Scala was inaugurated and 2,450 incandescent light bulbs were lit up thanks to the electrical wiring of the Pirelli brand. Thus, an association began that would lead to Giovanni Battista taking his sit at the table of the Board of Directors of Edison in 1889. But there is more. On the horizon we could glimpse a relationship of synergy allowing us to realise how many resources the world of electricity attracts to itself; this was an opportunity that a company specialising in the production of elastic materials could not ignore, at least until the change of direction, which took place soon afterwards, in the early 1890s, at the time when a new entrepreneurial adventure was inaugurated in the sector of tyres for velocipedes and, later still, for automobiles. While horses and carriages were moving around the city, undersea cables were the main pole of attraction of the company in Via Ponte Seveso. Italy threw itself into colonial policies, with disastrous results, yet the defeat in Dogali, in Eritrea, which occurred on 26 January 1887, did not discourage the plans, but if anything speeded them up. In order to rectify the mistakes leading up to the military defeat, the government of Prime Minister Agostino Depretis intended to resolve the problem of communications and the Milanese firm won itself the twenty-year contract for the manufacture, laying and maintenance of telegraph cables also capable of connecting up the military stations in the Red Sea, in addition to Sicily and Sardinia. There are two signs that point to how this entrepreneurial policy is the result of conviction. The first is the birth of a branch in La Spezia, the San Bartolomeo plant, completed a few months after the disaster in Dogali. The second

is the acquisition of the cable-laying ship *Città di Milano*, bought in England: a ship of around 1,000 tons, fitted with electrical and mechanical equipments and with enormous tanks capable of containing up to 400 kilometres of cables. This was a period of great activity and enthusiastic messages arrived at the address in Via Ponte Seveso saluting the Pirelli company as a promoter of civilisation. Later, after the Spanish government had entered into a contract for laying telegraph cables between the mainland and the island of Ibiza, the Italian Ambassador to Madrid sent a telegram of congratulations that concluded with 'Viva Pirelli'. There are images in Alberto's book reconstructing the phases in which the bottom of the Mediterranean is covered with a spider's web of lines and the *Città di Milano* is laying cables between Italy, North Africa, the Iberian Peninsula, Istria, Dalmatia, and Greece. This is the second time that the destiny of the Milanese company is interwoven with the adventurous world of ships, and two names must be remembered among the engineers playing a fundamental role in these operations: Emanuele Jona, who headed the technical office for undersea cables and electrical applications, and Leopoldo Emanueli, an expert in the production and laying of cables. We can see the photographs of both in Alberto's book. Leopoldo Emanueli seems to be the younger of the two: he has a pointed moustache, a receding hairline and an optimistic expression. Emanuele Jona has longer hair, white as lace in the manner of Giosuè Carducci; he gazes intently at the photographic shutter, his eyes slightly asymmetrical. He seems to have realised in which direction fate will push him, his collaborators and the *Città di Milano*. When the cable-laying ship went into action, almost twenty years had gone by from its date of foundation and Pirelli was about to spread beyond the boundary wall in Via Ponte Seveso. In a view by Antonio Bonamore from 1889, other buildings have been added to the old construction, complete with chimneys, large windows, canopy roofs, and gardens. The following year an additional lot of 6,428 square metres was annexed. The area was called Brusada, because inside there was a farmhouse that had been burnt down in a fire, and it was there that, in 1894, the production of the first models of tyres for velocipedes, the Stella and the Milano, began, intended to replace the heavy solid rubber rings that had been used until that moment. The factory founded by Giovanni Battista did not abandon the sector of undersea cables (and cables in general), but the desire to enter a new production sphere was a sign of design capacity and insight, ready to identify from what direction the wind of the future was blowing. Despite the signs of economic recession, the fact that in the early 1890s Pirelli & C. was investing in a new product such as tyres indicates a precise strategic choice in favour of the most significant (and sensational) among the elements of an age that was to make speed its distinctive characteristic. The world began to race on wheels operated by pedals and engines; horses were

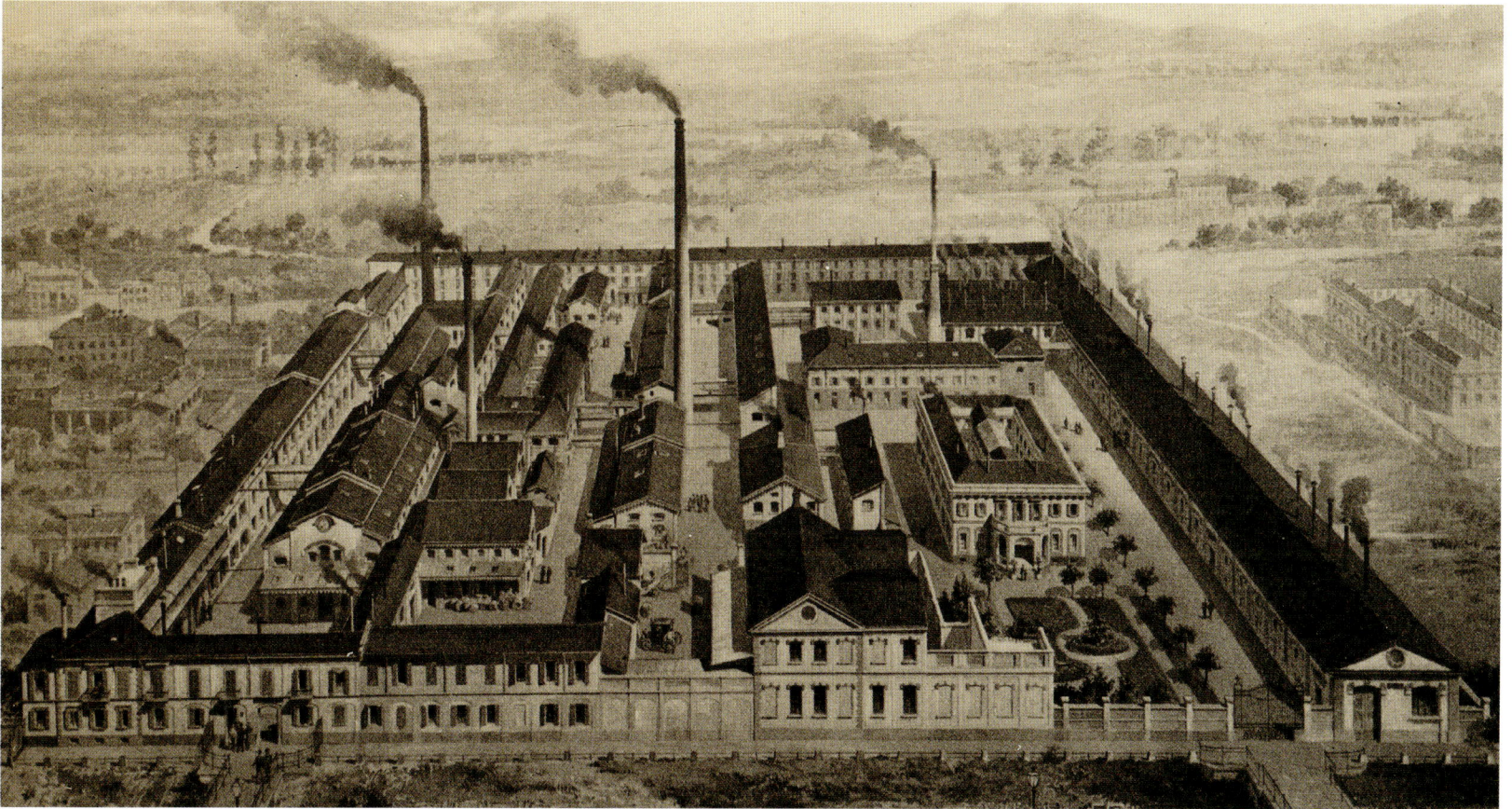

Antonio Bonamore, view of the Pirelli factory in Milan, 1889

Portrait of Emanuele Jona, 1887

Cable-laying steamboat Città di Milano, *1890*

ELASTICI CIRCOLARI PROFUMATI

Bracelets Élastiques Circulaires Parfumés

Si vendono in scatole composte di elastici uguali di un solo numero oppure assortiti in serie come al presente specchio.
Gli elastici della serie H si vendono sempre in serie complete.

La serie I è composta degli elastici dal N. 1 al 6
» L » » » 2 » 7
» M » » » 3 » 8
» N » » » 4 » 9
» O » » » 5 » 10
» P » » » 11 » 16

On vend ces Bracelets en boîtes composées d'un seul numéro ou assortis en séries d'après détail.
Les Bracelets de la Série H se vendent toujours en séries complètes.

La série I est composée de bracelets du N. 1 au 6
» L » » » 2 » 7
» M » » » 3 » 8
» N » » » 4 » 9
» O » » » 5 » 10
» P » » » 11 » 16

Serie H

Serie I   L   M   N   O   P

Grandezza naturale
Grandeur naturelle.

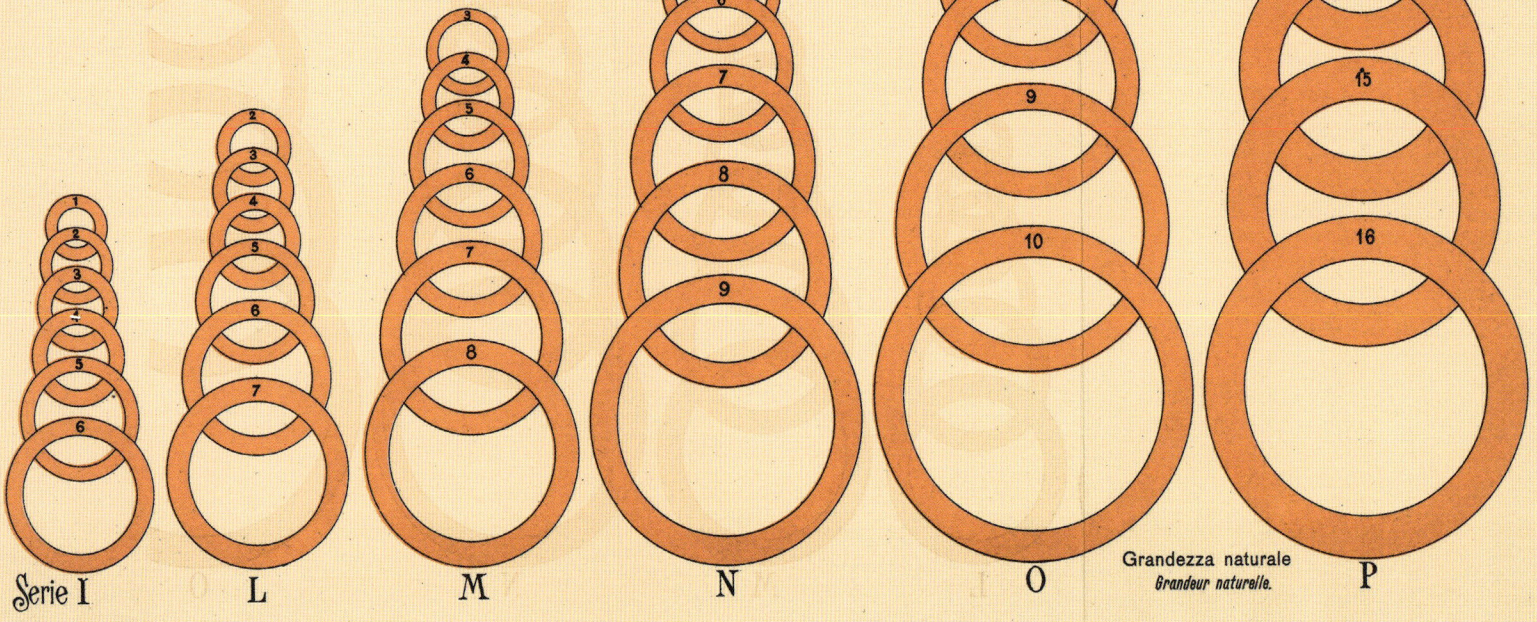

Illustrated plate from the Pirelli & C. catalogue of haberdashery, hygiene and surgery articles, 1894

Pirelli & C. catalogue of men's raincoats, 1920–1921

Price list of Pirelli rubber balls, 1927

no longer of use. Prisoners of an ancient sentiment of distrust towards technological innovations, the poets would only realise many years later, perhaps with guilty delay, but certainly not before the day when Filippo Tommaso Marinetti was to sing the praises of the wonders of the automobile in the *Manifesto of Futurism*: 'We affirm that the magnificence of the world has been enriched with a new beauty: the beauty of speed'. A few words, published in Paris, on the front page of *Le Figaro*, on 20 February 1909. The twentieth century had already arrived a decade earlier. Few had realised it, but in Italy too modernity seemed to seek consent in the imagination not only of men.

This is confirmed by the oil on canvas *Workers Leaving the Pirelli Factory*. It was painted by artist Giovanni Sottocornola between 1891 and 1897: it tells of a moment in the day when the end of work in the factory arrives and a ray of sunlight illuminates the gate, from where, in couples, in groups, the skirts, blouses, scarves and hairstyles of the female employees abound. Life far removed from the machines regains its afternoon liberty and in the extended goodbyes, in the expectation of returning home, there springs forth, along with the tiredness, the enthusiasm over participating in this new, emancipatory experience. It may be a coincidence, but the subject of the painting anticipated by a few years the panoramic view that photographer Luca Comerio was to create in 1905: workers leaving the factory in Via Ponte Seveso—as the photograph is identified generically—captures a much more populous parade of employees than the initial forty blue-collar and five white-collar workers, and once again in the foreground we note a significant presence of women. The statistical data confirm this: in 1908, when the move to the Bicocca area had already taken place, the share was to reach 47 per cent. It may well have been a factory for male markets, but it talked with a woman's voice.

The imposing crowd of faces is a sign of growth. Behind each of them there are family ties, feelings of hope and future uncertainties. It appears that everything is proceeding well in the passage between the nineteenth and twentieth centuries, yet this is not so. The photograph does not express the managers' concerns. While the undersea cable sector continued to be successful, rubber tyres for velocipedes and automobiles were a sore point. The problem was a double one: it is not easy to become experts in a short time, just as it is not easy to challenge the competition of foreign brands, above all the British ones. 'The production of tyres for velocipedes gave rise, originally, to more trouble', confesses Alberto in its book. And he admits: 'there were complaints and lawsuits". Something was clearly not working properly and the biggest problems occurred with tyres for automobiles: 'broken beads, bends in the frames, burst carcasses, cracks, rapid wear, detached tread, early aging', again it is Alberto who writes, reconstructing the pioneering endeavours of those years and the first, tentative attempts to establish contact with Fiat, Pirelli's ideal partner. Giovanni Battista visited the Turin factory for the first time in 1899, the very year it was founded, but he came away with a feeling of having experienced hostility. 'Fiat proved to be a difficult customer to win over', remembers Alberto. 'More than once we had to go to tell the bosses of the great Turinese company: "Do us the favour of trying again; now our tyres work well"'.

There was no shortage of competitors on the European markets, and these were considered much more competitive because they had an unquestionable advantage: they had been producing for longer and they were more experienced. The frustration of those years is contained in Alberto's words, but so too is the desire for the time to soon arrive when the doubts would finally be swept away as regards a company that was still young, and mostly Italian, with all the mistrust that its being Italian carried with it. The fate of the future Pirelli lay in tyres: Giovanni Battista was more than sure of this and his efforts were focused on this sector, the most fascinating and the one with the largest impact on the emerging modernity. Thus, there began the turbulent period that accompanied the nineteenth century to its definitive decline: a period of economic crisis that not only involved Italy, but was manifested in Italy in a particularly cruel way, through a serious recession between 1890 and 1891. This did not prevent the expansion programme from continuing and in 1894 Pirelli bought a company that manufactured rubber and gutta-percha objects and similar from the Ansaldo group. The company had its headquarters in the town of Narni, in Umbria, beside the River Nera, and soon changed its name to the Società del Linoleum, because the plan of the Pirelli group was for a material to be produced by the establishment that was practically unknown in Italy—linoleum, in fact—but that was destined to dominate the competition from marble, granite, tiles and wood as regards flooring for schools, offices, hospitals and court buildings.

Following the vicissitudes of that decade, the impression was gained that the wall surrounding the workshops in Via Ponte Seveso was not only a division between industry and countryside, but a genuine diaphragm between the feverish air that was being breathed inside the workshop and the social tensions that were about to explode. In May 1898 Milan became the stage for strikes and disputes that were to result in violent events, to which General Bava Beccaris reacted by ordering his troops to shoot on the crowd. While the city was in a state of military siege, Filippo Turati, the leader of the Socialist movement, went through the gates to meet the workers personally. 'Some of the older ones will certainly remember his characteristic features', Alberto notes in his book: 'unkempt hair and beard, intelligent eyes, impassioned speech'.

Alberto describes the first attempts at employee welfare in his book: the reduction in the number of hours per week from seventy to sixty in 1881, the granting of support for medical care between 1900 and 1905, paid holidays and the introduction of redundancy payments in 1917, and even profit-sharing for employees with more than five years of service in 1919. The disparities in the economic treatment of men and women remained significant, but this was a phenomenon in line with the principles of a sexist society and it would take some time before these differences were reduced; it would be necessary, that is, for the twentieth century to take its course, composed of successes and failures, of accelerations and slowdowns, and new faces were to make their entrance in the factory, to reinvigorate the work begun three decades earlier. This occurred on 1 January 1905, when Piero and Alberto, Giovanni Battista's sons, aged 24 and 23 respectively, joined the company as managers; they were both graduates in Legal Sciences in Genoa, and were entrusted with different roles: Piero with organisation and administration, Alberto with external relations.

This was not yet the moment for Giovanni Battista to pass the baton on to the second generation, but the amending of the company structure was a sign of courage and trust in the new recruits. 'We felt the responsibility deriving from the opportunity that was offered us—young as we were—by the trust of our Father, the Partners and the Workers', writes Alberto again in his book, 'to the point of always and continually being tormented by the thought that we might prove not to be sufficiently worthy'. The new century, which began with change as the watchword, confirmed its innovative character. Before Piero and Alberto entered the firm, the production of tyres for automobiles had finally begun with an attempt to rectify the problems of the first models and patent the resolutions: the attachment of the rim, the perforability and lacerability of the tyre itself, the problem of skidding. And then there was another important innovation: in 1902 in Spain the plant in Vilanova i la Geltrú, near Barcelona, was built, to be used for the production of electrical conductors and sanitary and rubber goods. This was the first to be created abroad. There would follow the plant in Southampton in 1913 and that in Buenos Aires in 1917. This was an international vocation that Pirelli had followed from the outset and this was its definitive confirmation. Alberto indirectly became the face with which the group represented itself in the world. In 1904, Giovanni Battista asked him to participate in the US exposition in St. Louis, in order to get to know the US rubber companies, to sign contracts for the purchase of raw materials and to launch negotiations for the supply of cables at Niagara Falls, and from there to go on to Amazonia to visit the rubber forests. 'I was 22 years old', he remembers in the book. 'In a letter that he [his father] sent to me in New York, with his instructions, he said: "you will not be displeased to find the opportunity for a hazardous, extensive mission, worthy of a young man who wants to get ahead"'.

Implied in Giovanni Battista's words is the hope that it will not only be his children who will get ahead, but also the company in which they are involved and to which they should devote every effort, every attention. In effect, the most delicate aspect in being entrepreneurs

in the manner of the Pirellis was the capacity to be in step with the times, to accompany the phenomena of modernity or even to anticipate them. The challenge no longer concerned underground and undersea cables, but the world on two and four wheels. The evolution of velocipedes generated a type of pedal vehicle that eventually lost its rather comical circus image, to transform itself into a less striking structure, more suited to making it a practical, fast means of transport, as was demanded by the pragmatism of the new century. On the cover of the *Rivista Mensile del Touring* dated December 1908, a man is seen on a bicycle, along a road bordered with snow, as he stands beside an advertising hoarding with the words: 'la Semelle Pirelli. Also, for bicycles. Anti-skid, unpierceable, smooth'. Two words are striking, and for different reasons: one is 'bicycle', the other is the brand of the tyres, Pirelli. It cannot be stated with any certainty, but this could be one of the last times when the word appears in its original form. In fact, the invention of the capital P that—as Vittorio Sereni was to write much later—'by lengthening horizontally covers the other letters that make up the name like a roof', dates back precisely to those years.

The roof-shaped P is an invention attributed to an anonymous representative of Pirelli when he was in New York, but it immediately took on a symbolic value because it prefigured the advent of the Futurist graphics to which the Milanese firm, due to its links with the icons of speed, appears to be doubly tied. The manufacture of balls for playing games, raincoats, elastic thread for weaving, rubber soles and heels, tubes, carpets and drive belts certainly had not stopped, but tyres catalysed the main efforts and became the key products, and sports events contributed to the diffusion of these: particularly the most important race in stages that came about in those years, the Tour de France, which made its debut in 1903, attracting everyone's attention, both the working and middle classes. In an advertisement by Aleardo Terzi we see an elegantly dressed woman holding a bicycle tyre who has the red, white and green tricolour fluttering behind her. At the bottom there appear the reassuring words: 'Pirelli tyres stand out as the best in the "Giro d'Italia" race'. The advertisement dates back to 1909, the year when the competition for the pink jersey began. The interweaving of industry and sport was becoming an interesting phenomenon, also involving the world on four wheels. The Peking-to-Paris Race took place between June and August 1907: 16,000 kilometres, in which the team composed of Prince Scipione Borghese and the journalist Luigi Barzini triumphed. The car they were travelling in had Pirelli rubber tyres. This was the definitive payback for the time when Giovanni Battista was forced to ask Fiat: 'Do us the favour of trying again'. A new tyre was introduced onto the market that year. It was called Neroferrato: it used carbon black in the compound for strengthening purposes.

The twentieth century launched itself into its dizzying technological conquests and the old factory in Via Ponte Seveso required extra space. The inability to expand

Aleardo Terzi,
advertisement for Pirelli
tyres, postcard created on
the occasion of the Giro
d'Italia, 1909

Gian Emilio Malerba,
cover of the Rivista
mensile del Touring,
December 1908

The motorcycle rider
Carlo Maffei, winner of
the Italian Motorcycling
Championship on a number
of occasions, on a Bianchi
motorcycle with Pirelli
tyres, 1919, photo Strazza

The Itala car with Pirelli tyres, winner of the Peking-Paris Race, on display at the editorial office of Le Matin *newspaper in Paris, 1907*

Alberto Pirelli on the ship sailing up the River Amazon, 1904

further made it necessary to move to the locality of La Bicocca, in the north-east of the city, between the municipalities of Niguarda and Greco Milanese. In that area a plot of 115 hectares was purchased by the family of Count Sormani. It was no longer city and not yet suburban, but countryside that gradually began to be filled with railway tracks, roads, warehouses and chimneys. The work on the construction of the new workshops began in 1907 and concluded two years later, precisely when Giovanni Battista was named Senator of the Kingdom. The first decade of the new century consolidated the brand he had founded, and not only at national level. The success that he finally enjoyed repaid the sacrifices of the entire community over the previous forty years and, even if on the horizon the causes were accumulating that would soon lead to the Great War, the conviction was prevalent of being on the right road as regards entrepreneurial choices. In Italy the projects were multiplying, with branches to appear in Monza, Tivoli, Rovereto, Pizzighettone and Vercurago. In London, in 1909, the subsidiary Pirelli Ltd was founded, with the aim of handling the sale of all the group's products in the British Empire. In Paris, in 1913, the Société Française Pirelli was established with commercial aims. In England Pirelli General Cable Work Ltd also came about, thanks to the alliance with General Electric.

These are simple news chronicles, but they do give the measure of an achievement. The challenge was now a more ambitious one and was to be directed at the rubber plantations: in the East, in Java and Singapore, or in South America. The war that began in 1914 proved to be slow and draining, quite the opposite of how it had been announced, but it resulted in orders arriving at the addresses in La Bicocca, where the female labour force predominated over the male. Yet the war did not go unnoticed. The twentieth century was not only a festive and rhetorical race for progress and on the day after the armistice the whole world was to begin to understand that modernity is also suffering, disappointment and pain. On 16 June 1919 the cable-laying ship *Città di Milano* struck a rock off Filicudi and sank into the sea. The path of Pirelli's destiny had encountered the sea for the third time. Twenty-six employees died, including Emanuele Jona, the chief electrician, the engineer with the sad gaze. He was succeeded by Luigi Emanueli, Leopoldo's son, demonstrating the fact that the history of an industrial firm resembles a large spider's web of interwoven kinships. The Italy of those years had little in common with the young nineteenth-century nation in which Pirelli had taken its first steps and was already showing some signs of attrition in the relations between political class, entrepreneurs and work force. The shapes looming on the horizon promised nothing good and tensions would soon explode. The country was walking dangerously on the edge of a precipice, which a few years later would go by the name of Fascism.

THE ORIGINS OF A LONG HISTORY OF INNOVATION

The story of Pirelli has often influenced Italian history, pushing it towards avant-garde perspectives. Not only in the technological field, in which the company has had the capacity to value excellent materials and production processes from its very beginnings, but also in the social field, for example by entering into the first agreement with workers to improve salaries and working conditions. And again, without losing its distinctive character, it has been able to look beyond its own 'production' dimension, forging dialogues with the great artistic, literary and intellectual voices of the twentieth century. A dialogue that has never been broken off and that still makes it possible to write and to analyse the present, but also to imagine a future made of innovation.

In the letter from the engineer Giuseppe Colombo to Giovanni Battista Pirelli, written on 16 March 1871 and saved in Alberto Pirelli's private archive, the professor exhorts the future founder of the Milanese company not to become distracted by easy and well-tried and tested markets, such as that of silk, but rather to continue his research into the processing of rubber in Germany. Its importing into Italy could foster a much more promising entrepreneurial initiative: 'Your idea of devoting yourself to the silk industry is good in itself; but do not lose sight of the objective of Caoutchouc: this would be a wholly new industry, while that of silk is already so much exploited by us that it leaves us very little margin'.

G. COLOMBO
INGEGNERE INDUSTRIALE

PROGETTI
di impianti industriali
Macchine e materiale
delle industrie e delle costruzioni

UFFICIO
pei brevetti d'invenzione
per l' Italia e per l' estero
(Ing. P. GUZZI)

Milano, Via Rugabella, 10.
16 Marzo 1871

To my work colleagues

In the recent period, in which I have been away from the work that I did for over forty years in your midst, I have felt more than ever how strong the feelings of affection are that connect me to this work, to the company founded by my father and that bears my name, and to the entire family of Pirellians. It seemed to me to be appropriate to move closer to this great family by recalling some events of company life, and the spirit in which I wrote prompted me to give the narration a tone of particular intimacy, accompanying the exposition of the facts with personal memories and comments springing from a long and varied experience of work. My thoughts are directed not only at today's and tomorrow's Pirellians, but also at those who have left the work, for whom I hope this book may be a source of pleasant and perhaps touching re-evocations; and they are also directed at the family members of the company's current employees, who, through conversations within the family, are living the life of the company, and among whom there are, I hope, some future Pirellians.

Nobody will be surprised at this attachment of mine: I was born within the walls of the first old factory in Sevesetto. In 1882 my mother escaped unscathed from a fire at the plant a few weeks before my birth, carrying in her arms my brother Piero, who was just a year old. As children my brother and I felt the pulsating of the machines through our bedroom wall. Already at the age of 10-12—since we still lived at the factory—we frequently went around the workshops accompanied by our father; at 15–16 we participated in some campaigns of the ship *Città di Milano* to repair and lay undersea cables; at 17–18 our father took us with him on some business trips abroad. So we were born and grew up in the midst of the workers, the machines and the developments at the company, and very soon learned to love the work, the workers and this company, which has never been 'ours' due to some hereditary privilege or some predominance of stock, but the best of our lives is tied to it.

Founded at the dawn of Italian state unity, Pirelli was one of the first manifestations of this country's industrial development. In its long life, it has been witness to and a participant in the progress of the Nation, but it has also seen crises and misfortunes of the Nation, and has suffered momentary crises itself. Today the situation is serious as never before in the past. After the wretched period from which the country is emerging defeated and exhausted, we are living through a phase in which, adding to the lasting concrete difficulties, for many, above all for young people, there lie uncertainties and spiritual turmoil. Questions crowd the mind and doubts the awareness. But faith will return, our country will be born again and we will resume the path of progress. I am certain of that. And our company too will emerge victorious from the present depression if we are animated by that honesty of intentions, by that desire for industriousness, technical efficiency and social justice, and also by that healthy optimism, that were the characteristics of the man from whom our company derived its life, name and success and whose personality is imprinted, in his children's memory, on the pages that follow. In addressing this message to the members of the Pirellian family, I have therefore also had the hope of being able to reinforce this confident optimism in them, through memories of the past and perspectives for the future, together with the feeling that the company to whom they give their work is very worthy, on account of all the strengths and experiences, the traditions of honesty and integrity, the prestige internally and externally, of being considered by them to be a flag in which to wrap themselves, to be a secure point of support for their faith in the future. The executives, for their part, fully feel their responsibility in the social no less than in the economic field.

Giugno 1946   *Alberto Pirelli*

Returning to the company after the end of the Second World War, Alberto Pirelli addresses his employees and collaborators recalling the figure of his father, his own growth 'among the machines' at the factory, but above all encouraging those qualities of cohesion, strength and resilience that the whole group of workers was able to demonstrate in a tragic period of Italian history. The text, addressed to 'my work colleagues', is the premise to the book by Alberto himself La Pirelli. Vita di una azienda industriale (Milan, 1946), in which his natural attachment to the company founded by his father and his feelings of affection for having run it for over forty years amid national and personal events clearly emerge.

The Concordato fra la Ditta e la Commissione Operai per miglioramenti di trattamento e disposizioni varie in seguito alla presentazione del Memoriale Operai [Agreement between the Company and the Workers' Commission for Improvements in Treatment and Various Provisions Following the Presentation of the Workers' Petition] *is the first agreement between a company and its workers to be signed in Italy. Printed in Milan on 3 May 1902 by the Tipolitografia Angelo Restelli, the certified copy of the agreement, conserved by the Fondazione Pirelli, also contains handwritten indications of major historical-social value.*

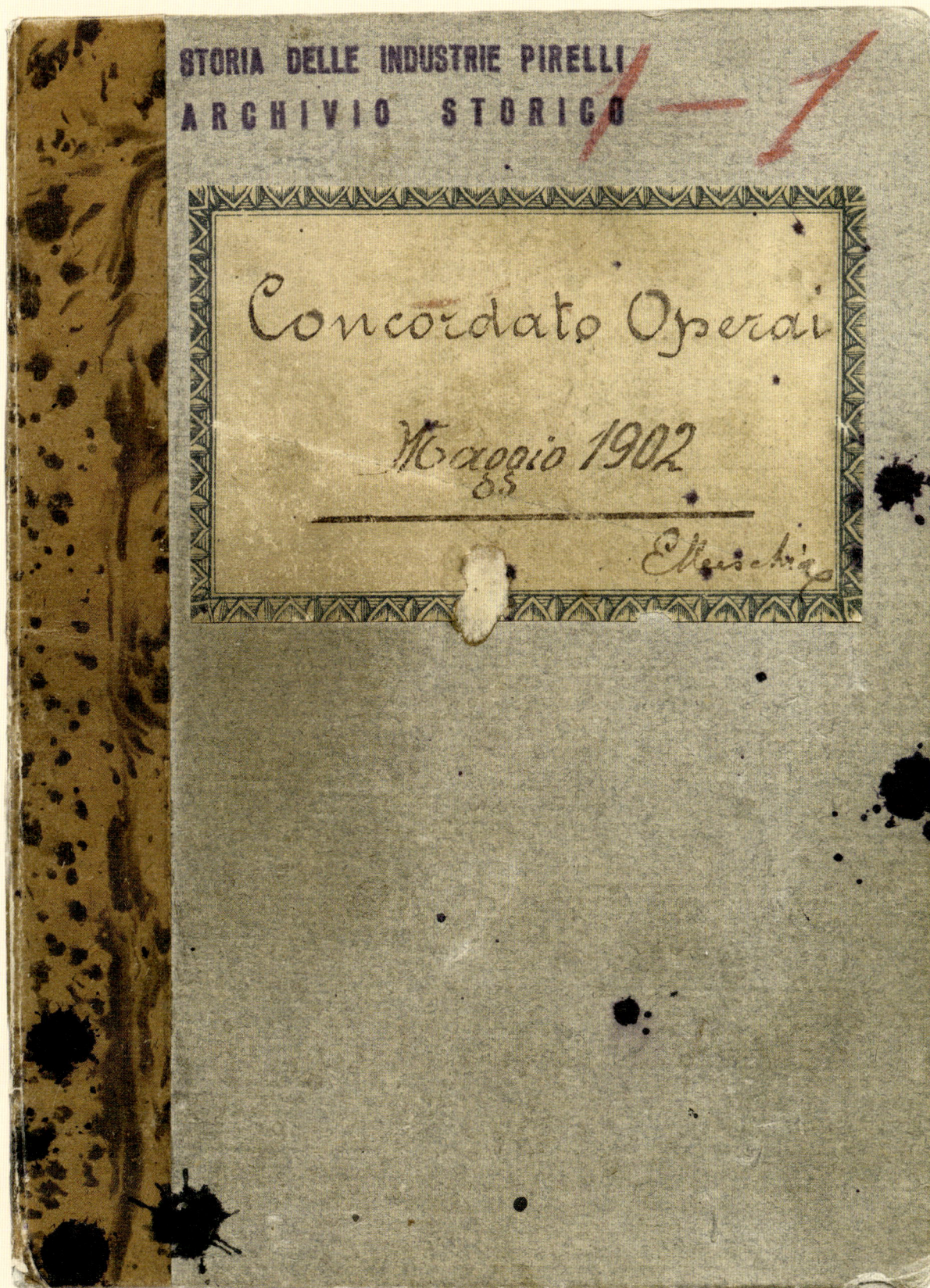

STORIA DELLE INDUSTRIE PIRELLI
ARCHIVIO STORICO

Concordato Operai

Maggio 1902

1175

<u>Relazione sul naufragio della R. N. " Città di Milano</u>

Messina 18 Giugno 1919.

Sigg. Pirelli e C.

                Milano

     Soltanto stamane mi trovo sistemato ed in condizioni di potere riferire dettagliatamente quanto avvenne e prego ritenermi scusato se non l'ho fatto prima come sarebbe stato mio desiderio.

     Siamo partiti da Milazzo lunedì mattina 16 corr. col programma di visitare dapprima gli approdi di Salina e Filicudi (del cavo Salina-Filicudi) per constatarne lo stato ed eventualmente eseguire qualche lavoro, si sarebbe poi andati all'altro approdo di Filicudi per compiere la riparazione del cavo con Alicudi che sapevamo rotto fra gli scogli all'atterraggio.

     Alle ore II eravamo a Salina dove sono sceso trovando tutto in ordine. Proseguimmo per Filicudi x ove arrivammo verso le I3. Anche qui scesi constatando che il cavo non aveva bisogno di nulla. Ritornato a bordo verso le ore I3,30 la nave si rimise in moto a tutta forza dirigendo a levante per girare l'Isola da sud onde vedere la boa d'ormeggio posta davanti il grosso dell'abitato di Filicudi e giudicare se potervi venire con la nave e passarvi la notte se prima non si fosse ultimata la riparazione all'altro approdo.

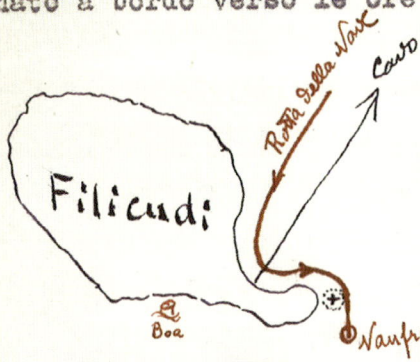

     Io mi trovavo in Gabinetto Elettrico e stavo scrivendo nel rapporto gli appunti circa la visita all'approdo, quando sentii la nave urtare due volte a breve distanza (ore I3,40) e tosto l'ordine di fermare la macchina seguito da quello di mettere indietro. Uscii dal Gabinetto e vidi in coperta gl'Ingg. Jona, Pinelli, Vitali ed il Comm. Brunelli. La prua incominciava già ad abbassare, mi precipitai a poppa dove ho il camerino per provvedermi di salvagente seguito dal Comm. Brunelli. A poppa vi era il Tenente che raccomandando la calma ten-

Having survived the wreck of the cable-laying ship Città di Milano, *which occurred on 16 June 1919 off the coast of the island of Filicudi during an expedition to check on the work, Ernesto Del Grande, a Pirelli employee, sent a report to the owners on what had happened. The rescue operations did not prevent the deaths of the engineers Emanuele Jona and Ettore Pinelli, among others.*

(2

tava mettere la gente in riga. I nostri operai invece di loro iniziativa
stavano mettendo in mare le imbarcazioni. Aiutai il Comm.Brunelli a met-
tersi il salvagente,poco discosto era l'Ing. Jona che ci guardava senza
dire nulla. Visto che nella barca vela a sinistra vi erano già i nostri
operai Saioni,Porini,Maggiani e qualche altro aiutai a scendere il Comm.
Brunelli e poi mi filai giu io. Il bastimento era giàn per metà sommerse
intravidi la poppa che si alzava,vidi che qualcuno dei nostri vedende
che non si riusciva a scostare l'imbarcazione si buttaranoin acqua e ne
seguii l'esmpio nuotando disperatamente per allargarmi.Ho l'impressione
di aver visto la poppa tutta fuori con l'elica inabissare rapidamente.
Sono rimasti in acqua fra i rottami forse per una quindicina di minuti
poi sono stato preso da una lancia in cui era il Capitano De-Ferrari e
sbarcammo sugli scogli della punta. Intanto soppraggiungevano pescatori
ed abitanti di Filicudi che avevano visto il disastro e si diedero a
prestare soccorso. Altri animosi dei nostri con la lancia ripresero il
mare. Poco dopo vidi portare a terra l'Ing.Pinelli trovato svenuto e
sostenuto da un fuochista (Napo) che cercava di porgergli inutilmente
un cuscino di poltrona che galleggiava. Imbarcato in un batello borghese
venne poi deposto su uno scoglio della punta dove gli si praticò invano
per circa 3/4 d'ora la respirazione artificiale.

Mentre andavo a terra vidi la barca a vela capovolta su cui stavano appollaiati Saioni e Locori,appena fu possibile andarono a prenderli
e rimessa a galla l'imbarcazione vi trovarono un fuochista della R.M.
ancora vivo e impigliato sotto i banchi il cadavere del povero Comm.
Brunelli che non ha avuto,si vede,il coraggio di seguirmi quando mi sone
buttato a mare. La barca vela deve essere stata rovesciata dalle grue
dei paranchi quando la nave affondò.

Degli Ingg. Jona e Vitali nessuna traccia. Il Comandante e l'Uffi-
ciale di rotta dicono di averli visti in coperta a poppa fino all'ultimo
quando loro si buttarono a mare. L'Ing.Jona aveva il salvagente ed il
binocolo.

L'Ing.Vitali,nuotatore abilissimo,deve avere perduta la testa,ed é

(3

rimasto a bordo precipitando poi nel gorgo forse come l'Ing.Jona,tratte-
nuto dalla tenda.

Il Comandante si salvò agguantando uno dei nostri palloni che ri-
masero a galla perchè il nostromo pensò a slegarli. E per questo forse
oi rimase la vita. Appena giunto a terra,cioè verso le 15,mi dettò il
telegramma per il Comando della Difesa Marittima di Messina che tosto
consegnai al guardiafili di Filicudi da portare all'Ufficio che sta in
alto a quasi mezz'ora di aspra salita dall'approdo.

Dopo che mi sono fatto asciugare al sole quanto tenevo in dosso,
verso le ore 16 mi diressi all'approdo dove poco alla volta si raduna-
rono tutti i superstiti e quando fui certo che nessuna speranza vi era
più di rintracciare,almeno per allora,i mancanti risultanti dall'appel-
lo,mi recai personalmente all'Ufficio e telegrafai d'urgenza a Voi a
Spezia e al Ministero Poste e Telegrafi.

L'Isola,come è facile immaginare,non ha risorse,quindi ben pochi
hanno potuto trovare di che coprirsi e rifocillarsi. I soccorsi giunse-
ro dopo il tramonto. La Torpediniera N°24 che prese a bordo le due salme ritrovate,il Comandante e parte dell'equipaggio militare.

Più tardi giunse un vaporetto da Lipari sul quale imbarcammo noi
della Ditta ed il rimanente dell'equipaggio. Più tardi ancora essendo
arrivati anche il vaporetto di Milazzo vi fummo trasbordati.

Si partì dopo le ore 23 noi diretti a Milazzo,la torpediniera a
Messina. A Milazzo arrivammo alle 3 del mattino ma non trovammo la torpediniera "Cigno" che,secondo gli accordi,avrebbe dovuto portarci subito
a Messina. Verso le ore 7 ottenemmo dalla Capitaneria di Porto di farci
proseguire per ferrovia e giungemmo a Messina verso le ore 9,30. Alla
stazione trovammo un Tenente della R.M. che ci portò alla difesa Marittima,ove finalmente potemmo avere un po' di ristoro.

Gli operai,per equivoco,furono dimenticati e asixxxxxx non man-
giarono che a mezzogiorno passato.

Intanto per disposizione del Comando fummo provvisti degli indumen
ti più necessari e analoghe disposizioni vennero date per gli operai;ma

(4

purtroppo anche per questo sorse equivoco e gli indumenti (militari:maglie,calze,scarpe,divise grigio-verde e berretti)non gli ebbero che verso le 17.- E qui non vi posso nascondere che il nostro personale ha tenuto un contegno poco corretto,dimostrando una irrequietezza ed anche prepotenza fuori luogo.

Fummo tutti quanti sottoposti ad un interrogatorio da parte dal segretario della Difesa. Dopo di che il Comando dispose di lasciare libero il nostro personale,tranne Lagomarsini che rimane con me e De-Ferrari a disposizione del Comando per l'inchiesta che sarà fatta,pare, dall'Amm.Resio che giungerà da Roma.

Per cura del Comando stesso i tredici operai vennero messi in treno ieri sera alle 18,con foglio di via per la 2°classe e per Spezia. Ad ognuno vennero consegnate L.50.-

Ieri sera poi,per cura delle autorità civili e militari,venne fatto il trasporto funebre,su camion,dal Viale S.Martino a Cimitero,per una tumulazione provvisoria delle salme dell'Ing.Pinelli e del Comm.Brunelli. Per questa cerimonia,nè io,nè il Cap.De-Ferrari fummo interpellati. A quell'ora,trovandomi casualmente aterra,seguii di mia iniziativa,il corteo accompagnandomi col Direttore delle Costruz. di qui,Cav.Maresca. Al ponte Americano il corteo sostò e si ebbero discorsi del Prefetto,del Direttore Ufficio Telegrafi,del Generale Vagliasindi e del Comandante Casabona.

Io sono alloggiato bene,qui al Comando della Difesa Marittima.

Il De-Ferrari con Lagomarsini hanno preferito stabilirsi all'albergo in Città.Non ho creduto fare altrettanto giudicando essere meglio tenermi in contatto con le Autorità per qualunque convenienza.

Ieri sera vi ho telegrafato estesamente ed altrettanto ho fatto per Roma in risposta ad un telegramma del Sig. Alberto.

Spero avrete informata e tranquillizzata la mia famiglia alla quale non ho potuto telegrafare che ieri mattina. Ora non ho tempo di scrivere anche per loro dettagliatamente.Vi prego quindi comunicare a mia moglie,stralciando dalla presente,quante giudicate possa interessarle. Ringraziamenti e distinti saluti.

La metà del mondo vista da un'automobile.
Da Pechino a Parigi in 60 giorni
[Half the World Seen from an Automobile.
From Peking to Paris in 60 Days]
by Luigi Barzini

La metà del mondo vista da un'automobile. Da Pechino a Parigi in 60 giorni [Half the World Seen from an Automobile. From Peking to Paris in 60 Days] by Luigi Barzini is the first reportage in the history of Italian journalism and, at the same time, a direct testimony of civilizations and peoples gathered before the modernization of the twentieth century. Published in 1908, it contains episodes and events experienced by the journalist alongside Prince Scipione Borghese in what, the previous year, represented the first transcontinental ride in history. Tackling bad weather and territories unexplored on four wheels, the Itala with Pirelli tyres driven by the prince arrived in Paris over fifteen days earlier than its adversaries.
The victory marked a fundamental watershed for Pirelli, who thus began its history in the world of racing, on the track and on the road.

All the parts then—and I am not talking about the wheels and the springs, which had to undergo fatigue—were tested to the limits. It was an unprecedented trial.

- From Italy the tyres arrived at pre-arranged stages. [...] From Irkutsk onwards Pirelli tyres awaited us every thousand or fifteen hundred kilometres. And we were lucky. Not once were we short of fuel or lubricant; we were never without a supply of spare tyres, which, incidentally, we barely used.

- We jump into the car and away! Away, along a winding, uneven road, without worrying about the jumps, the jolts, the bumps, as long as we are racing along. The automobile is only in second gear, but we feel like we are flying. We are presented with huge puddles formed by the rain. Onward! We hurtle into them, ploughing through and raising a storm of water and mud; the wave is regurgitated into the compartment in the chassis and soaks us through. We laugh. We talk in loud voices, overcome by a strange exuberance.

- The car was in excellent condition—from the departure from Peking we had not needed to change more than one tyre, the one on the left rear wheel—, we had fuel and lubricant for a thousand kilometres, provisions for three days; we could therefore even venture into completely uninhabited regions.

Una P lunga cinquant'anni [A P fifty years long]
by *Vittorio Sereni*

A poet, writer and translator, Vittorio Sereni was one of the most powerful literary and intellectual voices on the Italian panorama in the period following the Second World War. Like many other writers, artists and thinkers of the period, he contributed to the contents of Rivista Pirelli. In the article from which we reproduce some passages here, he considers the topic of the evolution of the 'Long P', the logo that has been part of the company's history since 1908. The three pages by Sereni grace the second issue of the magazine, published in 1958.

- The idea for the capital letter that, being elongated horizontally, covers the other letters that compose the name like a roof, came about in New York one day back in 1908. It was a brainwave of that moment, due to a request from the representative that Pirelli had there at the time.

- —Does this work for you? —asked the visitor who had just arrived from Italy. And he drew on a sheet of paper, very roughly, a P with a wholly unusual shape.

- —Yes, it could work—the other replied after a first glance. —Indeed, it works very well. —He looked and looked again at that P standing out on a poster or against a background of sky.

- Look at the hole of the elongated P and tell me if it doesn't remind you of the definition studied in the physics book on the subject of that property whereby bodies resume their original shape after a deformation.

- The elastic hole that extends and stretches, thickening at the round end point where an invisible finger holds it in place, preventing it from springing back and taking on its initial appearance, is a kind of Disney-like insight before the term existed.

Restarting in the Aftermath of the World Wars

After the end of the world wars, Europe finds itself having to rewrite and redefine its equilibria. Alberto Pirelli is one of the key figures of the international reconstruction: entrepreneur, diplomat, international finance expert. With energy and a positive spirit he takes up the reins of Pirelli again.

by Monica Maggioni

-

**JOURNALIST, WRITER
AND DOCUMENTARY-MAKER**

I t was the month of June 1946. Europe, devastated by the violent wave of two world wars, was dominated by uncertainty. Restarting meant being able of rewrite the internal equilibria of countries, the relationships between states and the global order. The view was dark. There were no answers. The scene was populated by the rubble of History.

Alberto Pirelli, having returned to run the family business a month earlier, after suffering from the purge and the commissariat system, felt that the moment had come to put black on white concerning some key elements of the relationship between the company that embodied the history of his family, Pirelli, and the country: this was a reflection that perhaps led to the exploration of the very reasons for the existence, and of the need for survival, of one of the greatest and most representative Italian industrial firms.

So, he sat at his writing desk and wrote down a series of considerations.

The idea of bringing together the life of Pirelli up to that moment in a small book also enabled the Milanese industrialist to establish some fixed points regarding the relationship between himself, Pirelli and, fundamentally, Italy: it was then that *La Pirelli. Vita di un'azienda industriale [Pirelli. Life of an Industrial Company]* came about.

Pirelli—he writes in the preface—has represented one of the first manifestations of this country's industrial development. In its long life it has borne witness to and participated in the progress of the Nation, but it has also seen crises and misfortunes strike the Nation, and it has suffered momentary crises itself. Today the situation is serious as never before in the past. After the wretched period from which the country is emerging defeated and exhausted [...] questions crowd the mind and doubts the awareness. But faith will return, our country will be reborn and we will again follow the path upwards of this I am sure.[1]

This was a sense of optimism and faith that he also projected into the future of the company, provided it was animated 'by that honesty of intentions, by that desire for industriousness, technical efficiency and social justice'[2] that Alberto identified as 'Pirellian' values transmitted by the founder—his father Giovanni Battista—to him, to his brothers, to all the executives.

This state of mind was that of someone who, after a profound trauma, decides to try to look the future in the face with energy and a positive spirit.

Only a few days had passed since that 2 June in which, from the very first light of dawn, almost 25 million Italians had joined the long queues to choose between Monarchy and the Republic. The vote marked the future path of an Italy yet to be built. On 13 June Umberto di Savoia left the country; the page of the monarchy was closed forever. A collective liberatory ritual seemed to be performed to leave the twenty years of Fascism, the years of the war, of the thousands of deaths, of the horror of the concentration camps behind. Time to start again. With a country covered in dust and rubble.

In that setting, for the industrialist Alberto Pirelli the reconstruction of cities, the country's economy, production, was equivalent to the effort to overcome trauma: a journey that is collective and personal. Industrial and human. He too had to succeed in thinking about the future leaving behind him what he had experienced in recent years.

On 7 May he returned to the factory after being forced to hide in Rome because he was threatened with arrest and purging ('epurazione' in Italian). Many people, including his son Giovanni, a partisan fighter, worked to have him exonerated from the unfair accusation of having

Piero and Alberto Pirelli,
1954

The Pirelli Headquarters
in Viale Abruzzi
in Milan, 1948

previous pages
The driver Tazio Nuvolari
on the Monza racing
circuit with an Alfa Romeo
P2, circa 1930

The Pirelli area after the
bombing in 1943,
photo Crimella

wholeheartedly collaborated with the régime, among other things, by agreeing to be a minister with Mussolini, brought against him by the Committee of National Liberation of Northern Italy. Pirelli was subsequently declared not chargeable, but the company—as indeed the vast majority of Italian businesses with over two hundred employees—was placed in the commissariat system. It was only in May 1946 that the extraordinary shareholders meeting was to order the return of the two brothers to the factory: Piero took on the role of president and Alberto that of managing director. In this context the role of Cesare Merzagora proved decisive. Recruited by Pirelli in 1938, in the post-war period he was named commissioner of the company, thus representing the interests of the industry in the delicate recovery phase. In 1946, appointed as a board member of the IRI [Institute for Industrial Reconstruction; in Italian 'Istituto per la Ricostruzione Industriale'], he presented a plan for its reorganisation. He was subsequently to be named Prime Minister and then Senator under the De Gasperi Government.

For Alberto Pirelli, who had been one of the most brilliant European industrialists, it was a matter of coming to grips with the gazes of those who had considered him too close to Fascism, despite the positions he had adopted more recently, during the war and the bombing of the factories, in the battle against the deportation of his workers. Alberto felt the weight bearing heavily on his shoulders of the long years lived following a path that grew increasingly narrow in the attempt to survive, and to enable the company to survive, in an Italy crushed by the Fascist vice, avoiding clearcut support for the *régime*, but without expressing—except on a few occasions—positions that were so decidedly different as to jeopardise the possibility of continuing production.

Starting up again, in that 1946, meant overcoming the anguish of the rubble and knitting contacts with the world back together. With that history that for twenty years, between the wars, had transformed Pirelli into a colossus acting on the global market. To renew relationships with that international context that for Alberto Pirelli and the leading executives at the company had been a kind of natural horizon of doing business and being Italian. Perhaps Italians different from many others, passionate about innovation and discovery, research and ambition, open to the planet and to business, ready to move ever slightly forward the boundary line already drawn for their businesses, their projects. For their dreams.

The path between the two wars had begun for Alberto Pirelli with the awareness of the gravity of the moment that Europe and the world were preparing to go through, after the beginning of the conflict. 'The war will allow situations to rise again and will leave traces of them that seemed over, and, along with every sort of new problem, will trouble the souls of those who, by orientation and by their studies completed, belonged to the liberalist school.'[5] When he wrote these lines to his friend Luigi Einaudi it was Wednesday 12 January 1916. He had just leafed through the morning edition of *Corriere della Sera*, which

opened with the headline: *Lovcén occupied by Austrian troops*, and reported that 'a French detachment has disembarked in Corfù to prepare for the arrival of Serbian units on the island. The dispatch from Petrograd by the correspondent of *Le Temps*, taken from the Milanese newspaper, stated that 'the progress of the Czar's troops is slow everywhere, but sure'. In his daily bulletin General Cadorna reported that 'from Monte Ghello, northeast of Rovereto, on the evening of the 9th, the enemy launched incendiary grenades against our positions…'.

In the hours when King Vittorio Emanuele II arrived in Rome from Florence privately for talks with the Prime Minister in Villa Ada, Italy seemed to be just a small piece in a European mosaic riven with conflict. Indeed, the front page of *Corriere* was a war bulletin.

Yet, while the chronicles of those hours offer a precise description of the actions in the war, the daily difficulties, the tactics of the armies pitted against each other, Alberto Pirelli's gaze already seemed to be directed towards the world that was to be. And the personal—and business—advantage resulting from the international turmoil it seems to be worth little or offer little consolation, in his words. It is clear that precisely the years of the war, and of the immediate post-war period, were destined to mark a decisive growth for the company, which would end up also playing a leading role on the global scene. His nature, his passion for the world, instead prompted him to direct his gaze forwards, beyond the circumstances of his family and even the nation. Alberto Pirelli had a natural political vocation; he often crossed swords with Luigi Einaudi, who, those days, was teaching Science of Finances at the Bocconi. With him on a number of occasions he discussed the challenges that awaited liberalism and a political class that was unprepared to come to terms with a world that had definitively ended with the nineteenth century and had been overwhelmed by the impact of the war.

The grave consequences of the conflict on the world order, and particularly on western societies, were clear to his eyes. For this reason, the efforts of everybody, in his view, had to be directed at transforming the economy marked by the war into an economy and a society of peace. He, who with his brother Piero continued to push Pirelli out into the world and towards innovative industrial paths projected into the future, already sensed what social imbalances, what issues of overall reorganisation, would be involved in the return to an economic rhythm no longer powered by the frenzy of war.

It was with this awareness that, in 1917, he set off for London. The House of Lords had called upon him to illustrate his position on the future of the commercial relations between Italy and Britain, on the basis of the elements discussed within the Italian Committee for Customs Tariffs and Trade Treaties, of which he was a member. London was a familiar environment for Alberto Pirelli. With Piero he had travelled at length over all the early years of the century, in the Americas and in Europe. In England he already had friends and a lifestyle, in addition to his company's factories. When he entered the House of Lords, many of the faces there were familiar and he was met with warm greetings. He brought them, passionately and knowledgeably, his concerns about the world that was to come.

In the meantime, however, Italy's entry into the war, for Pirelli, corresponded to a significant increase in orders, above all from the market of solid rubber tyres, which were essential to the Navy and the Air Force. In the years of the war sales revenue quadrupled. At the end of December 1917, the company had 11,000 employees, of whom 2,000 had been called up.

The period after the First World War seemed to revolve around the existence of this contradiction: the drive towards progress of the new century and fears over a world that had become bigger and more fragile.

In Milan, amid the Pirelli sheds and offices, every choice seemed to speak of the future: the international acquisitions, the research into new products, the collaboration with artists who began to build a recognisable image and made 'propaganda' (as this form of company advertising was called at that time) the company's distinctive feature.

In those days there was already the 'long P' defining a brand (the P that the two Pirelli brothers would become used to using even in their own signatures), but it was the collaboration with the most visionary artists of the age that gave the company image total recognisability. This is a distinctive feature that continues to this day. Therefore, in the gallery of advertising images there also appears the design by Marcello Dudovich, an artist who had already characterised the appearance of the Universal Exposition in Milan in 1906 and who now, in the early 1920s, had devoted his energies to cinema posters and advertising for the major Italian brands. In the Pirelli advertisement from 1919, it was he who portrayed a woman in a blindfold resting securely inside a tyre. This was a fashionable young woman, with the Parisian air of a muse of Toulouse-Lautrec. In the portrait by the great artist of Trieste, Pirelli becomes the emblem of a world full of charm and seduction that transcends the narrow confines of the Milanese limelight. The innovation also lay in this. In already knowing how to present itself, in the early twentieth century, as a visionary brand in which the reference is not to a product but to a lifestyle, in which the communication is not directed exclusively at the illustration of the object but at the story of a vision of the world. To the public it described not only an object, but an industrial system.

At the age of thirty-five, Alberto Pirelli was certainly one of the most outstanding figures of Italy, and not only on the industrial plane, thanks to his constant relationship with the foreign markets. With the end of the First World War there began for him, and for the company, a phase of further international recognisability. The need to increasingly extend the market of raw materials, to expand the branches of activity, led to the Milanese entrepreneur entering conversations with producers and industrialists from all over the world, devoting his energies to the development of the sector of rubber and electric cables, in addition to that of textiles and chemicals, in Italy and abroad.

In reality, already before the outbreak of war Alberto had understood that the time had come to move more effectively on the international market. The competition from some European companies, and even more of American ones, had to be managed with a strategic vision. Although in Italy there were very few industries capable of projecting themselves effectively on an international scale, Pirelli was already ready—with choices ahead of its time—to move even beyond European confines. The commercial network was extended through the establishing of a series of autonomous companies that acted as branches for the mother house. A series of new production plants with the brand of the 'long P' saw the light of day in foreign countries. The quality of the management, the presence of the two brothers who were used to travel, their personal contacts and naturally diplomatic approach favoured the development of relations with the rest of the world.

It is no coincidence that when Alberto made his aforementioned speech to the House of Lords, he was not seen as someone extraneous, but as a habitual frequenter of London and the world of British finance, as that Italian entrepreneur who, in 1913, was the first to conclude a joint venture with London's General Electric for the creation of two factories to manufacture cables, in Southampton and Eastleigh.

On the other side of the ocean, the case of Argentina is emblematic: Alberto had decided that he wanted to establish himself on the cable market in the South American country, but the German competition seemed impossible to outperform. Again, he worked with the local entrepreneurs to find a way round the problem. He founded the Compañía Ítalo Argentina de Electricidad, which would gain significant orders. The South American market was also open. Despite the international political turbulence, it was a period of growth and the construction of what would be destined to turn into the global market. Alberto Pirelli summarised the energy of the moment in the definition 'optimistic prospects for the industry' when he spoke of them, looking at them retrospectively, in his text from 1946:

Added to the general awakening of the Italian economy was the development of many industries consuming our products, such as mines, sugar mills, paper mills, and so on, and some new discoveries in the field of miscellaneous rubber articles were being introduced.[4]

There was a sense of energy and change that was pervading the century just born. In the 1920s the effect of war events on the economy was a fact; but in reading Pirelli we can grasp an element that went beyond contingency. It was almost a matter of personality. The expansion beyond the national confines with unusual methods certainly corresponded to a strategic calculation of an entrepreneurial type. Yet, factually speaking, it underlined that the company story was not sufficient for a spirit such as Alberto's. A man marked by a strong passion for politics, travel, and the world such as to take

Advertisement for Pirelli
tyres on the cover of the
English magazine
Land & Water,
7 May 1913

Marcello Dudovich,
advertisement for Pirelli
tyres, 1920

*Advertisement for Pirelli
tyres on the cover of the
English magazine*
Land & Water,
7 May 1913

*Marcello Dudovich,
advertisement for Pirelli
tyres, 1920*

LE ORGANIZZAZIONI PIRELLI NEL CINQUANTENARIO DELLA DITTA

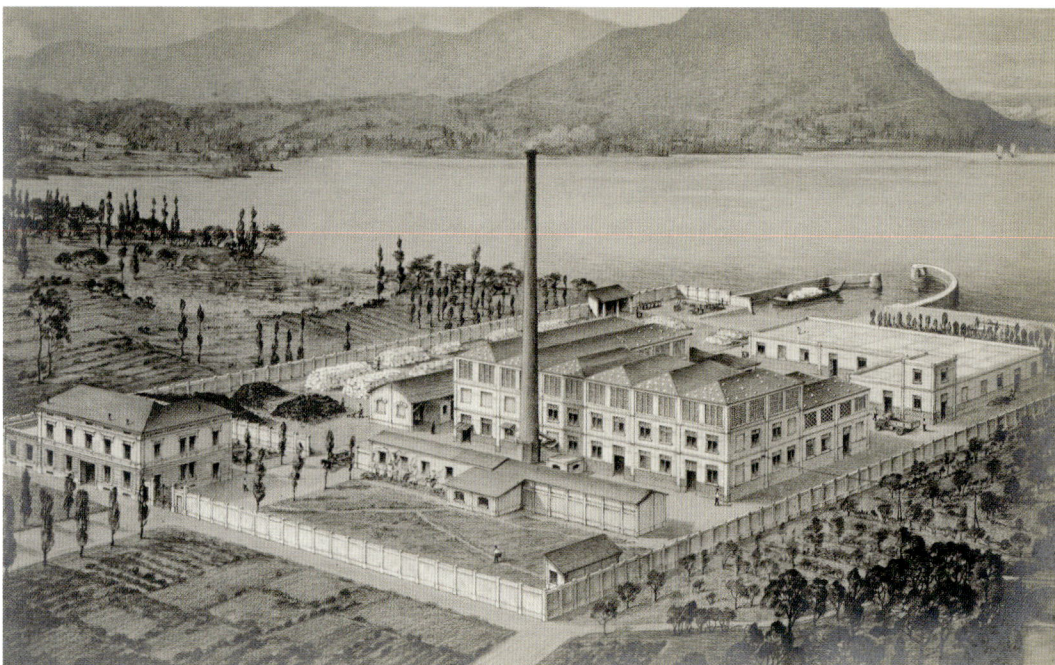

Domenico Bonamini and Umberto Ubaldi, Le organizzazioni Pirelli nel Cinquantenario della ditta [The Pirelli Organisations on the Fiftieth Anniversary of the Company], *1922*

The Pirelli factory in Vercurago, 1922

into consideration, at a certain point, even the eventuality of putting his company commitment to one side in order to devote his energies precisely to diplomacy, to international politics. This was not to be the case.
Yet he would continue to be involved on the world scene. 1919 was the year of the restructuring of the post-war global order. Again, it was one of Pirelli's advertising posters that told of the relationship between industry and reality: at the centre of the poster there appears the tyre of a racing car. Radiating from the spokes are the flags of the whole world. The representation is powerfully symbolic. What seems to emerge from those rays is the image of the drive towards internationalisation of Milanese industry—of course—but also the evocation of a world community reunited in the negotiating effort of the Peace Conference in Paris, in which Alberto participated as a technical member of the Italian delegation.
He was called upon by Ettore Conti, a major industrialist in the field of electricity, who in the meantime had become Treasury Undersecretary for the liquidation of arms and munitions services and aeronautics. He asked Pirelli to deal first of all with the liquidation of ministries in Italy and then, more generally, with relations with the Allied powers. So it was that, for Pirelli, the doors of the Peace Conference in Paris were opened.
The Italian delegation in the Reparations Commission of the Peace Conference included former Prime Minister Antonio Salandra, parliament member Eugenio Chiesa and the jurist Mariano D'Amelio. In Versailles, Alberto sat on the Supreme Economic Council and in the economic and financial commissions for the concluding of peace treaties, dealing with the determining of reparations for war damages from Germany, Austria and Hungary payable to the winning countries and the regulations for war debts. He was the *de facto* negotiator for Italy.
Accustomed to methods of decision-making and their necessary rapidity in the industrial sphere, Pirelli very soon found himself in total disagreement with the distracted way in which the political members of the Italian delegation tackled the issue of war reparations. But he was even more critical of the absent attitude towards the definition of the country's future, which would depend precisely on the outcomes of the Peace Conference. His way of representing Italy, in contrast, was present and passionate, entirely different from the style of the rest of the government delegation. In March 1919 Alberto Pirelli found himself forced to write a letter to Treasury Minister Bonaldo Stringher in which he decided to express all his disappointment at how things were going in Paris. It is an extremely explicit text, from the title onwards: *Insufficient and ineffective Italian presence in the negotiations on reparations.*

Paris, 3 March 1919
Your Excellency, please allow me to offer Your Excellency some considerations suggested to me by the impressions and experiences of recent days, which broadly speaking confirm the opinions already developed in my previous stay in Paris. Anxiety grows in me when faced with the fact that, while

negotiations of a territorial and military character are proceeding, and while those of an economic character are being launched (raw materials, commercial treaties, etc.) and also financial ones regarding certain specific problems, the problem of the international structuring of war costs and the parallel one of the structuring of inter-allied credits does not seem to be making any step forward. [...]
But please allow me to state to Your Excellency, in all frankness, my conviction that the almost complete absence of the Italian Government from Paris, as regards these kinds of negotiations, cannot continue without serious damage to our country. [...]
For my part, I will close this already too long letter by confirming my displeasure at seeing this serious matter of the arrangements for war costs and inter-allied debts not properly begun in the international field. America and England would assume a grave responsibility towards history by refusing to resolve this matter equitably.[5]

The result was that very soon Alberto would abandon the works of the Conference, indeed practically at the same time as the English economist John Maynard Keynes, who was equally critical of the formalities with which discussions were proceeding.
Keynes was participating in the Peace Conference as a delegate of the British Chancellor of the Exchequer but, unlike the British government, considered that peace conditions had to be pursued that were more generous than those that were actually agreed in Versailles. Before leaving, he too wrote to one of his friends from the Bloomsbury group, the painter Duncan Grant: 'I work for a government that I despise and whose objective is criminal.'
There is a reason why, talking about the Pirelli industrial firm and its relationship with innovation—and with the country—, it is not possible not to devote such a large space to Alberto's political-diplomatic activities. In his intransigent attitude, strongly aligned in the defence of the national interest but at the same time cosmopolitan and open to the world, we can grasp a characteristic of his way of 'doing business'. Pirelli was attentive to the world, to innovations, to stimuli also coming from contexts less close to the Milanese industrial milieu; yet he was able to find an equilibrium in his relationship with the national institutions and politics. Vision and pragmatism coexisted in him. And this, perhaps, will help us better understand the complexity—and the meaning—of the subsequent phases of his life.
The 1920s saw industrial relations become increasingly complex and full of conflict. The inequality gap was widening since the huge circulation of capital was not being translated into social justice. This applied to Europe and, even more, beyond the ocean, in the United States pervaded by a hyper-energetic race towards the future and totally blind to the profound malaise experienced by a large part of society, who were left completely excluded from the benefits of a progress of which they could only glimpse the far-off splendour.
The century came of age and Pirelli raced forwards,

The driver Alberto Ascari
photographed beside
his Ferrari, 1953,
photo Giorgio Calcagni

driven first by the war effort and now by the reconstruction. It opened a new chemical ingredients plant in Vercurago, near Lecco, and acquired new land in Bicocca. Cable laying activities were expanded throughout the Mediterranean, the Atlantic and South America.

Cables and tyres could count on significant growth margins. Both Pirelli brothers spent long days at sea, on board the cable-laying ship *Città di Milano*. And cables were the true moment of interweaving with the business of the future: on 26 November 1921 Pirelli took part in the establishing of the Società italiana reti telefoniche [The Italian Telephone Networks Company]. It had actively entered the world of telephony.

Six months later, in June 1922, the fiftieth anniversary of the birth of the company was celebrated, on the eve of the beginning of fascism. The dark view, the features of which Alberto Pirelli had sensed back in January 1916, revealed itself in all its gloom six years later. The liberal ruling class, the protagonist of the country's government starting from Unity, proved itself increasingly unsuitable to manage the difficult post-First World War period. This happened in Italy and in the vast majority of states built on the liberal model. Contact with the masses and the working class seems to have remained an exclusive characteristic of the socialists, who became the interpreters of the need to respond to the impoverished, hungry, and uncultured masses, and were rewarded by electoral growth. For these reasons the shadow of Bolshevism worried the liberal circles, who were incapable of managing the contradictions and social imbalances of the immediate post-war period. The reactions of the employers, still landowners to a large degree, were of panic. The premises were thus being created—in the days of the occupations of the factories in the 'two red years' 1919–1921—for the change towards fascist dictatorship. In all these years politics nevertheless succeeded in being kept decidedly outside of the gates of the Pirelli plants, while the company structure was revised as a result of the continuous expansion of international activities.

Alberto continued to be committed to developing the company and to building an authoritative and credible image of Italy in the world at the same time, with inevitable positive implications also for the government, from which, however, Pirelli did not wish to have public recognition. Not even a trace of all this, formally or informally, appears in the company archives, which instead abound with information concerning the new products and achievements of Pirelli on the market. In the historical story 1921 and 1922 remain as years of major growth.

The impetus of scientific research, essential for a potential war scenario, produced a strong push for innovation as an indirect result. A series of new products were emerging on the international market.

Mobility and communication between people were changing. The structure of society was being rewritten. Distances were being shortened. Ways of dwelling were being modified. Europe was setting out on the path of reconstruction, but it had to come to terms with the collective trauma over the loss of human life in the First World War. European war economies were struggling to be restructured. Therefore, when Germany did not succeed in making payment for its war debts, the United States intervened, and Wall Street invested to keep the economy of the Old Continent afloat. An extraordinary new *de facto* market opened for US consumer goods. In the 'Roaring Twenties' energy, cultural, and artistic dynamism certainly had the US brand, but the repercussions also reverberated in Europe, traversed by the winds of modernity, from the drive to break with tradition in the passage—which would not be painless—from primarily agricultural economic systems to industrial economies.

On 22 September 1922 the first Grand Prix took place at the new track in Monza. Pietro Bordino took the chequered flag, followed by Felice Nazzaro. They were driving two Fiat 804s fitted with Pirelli Superflex Cord tyres. In 1924 the pairing with Alfa Romeo was inaugurated that would lead to a series of extraordinary victories: from the P2 of Giuseppe Campari and Antonio Ascari to those of Tazio Nuvolari in the 6C 1750. These were the years in which the market of 'tyres for automobiles' increasingly flourished, the number of private cars grew, races and the myth of speed unleashed passions and drove consumption.

As the decade advanced, Alberto Pirelli was still a protagonist on the world scene: in 1927 he became president of the International Chamber of Commerce in Paris. The two years of his presidency had the reduction of the obstacles to international exchanges as their main objective.

This was the year when the first Transatlantic telephone service was created between the United States and Great Britain. Italians who already had a radio device in their homes and all the others, the vast majority, who met up in the bars and clubs, listened live to the first radio commentary of a sporting event, the Gran Premio di Galoppo horse race that took place at the San Siro stadium.

On the roads of Europe, still characterised by uneven surfaces and asphalt providing unsure grip, very few cars circulated, mostly luxury or sports cars. The most popular models (the Alfa Romeo 20-30, the Itala 61, the Lancia Lambda, the OM Superba, the Fiat 525SS) already provided a very respectable performance and required the perfecting of new tyres suitable for high performance. It was precisely spurred on by this that the Stella Bianca tyre was created, which was so innovative for the period that it continued to be used on sports cars until the 1950s. Indeed, the Stella Bianca model was the first, and the most long-lasting, modern tyre by Pirelli: in 1950 in Silverstone it would win the opening race of the World Championship and in Formula 1 in 1952 it would again be fitted onto Alberto Ascari's legendary Ferrari 500 that was to triumph at the Italian Grand Prix.

Meanwhile the group was growing abroad, in Spain, the United Kingdom, and South America.

In 1929 a new Pirelli plant was built in Burton-on-Trent. It was the third English factory, the first for tyres, after those for cables. Alberto mentions it in his 1946 text: 'Burton-on-Trent is a town situated in the industrial zone of the North of England and is known as the site of the major English breweries, whose beer the drinkers call "Burton water".'[6] For the inauguration of the plant, even Edward VII, Prince of Wales, travelled there from London.

Comparison with foreign experiences enabled the executives of the Pirelli factories to have points of reference as to where to go. The company structure evolved, undergoing continuous changes until 1928. The Milanese industrialist's links with the United States grew ever closer and more frequent. A note in *The Foreign Service Journal* from early 1929 recalls that 'the US Chamber of Commerce held its annual Thanksgiving lunch at the Cova restaurant in Milan', where a large number of members and Italian and American friends of the Chamber of Commerce met. 'Senator Pirelli and Commendatore Vanzetti made speeches appropriate to the occasion.'[7]

In the meantime, the placement of bonds for 4 million lire on the US went particularly well.

On Monday 18 February 1929 Pirelli was quoted on Wall Street. It was the first share in an Italian company to be listed in the US stock market, but the euphoria had a short duration. The following month, at the New York Stock Exchange, the first creaks in the system began to be heard. There were some signs of incumbent troubles in March, and then again in May. It only seemed to be a passing moment, but then the stock market seemed to resume its unstoppable course. Along with the smoky jazz joints and fashionable clothes that populated the trendy environments, the 'Roaring Twenties' were about to present a very big bill, due to the excess of optimism and to having underestimated the energy of the social claims of the masses, who had left the countryside attracted by the bright lights of metropolitan life.

At 11 in the morning of Thursday 24 October 1929, selling orders vastly exceeded those for buying. This sparked panic: after months of euphoric prosperity, on Wall Street the Dow Jones crashed. At the weekend the situation seemed to calm down, then on Tuesday 29th the world witnessed the inappellable collapse of the US Stock Exchange: the most disastrous day in the history of stock markets.

In the two years that followed the GDP of the industrialised countries fell by 20 per cent. Almost 9000 credit institutes would be forced to close. The Great Depression forced the liberal foundations of the West to be questioned: the crisis, which was born as an economic one, was quickly being transformed into a political and civil one.

The illusion, or rather the unspeakable thought of many, was that totalitarian states were able to react more effectively to the counterblow of the war compared with fragile liberal democracies. Europe had not recovered from the adverse effects of the First World War and

was paying the price for the errors that had marked the dynamics between the winners and the defeated. For Italy, then, the structural weakness, which fascism was not able to tackle, but, if anything, camouflaged, was evident. Despite this (or perhaps precisely because of it), for the first time we read a political evaluation, even if indirect, of the actions of the government in the official reports of a Pirelli board of directors. On the company balance sheet, on 14 March 1932, the directors wrote: 'The action of the national government has contributed to making the effects of the general depression less serious than elsewhere'.

Six months later, the founder, Giovanni Battista Pirelli, passed away.

In the meantime, Alberto's national and international profile continued to be raised. Indeed, even Mussolini recognised his status. Relations with the Duce were hard to define. In the early years after the 'March on Rome', Pirelli maintained quite a prudent position with respect to fascism, as did the vast majority of Italian industrialists, who were inclined towards what historian Giovanni De Luna has defined as a 'marriage of interest'. In 1925, after Matteotti's assassination of 10 June 1924, Pirelli was part of the delegation of entrepreneurs who addressed Mussolini requesting respect for trade union freedoms and, like many others, would avoid joining the National Fascist Party until 1932.

Yet, despite the distance between the worlds of origin and—for the most part—the visions, during the 1920s, of the leader of Fascism and the Milanese industrialist, an unusual personal relationship was created. Mussolini made no secret of the fact that he appreciated the entrepreneur's diplomatic nature and extensive network of contacts: there was a kind of fascination for that man, who moved in the world as though it were his home, a man capable of dealing with governors and economists in Paris and London, a protagonist of the New York scene while, for the vast majority of Europeans, New York seemed to be on another planet.

When, in 1935, Pirelli accepted the presidency of the Institute for the Study of International Politics (ISPI) in Milan, founded the previous year by a group of scholars in Pavia, the ISPI became one of the most important cultural institutions of the period, with significant publishing activities, a point of reference for an intellectual class in search of 'information on the world', and it took on a central role in the training of diplomats. On one hand Alberto Pirelli guaranteed the input of funds necessary for the institute and, at the same time, he built strong links with the entrepreneurial world. Diplomats and the business world learned to talk together in these very rooms of the ISPI, where there was discussion of the war in Ethiopia, which was about to break out, of the international tensions, of the interconnections between business and planetary instability. It was precisely the evaluation of the war in Ethiopia that prompted Alberto Pirelli to assume a position of open disagreement with the régime's choices: a war commitment that nevertheless pushed the company's production to levels never reached before.

*Pietro Todeschini, price
list of Superflex Cord
Pirelli tyres, 1924*

*Mario Bertoglio, sketch for
the advertisement for the
Stella Bianca Pirelli tyre,
1931–1935*

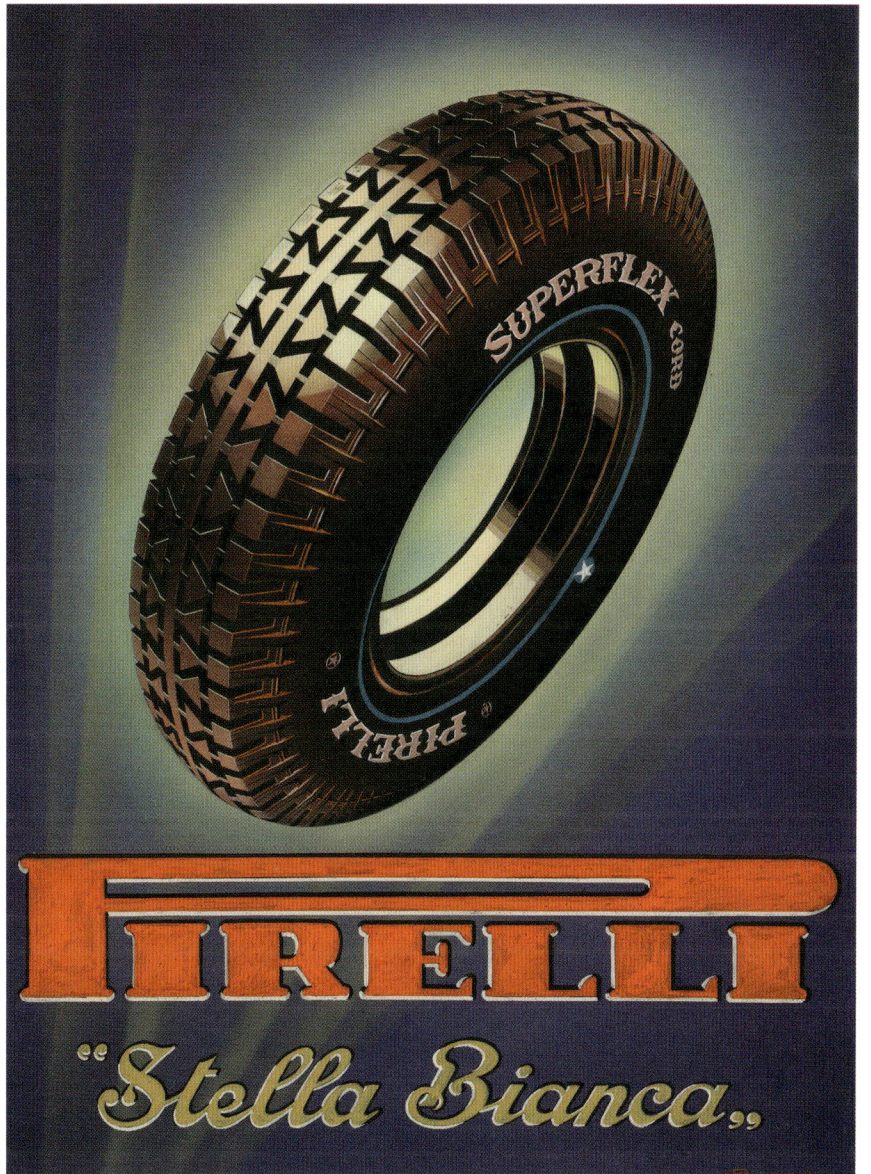

The Pirelli stand
at the Milan International
Motor Show, 1937,
photo Ancillotti & Martinotti

The Fascist government, meanwhile, imposed the idea of self-sufficiency on the country and conditioned industry's choices: it was necessary to be independent from the states supplying raw materials so as not to be held to random by them; it was necessary to be autonomous with respect to the importing of raw materials so as not to run the risk of shortages. It was precisely this idea of independence that ended up profoundly conditioning the rubber industry. Pirelli was the key example of this.

In June 1937 the Council of Ministers approved a decree-law that had the objective of creating favourable conditions for the production of synthetic rubber in Italy. On the basis of a series of agreements between the IRI and Pirelli, an Institute for the Study of Synthetic Rubber and a Company for the Production of Synthetic Rubber was created, with a view to producing on an industrial scale. The protagonist of this venture was to be the chemist Giulio Natta: aged thirty-four, recently named full professor of Industrial Chemistry at the Politecnico di Torino. That same June, the collaboration was formally agreed between the Milanese company and Natta: Pirelli paid him 4000 lire a month and a series of patents from those years bear his name. The decade that Natta lived between the Politecnico di Torino and the Pirelli laboratories was to be particularly important in his research path, to the point of being considered—as he himself said—a fundamental stage in achieving the 1963 Nobel Prize.

Natta, a scientist with a profound theoretical culture and endless technical passion in the application of his discoveries, devoted himself to studying synthetic rubber and designed a pilot plant in the industrial area of Bicocca. This was Building 131, described in the issue on the Institute for the Study of Synthetic Rubber conserved in the historical archive of the Milan Chamber of Commerce as follows: 'A complete modern laboratory split into four sections: analytical chemistry, organic chemistry, technology, compounds and vulcanisation, plus a fifth section for physical tests.' In that period, Pirelli could already count on the collaboration of Alexander Maximoff, a Russian chemical engineer who had fled the Soviet Union: he had worked on the synthesis of butadiene and had been director of the Bogatyr rubber factory in Moscow. He went to the USA first and joined Pirelli in 1934. He was entrusted with following the studies on synthetic rubber and when the Institute for the Study of Synthetic Rubber was created, he became director of the chemical research laboratory. Alexander Maximoff was a character who was something of a mystery; his work colleagues said he was infallible on the technical level, but they emphasised his toughness of character and stubbornness. The chemistry of rubber was his sole, true passion and, after almost a decade lived as stateless, he decided to request Italian citizenship precisely in the years of the Pirelli laboratory. In that laboratory Natta studied the basic intermediaries for the production of synthetic rubber that, at that time, was already being produced in Germany with the name 'Buna S'. In 1938, he perfected the process known as

'fractionated absorption', which was to be registered as Italian patent number 364.722. It was on the basis of this patent that, in a plant in Ferrara, the production of Italian synthetic rubber was launched, 'an excellent rubber'— even according to the Germans. It was 1939.

But what did synthetic rubber represent in those years for the Italian industry? Certainly, it was an incredible opportunity for scientific and technological research, but above all was a precise response to the government's requests, committed as it was to fully go down the route of self-sufficiency. It was certainly not the market that was pushing in this direction. We need only consider that the production costs were so high that they took the price of the finished product to almost double that obtained with natural rubber.

This contradiction was underlined by Alberto Pirelli:

In the current state of technology, synthetic rubber is of inferior quality to that of natural rubber and—in Italy—is much more expensive. [...] As we, even though indirectly and partially, were interested in rubber plantations, we did not have any interest as an industry consuming rubber; rather, we had an interest in opposing the rise of this industry in Italy, an industry that, moreover, needed major capital investments. [...] But the production of synthetic rubber had already been developed in Russia and Germany, and our military Ministers, then also other Ministries, judged it essential that in this country too we should move on to the industrial phase. We therefore decided that we had to participate in the enterprise, also because others were ready to follow-up the government programme.[8]

It is, however, a fact that, in the evolution of Pirelli, the research into synthetic rubber introduced another element of innovation: the interaction between major industry and the university, between theoretical and applied research, that became a model for subsequent decades. A report published in the *Annuario* [Yearbook] of the Politecnico di Milano underlines 'how much the collaboration between university scientific institutes and industry can lead to important results, particularly at the current time, in which all the energies must contribute towards the self-sufficient resolution of the numerous problems affecting the industrial life of this country.' Thus, the history of Pirelli is confirmed as a place of technological research in which engineers such as Emanuele Jona, Luigi Emanueli, and Giuseppe Bruni found space for action and experimentation.

The results of the laboratories soon offered the opportunity for public pride: the first artificial rubber tyres were exhibited in 1937 at the Pirelli stand at the Motor Show within the Fiera Campionaria in Milan. There were samples that were not on sale, to publicise the joint venture with the IRI: two twinned tyres for lorries and one low-pressure tyre for cars of the Aerflex type. At the Fiera Campionaria and the Textile Show in Rome in 1938, on the other hand, there was a wide range of articles on display that were now in production: accessories and tyres for cars, motorcycles, velocipedes, special

Rubber collector
in Amazonia, 1904,
photo Alberto Pirelli

synthetic rubber pipes for fuel, together with unprocessed samples of synthetic rubber. But the first completely self-sufficient tyre made its debut in the summer of 1939 at the Inventions Show that was held in Milan, where the first prize for synthetic rubber was awarded to Pirelli. When the new tyre was officially presented to the Duce, who was ready to order a pair immediately—in the presence of the rejoicing public—to be fitted onto his car, the magazine *La Chimica & l'Industria* added the details of the product: it was a model of tyre containing solely synthetic rubber, with rayon to replace cotton and carbon black produced in the Pirelli laboratories.

The synthetic rubber presented to the Duce has been achieved with procedures studied in Italy in the laboratories of the Pirelli company and subsequently in those of the Institute for the Study of Synthetic Rubber. During the studies conducted for the purpose, the various alternative procedures that can lead to butadiene and the various raw and intermediary materials, all Italian, have been investigated.

In the meantime, once the plant in Ferrara had been started up, Natta had gone on to study the German technology of synthetic rubber by going to Germany a number of times to visit the factories of the Ruhr Valley. The experimentation and production of this type of rubber, in fact, had already begun in other countries, in Germany and Russia in particular, due to fears over the prospects of war. In the early twentieth century, natural rubber was mainly found in Brazil, in the Congo and in the British, Dutch, and French colonies. On the eve of the First World War Russians and Germans identified the problem of dependence on these countries in the procurement of raw materials; for this reason, scientists set about studying how to produce rubber synthetically. And the first real success in this field was in fact German. In 1910 Fritz Hoffmann, a chemist at Bayer, registered the first patent, thanks to which Continental produced the first synthetic rubber tyre. Germany shared the fear for its independence from the supplies of raw materials from potentially hostile countries. Tyres and all the other rubber components became, *de facto*, a fundamental strategic structure for the country's independence and military efficiency: with the Nazi government, in fact, the process of motorisation of the armed forces was completed.

In 1940 Fritz Todt, director of the construction company of major roads in Munich and general in the Luftwaffe, became Minister of Armaments and Munitions of the Third Reich and organised a government motorway construction programme, in which hundreds of thousands of workers were employed, to a large extent recruited in the occupied countries, and prisoners of war. In February 1935, the results of the laboratory experiments on synthetic rubber, by now in their advanced stages, were submitted to the Minister of War of the Reich and the latter decided to earmark huge resources for the launch of production.

In issue 14 of the *Zeitschrift des Vereines Deutscher Ingenieure* of 3 April 1937 we read that 'At the Motor Show [of Berlin] in 1936 the Army exhibited various types of vehicle [...] also synthetic rubber products, known as BUNA, including tyres in particular. The BUNA tyre was exhibited this year in the Pavilion of Honour at the Show.' The strategic importance of Buna is confirmed in all the documents of the period: in Germany new factories were built, but the management of the plants—which nevertheless also required specialist personnel—was at the centre of the strategies of the Ministry of War. The description of those days given by Primo Levi is extraordinary and distressing. The Jewish writer, a chemist, who survived the Nazi concentration camps, wrote to the editor-in-chief of *La Chimica & l'Industria* in 1947, telling of his experiences in the Buna-Monowitz camp in Upper Silesia.

Letter to the Editors
Dear Editor-in-Chief, the purpose of this letter is to submit to your kind attention some news of a technical character of which I became aware in the most direct way during my imprisonment in Germany. I am 28 years old; I graduated in chemistry in Turin in 1941. I was arrested as a partisan in Dec. '43, was then deported to an annihilation camp, of which not much has been said: Buna-Monowitz, in Upper Silesia. The whole camp was part of a synthetic rubber factory (hence the name); it is precisely about this that I intend to speak here. I do not believe that the western world has information on this fact: in the Silesian coal mining zone, 40 km west of Kraków, 12 km from the much better-known site of Auschwitz, the Germans planned, and almost fully completed, an industrial complex covering a rectangular surface area of around 5 km by 7. [...] 40,000 workers operated on the site, almost all non-German; of these, 600 were English prisoners of war, and 10,000 were Jewish of various origins confined at night in the camp named above. [...] The purpose of the industrial centre was the production of Buna starting from coal, through coking, calcium carbide, acetylene, butadiene and the process of polymerisation by emulsioning. Quantitative data on the anticipated production can be deduced from the dimensions of the building to be used for the storage of the finished Buna (rolled): it occupied a rectangle of 120 m by 60, and was six storeys high, of which two below ground. I am aware of many of the raw materials that were to be used (emulsifiers, catalysts, anti-aging elements, etc.); I also witnessed, and often participated in, the assembly of various plants, not always understanding their function. [...] In addition to Buna, the complex was supposed to produce (and partly had already produced) methanol, ammonia, compressed gas, acetic acid, styrene and stilbene. The date of commencement of the production of Buna had been set for 1 August 1944, but starting from 20 July, the site was subject to Allied bombing [...]. As a result, not a kilogram of Buna ever left the huge factory; it was relatively undamaged when it fell into Russian hands on 27 January 1945. Along the roads of the site the Germans resisted bloodily for various days. I know nothing about the subsequent destiny of the Buna-Monowitz factory. [...]
Turin, November 1947
Dr Primo Levi

This letter by Primo Levi, in all its drama, throws a distressing shadow over the story of the production of synthetic rubber, placing it in the context of the darkest moment of the twentieth century.

The great intellectual, who told of all his experiences in the extermination camps in those years so the world would not forget, opens a particular window on his experience here. The technical and production aspects reveal his intention: to attempt to show every detail of how the Germans produced synthetic rubber; details that would perhaps be useful to the Italian industry of the immediate post-war period. An extreme attempt to give a meaning, some form of utility, to the horror he lived through.

Meanwhile, the end of the war made it necessary to come to terms with the destruction, with the factories reduced to rubble. Pirelli could rely on owning a number of patents, but significant capital was necessary to convert the factories to use the new technologies. The plant in Terni, for instance, had to be completely rebuilt, because after 8 September the Wehrmacht dismantled the machinery and took everything to Germany. The factory in Ferrara, on the other hand, had been bombed in 1942 by the Allied planes and had closed down. On 20 October 1944 it was the turn of the large factories on the northern outskirts of Milan, between Sesto San Giovanni and Gorla, to be the target of a massive Allied raid. La Bicocca was hit and among the buildings destroyed there was also that housing the laboratory of the Institute for the Study of Synthetic Rubber. Natta asked the director of the Politecnico, Gino Cassini, to transport what had been saved to his study centre and to rebuild the pilot plant that had been destroyed at the Politecnico in order to continue the research.

The story is in the report to the board of directors of Pirelli drafted by Alberto Pirelli on 22 February 1945:

following the almost total destruction of the experimental laboratory at La Bicocca due to the raid on 20 October, the Institute must for the moment have recourse, for its activities, to makeshift means: these activities will in fact be conducted using the Laboratory of the Milan Politecnico and a small improvised laboratory reconstructed near La Bicocca.

In the hectic days of the Liberation, an extremely difficult phase opened up for the industrialists.

In reality, in the years of fascism, Alberto had ably succeeded in avoiding a series of official tasks that Mussolini wanted to assign to him. In every conversation with the Duce, Pirelli attempted to dissuade him from following Germany into the adventure of war. Yet, when war was declared on 10 June, his motto became: 'It's my country, right or wrong'. But from that moment he expressly displayed his dissent towards the *régime*.

In 1943, on the fall of Mussolini, Pirelli had meetings with King Vittorio Emanuele II, with Cardinal Luigi Maglione (Secretary of State for the Vatican) and with the Swiss federal government, in the vain attempt to find a way to find a separate peace for Italy; he subsequently participated in the diplomatic manoeuvres aiming to establish peace negotiations with the Anglo-Americans. The efforts to participate in a phase of pacification were not considered sufficient; in July 1945, with the war ended, Pirelli, along with eleven other Northern Italian industrialists, was subject to a purging process and removed from his position as managing director. The company was subject to the commissariat system, although the process was to lead to a verdict of not chargeable for Alberto. It was only in April of the following year that his appeal was allowed and the industrialist was fully rehabilitated. This was his return to running the company: the extraordinary shareholders meeting of 1946 reinstated Piero and Alberto in the leadership of the company.

However, the years of fascism and the war had profoundly marked the Pirelli family. The decision by Alberto's son, Giovanni, a partisan of strongly left-wing views, to split from the company and not work there was to mark this separation even more. Yet the profound affection between father and son that was able to overcome the differences in views of the world was never lost; but Alberto would never succeed in convincing his revolutionary son of the goodness of his enlightened thought, which prompted him to affirm that 'it is to the constant evolution of social life, not to revolutions, that progress is due above all'.

And progress was knocking on the doors of the West after the devastation and the massacres of the war. In the spring of 1948 the US funds of the Marshall Plan flowed towards Europe, the premise for the rapid reconstruction of the country and then for the incredible growth of the subsequent years, which prompted talk of an 'economic miracle'. Pirelli was among the industrial firms ready to grasp all the opportunities of the new phase: the scientists returned to the laboratories, the technicians studied every kind of innovation, the market regained strength and required products of all types. The Italians looked to America, to all the technological devilry, to the new seductive objects that seemed specially created to leave the traumas of war behind them. Pirelli seemed ready to intercept the new spirit of the age immediately.

NOTES

1 A. Pirelli, *La Pirelli. Vita di un'azienda industriale*, Milan, 1946, p. 8.
2 *Ibid.*
3 Letter by Alberto Pirelli to Luigi Einaudi of 12 January 1916 (Private archive of Alberto Pirelli).
4 A. Pirelli, *La Pirelli. Vita di un'azienda industriale*, cit., p. 32.
5 The letter is taken from *L'Italia e il sistema finanziario internazionale, 1919-1936*, edited by M. De Cecco, Rome, 1993.
6 A. Pirelli, *La Pirelli. Vita di un'azienda industriale*, cit., p. 63.
7 *Ibid.*
8 A. Pirelli, *La Pirelli. Vita di un'azienda industriale*, cit., pp. 52–53.

*Silverstone Racing Circuit,
Great Britain, 1954*

*Leopoldo and Alberto Pirelli,
1958, photo Giancarlo
Scalfati*

NEW CHALLENGES AND MAJOR OPPORTUNITIES

Against the backdrop of the First World War and with the Second on the way, the climate of uncertainty in Europe was palpable. For Pirelli relaunching meant rewriting the internal equilibria, but also knitting back together its contacts with the world and with its own country. It was with a spirit of energy and change that the company negotiated the new century: around the sheds of the Milanese factories everything was speaking of the future and would continue to do so, especially in the post-war period. From international acquisitions to research into new products, to new company communication strategies.

The reputation of a continually expanding brand, in Europe and in America; the authoritativeness of the greatly respected entrepreneurial figure that was Alberto Pirelli; the old continent struggling to find the path towards reconstruction, albeit in the dynamic and international context of the 'Roaring Twenties'.

Under the guidance of Piero and Alberto Pirelli, the company continued to look to the future with an approach that we would define today as 'global'. It increased its investments abroad, focusing on research into new products and materials, but above all on the collaboration with artists who would launch the construction of a recognisable image at world level.

The 'long P' entered a new era, making communication an instrument to offer visions of the future and a lifestyle, even before the product proper. To do so, it called together great names from the world of illustration, design, advertising and culture and acted on a number of fronts: advertisements, posters, but also participation in exhibitions and national and international fairs.

The photograph showing the Pirelli Pavilion at the 1924 Fiera Campionaria in Milan demonstrates a communication strategy that is a homage to the greatness of the company, in total discontinuity with what would be the much more minimalist displays of 1940, 1951 and 1961. The image shows an exhibition space bursting at the seams with elastic rubber objects of every type, which document the diversification of products, and even two large rubber trees imported from the plantations in Java. To remind visitors that everything comes from raw materials, but also from the know-how and creative thought of the company.

PROOF No· 5

A-10220

COMMITTEE ON STOCK LIST
NEW YORK STOCK EXCHANGE

PIRELLI COMPANY OF ITALY
(SOCIETA ITALIANA PIRELLI)
(Incorporated under the laws of Italy, November 3, 1920)

"AMERICAN SHARES," REPRESENTING CAPITAL STOCK (SERIES "A")

Each American Share issued by the City Bank Farmers Trust Company, as successor Depositary, represents one Bearer Share (Lire 400 par value) of the Capital Stock (Series "A") of the Pirelli Company of Italy, deposited under the Deposit Agreement dated as of January 24, 1929, as amended.

CAPITALIZATION

(As of December 31, 1933, but giving effect to the capital readjustments approved by the General and Extraordinary Meeting of Shareholders held in Milan, Italy, on March 21, 1934)

	Authorized	Outstanding
7% Convertible Gold Bonds, due May 1, 1952	$4,000,000	......
Capital Stock:		
Series "A"—Par Value Lire 400	373,000 shares	351,975 shares
Series "B"—Par Value Lire 400	51,000 shares	48,025 shares

Milan, Italy, July 3, 1934.

The Pirelli Company of Italy hereby makes application for the listing on the New York Stock Exchange of "American Shares," representing 21,118 shares Capital Stock (Series "A") of the par value of Lire 400 per share in substitution for American Shares representing Capital Stock (Series "A") of the par value of Lire 500 per share, with authority to add American Shares representing Capital Stock (Series "A") of the par value of Lire 400 per share on official notice of issuance, pursuant to the terms of the Deposit Agreement as amended. Reference is hereby made to previous application of the Company, A-8437 dated as of January 24, 1929.

All the outstanding Capital Shares of the Pirelli Company are fully paid and non-assessable, and no personal liability attaches to the holders with respect thereto. The Pirelli Company of Italy has no liabilities other than those indicated in its balance sheets and is not in default of any of its obligations.

PIRELLI COMPANY OF ITALY
(SOCIETA ITALIANA PIRELLI)
By PIERO PIRELLI,
Chairman and Managing Director.

AUTHORITY FOR ISSUE OF "AMERICAN SHARES"

Certificates for 167,706 American Shares were issued pursuant to the Deposit Agreement dated as of January 24, 1929 between The National City Company as Depositor, The National City Bank of New York, as Depositary (on July 31, 1929 the City Bank Farmers Trust Company was appointed successor Depositary and has acted in that capacity since that date), and all holders of certificates issued and to be issued thereunder, and were listed on the New York Stock Exchange pursuant to said application A-8437. Of these, 21,118 American Shares were outstanding at the time of the change in capitalization hereunder described.

CHANGE IN CAPITALIZATION

By Resolutions adopted at the General and Extraordinary Meeting of Shareholders of the Company held in Milan, Italy, on March 21, 1934, there was authorized:

(1) An increase in the capital of the Company from Lire 191,986,000 to Lire 200,000,000 by the issue of 14,087 new shares of Capital Stock (Series "A") (Lire 500 par value) and 1,941 new shares of Capital Stock (Series "B") (Lire 500 par value) to existing shareholders in the ratio of one new share for each twenty-four shares of Capital Stock Series "A" or "B" already held.

(2) Reduction in the capital of the Company from Lire 200,000,000 to Lire 160,000,000 to be effected by reducing the par value of each outstanding share of Capital Stock from Lire 500 to Lire 400 and by distributing Lire 100 per share in cash to stockholders.

The Resolutions thus approved were published under date of March 26, 1934 in the *Foglio Annunzi Legali* (Official Gazette). Article 101 of the Italian Commercial Code provides that capital reductions such as referred to in (2) above become effective only three months after publication in said *Foglio Annunzi Legali*.

It was 18 February 1929. Piero Pirelli signed the document of membership of the New York Stock Exchange, with the company being quoted and guaranteeing it another primacy, that of being the first Italian company to be present on Wall Street. The choice, dictated by a profitable series of bonds placed on the US market for a value of over 4 million dollars, produced great satisfaction and promised further growth for Pirelli. However, already the following month, in New York the first signs of an imminent crisis began to be felt. On 24 October 1929, in fact, the Dow Jones crashed, bringing with it the most difficult financial challenge seen up to that point: the Great Depression, which started out as economic, but was quickly transformed into a reckoning at a political, civil and social level, above all in Europe, which was yet to recover from the First World War and was facing the challenge of the incipient Nazi fascism. But Pirelli looked to the future with faith and invested in the opening of its first factory in Brazil that very year.

In the political context of fascism, which imposed self-sufficiency on companies, Pirelli relied on the birth of the Institute for the Study of Synthetic Rubber and the Company for the Production of Synthetic Rubber on an Industrial Scale, where Giulio Natta worked in 1937. An industrial chemist, an innovator and a prolific promoter of the chemical industry during and after the Second World War, Natta was to win the Nobel Prize for Chemistry in 1963 thanks to his perfecting of the polymerisation of propylene for the production of isotactic polypropylene, a highly flexible material that is still used today in the manufacture of electrical appliances, kitchen utensils, gas and water pipes and is capable of withstanding high pressures. Giulio Natta's transversality and capacity for vision is summarised in a phrase taken from Le nuove grandi sintesi organiche [The Great New Organic Syntheses] (La Chimica & l'Industria, April 1938): 'In reality, even the farmer can be considered as a chemical worker, as he attends to the most important of organic syntheses that is known, chlorophyll synthesis, in which the energy is supplied by the sun, and the raw materials are water and carbon dioxide in the air, and many of the raw materials considered here, as well as by synthesis, can be obtained by decomposition or transformation of organic natural substances'.

ING. PROF. GIULIO NATTA
===== Milano
Via Mario Pagano n. 54

LI 31 Gennaio 1938-XVI

Spett.   Direzione Centrale Gomma
         Società Italiana Pirelli

                                    Milano

    Ricevo la V/ lettera del 21 c.m. relativa all'accordo per la mia consulenza e prestazioni inerenti agli studi, esperienze e ricerche per la gomma sintetica, per il quale, ringraziando, Vi trasmetto con la presente il mio benestare.

    Ricevo pure la V/ pregiata lettera del 24 c.m. con la quale mi confermate che detto accordo viene integralmente passato, come fu a suo tempo previsto, agli enti Istituto per lo Studio della Gomma Sintetica e Società Italiana per la Produzione della Gomma Sintetica.

    RingraziandoVi per le gentili espressioni a mio riguardo che avete voluto aggiungere a detta comunicazione, Vi prego gradire i miei migliori saluti

                        (Prof. G. Natta)

The Strain of Manufacturing Growth

From the reconstruction to today. Pirelli taps the energies of the reconstruction and begins the years of the Cinturato, racing drivers, the Giro d'Italia, the Pirelli Skyscraper and mass mobility. After the so-called 'Years of Lead' and the decade of 1980s advertising becomes increasingly international, driven by the slogan 'Power is nothing without control', and production is characterised by an increasingly technological approach with the revolution of the MIRS™

by Claudio Colombo
-
JOURNALIST

Renaissance, Risorgimento, Resistance, Reconstruction. The 'R' that recurs in the history of Italy also reared its head in the common feeling that permeated the country as it re-emerged from the two decades of Fascism (the *Ventennio*) and the tragedy of war. After the fall, the time had come for the Recovery. And, indeed, for the Reconstruction. Which meant building again, rebuilding: a house, a factory, a city, a nation. And not only in Italy: the whole world was attempting to do the same thing. But it was here, in the newborn democracy sprouting among the ruins, that the level of enthusiasm reached unthinkable heights, replacing the pain and the wounds of stories to be forgotten with a vitality and a dynamism that in a short time were to transform the country from being the 'Cinderella of Europe' into an industrial power admired the world over. The four years from 1945 to 1948 seem as long as a century, so traversed were they by extraordinary phases and events: the new Constitutional Charter, the basis of a new state, the popular choice of the Republic with an unequivocal referendum, the aid of the Marshall Plan (the correct wording is the European Recovery Program, something similar would also be seen many years later …), the first governments deployed in the name of resistance unity, the elections of April 1948, won by the Christian Democrats of Alcide De Gasperi. Four special years in which the country laid the foundations for a radical transformation: from farming to industry, replacing backwardness with modernity, paving the way for the major global processes of wellbeing. In this hectic period full of hope, the industrial society experienced a difficult transition, in which errors and omissions committed during the *Ventennio* were mirrored: public opinion issued a condemnation of it for collusion with Fascism. The verdict was already written: the Allied Military Government proceeded with the extraordinary

administration of the companies of the North. That of Pirelli lasted for exactly one year: decreed on 7 May 1945, it was revoked on 7 May 1946, prompted by the testimonies that encouraged Cesare Merzagora, one of the commissioners (and soon to be Minister for Foreign Trade), to recognise not only the good faith of the legitimate ownership structure but also its participation in resistance activities during the past régime. It had been Alberto Pirelli who set under way an intelligent resilience in relation to the flattery of Fascism and the German oppression, starting with opposition to the German indications to dismantle the factory and deport its workers. This was a choice with long-term implications: by collaborating with the Resistance, it had prefigured the new age of the factory, based on democracy and the free market.

A new beginning, therefore, amid a thousand difficulties but with all the 'Rs' in the right places: reconstruction, recovery, and finally restart. And so in 1947, the year that coincided with the 75th anniversary of its foundation, with the company back under the control of Piero and Alberto Pirelli, production recommenced strongly in the traditional sector of cables, driven by the resumption of construction activities, although a little less so in that of tyres, still suffering from the effects of a widespread and large-scale black market (but growth in this field too was only a matter of time, as we will see below).

These were the years when differences were marked, the years when project work, investments in technology, the capacity for vision projected towards unprecedented challenges and scenarios determined the success of a business. New players were bursting onto the Italian scene to stand alongside the major protagonists of the country's industrialisation. These are names that—alongside the 'historical' ones, Agnelli, Marzotto, Olivetti, Pirelli, Falck, Barilla—would become the protagonists of the new national entrepreneurship: Borghi, Zanussi and Merloni

Sketch for the celebration
of the 75th anniversary of
Pirelli, 1947

Inside the factory in
Settimo Torinese, 1962,
photo Arno Hammacher

previous pages
Advertising installation
in Piazza Duca d'Aosta
in front of the Pirelli
Skyscraper worksite,
1956, photo Giorgio
Calcagni

Alberto Ascari and Nino Farina in the Ferrari 375 fitted with Pirelli tyres at the Valentino Grand Prix in Turin, 1952

John Cage at the Centro Culturale Pirelli performing the Concerto for Prepared Piano and Orchestra, *1954*

Claudia Cardinale on the cover of the haulage contractors' magazine Vado e torno, *1962*

in the field of electrical appliances, Pesenti for cement, Monti and Moratti for petroleum. The development model was that of a family capitalism manifested not only in the companies of large dimensions but also in that capable and generous network of small and medium-sized enterprises that would become the backbone of the Italian economy.

The factory was the centre of Pirelli's world. And as such it absorbed the energies for a recovery that developed along various trajectories: new openings (a plant for tyres in Settimo, near Turin), the establishing or acquisition of companies abroad, the reorganisation of those already in existence (Spain, the United Kingdom, the South American pole with Brazil and Argentina) and, above all, the strong core idea that continuous innovation is the key to being found prepared to meet the demands of a market projected towards increasingly European and international scenarios.

The Cinturato Pirelli for cars, patented in 1951—one of the company's fortes, the first chapter in a long story of success stretching to the present day—, began to be devised and designed years earlier, in an Italy that was preparing for another revolution, that of mass motorisation. And pressing down on the accelerator of intelligent innovation was one of the fundamental personalities in the history of Pirelli, engineer Luigi Emanueli, the man who loved to understand things by looking inside them (*Adess ghe capisserem un quaicoss, andem a guardagh denter*, or 'Now, we'll understand if we look into it', he used to say in Milanese dialect: the phrase, still a very contemporary inspiration, appears at the entrance to the Fondazione Pirelli Headquarters in Milano-Bicocca). 'After five long years of studies'—we read in the 1952 annual report—'we have produced and placed on sale a new tyre called Cinturato, built on the basis of completely different criteria from the usual ones. The fundamental detail that characterises its structure is a strong belt of fabric positioned between the tread and the tyre carcass; this, thanks to unusual expedients, also has sufficient solidity to withstand the wear and tear of use in a superior way'.

The Cinturato is the exact representation of the spirit that guides the company, knowing how to conduct research having two objectives: the improvement of the products already on the market and the ambition to create new ones. Since its launch on the market, the Cinturato was recommended for the fast and powerful Alfa Romeo Giulietta Sprint, and also for the Lancia Aurelia B20, or even for the Fiat 8V: in other words, a tyre that seems specially built for winning, which is what happened regularly with the Mille Miglia road race, defined by Enzo Ferrari as 'the finest race in the world', the historic long-distance motor race from Brescia to Rome and back. Over the years, meanwhile, the power of the engines fitted in 'normal' cars also began to increase, as did speeds, with the prospect of new demands as regards road holding: it was in this context that the new 'jewel' of 'Casa Pirelli' began to show its superiority. Starting by being fitted almost exclusively

on sports cars or super-luxury cars, during the 1960s the Cinturato extended its range to other segments of the car market. Reliability, performance and a high level of safety were assets that decreed its commercial success, also suggesting a step change in the advertising of the product: it was travelling 'safely' that was to be precisely the *leitmotif* of the advertising campaign created by Arrigo Castellani, Head of Communications, and Pino Tovaglia, a much-appreciated designer. The famous advertising slogan 'un viaggio ma' [a journey but yet], made of puns and plays on words alluding to facts and personalities that were famous in the 1960s, would inspire writers and intellectuals such as Camilla Cederna, who would write an amusing article inspired by it for the *Rivista Pirelli*. There was also no lack of recourse to popular characters much loved by sports enthusiasts. 'Extraordinario Cinturato Pirelli!', exclaims Formula 1 world champion Juan Manuel Fangio in a very successful advert in 1966, who had made safety 'en velocidad' his trademark. It was the Italy of Carosello, a real milestone on a television adventure that would accompany the evolution of a 'medium' destined to revolutionise usage and customs, and society.

After what could be referred to as the great lethargy, the almost physiological need for new ideas and new initiatives re-emerged forcefully: the founding of the CISE (Centre for Information, Studies and Experiences), which Pirelli promoted together with Fiat, Edison and Montecatini, gave a new boost in the field of scientific research and anticipated the themes of the future associated with energy needs and the exploitation of the Earth's resources. But the meaning of and the reason for a business cannot stop here. Doing business also means promoting culture, interpreting the spirit of the time, being the spokesperson for the social, political and economic transformations of a country, of a community. Milan was at the centre of everything: the open and inclusive city *par excellence*, it was the metropolis of cross-contaminations of cultures, of the virtuous convergence between literature and industry, theatre and finance, music and science. Milan and the Milanese re-emerged from the darkness of reason, going back to cinemas and theatres, but also intellectual poles such as the Centro Culturale Pirelli, where the general public could interact with people of letters, musicians, scientists, stage and screen directors. Or by following the many publishing initiatives that blossomed in those years. In November 1948 the first issue of the *Rivista Pirelli* was published (*Pirelli. Rivista d'informazione e di tecnica* [Pirelli. Magazine of Information and Technology] was the exact title), founded by Giuseppe Luraghi and with 'poet-engineer' Leonardo Sinisgalli as its editor-in-chief: an open place for work and study, a training ground of talents of thought, the perfect synthesis of that polytechnic culture to which the outstanding figures of Italian and European culture would lend their genius for a quarter of a century: writers, scientists, poets, musicians and Nobel Prize winners such as Eugenio Montale and Salvatore Quasimodo. To interpret the spirit of the time, to tell of the processes of economic and social development, to create a bridge between business and culture, these were the outlines around which the magazine moved; in the years that followed it was to be joined by other periodical publications by Pirelli, such as the house organ *Fatti e Notizie*, intended for the workers in the group, and *Vado e torno*, a periodical devoted to the world of road haulage. An intense and fruitful publishing activity, for the sake of a mission that would never be abandoned by the company: to communicate about the business, to inform the public, to promote the product using unconventional means. And it was exactly from this perspective that the Pirelli Calendar came about in 1964, intended to stand out as a showcase for artistic photography, for female beauty and to bear witness to the changes in customs, in Italy and worldwide.

We were at the dawn of a decade of major development, of an extraordinary age in which a virtuous interweaving of economic and social factors would lead to Italy experiencing the season of the so-called 'economic boom'. From 1950 to 1960, the period in which GDP registered an annual growth rate of 5.9 per cent, the country changed its appearance, discovering wellbeing and the path of consumerism. We began to race, literally, along new roads and in new vehicles: in 1955 Fiat presented the 600, which was to become the emblem of the nation's road transport; two years later it was to be the turn of the 500, another cornerstone in the automobile field; Piaggio and Innocenti turned out tens of thousands of Vespas and Lambrettas and Pirelli launched the Motor Scooter onto the market, the small tyre capable of bearing exceptional wear and tear due to the high rotation speed of the mini-wheels.

Private mobility was the key to modernisation. Pirelli was not found to be unprepared on a market that had become effervescent: it turned out new products (the BS3 tyre) and extended its international spread by opening new factories in Greece and Turkey. This was also the moment of major sports events, a formidable showcase for products intended for mass use: on circuits the world over Ferraris and Maseratis fitted with Pirelli tyres reaped victories in Formula 1, and this was only the beginning of a great adventure that, to the present day, would associate the brand with the most important motor race in the world. There were also close relationships with icons of sport such as the former cyclist Alfredo Binda, five times winner of the Giro d'Italia and three of the

World Championship: he was entrusted with organising the Gran Premio Pirelli cycling championship, a kind of national event for *amateurs* that in the nine editions that took place was to feature thousands of aspiring champions. The brand spread thanks also to the major names in design that Pirelli called upon to collaborate with it: this was the point of departure towards a series of national and international awards that would reward that culture of the beautiful and 'know-how' that has always been pursued by the company.

The economic boom was the setting that served as the backdrop for increasingly ambitious projects. Now Italy was thinking big and Milan was looking upwards: at Pirelli the idea was born and grew of concentrating the firm's business and administrative centre and grouping together in a skyscraper in the city centre the offices that, due to the Second World War, had been spread around various zones of the city: the definitive project was dated 1954, while the inauguration took place in April 1960. The visual impact on Piazza Duca d'Aosta of the new, highly imaginative Pirelli Skyscraper was extraordinary. The building, designed by Gio Ponti with the collaboration of Pier Luigi Nervi, 31 storeys and 127 metres high, was a celebration of modernity. It rises up to the sky indicating new horizons and offers a scathing comparison with the nearby, low and stumpy Central Station, built by Fascism. The skyscraper was the symbolic postcard of the passage from the old to the new world. 'This is a building'—writes Walter McQuade in *The Architectural Forum*—'that would honour every city in the world and especially the vertical New York. It is a building capable of teaching something to those who still knowingly practise architecture'. For the company the work was a powerful vehicle for the image of progress, impetus towards the future, internationalism and, at the same time, profound Milan-ness. In the city they christened it 'the Pirellone' and the use of this term is evidence of the 'fondness' with which the futuristic construction was immediately welcomed by the Milanese: to this day it is still one of the symbols of the Lombard metropolis and the economic boom. The company's choice of a prestige name such as Ponti, an architect known in Italy but also abroad and already the designer of important business complexes such as those for the Montecatini company, again in Milan, fitted in fully with the strongly promotional character that the operation immediately took on. Ponti also left his mark on the

Advertisement for the Rolle Pirelli tyre for the Fiat 600, 1955

Pino Tovaglia, advertisement for the Cinturato Pirelli tyre, 1966

Start of the Gran Premio
Pirelli, Lazio qualifier,
1956, photo Keystone

interiors and furnishings of the building, according to a stylistic identity that had to involve all the environments, in the 'democratic' conviction that all the 'inhabitants' of the building, from the company president to its employees, had to live in the same spaces. Ponti's design therefore involved the walls and the floors, all covered by Pirelli rubber and linoleum, the furniture, the doors, the lifts, the clocks, the lighting equipment. With a special attention devoted to the colours, used, Ponti argued, 'as a corrective to the monotony and impersonality of the spaces'. Therefore, the green light was given for doors covered in red linoleum and floors in an amazing blend of yellow and black. These were also the years of renewal in the leadership of the group. On 7 August 1956 Piero Pirelli, president of the company, passed away aged seventy-five. His brother Alberto assumed that role, leaving that of managing director; he was joined by his son Leopoldo and engineer Luigi Emanueli as vice presidents. Franco Brambilla, Emanuele Dubini and Luigi Rossari became managing directors and general managers. This was an important phase for the company: Leopoldo, who had already been at the group for two years as a consultant, represented the third generation of the family. Alberto's other male son, Giovanni, had made different choices, giving precedence to the humanistic disciplines over economic ones: moving to Naples, a student of Federico Chabod at the Italian Institute for Historical Studies—founded by Benedetto Croce in 1946—, he was to become one of the most significant figures in twentieth-century Italian culture (in 1959, for the *Rivista Pirelli*, with the pseudonym of Franco Fellini, he was to write a series of articles on a visit made to Egypt together with his friend, painter Renato Guttuso). But the changes at the head of the company did not end there: less than three years later, in the spring of 1959, Alberto Pirelli suffered a stroke. This serious disability was to speed up the transfer of operational and managerial duties to his son Leopoldo.

The favourable climate, which was still in existence in the early 1960s, provided a push towards new investments and towards a general restructuring of production poles in Italy: for tyres in Settimo Torinese, Figline Valdarno, Villafranca Tirrena, Rovereto and Pizzighettone, while for the construction of cables the installation in Arco Felice in the Naples area was completed. There was also a strong presence abroad, with the construction of new plants in Greece, Turkey, Spain and Brazil, in addition to the expansion of the English factory in Eastleigh, used for the production of high-tension cables. This was another of Pirelli's vocations, the distinctive feature of a company that knows no bounds: Italian history, international scope. This also led to innovative solutions to extend the business. Arrival on the German market, for example, came about with an unprecedented procedure: a brand-new factory was not built, but rather a structure already operating in the territory was acquired, Veith-Gummiwerke in Sandbach, in the Federal Republic of Germany, which at that time possessed a 7 per cent share of the tyre market.

This climate, already to a large extent positive, even reached moments of euphoria, thanks also to resounding successes in the international field: in 1963 the engineer Giulio Natta, together with German Karl Ziegler, received the Nobel Prize for Chemistry for the invention of polypropylene, a type of plastic that revolutionised the world of consumer products: toys, kitchen utensils, recipients and containers for food were now made using moplen. This was a Nobel Prize that also 'rewarded' Pirelli: at the end of the 1930s, a couple of years before the outbreak of the Second World War, the firm had commissioned the Italian chemist—within the sphere of operations of the Italian company for the production of synthetic rubber that had recently been created together with the IRI [The Institute for Industrial Reconstruction]—to find an alternative approach to the increasingly difficult problem of importing natural rubber from the major South American plantations and from the British, French and Dutch colonies of the Far East. This magical moment in Italy, however, was destined not to last long. The economic boom, with all its baggage of unresolved contradictions, was beginning to prepare its bill. Development was impetuous but abounding in incongruities: first and foremost, the significant presence of the State on the terrain of the economy became increasingly cumbersome, in its role as regulator and also as a player with its multiple government-owned corporations. Then the political frame of reference also changed: after years of centrist governments led by the Christian Democrats, the Socialists joined the first centre-left executive that saw the light of day in late 1963, opening up an era of 'economic planning' that in reality was to plan very little and, rather, was to highlight its own substantial incapacity to tackle a phase of recession that struck Italy in 1964, after a sudden yet significant decrease in the growth rate of the economy. The psychological backlash that hit the country was clear: from widespread wellbeing there was a shift towards the uncertainty of the present and worries for the future. It was no longer development that was growing, but social tensions, which were increasingly evident and, with the passing months, less and less under control: a creeping, unstoppable unease that would lead in Italy to protests by students and workers and to the so-called 'Hot Autumn of '69', one of the moments of transformation for the youthful Italian democracy.

It was in this phase that Pirelli experienced a growth dynamic with an asymmetrical development: it implemented its business plan and supported new investments abroad—where, in the twelve months between March 1967 and March 1968, an 'Eastern front' with new production structures in Romania and the Soviet Union was opened, in addition to the opening of a factory for radial tyres in Carlisle, in the United Kingdom—, while in Italy it was at the centre of a clash with the trade unions that was to continue throughout 1969, despite the signing, in December 1968, of the so-called 'decretone' [big decree] on the reduction of working hours, an agreement in which the owners accepted some of the demands of the workers' representatives. This, however, was not enough to stop the wave of unrest that culminated, in September 1969, in the sabotaging at the plant in the Bicocca area in Milan of the stocks of tyres coming from the Greek and Spanish subsidiaries: spread out throughout the plant, the tyres were also used to erect obstructions at the entrances, before launching a night of destruction in which thirty or so cars were overturned and destroyed, the windows of offices broken and some production departments damaged.

The 1970s announced themselves as tough and complex, but even the bleakest forecasts were exceeded by the crude reality of the facts. Two powerfully destabilising phenomena occurred on the Italian scene, namely terrorist acts in a Neo-fascist mould and red terrorism, which would leave a heavy toll of dead and injured in their wake. These were the so-called 'anni di piombo' [literally 'years of lead'], difficult years in which, added to the uncertainties as to whether the democratic institutions were watertight was a clear worsening of the general economic framework. In the ten preceding years the country had experienced a dangerous illusion of wealth: once the economic boom had been consigned to history, there was a vain pursuit of another one, without having laid the foundations for it in terms of the accumulation of knowledge, research and investment. This was a reality clearly present in the eyes of the industrial society: and above all in that component that looked at the Confindustria [Italian Confederation of Industry] not only as an association providing services to its associates, but also as a body of political representation capable of orienting the economic choices of the government. In this regard it discussed what is considered to be the manifesto of entrepreneurial reformism, that 'Pirelli Report' (Leopoldo was the president of the Confindustria's commission entrusted with drafting it) that was circulated in early 1970 in which the guidelines for the transformation of production dynamics in a democratic direction and for the promotion of a modern industrial culture were contained.

In the meantime, after Alberto's death on 19 October 1971, the company sought new paths under the guidance of Leopoldo, orienting itself towards the search for aggregations and integrations between producers of tyres, a necessary step also in response to the challenge of the French company Michelin, which had just introduced the successful innovation of the 'metal radial tyre': the choice of partnership settled in the end on the British firm Dunlop, whose integration with Pirelli led to the creation of the third player on the world rubber market.

The new group—called Dunlop-Pirelli Union—was to have a life of misfortune, also on account of the decidedly turbulent economic, social and political context in which Pirelli found itself operating in this country. The worldwide situation was also not helpful, suffering as it was from the shock of the two oil crises of 1973 and 1979. These were crisis that, in the western quadrant, struck Italy particularly badly. These were the years when it was necessary to cope with a new word, 'stagflation', that

is, the contemporary presence of economic stagnation and high inflation. But these were also the years in which, even though in a patchwork manner, a new entrepreneurship began to take shape in this country, committed to constructing a different civil society. Doing business also meant fighting against an unfavourable general climate, aggravated by a political context the choices of which, increasingly inspired by the logic of consensus, dragged Italy towards a situation dominated by uncertainty and by one decisive factor: the burgeoning of public finances. Pirelli deployed its growth strategy to overcome the dramatic climate that was crippling *de facto* the tyre market, but it was immediately clear that the alliance with Dunlop could not give the results hoped for, both on account of the evident cultural differences between the respective entrepreneurial visions and of objective difficulties in governance caused by a 50 per cent merger. The final blow was also to be delivered through the refusal of the British partner, also in a profound crisis, to give its support to the process of financial readjustment undertaken by the group, to all intents and purposes emptying the merger agreement of any meaning. What happened in the spring of 1981 therefore appeared inevitable: the Union was officially dissolved. Aiming at a rebalancing of finances, Pirelli was also forced to make painful choices, such as that, in 1978, of selling the prestigious and iconic company head office, the Pirelli Skyscraper, transferring it to the Lombardy Regional Authority. Nevertheless, despite the difficulties, the company did not give up its role as protagonist in the rubber industry: the 1970s were the period in which, thanks to a prodigious leap in technological terms, new models were to be built of the Cinturato, a successful 'series' that in the early 1980s was to give new energy to the competition with Michelin. The move towards the motorcycle market was in full development; this had begun in 1974 with the establishing of the Pirelli Motovelo group for the study and production of tyres: in 1983 the first radial tyre devised for the new generations of two-wheelers was launched. Again in that period, the focus was accentuated on the sector of optic fibre, the natural technological evolution of cables for telecommunications: the first studies were conducted in 1974 in the Bicocca laboratories, and things speeded up in 1984 with the acquisition of companies already active in the sector (especially in the United Kingdom and the USA) and with the decision to concentrate the experimental activities carried out in various countries in a single research centre.

The mid-1980s marked two important innovations. The first was the launch of a major project for the upgrading of the Bicocca area, which had been an element of identification of the company ever since the early twentieth century: with the moving of the most recent production activities to the new plants (in Bollate and in Settimo Torinese, the latter the source of greatest pride for the company from the two thousands, thanks also to the project by architect Renzo Piano), the role of the establishment occupying a vast area in the north zone

Alberto and Leopoldo Pirelli on the Pirelli Skyscraper under construction, 1958, photo Publifoto

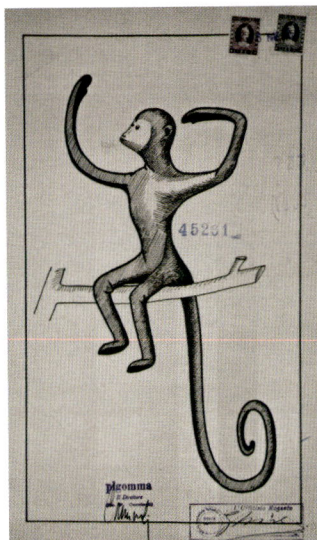

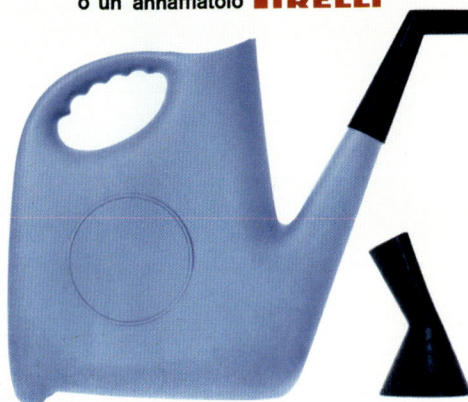

Agenzia Centro, advertisement for the Cinturato CN54, 1972

Patent of the Scimmietta Zizì toy by Bruno Munari for the Pigomma company, 1953

Raymond Gfeller, advertisement for the jerrycan ('canestro') by Roberto Menghi and Pirelli watering cans, 1961, photo Aldo Ballo

of Milan had to be rethought. The company was not new to operations of this kind: we need only think of the dismantling, between the two world wars, of the area around the Central Station, where the first production plants were located and where, as has already been recalled, the skyscraper-symbol of the industrial brand was built in the 1950s. The upgrading of Pirelli was an ambitious programme bringing together tradition and the future, and matching the company's needs (the technical headquarters of the group and the research laboratories still remain there today) with a broader vision of the relationship between industry and territory: the construction of a technological pole envisaging the presence and contribution of other Milanese players such as universities and research centres.

The second innovation directly concerned the ownership structure, with the entry onto the scene of Cam Spa (later to become Camfin), which controlled a group of companies active in the sector of energy, petroleum and raw materials and was headed by Silvio Tronchetti Provera. His son Marco, at the time the husband of Cecilia Pirelli, daughter of Leopoldo, was one of the most convinced supporters of the decision to invest Camfin's profits in Pirelli & C., even becoming its fourth shareholder, after Mediobanca, Gim and Gemina. This was the moment when, exploiting a recovery in the economic outlook, industrial events also took on a new dynamism with the acquisitions, as regards tyres, of the German Metzeler and the French Filergie in the cable sector. The acquisition of Metzeler, the German leader in the production of tyres for motorcycles, enabled Pirelli to achieve two objectives: the doubling of the European market share in the motorbike segment (in 1985 this reached 44 per cent) and the exploitation of sound research activity in the new materials in which the firm from Munich excelled.

But the growth strategy of the group aimed at more ambitious targets in a period in which the first outlines of globalisation began to be perceived. It is in this direction that the idea of a possible integration with Firestone, the US tyre colossus, must be read; this took shape in early 1988 and was to be at the centre of intense negotiations, which, however, were destined to fail after the entry onto the scene, thanks to its relaunch, of the Japanese Bridgestone. 1988 was also the year of an extensive reorganisation of the group: the new architecture envisaged the concentration in Pirelli alone of the ownership and management of all the companies that were operational, leaving the financial coordination to the Société Internationale Pirelli, of which Marco Tronchetti Provera became managing director. A new company was created, Pirelli Tyre Holding, within which all the companies of the group active in the tyre segment were gathered. The change of pace was significant and coincided with a success in operating results that rewarded the efforts made in

recent years to position itself, as one of the few Italian multinationals, in an international context: consolidated sales revenues reached 10,000 billion lire, 4,000 billion of which generated by the rubber tyres produced in the thirty-one plants located in ten countries and 4,320 billion deriving from the cable sector, manufactured in the seventy-one plants distributed over thirteen countries. The idea was alive in Leopoldo Pirelli's mind of the so-called 'dimensional leap' of the group, a step considered necessary in order to respond to the new dynamics of competition on the international markets. New because, between the 1980s and '90s, the worldwide geo-political scene changed radically with the fall of the Berlin Wall, the implosion of the totalitarian régimes of Eastern Europe and the taking shape of European integration, which opened up new and more global perspectives to the development of companies and their businesses. The disappointing experience with Dunlop now consigned to history, Leopoldo Pirelli focused on a new integration project, identifying the German brand Continental as a possible partner. This was a choice that took account of the overall panorama and that was implemented after careful exploration of various options: 'opening up' to the French Michelin or to the US Goodyear, companies that were far superior in terms of dimensions, would have meant 'handing over' Pirelli *de facto* to the two biggest international players. Just as seeking an agreement with the main Japanese firms in the sector would make no sense in geographical or logistical terms. A merger with Continental, on the other hand, would bring considerable benefits, starting with the doubling of the share of the world tyre market (estimated at 13 per cent), to arrive at a better logistical coverage of the market (Pirelli is leader in Italy and Latin America, Continental in Germany, Austria and part of the USA).

Negotiations with the German brand were long and stressful, not without surprises and unexpected developments, with alternating possibilities of success and failure, until the conclusion was reached in late 1991. The game ended with huge losses for the company. After the negative epilogue, there was a move towards a new structure at the top of the company, where from June onwards Pietro Serra and Marco Tronchetti Provera operated as managing directors and general managers: in the statement of Pirelli's board of directors on 30 November 1991, in declaring negotiations with the Hanover firm concluded, direct reference was made to the future and the need to study the measures to be taken to safeguard the integrity of the group's business and assets. These were the years of standing at a turning-point, at the classic crossroads faced with which urgent and definitive choices were made necessary. This was the great challenge that the company was called upon to take up on the eve of the 120th anniversary of its foundation. An epic challenge upon which the destiny of Pirelli would depend.

TRANSFORMATIONS OF THE COUNTRY FROM AFTER THE SECOND WORLD WAR TO THE 1980s

The history of Pirelli side-by-side with that of Italy, also from after the Second World War to the 1980s. In various crucial moments of contemporary history, the group contributed to the reconstruction of the country, to the changes under way and to the drive towards an increasingly technological future. And it did so not only through the innovation of products and production processes, but also thanks to an avant-garde vision at a cultural, urbanistic and architectural level. From the years of the economic boom, in which Milan was the centre of everything, to those of the trade union struggles, to then arrive in the 1980s.
In each of these decades, Pirelli, with its polytechnic culture, embodied the innovative spirit of the country and established a dialogue with the world thanks to a high-profile creative, engineering and communicative strength.

Made by the genius of engineering Luigi Emanueli, the Cinturato became the protagonist of mass motor transport in the mid-1950s. Pirelli holds the patent, taken out in 1950, for this radial tyre. What differentiates it from the previous examples is a 'belt' that squeezes the plies together longitudinally, ensuring the maximum grip in the curves and guaranteeing safer travel. This is how Alberto Pirelli describes its birth: 'After five long years of studies, we produced a new tyre called Cinturato and placed it on sale, a tyre built on the basis of completely different criteria from the usual ones. The fundamental detail that characterises its structure is a strong fabric belt positioned between the tread and the carcass; thanks to special design solutions, the latter is also so solid that its resistance to wear and tear is superior.'

GIO PONTI ARCHITETTO

Milano, 5 Agosto 1957

GP/gm

A Sua Eccellenza

Dr. ALBERTO PIRELLI

Presidente della Soc. PIRELLI

V.le Abruzzi N. 94

M I L A N O

Illustre amico,

         parto in questi giorni, assieme a Valtolina, per
Bagdad.

         Nella attribuzione delle opere mi è stato assegnato
il Palazzo degli uffici del Development Board, e ciò deriva certo
dalla eccezionale possibilità di manifestarmi che la Pirelli mi ha
dato col suo grattacielo. Il mio pensiero, partendo, va a Lei con
commossa gratitudine.

         Mi creda

Suo

Seen from above, the unique diamond-shaped plan of the Pirelli Skyscraper recalls the shape of a grain of rice. Known to the Milanese as the 'Pirellone', it is the most authentic expression not only of the ideology that moved the hand of its inventor, architect Gio Ponti, but also of the values of the company it represents.

Ponti writes in 'Perpetuità di un edificio' in the Rivista Pirelli:

'We entrust this work, writing about it at the beginning of its conception, to those principles that, before Pirelli and after it, have inspired and continue to inspire our work in its truest expressions; these are the principles of formal unity, the finished form, essentiality, representativeness, and finally, 'illusiveness', with which, in looking at architecture that, if it is such, after fulfilling and perhaps discharging the function that gave rise to it, takes on a reality of appearance and art beyond material reality'.

Leopoldo Pirelli
on top of the Pirellone,
1967, photo Publifoto

Le 10 regole dell'imprenditore
[The Ten Rules of a Good Entrepreneur]
by Leopoldo Pirelli

1. I have always been convinced that free private enterprise is an important pillar of a free system and an irreplaceable means of social progress. Albeit with facets that vary from country to country, depending on the local socio-political situation, I believe I can state that a huge and radical transformation process is under way everywhere that traverses the sphere of the economy and affects the whole of society, overturning its traditional orders and setting it in motion, in search of new equilibria. Everywhere a close correlation is emerging between the process of innovation and the initiative of the entrepreneurial forces. Our credibility, our authoritativeness, I would say our legitimacy in the public awareness, are directly related to the role we are fulfilling in contributing to overcoming the social and economic imbalances of the countries in which we operate: business is increasingly presented as a place of synthesis between the tendencies oriented towards the maximum technical-economic progress and the human tendencies for better conditions of work and life.

2. I have always believed that a chief executive officer, who is also a shareholder, must privilege the former qualification, that of chief executive officer, with respect to the latter, because his duties are not only towards his shareholders, but also towards all those who work at the company, towards the communities that surround it, towards the countries (in the case of the Pirelli, no less than 16) in which the Group operates.

3. I firmly believe that in a group of our dimensions (but I think the concept is also extendible to smaller units) the chief executive officer must be supported by professionally capable and morally unexceptionable collaborators. I think, furthermore, that with them he must clearly establish what the problems are concerning which he intends to decide in the first person, naturally after having listened to and examined their opinions, and what the problems are regarding which he delegates his decision-making (and they must be many). And, among these delegated problems, which are the ones of which he wishes to be informed *a posteriori* and which are the ones of which he does not even wish to be informed. It remains clear, nevertheless, that, whatever the degree of delegation is, the chief executive officer remains responsible for everything that happens in the Group, because he is the one who has chosen the people and the delegations and, therefore, he covers them always and in any circumstance.

4. I am convinced that among the first tasks of the chief executive officer there is continuous care in the training of future line managers, from his succession to those of his closest collaborators, concerning himself that these in turn give the problem the same importance, and so on down through the pyramid.

LE 10 REGOLE DELL'IMPRENDITORE

It was 3 October 1970 when the College of Engineers of Milan handed three gold medals as honorary associates to three engineers who particularly distinguished themselves in the performance of their activities. Among them was Leopoldo Pirelli, who, during his acceptance speech, remembered the responsibilities taken on in his thirty-five years of work and summarised the rules that a good entrepreneur should follow in ten points, starting with the experience accrued as executive head of the Pirelli group.

5. Though being the head, the chief executive officer must try to understand the human personalities of his colleagues, with their personal problems concerning health, finance or family, and he must always remember that, if a colleague does not prove to be up to the tasks entrusted to him, it is he, the chief executive officer, who has made the first mistake by appointing them.

6. I am convinced that an entrepreneur must be honest in the broadest sense of the word (it is not enough, that is, that he does not steal and does not bear false witness). Speaking of honesty in a broad sense, I am thinking of a given conduct in relation to shareholders and employees, but also to customers, suppliers, competitors, tax authorities, parties and the political world. I think that—apart from any moral principle—being honest benefits both the entrepreneur as a person and the company he runs.

7. I am convinced that the chief executive officer must know how to evolve with the times, though keeping faith with the 'sacred principles' I have just mentioned. One example: that of relations with workers and their representatives. I joined the company when paternalism, even the most enlightened, already had no place in the industrial reality any longer. I went through the times of the bitter conflicts of '68/69, managing relations with the trade unions personally, when the walls of Milan were covered with slogans: 'Agnelli and Pirelli the thieving twins' and personally having very harsh words and attitudes towards those who wanted 'everything and now'. But already then I had faith—and this is evident from the new Statute of the Confindustria drafted by the so-called 'Pirelli Commission' in 1969–1970—that it would be possible to change from a conflictual relationship to a collaborative one, something that today—even if I do not manage these problems anymore personally—I am pleased to see realised to an important degree, even though this could certainly be further improved. Well, if all this has been able to happen, it is because both parties have known how to mature and to evolve on the basis of changes in the social framework and living conditions.

8. It is my opinion that the entrepreneur must not regret decisions that have been taken in the conviction of being right and that have proven to be wrong: here too, just one example, without of course claiming that there are not any others that I could give. I am referring to the marriage between Pirelli and Dunlop that came about in 1970 with the aim of making their respective tyre-making activities, once working together, reach dimensions comparable to those of the three majors in the sector: Goodyear, Michelin and Firestone. It seemed like an ideal union, but unfortunately, despite the respect and friendship between the Pirelli and Dunlop people and, particularly between the two presidents, the marriage failed: perhaps in reality it was never consummated. And this was for a series of reasons: crisis of Pirelli in Italy in the 1970s, then crisis of Dunlop in England; the impossibility of managing jointly; the difficulty of interpenetration between the Anglo-Saxon mentality and the Latin mentality. And perhaps a little bad luck. In any event, it failed and then came the divorce. For Pirelli (and also for Dunlop) it was a major negative experience: I feel fully responsible for it, but if I went back to 1969–1970, I would join with Dunlop again. I do not regret the decision taken then, therefore, even though I would try to consummate the marriage on the evening of the wedding, or perhaps—to be in step with the young people of today—even a little earlier.

9. I believe that entrepreneurs must not boast merits that are often not individual but collective. If I have to attribute a merit to myself, I would choose that of having remained calm and serene at the helm in the moments when the boat was in rough seas, when the hull was showing signs of collapsing. But I was certainly not alone in bringing the boat out of the storm: while I stayed at the helm, others hoisted the sails and together we started sailing again. Better than before; quite well; why not say, today, not bad at all?

10. I will stop here, recalling finally the first quality that an entrepreneur must always have: to try, to try with all his might, to close the balance sheets well. If you do not succeed once, try again. If you do not succeed a number of times, then go. And if you do succeed, do not think you are God Almighty, but simply someone who, given the trade chosen, has done his duty.

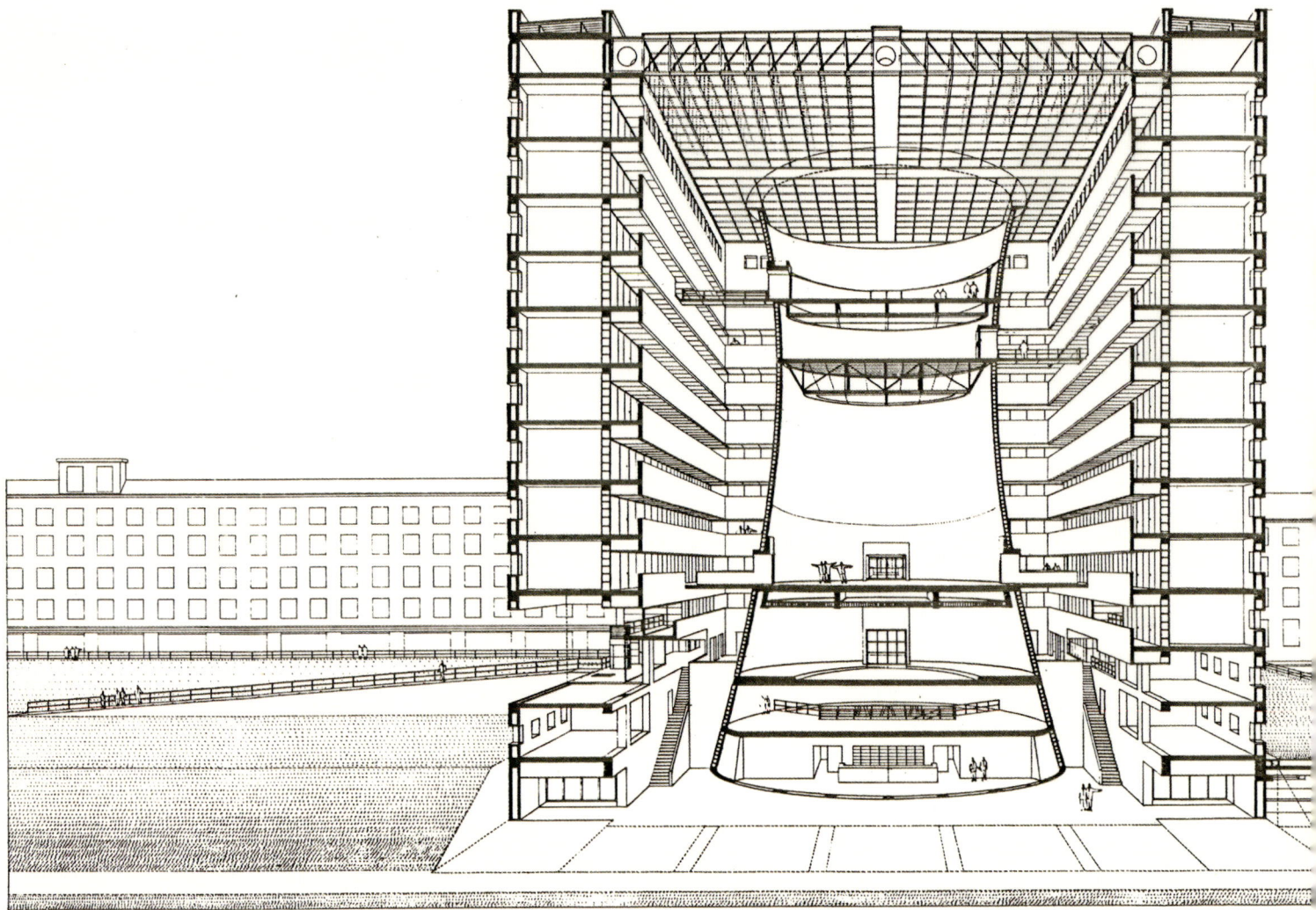

Veduta dello spazio interno della nuova Direzione Pirelli, sullo sfondo l'edificio n° 45.

Progetto Bicocca
Pirelli

Progetto urbanistico
ed architettonico
di un centro tecnologico
innovativo

Secondo grado
Milano, Febbraio 1988

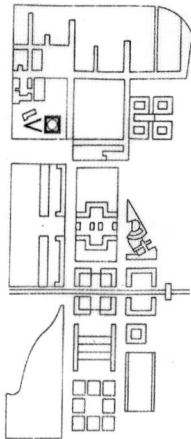

Tavola n.   55

Comparto   L

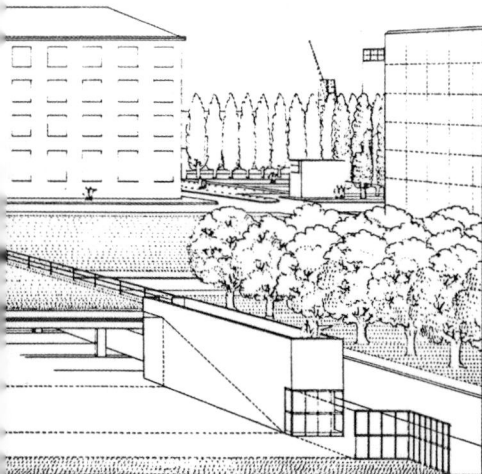

Gregotti Associati

Augusto Cagnardi
Pierluigi Cerri
Vittorio Gregotti
Architetti

20123 Milano
Via Bandello 20
telefono (02) 4814141/2/3

30121 Venezia
Cannaregio 2179
telefono (041) 720996

The project for upgrading of the Bicocca neighbourhood, entrusted, following a competition of international scope, to the Studio Gregotti Associati International (1988), also presupposed an architectural rethinking of the headquarters of the Pirelli group with the aim of integrating it into the social reality that would grow around the industrial pole.

Thus, in the introduction to the volume Progetto Bicocca, Leopoldo Pirelli explains his vision: 'The Bicocca in the 1990s must not be a space that is closed and inaccessible to citizens, but rather an open place, rich in possibilities of communication and economic, social and cultural interchange.

An area where the new technologies 'will speak the language of people', giving back an urban value to the old city-factory of the Bicocca'.

The project for building HQ1 shows the pre-existing cooling tower, created in the 1950s in the factory in Milan Bicocca, in its new conception: at the centre of a cube composed on three sides of offices and on one of a glass wall, the tower takes on the role of an auditorium on the lower floor and of conference rooms on the upper floors. Today the building is the heart of the current Pirelli group Headquarters.

Changing Pace between Power and Control

Marco Tronchetti Provera succeeds Leopoldo Pirelli and reorganises the entire group with the turnaround to relaunch the company. He invests in Research and Development, in culture, but especially in the progressive transformation of Pirelli into a 'pure tyre company'. And he succeeds in his aim to change course.

by Bruno Arpaia

-

WRITER

Many years later, speaking into the microphone of Fabrizio Spagna, Marco Tronchetti Provera would recall the 'turnaround', the major process of reorganisation of the Pirelli group that occurred between late 1991 and late 1994, as follows:

It was necessary to employ all the available levers to begin a restructuring and a simultaneous relaunch of the company. The situation was one of such demotivation and crisis that it was necessary to succeed in reconciling the vision of the future with sacrifices in the here and now. We had the urgent need to focus everything on innovation and to set back in motion the most vital forces of the company with a team of motivated people.[1]

To focus everything on innovation: as had always happened over the course of its history, at that point of more than a hundred years, even in moments of difficulty Pirelli focused on research and productivity. This is a company characteristic evidenced by the fact that, more or less consistently over recent decades, the group at the Bicocca has devoted around 4 per cent of its sales revenue to R&D, a share that is considerably higher than that of its international competitors and ten times more than the average for Italian industry.
In the 1980s, the market sectors in which the group was involved had had an up-and-down performance, and Pirelli had responded both with the attempt to increase its sizes and areas of action with acquisitions and integrations, also with a view to the possibility of more investments in research, and also by once again backing the quality and innovation of its products. In 1981, once the association with Dunlop was over, the Bicocca company had returned to Formula 1 after twenty-five years of absence, providing tyres to Brabham, Lotus and

Benetton. Formula 1 was the perfect laboratory to trial new construction processes, new forms and structures of tyres, new materials and new compounds, to then transfer them onto standard tyres. That experience, moreover, was integrated with the work of the research and development division at the Bicocca, where tyres, casings and compounds were tested on the simulator, with loads and tractions even higher than those of racing vehicles.
So it was that, in the 1970s, entering the rally field, Pirelli had developed the revolutionary P7, a 'super-low-profile' with a more rigid shoulder and reduced drift that had succeeded in surpassing all the limits to which the tyres of the time were subjected to and all the prejudices whereby a radial would never be able to satisfy the requirements of a racing tyre. After success in rallies, the P7 belt tyre had also been used on the track, first in Formula 2 and then in Formula 1. The creator of that success had undoubtedly been Mario Mezzanotte. After joining the firm in the 1950s, in the technical tyre department, he had gradually become the man who had enabled Pirelli to establish itself in the segment of high-performance tyres. Following in the wake of the P7, applying the experience accumulated in the racing world, in the mid-1980s Mezzanotte's team had perfected a new low-profile road tyre, for which para-aramid fibres and silica were used for the first time in production. It was named P Zero, meaning the absolute, perfection. Created as the first kit for the Lancia Delta S4, it was officially launched in 1986 as the exclusive kit for the Ferrari F40, to then become the founder of a prestigious family of high-end tyres.
Also, in the group's other main business unit, that of cables, during the 1980s Pirelli's research had not remained idle, but was among the first firms in the world to commit to photonics, which is the branch of science that studies light. More than a decade after the invention of the laser, which occurred in 1960, the possibility that data for telecommunications could travel not in cables in

Technical drawing
of the P7 Corsa
Montecarlo tyre, 1977

Tomás Gonda,
advertisement
for the Cinturato
Pirelli tyre, 1971

Check on Pirelli tyres
on the Formula 1
track, 1983

previous pages
Maestro Salvatore
Accardo and the Italian
Chamber Orchestra
performing Il Canto della
fabbrica at the Pirelli
Industrial Pole in Settimo
Torinese, 2017,
photo Ippistudio

The driver Miki Biasion in the Lancia Delta with Pirelli tyres in the Rally Argentina, 1986

Michael Schumacher in his Benetton with Pirelli tyres, 1991

the form of electric pulses, and therefore of electrons, but rather as light pulses or photons, began to be glimpsed at the speed of light. Thus, Pirelli had already begun experimenting with optical fibres in 1977, and in 1981 the first telephone line of this type was installed between Venice and Mestre. In 1984 a single research centre was founded, bringing together the projects previously spread around in Italy, the United Kingdom, the USA and Brazil. It was in 1987, prompted by Giorgio Grasso, that the Pirelli Photonic Unit was founded.

Furthermore, perceiving the importance of photonic technologies for telecommunications from the very start, Pirelli had investigated and also adopted a strategy of international alliances based on those optical fibre manufacture technologies that appeared most interesting and complementary to each other. Then, original innovations were grafted onto them, succeeding in resolving a real 'bottleneck' for those technologies: the need often encountered for the light signal to pass through electrical equipment in order to be regenerated and repowered. This difficulty was brilliantly overcome through the creation of the first optical amplifier, a piece of equipment based on a special active optical fibre, 'drugged' with erbium (a chemical element in the category of rare earths), and on laser micro-pumps that enabled the signal to travel for thousands of kilometres without intermediary regenerations. They were now ready to provide high-quality ultra-wideband services, with potentials that could barely be imagined at that time. Meanwhile, the world around was changing at dizzying speed. The fall of the Berlin Wall opened up scenarios that were not easy to foresee, while the Maastricht Treaty and the single market, which was to come into effect in 1993, speeded up the process of European integration. The future appeared uncertain, but for Pirelli that future could offer a challenge and at the same time an opportunity for investments in the new markets that were opening up beyond the former Iron Curtain and in the Far East. In the meantime, however, still following the rationale of dimensional expansion, the group was committed to the attempt at integration with Continental. The 'Continental saga', the lengthy negotiations with the German company, which ultimately proved fruitless and concluded in nothing at all, weakened the resources at La Bicocca, contributing to bringing all the critical issues that had accumulated in the preceding years to light, mostly in an international economic situation that was not at all favourable and, as regards Italy, also in a political climate that was increasingly heavy.

According to Carlo Bellavite Pellegrini, 'for too long the Group had focused its attention predominantly on tyres and had insisted on almost exclusively seeking advantages deriving from the dimensional factor'.[2] This 'dimensional obsession'[3] had ended up sacrificing productivity and, although the company had continued to conduct research and to innovate, it had reduced the capacity to obtain more competitive products than those of its competitors. The capacity to identify and exploit technological discontinuities has gradually grown weak.

For Marco Tronchetti Provera, who was about to take over at the helm of the group from Leopoldo Pirelli, the situation was clear. He knew that the company needed a profound restructuring and he also knew that this would happen in an unfavourable context. Therefore, even before the conclusion of the Continental episode, with great energy he launched the *turnaround*, that is to say, 'an enormous, prodigious reorganisation', according to the definition by Carlo Bellavite Pellegrini,[4] which affected the economic, financial, institutional, managerial and research aspects all at the same time: profound changes in management and in the company structure, divesting of the so-called diversified activities, focusing on the group's two main business units, cables and tyres, upgrading its products and increasingly orienting itself towards the high end. Innovation also concerned IT systems, entrusted to Arrigo Andreoni, who, years ahead of the competitors, adopted Sap, a software able to manage all the resources and to plan business activities highly effectively. No less important was the introduction of Total Production Manufacturing, a methodology based on the continuous improvement of quality and productivity and on the active involvement of people.

And so, after the *annus horribilis* of 1992, the first results began to be seen, with the beginning of the relaunch with new technologies and new products destined for the high-end segment, as well as the opening up of new markets, especially in China, South-East Asia and Africa. In the tyre sector, first the models P 200 Chrono and P 5000 Vizzola were presented for the spares market, then the worldwide distribution began of the P Zero System, an ultra-low-profile tyre to be used on the most prestigious car models, and of the 'mass market' low-profile, the P 6000, the first tyre entirely generated by computer, proving the company's attention towards computerised systems to assist design and the ever greater capacity to achieve a high degree of flexibility in production. In Building 43 in Viale Sarca, researchers also coming from the university world worked to reduce costs by shortening study and design times, arriving at the prototype as soon as possible and avoiding many indoor and outdoor tests, thanks to complex mathematical models capable of predicting the behaviour of a tyre under the various conditions of use. The new Pirelli products came about above all from intense research activity in order to reduce their noisiness, to endow them with low rolling resistance, to use materials with reduced environmental impact, with a view, which was then futuristic and almost visionary, to the introduction of the electric car. Very soon, in the field of the chemistry, for materials and compounds, the work of Enrico Albizzati proved fundamental; he was an expert in polymers, coming from the academic world, whose work contributed to creating ever closer relations between the company and universities. And with the new products, particularly with the Dragon series, capable of complete mastery on wet or snowy surfaces, thanks above all to the incisive action of Maurizio Boiocchi, today executive vice president & strategic advisor Technology and Innovation, Pirelli succeeded in regaining approvals at BMW, Mercedes and Porsche and to obtain that of Audi.

On 31 January 1995, presenting the P 6000 in Lisbon, Giuseppe Bencini, head of the tyre sector, stated: 'The cure has ended and 1995 will be the year of the attack. The products have been the major resource that has enabled Pirelli first to emerge from the crisis and then to attack the market'.[5] An attack that also availed itself of innovative communication tools: the fascination of Sharon Stone in the advert *Driving Instinct*, and the elegant power of Ronaldo and Carl Lewis marked an advertising campaign around the slogan 'Power is nothing without control'. And the iconic image of Annie Leibovitz portraying Lewis, the Olympic multi-gold medallist, in running spikes on the starting blocks, is imprinted in the minds of millions of people.

However, between 1993 and 1994, while definite signs of improvement were coming from tyres, the cable sector underwent an almost pre-announced crisis, an abrupt fall in demand, also due to the reduction in the price of optical fibre. What was supposed to be an important technological advance was quickly to become a commodity, that is, a goods item exchanged on the market without qualitative differences. Despite this, Tronchetti Provera continued to glimpse speedy development in the telecommunications sector, associated above all with the new computer technologies and the Internet. Cables offered the group the opportunity to tackle those segments of major innovation, provided technological advances could be optimized. Very soon, in fact, the world was constantly talking about the new information highways and the G7 Ministerial Conference on the Global Information Society of February 1995 in Brussels ratified their launch in great style. Marco Tronchetti Provera was one of the four Italian entrepreneurs who were invited to the summit, and he expressed the Pirelli group's agreement with the aim of creating an integrated worldwide telecommunications system. In that period, the Pirelli leadership considered that 'the transition from

electronics to photonics in telecommunications networks is a genuine revolution comparable to the passage from traditional copper cable carriers to optical fibres'.[6] A large part of the possibilities of development of a number of industries and services was based, in fact, on the cable sector.

Thanks to the research developed for decades, Pirelli was in pole position in that race. The frontier was still represented by photonics, but further scenarios were already being glimpsed. Anticipating them was fundamental. And so it was that in May 1995 Pirelli created a consortium with the Milan Politecnico, CoreCom (Milan Consortium for the Research and Development of Optical Switching), first with a five-year duration, then extended to 2008, which soon became a point of reference at European level for all the research topics connected with optical communications and beyond, also conducting pioneering activities in the fields of optical networks, wavelength conversion, optical amplification, high-contrast integrated optics, nanomaterials and special optical fibres, producing no less than forty-six patents deposited, with equipment that would form the core of the newly developing information highways.

The innovation, however, did not only concern the products and materials. The Bicocca company, in fact, was moving decisively to bring about a radical change in the production process.

'On 17 May 1997', Renato Caretta told Maurizio Maggi of l'Espresso *magazine, 'when I was about to retire after forty-five years of work, the Dottore called me and told me: 'Caretta, you must not leave before making Pirelli take an epic step forward in its way of manufacturing tyres. Do what you want, but bring the result home to me'.[7]*

The 'Dottore' is obviously Marco Tronchetti Provera, and at that time Renato Caretta was Head of Research and Development for tyres. A workshop mechanic who

POWER IS NOTHING WITHOUT CONTROL.

Carl Lewis is a member of the Santa Monica Track Club

IF YOU'RE GOING TO DRIVE, DRIVE

PIRELLI

Young & Rubicam,
Carl Lewis for the
advertisement
for Pirelli tyres, 1994,
photo Annie Leibovitz

Young & Rubicam,
one-page advertisement
in Pirelli World,
issue 11, 1997

POWER IS NOTHING WITHOUT CONTROL.

P6000.™ The latest wave in tyre technology has broken. Silica based compounds, developed with the world's top car manufacturers, ensure maximum adhesion in the wet. A dramatic improvement in braking, cornering and steering power ensures maximum grip. The P6000™ ensures maximum envy. Pirelli. Power is nothing without control.

http://www.pirelli.com

had gained a diploma as an expert technician by studying at evening classes, Caretta had joined the company in 1953 as a mechanical designer. He had worked hard and observed for a long time until he became the key man in most of the company's successes. After that conversation with the Dottore, Caretta was not seen around very much, but was shut away in his office in La Bicocca, gradually assembling a team of mechanics, engineers, designers and IT experts around him, working starting from an idea that he had already studied in the 1970s, back then still too far ahead of its time. Until, in 1999, Caretta was able 'to bring the result home' and to officially present the MIRS™ (Modular Integrated Robotized System), which, starting from the following year, was gradually installed at La Bicocca, and then at the plants in Breuberg, in Germany, in Rome, the USA, and at Burton-on-Trent in Great Britain.

What was it? A production process, protected by twenty-two patents, fully automated and managed by integrated software, enabling high-end and very high-end tyres to be produced in small quantities, with very fast development times, making logistics and a wholly innovative customer service possible. The robots that comprised it produced the tyre in a single working cycle, from the production of the various materials to vulcanisation, improving quality standards thanks to the elimination of rapid changes in temperature, intermediate storage, the transportation of goods in process in the various zones of the plant and non-homogeneous vulcanisation conditions.

This was a genuine revolution compared to the traditional production process. MIRS™ reduced the lead time from 6 days to 72 minutes, cutting the production phases from 14 to 3, without wastes of energy and running at unprecedented speed: one tyre every three minutes, producing a 25 per cent saving on costs and offering the possibility of managing the variations in demand efficiently thanks to its intrinsic flexibility. If so desired, in fact, in a few minutes the MIRS™ can be adapted to produce even just a single unit per type of tyre. For a company like Pirelli this is a fundamental trump card, since the high-performance market, on which it decided to focus, requires great quality and production volumes of small dimensions with ever differing requisites. And it was precisely this characteristic that enabled Maurizio Boiocchi, returning from Germany, where he had led the local research, to enable Pirelli to take on an important role among the leaders in the Prestige and Premium sectors, that is, the high end and very high end for tyres. After all, MIRS™ was not created to replace all the traditional systems, but to run alongside them in the production precisely of high-performance or of 'run-flat' tyres (those capable of travelling a long way even in the event of a puncture), giving the La Bicocca company a major competitive advantage and the possibility of continuing to produce in countries with high costs, such as in Europe or the USA.

Yet it did not end there. In 2002 MIRS™ was, so to speak, complemented by CCM (Continuous Compounding Mixing), protected by seven families of patents, an integrated and flexible system for managing compounds, also designed for production in the cable sector. CCM reduces the lead time from 24 to 7.4 hours, permits energy savings of 20 per cent, reduces the variability of the physical properties of components by 70 per cent and cuts dust emissions. Above all, in a complex compartment such as that of compounds, where around 160 components are involved, often calibrated almost as though with a pharmacist's scales, the production is permitted of so-called 'green' compounds, where a large quantity of silica replaces a certain percentage of carbon black, the by-product from the combustion of petroleum that is always necessary to produce tyres. The advantage is undoubtedly in environmental terms, but also involves reduced consumption for the car, considering that silica reduces rolling resistance on asphalt. The working process is more complex, however, as it needs more energy and greater control of temperatures. CCM also resolves these problems, and was very soon adopted upstream of MIRS™.

A further development of the revolutionary production process was subsequently installed in the new factory in Settimo Torinese: Next MIRS began operating in 2010 in the 'beautiful factory', or 'fabbrica bella', designed by Renzo Piano according to a green philosophy, alongside other very advanced production lines, always specialising in high-end and very high-end tyres. In addition to the futuristic 'spina' [backbone] that connects up the various departments, running for almost five hundred metres between two rows of cherry trees, the natural light that bathes the plant is impressive. Historically, in fact, the sites for the production of tyres had blacked-out windows as light affected the compounds and the vulcanisation process; at Settimo, on the other hand, the Pirelli researchers studied special glass that does not compromise production and gives light and liveability to the factory environment.

In the years around the turn of the century, however, the La Bicocca group also experimented with other innovations. In 1999 an agreement was signed with Michelin for the production of the Pax System, a particular type of run-flat based on a newly conceived asymmetrical wheel. And the underground optical systems were sold to Cisco, with an unprecedented creation of value, and optical components to Corning, for a total sum of more than five billion euros, which would later be used for the purchase of Telecom Italia; the company decided to invest around 135 million euros in the creation of Pirelli Labs, a research centre that is among the most advanced in the world, with the purpose of becoming a knowledge company, or, as Marco Tronchetti Provera explained, 'a company that evolves and creates value through the development of new knowledge and technologies'.[8] A company, that is, that sells discoveries. Behind the long brick walls of the old Pirelli plants in Viale Sarca in Milan, where at one time thousands of workers came together in a desolate peripheral zone just like in the old images of the industrial revolution, stand the so-called Case Bianche [White Houses].

You can only enter wearing an antiseptic diving suit to study the infinitely small and the infinitely fast. To study the future. Under the guidance of Giorgio Grasso and Enrico Albizzati, first, and then of Maurizio Boiocchi, in constant connection with the other Pirelli research centres and with Russian, British and US researchers of the Massachusetts Institute of Technology Microphotonics Center, scientists coming from all over the world, physicists, engineers and mathematicians, experimented with components of dimensions in the order of microns and nanometres for optical technologies, in order to give 'more band' to bits in data transmission. And when the research had not yet finished experimenting with every possible application of optical nanotechnologies, maximising the quantity of data transmitted in the single fibre and revolutionising the broadband telecommunications sector to end users, the researchers set off to explore new frontiers: superconductor materials and the transmission of bundles of neutrinos applied to telecommunications.

The group's innovative drive has not diminished even in recent years, which have been marked by profound changes in the company's structures, with the abandonment of the control of Telecom Italia and the entry of ChemChina as main shareholder, as well as the transfer of the other branches of activity and the decision, in 2010, to focus on the core business of tyres to become a 'pure tyre company'. New factories emerged in Russia, Romania, Mexico and China, while Pirelli returned to Formula 1 as the exclusive supplier to all the teams and sponsored the first Emirates New Zealand sailing team and then Luna Rossa Prada for the America's Cup. In the meantime, it continued on the path of research and new agreements were entered into of collaboration with universities, from the Milan Politecnico (with a new professorship in innovative materials) to that of Turin, from the Università degli Studi di Milano Bicocca to Berkeley. And there was no shortage of results in terms of innovation in the field of production processes.

In this sphere, the researchers at the laboratories of Milan Bicocca, in collaboration with the Department of IT, Science and Engineering of the University of Bologna and the Department of Automatics and IT of the Turin Politecnico, developed the prototype CVA for the automatic visual control of tyres, receiving the Oscar Masi Prize for Industrial Innovation in 2015. This was a system, covered by a family of around forty patents, for the recognition of possible defects in tyres, fully automated and based on complex algorithms and avant-garde computer vision technologies.

After long years of studies and prototypes in collaboration with the Milan Politecnico, the Cyber Tyre has recently entered production, as was announced by Marco Tronchetti Provera in 2017 at the Geneva Motor Show and in an interview with *Corriere della Sera*:

We have developed a different tyre that, thanks to digitisation, is capable of rendering a constant flow of information. The digitisation process allows us to predict possible anomalies that could compromise the quality standards of our tyres.[9]

Thanks to a highly advanced sensor, a little less than a centimetre in size and applied directly to the inner liner, and not to the valve, as was previously done, the tyre not only records the data on its performance, also allowing retrospective tracing as far back as the production batch, but also 'reads the road', identifying the conditions of the asphalt and then communicating the data with a wireless connection to the on-board control unit and the car's instrumentation. The latter, acquiring a greater 'sensory awareness', can therefore adapt to the type of driving selected. Cyber technology has made use of various innovative solutions that have considerably extended the number of patents deposited by the company. A first for Pirelli, a continually evolving system, already fundamental for safety in mobility, which will become crucial in the management of the autonomous drive cars of the near future, also increasing their sustainability at the same time. These days, in fact, any respectable innovation must take the environmental impact of production processes and products seriously into account. From this point of view, starting from 2004 Pirelli has endowed itself

The 'Spina' by Renzo
Piano in the Pirelli
Industrial Pole
in Settimo Torinese,
2016, photo
Carlo Furgeri Gilbert

*Pirelli APAC R&D Open
Innovation Center, 2020*

*The Pirelli factory
in Mexico, 2016*

with a sustainable management model inspired by the principles of the United Nations Global Compact and the guidelines on the social responsibility of enterprises dictated by international standard ISO 26000. In January 2012, furthermore, it signed a voluntary agreement with the Ministry of the Environment to reduce the impact of its activities on the climate. Hence, as highlighted by the young researcher Salvatore Scaletta, the major work undertaken in the development of tyres that, yes, are high-performance, but also with reduced environmental impact, in the research into new polymers based on biomaterials such as renewable source silica or on biofillers such as lignin, or on plasticisers or resins of vegetal origin and new vulcanisers and stabilisers for the production of sustainable products. Research agreements for experimentation on the use of natural rubber from guayule, on silica derived from rice husks and on other innovative materials were entered into with Versalis, from the Eni group, and with the University of Milan-Bicocca, within the sphere of the Consortium for Research into Advanced Materials (CORIMAV) and the Silvio Tronchetti Provera Foundation. 'The aim', writes Salvatore Scaletta, 'is to diversify the sources of supply available, so as to decrease the pressure on biodiversity of the producing countries and to allow a more flexible management of situations of possible scarcity of raw materials'.[10] Meanwhile, the introduction of materials of mineral origin into industrial procedures to partially replace silica and carbon black has allowed a reduction in the environmental impact associated with the production of raw materials of over 75 per cent in terms of carbon dioxide emissions and water consumption. It is thanks to these results that Pirelli is at the top of many stock-exchange indexes on sustainability and that, recently, in China the government of Shandong attributed Class A certification to the plant in Yanzhou for its commitment to waste recovery, energy use with low carbon emissions and the reduction of water use.

Finally, it would be impossible to fully shed light on the concept of innovation in a company such as Pirelli without considering the great attention devoted to enterprise culture, comparable to that, rightly much celebrated, of Olivetti.

Stressing the fact that doing business means making culture at the same time, as Antonio Calabrò, Head of Institutional Affairs and Senior Advisor for Culture at the company, has written, *means underlining the strong cultural value of scientific research and technology, giving the term 'innovation' a long series of connotations that affect new products and new production systems, experimentation on materials, new physical and chemical combinations, but also languages (from communication to marketing), industrial and working relations, the rules through which a company is governed, the relations between the business and the territories in which the economic activity is developed.*[11]

In the knowledge age, in fact, culture, first and foremost that deriving from creative activities, is (or should be) one of the fundamental assets of the new economic paradigm, a crucial factor for the development of innovation, to encourage new investments, new production chains, involving more thought, more social and environmental responsibilities. In substance, new models of production and consumption. However, in order for the relationship between culture and the economy to be fruitful, environments suitable for innovation must be created. A habitat is needed , a cultural ecosystem in which innovation can take root, grow and develop. The 'knowledge revolution', in fact, does not take place by the simple transfer from a university research laboratory to a more or less robotic industrial shed.

As the Measuring Third Stream Activities report by the Russell Group representing most UK universities explains, it is not enough to set up major scientific centres beside dynamic industries and then all you have to do is optimise the 'transfer of know how'. [...] The passage from the classical industrial economy to the knowledge economy is realised, rather, solely and exclusively where there is a cultural and human environment that is 'creative overall.'[12]

It is no coincidence that in the 1970s and 1980s one of the most important centres, the very emblem of the dawning economy based on knowledge, was California: with its major universities, its research centres, its Silicon Valley, but also with its movie studios, its artistic and literary avant-garde. Its lifestyle. In other words, its cultural industry.

And it has been precisely within this perspective of increasing integration between industrial production and cultural and creative production that Pirelli seems to have moved throughout its history, going beyond the model of relations between culture and enterprise that sees culture solely as economic investment or as a tool of business communication. Already between 1948 and 1972, the *Rivista Pirelli*, founded by Leonardo Sinisgalli and Giuseppe Luraghi, had brought the best of Italian culture into play (Montale, Quasimodo, Ungaretti, Sciascia, Gadda, Guttuso, Eco, Calvino...) to establish, surprisingly ahead of its time, a constant dialogue between science and humanistic knowledge. From 1994, moreover, Pirelli published the periodical *World*, created as a house organ, which became, through interviews with authors such as Zygmunt Bauman, Marc Augé and Franklin Foer, a place of reflection and encounter between science, technology, innovation, art, economics and customs. In recent years even the Pirelli balance-sheets, the company's Annual Reports, have been characterised by collaborations with authors such as Javier Cercas, Hans Magnus Enzensberger, Adam Greenfield, Lisa Halliday, Javier Marías, John Joseph 'J. R.' Moehringer or Emmanuel Carrère, also benefiting from the contribution of graphic designers and artists of international renown. Not to mention *The Cal*, the famous Pirelli Calendar, created in 1964 and featuring the most established photographers of the time, which has never been a simple marketing tool, but over the years has become increasingly established as an artistic object capable of capturing and interpreting contemporary culture and, often, of inspiring new trends. Stemming from the same source is the ambitious programme of upgrading of the areas of Bicocca for the creation, in cooperation with the territorial institutions and the trade unions, of a 'citadel of science', a technological and research pole, today known as Tecnocity or Progetto Italia, developed at the time of the company's presence in Telecom, based on the capacity for collaboration between the 'two cultures' and on recourse to creativity as a strategic lever for enterprise. Subsequently, Pirelli HangarBicocca, formed in 2004 in the large spaces once used for the manufacture of locomotives and high-power electrical machines, was immediately characterised as one of the most important European institutions devoted to the production and promotion of contemporary art, while the Fondazione Pirelli, founded in 2008, is intended to showcase the company's history and values, giving space to thought bringing together concrete industrial experiences and the memories held in the historical Archive with the drive for planning, valuing what is topical as it gradually becomes history. In recent years, ever closer links have been forged with prestigious musical and theatrical institutions, and the cultural activities promoted by the long P have become increasingly intense, especially at the factory in Settimo Torinese, where, amid cherry trees, calenders, mixers and robots, many theatrical groups and orchestras have performed, from Moni Ovadia to Marco Paolini, to the enthralling execution of *Il Canto della fabbrica*, a musical composition by Francesco Fiore, which came about inspired by that workplace and was performed in September 2017 inside the plant by the Italian Chamber Orchestra conducted by Salvatore Accardo. Another strong sign of the centrality of culture and creativity for the Pirelli group as the main drivers of innovation in the years to come.

NOTES

1 In C. Bellavite Pellegrini, *Pirelli. Innovazione e passione 1872-2017*, Bologna 2017, p. 217.

2 *Ibid.*, p. 204.

3 *Ibid.*

4 *Ibid.*, p. 208.

5 In *ibid.*, p. 247.

6 In *ibid.*, p. 254.

7 M. Maggi, 'La mia rivoluzione l'ho fatta di gomma', in *Fatti e Notizie*, 343, 2000, p. 3.

8 *I nuovi Pirelli Labs*, Pirelli press release, 3 May 2001.

9 M. Tronchetti Provera in an interview published in *Corriere della Sera*, 8 March 2017, highlighted in a note by C. Bellavite Pellegrini, *Pirelli. Innovazione e passione*, cit., p. 577.

10 S. Scaletta, *L'innovazione industriale e gli impatti sulla performance. Il caso Pirelli tra Next MIRS e CVA*, degree thesis, Luiss Guido Carli, Department of Law, Professorship of Company Economics, academic year 2017-2018, p. 180.

11 In C. Bellavite Pellegrini, *Pirelli. Innovazione e passione*, cit., p. 585.

12 B. Arpaia, P. Greco, *La cultura si mangia!*, Parma, 2013, p. 53.

Exhibition Pirelli,
When History Builds
the Future, *Fondazione
Pirelli, 2022,
photo Ippistudio*

Anselm Kiefer,
The Seven Heavenly
Palaces, *2004–2015.
Installation view, Pirelli
HangarBicocca, Milan
© Anselm Kiefer;
Courtesy Gallery
Lia Rumma, Milan/
Naples and Pirelli
HangarBicocca, Milan,
photo Lorenzo Palmieri*

HI-TECH LAB CHALLENGES AND DEVELOPMENT OF NEW PRODUCTS

Research, talent and a spirit of belonging are constants in the Pirelli identity. An identity based on the capacity to project itself into the future, pursuing a vision, but above all based on a concrete approach to innovation. The designing of MIRS™, Next MIRS and CCM (Continuous Compound Mixing), the Cyber Tyre, virtualisation. A long path with research and sustainability as the watchwords. To achieve the objective, Pirelli can count on long-standing relations with the major car producers, the academic world and all the scientific players capable of innovating products and processes.

Armando Testa,
advertisement for
Pirelli high-speed fibre,
1999

Felicitous Patents

Maurizio Boiocchi, Executive Vice President
& Strategic Advisor Technology and Innovation of Pirelli

It has been over fifty years since I first joined Pirelli. On 16 February 1970 I crossed the gate at Bicocca and as a twenty-year-old full of aspirations, the initial impact was quite traumatic as in those days, a rather traditional spirit pervaded Pirelli.

This involved not only human relations but also the physical geography of spaces: office interiors were classical, the furniture dark and sombre, and with heavy doors tending to shut out everything. It was just a matter of time, however, and in a few years everything would change, and I would witness some key transformations first-hand.

The first change happened in the post-1968 years; this was a complicated period and sometimes accompanied by violent events, but also an important turning point in Pirelli's history as this marked the company's acceleration towards new product lines. For me that change coincided with a period of consolidation of the Pirelli culture firmly rooted on innovation and technology. That new acceleration allowed Pirelli more than other 'giants' in the industry to innovate and be pre-emptive in identifying and experimenting with new solutions neglected by other competitors and which proved to be a truly winning strategy over time.

Few people know for example that we were the first to use the zero-degree nylon belt which is basic for the Premium technology that years later would become a world standard adopted by all our competitors. Also, we were the first company to develop and produce winter tyres: for an entire month our engineers and workers moved to Sweden to design and incise rubber, which required not only technology but entrepreneurship, team spirit, and first-hand experience in the field.

Another decisive step was taken in the mid-1980s when we took the decision to focus more on quality than quantity and by focusing on the high-range market. This transformation not only reconfigured our corporate strategy but also our relationship with workers, internal dynamics, production processes and even our machinery. This bold choice would bring rewards and soon important contracts were signed with Audi, BMW and Mercedes. We also received great appreciation for the P6000 tyre from the leading global automobile manufacturers at that time. This is why those years were so important as they marked the company's change of direction, repositioning the Pirelli brand as a synonym for quality.

In the 1990s and following attempted but unsuccessful merger with the German counterpart Continental, there was another key moment: the attack on the so-called 'Premium segment'. This choice was a truly radical change in direction as it relegated the Standard segment (and consequently its two main markets in Italy and Brazil) to second place while launching the company into a complex but fascinating challenge.

In keeping with the now changed objectives, the configuration of the factories also changed both in Italy and in other nations where Pirelli was present. The task was to produce the same product in different plants in far-flung parts of the world such as Europe,

China or Mexico and often with different suppliers of raw materials. This structural transformation involved all sectors of the company, from Research & Development to Manufacturing and Quality Assurance. New challenges in the technological and innovation fields are always fascinating for Pirelli. In the mid-1990s, the adoption of silica in the production of rubber mixtures forced a step-by-step replacement of the old Banbury machines—a sort of large-scale food mixer used to blend various ingredients—with new machinery. Indeed, it is no coincidence that the Formula 1 tyres are the 'children' of mixes produced by these new machines.

In any case, Pirelli has a long-standing tradition in machinery: until the 1990s, these were entirely built in house. Still today and taking as an example the Next MIRS plant— the flagship of our industrial pole in Settimo Torinese—we have amply demonstrated to be excellent tyre makers but also highly-skilled in mechatronic systems.

Now an epochal change is on-going, and sustainability is to play a vital role as this is perhaps the primary demand of the market. It will take many years to reach almost zero emissions from vehicles that transport goods and people: technologies are evolving towards electric or hydrogen power but as these processes have already started, we must keep pace with this evolution by identifying solutions to new problems such as the increased weight of vehicles due to batteries, more marked torsional resistance, noise of rotating tyres now audible with the advent of soundless electric motors and so on. These are unavoidable technological choices and our Research & Development division is at work on at least one thousand projects. Now the Cyber Tyre chapter has started involving software to supply data on a series of criteria such as performance or safety through in-built sensors; we are already in the game and will continue to be until the end.

Materials will change; not only the silica used in the mixtures but also nanocharges of clay, new hybrid fibres, no more mineral oils but plant-sourced oils and resins. In this field it is fundamental to hit on the 'innovation button' as often as possible, something we have already started doing through our collaboration with universities, research centres and scientific laboratories and which has already produced significant results. Factories will also change: new technologies require new production processes that take into consideration the use of energy, water, and renewable raw materials. Pirelli

is already allocating significant funding for the transition towards a digital culture which will take on an ever more fundamental role. Diverse sectors from Research & Development to Production all require the handling of huge amounts of data and information for digital optimisation and production control, to minimise waste and breakages, and to propose maintenance or interventions on machinery or plants. This change of stance will necessarily involve the services that we offer through our sales network: to understand exactly what the market needs, what products are required and how to produce these in real time. Our aim is to reach maximum efficiency, reduce warehouse stock, and minimise shipment time for our tyres. Another project that Pirelli is working on is the TAAS (Tyre As A Service) project, a business model based on offering a personalised subscription plan to give clients access to a wide range of ancillary services in addition to a regular change of tyres.

In the next few years mobility will drastically change our way of designing and constructing our means of transport. I willingly leave myself to be guided by a purely personal opinion: Pirelli will definitely be ready to take on this new revolution.

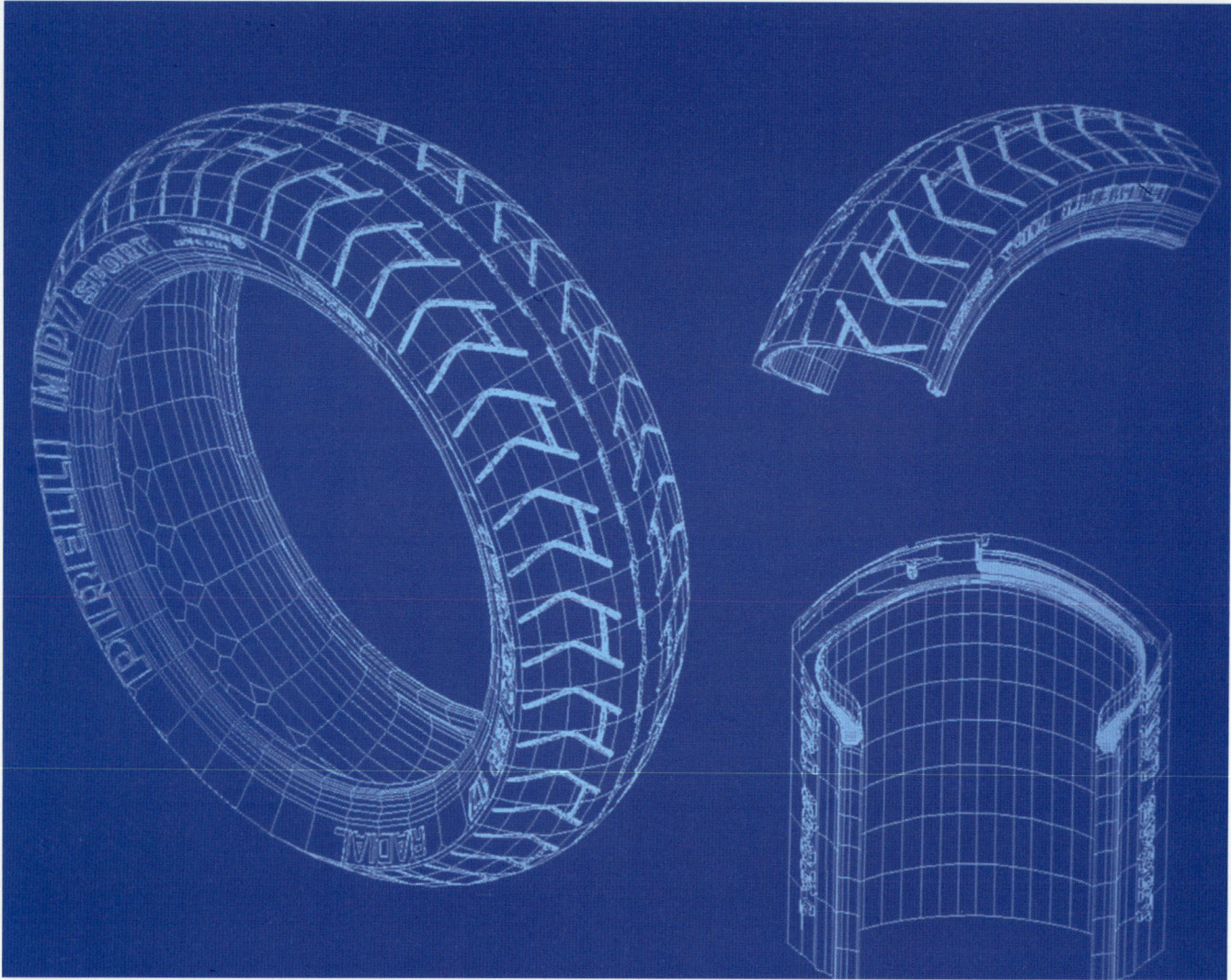

Designing of experimental tread using CAD, 1980s

*Designing of
experimental tread
using CAD, 1989*

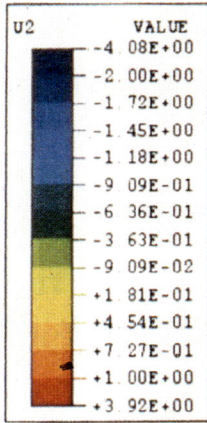

U2	VALUE
	−4.08E+00
	−2.00E+00
	−1.72E+00
	−1.45E+00
	−1.18E+00
	−9.09E−01
	−6.36E−01
	−3.63E−01
	−9.09E−02
	+1.81E−01
	+4.54E−01
	+7.27E−01
	+1.00E+00
	+3.92E+00

The Fascination of Photonics

Enrico Albizzati, Director CORIMAV and Scientific Advisor of Pirelli

Research, genius and future vision are the three key concepts that are part of what I call the 'Pirelli spirit' and are the foundations on which the success and progress of the past thirty years are based.

But these alone are not enough.

There is another element that is called on in decisive moments—a sense of belonging. This, together with our common values and shared passion for what we do, is what helps us solve problems.

So, here I am after almost thirty years at Montedison where I started at an early age in the group guided by the Nobel Prize winner Giulio Natta.

While there, I accumulated a series of professional qualifications and experience and when I joined Pirelli, I immediately identified fertile ground to develop innovative ideas and future-oriented projects.

In those years, our world was definitely very closed and did not readily welcome comparison with the outside, but already one could sense the quest for a necessary and unpostponable confrontation. I joined the Pirelli Cavi plant at Bicocca in 1996 and it did not take long to understand that I was somewhere special. I first felt this following an episode involving me directly: in one of my first days at work, the then director general Giuseppe Morchio called me to his office and handed me a small electric cable—something very ordinary, a copper wire sheathed with some PVC—and he said: 'See this? Let us make it simpler'.

I thought he was making fun of me. The problem was the PVC: when it burned, it produced hydrochloric acid and dioxin. The terrible accident at Düsseldorf airport had just taken place, a fire had broken out causing about twenty victims due to toxic fumes.

We developed a sheathed cable made with a mixture that when burnt, did not generate any smoke. This product is still in production today.

When speaking of mixtures, I remember a telephone call many years ago from 'Dottor' Tronchetti Provera. He asked me if it were possible to simplify not just a product but an entire working environment. He was referring to the mixing room.

For those that are not familiar with the environment, traditionally the mixing room was a sort of coal mine, with soot and coal dust coating everything and everywhere.

We put together a methodology that we called CCM (Continuous Compound Mixing) which was able to 'mix' the components in an optimal fashion and more importantly, 'cleanly'. Indeed, we hosted a small reception with the King of Sweden and some academicians in the same room where we developed the prototype.

In short, as I said previously, research, genius and passion.

We wanted to target real objectives, pursue a vision and then make it reality.

I believe that there are two ways of conducting research: one is to follow a business objective and the other is to go beyond business and try to identify new products so as to be ready to meet future market demands. Just think of MIRS™, and how this has changed how we work by taking into consideration the safety and health of workers, and how this was from an innovation perspective one of the greatest ever moments of discontinuity with the past. Opening a window onto the outside world has been one of my priorities and interpreted as a constant commitment to measuring oneself against the academic and scientific worlds and to understand in what way they can cooperate in our production processes.

An example is Corimav, the Consortium of Research into Advanced Materials that we founded in conjunction with the Università di Milano-Bicocca.

Then there is Joints Labs, created in collaboration with the Politecnico di Milano, or the Fondazione Silvio Tronchetti Provera which is another pole of excellence for research. These have been and still are important motors for research and culture, taking Pirelli to the forefront in innovative research into new materials and production processes.

Now the challenge of the future has a name, environmental sustainability. This is a challenge that we have met with great conviction—we now use significant quantities of plant-sourced materials in the construction of our tyres. Our hoisting the environmental banner is not mere rhetoric. Let us take the case of silica: we have been using this for about thirty years, normally sourced from sand heated to 900°C, but we have managed to source this from rice chaff. Also, the textile fibres used in our tyres are sourced from recycled material.

In short, the path has been marked out and we are following it with conviction in our task of identifying a point of equilibrium between sustainability, cost-saving and meeting performance requirements because, at the end of the day, a tyre must have characteristics of durability, resistance and safety.

Another example are the new carbon tubes that we are now using which some years ago would have been unimaginable but now are giving extraordinary results and represent a viable strategy to adopt to offer our clients the best that technology can give. This is how Pirelli can take advantage of a winning card: its extraordinary or special relationship with automobile manufacturers.

The exchange of information is a fundamental element in the development of products. This helps us understand the direction to take, the importance of research, the continual innovation that is functional to improving and bettering our work. This is an important strategy resulting in about one hundred homologations per year for the production of tailor-made tyres for specific car models and all that this entails in terms of product design and study. This has given us the opportunity to study materials in a different manner, conducting our own studies with our in-house research laboratories, a task which previously was undertaken by the supplier. We operate through a series of collaboration protocols which continue to give positive results and with the conviction that our work—independent of what the future of mobility envisages—will continue to be irreplaceable, or at least until the widespread adoption of magnetic levitation....

The future of the tyre has already started, and this process will continue, transforming it into a more active rather than 'support' function for the vehicle. I believe that the world of electronic sensors is the new frontier, facilitating 'dialogue' between the vehicle and the tyre to provide information regarding the conditions of use. Keeping apace with times and the evolution of mobility is an issue which is high in Pirelli's list of priorities. And how? By anticipating reaction times, by encouraging continual research and a passion for our work, being ready to take on the challenges that are waiting just over the horizon.

Article devoted to the birth of the new Pirelli laboratories in World *magazine, 2001*

TECHNOLOGY

Pirelli's new advanced research centre in the Milan-Bicocca area

The Birth of the New Pirelli Labs

The Group presents its new state-of-the-art laboratories,
a centre of technological excellence for new ideas and innovations

The third of May: there were more than 100 people, among them journalists from top Italian national and international newspapers, scientists and financial analysts. At the Bicocca complex in Milan, it was announced that the Group is to build its new research laboratories: the Pirelli Labs. They will cover an overall area of more than 13,000 square metres and will specialise in projects in the fields of photonics, optical fibres, superconductivity, new materials and undergrounding.

Marco Tronchetti Provera, Chairman and Chief Executive Officer of the Pirelli Group, opened the conference at which the laboratories were announced, outlining the significance of the project and its main characteristics. He said, "The Pirelli Labs represent the cutting edge of our advanced research. Through these laboratories, Pirelli aims to become a genuine 'knowledge company', evolving and creating value through the development of new know-how and technologies.

Bicocca, once the very heart of the Italian industrial manufacturing system, has today become the hub of this major project, a centre of technological excellence equipped with state-of-the-art laboratories that will play host to the creation and development of new ideas and innovation for the next-generation products that will be born in the medium and long term, the next 2 to 10 years".

This new structure integrates and completes the large network of Research and Development laboratories of the Group currently operating in the most important countries world wide. The Pirelli Labs will provide the reference point for all Pirelli's research activities throughout the world. They will be directly linked to all the Group's research centres as well as to leading private and university research centres in the USA, the UK, Russia and Italy, thanks to a series of special agreements and consortia. The new laboratories aim to further strengthen the Group's leadership in the sector of research and development of increasingly advanced technological products and solutions, both in Italy and abroad.

There are two main areas involved, Optical Innovation and Materials Innovation. Giorgio Grasso, head of the optical section, commented: "On the optics front, the efforts of the new laboratories will be concentrated on photonics and the development of new optical components based on nano-technologies, as well as on the industrialisation of new super-high performance optical fibres, able to transmit up to 10 Terabits per second

over

PIRELLI LABS

Cover of World *magazine devoted to the future of photonics, 1994*

W🌐RLD

The quartely magazine for Pirelli's management throughout the world - October 1994 - n.1

The Shining Future of Photonics

Pubblicazione non in vendita. Spedizione in abbonamento postale 50% - Milano. Registrazione presso il Tribunale di Milano n. 494 del 24.9.1994

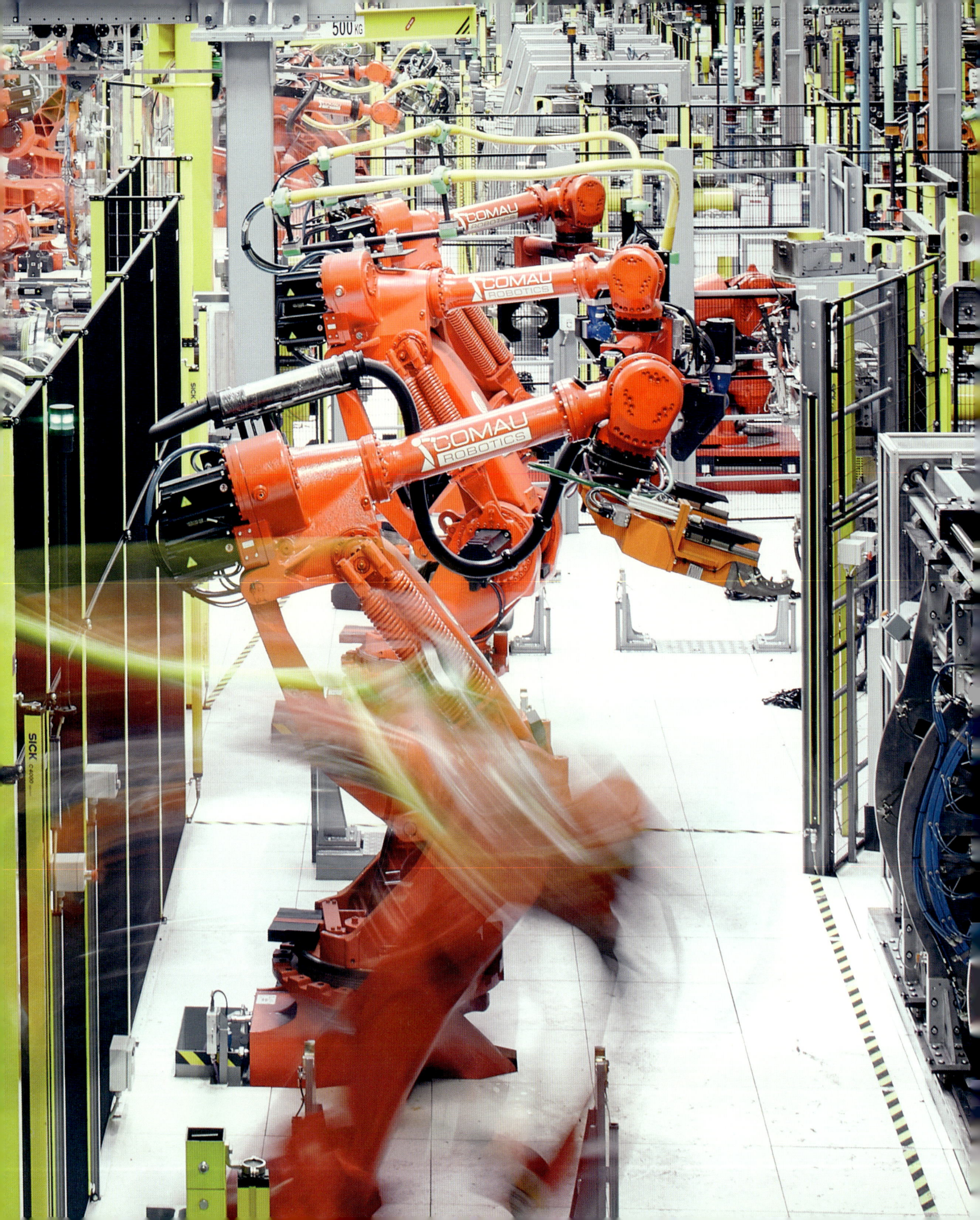

Digital Technologies for Development

The future calls upon the world of Research and Development to come to grips with new needs, new realities, new solutions. Performance, so greatly appreciated by the car producers, is joined by sustainability, also social, in terms of safety, materials and automation. The drive towards progress, which has always been in the Pirelli DNA, is not halted.

by Pierangelo Misani

-

**SENIOR VICE PRESIDENT
RESEARCH & DEVELOPMENT
AND CYBER OF PIRELLI**

We are not alarmed by the great challenges that we are to face in the coming years. Indeed, they help the implementation of measures and mindsets that Pirelli has proved to possess over the last few decades: velocity of innovation, a profound understanding of the market, and always first off the blocks thanks to a level of flexibility unknown to our competitors.

Please be indulgent if I show a little corporate pride but the passion that each of us possesses is transferred to our jobs. This is a fundamental element which, from the planning to the production phases, is an added value and makes one product better than another.

The near future almost obliges the pneumatic tyre to take on the challenges and requirements of new situations and so we must be ready to respond.

Today Pirelli is seen as a beacon of excellence in the field of pneumatic tyres, and more so in the field of performance. This is confirmed by hard data: in our core segment for high-range vehicles—specifically the Prestige segment for Ferrari, Lamborghini, Aston Martin, and McLaren or the Premium segment for BMW, Mercedes and Porsche to name some more recognised brands— we have twice as many homologations as our nearest competitor. This means that vehicle manufacturers choose our tyres as the best possible option for that particular model, and thus homologate their choice by applying their mark or distinctive sign which indicates that item of equipment as being ideally suited in terms of innovative materials, performance and safety. This is exactly what we have been doing for many years. Indeed, it is no coincidence that one of the best slogans of our extraordinary publicity campaign, 'Power is nothing without control', has accompanied the company's growth for the past thirty years.

Yet, today this is no longer enough: performance now needs the support of sustainability which is revolutionising our way of designing and testing tyres, an approach shared across the entire company.

Sustainability is a term that immediately makes one think of the environment, but this is a rather reductive vision. I prefer to widen the concept to encompass social sustainability or rather, the responsibility that we must have in proposing to our clients a product which satisfies all requirements in term of general safety or in emergencies such as sudden braking or a problem of stability on wet surfaces. We must also remember that there is another type of sustainability which I define as economic and synonymous with responsibility towards all those persons who work for Pirelli. Guarantee their future must be our priority: their jobs but also their workplaces which must embody the criteria of safety and comfort. Then, we have a third axis directly associated to the environment, an issue dear to public opinion and towards which I feel optimistic in terms of what we have done and what we intend to do in the future. The drive towards sustainability in the production of tyres starts with the raw materials. I would like to give a brief 'résumé' of how Pirelli in a successful publicity campaign for the German market defined the tyre as being 'your car's shoes' ('Die Beine Ihres Auto').

The inner structure of tyres is made of textiles and metal: this is the carcass that sustains the load. Then we have steel belts used to counteract the tyre's expansion due to centrifugal force at high velocities, but also give added strength to determine the drivability of the vehicle. Then we have the mixtures, a combination of polymers and natural rubber which before was mixed with Carbon Black to give the tyre its distinctive colour.

I understand that the lay person may find it impossible to believe that the inner tyre is made up of from ten to twelve different mixtures, each with its specific characteristics; the tread that needs to balance the resistance and grip to

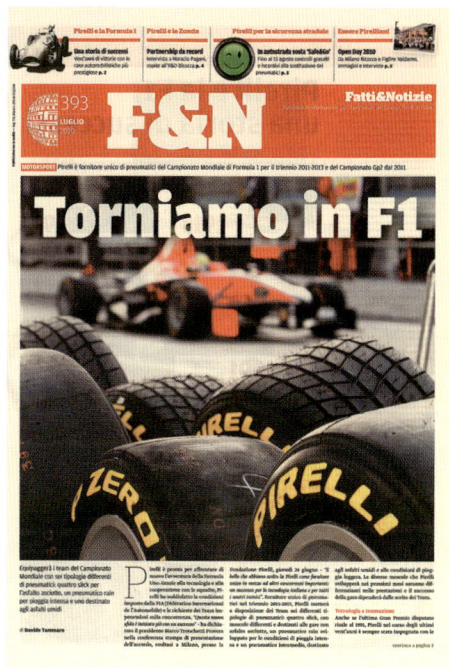

Cover of the Pirelli house
organ *Fatti e Notizie*
devoted to Pirelli's return
to Formula 1, 2010

*Formula 1 Portugal
Grand Prix, 2011*

previous pages
*The Next MIRS
production process,
2016, photo
Carlo Furgeri Gilbert*

Saatchi and Saatchi Compton, advertisement for Pirelli tyres, Die Beine Ihres Autos, *Germany, 1988–1990*

the road surface and the inner structure that must impede air from escaping. Previously Carbon Black was used but the 1980s and 90s saw the arrival of silica: these were the years in which carbon black started to be substituted by this new material. This would bring great benefits for the final result: silica has the characteristic of reducing the dissipation of energy, favours fluid movement and as discovered later, offers true advantages for safety on wet surfaces.

Our first *green* tyre, the P3000, represented a true turning point. I remember the resounding press campaign featuring the footballer Ronaldo—then striker for Inter—dominating the Bay of Rio de Janeiro.

Then there are what we call the 'chemicals' used to transform the tyre from a plastic to an elastic consistency—its final and definitive format—when the final design of the tread and markings on the sidewall are added. Lastly there are certain final treatments to protect the tyre from ageing, ultraviolet radiation and atmospheric agents.

Having understood how a tyre is made, now we have to answer the following question: what does this mean in a perspective of greater sustainability for people like us engaged in research and development? First of all, this means focusing on materials from natural or renewable sources. Although we can argue that mineral oil is from a natural source, it is not renewable whereas rice is renewable as it can grow again year after year. But why use the example of rice? Because this was our first and very simple experiment to show how we are moving towards materials from natural resources and rice is a good example. Indeed, we are the first to use by-products from rice in an experimental pilot plant set up about ten years ago in Brazil to extract silica from natural sources instead of extracting it from sand through chemical processes.

We are also studying other similar processes; e.g. we are examining another element called lignin which is a plant-sourced material obtained from by-products in the paper production process. Similar to silica, this is a strengthening element which allows the tyre to resist powerful deformities. Very often nature offers us a solution or even inspiration: what happens to a tree when exposed to strong winds? It bends, but it still maintains a great capacity of resistance. This is where the idea of using lignin started. Although we are not yet at an industrial level like in the case of silica and it is still an on-going project, there is a tangible result in the tyre we recently marketed with FSC certification—Forest Stewardship Council, the international organisation for the safeguard of forests—in line with our understanding of sustainability and the new emerging scenarios.

Also, the factory is at the centre of this discussion because to produce a sustainable tyre means to transform our way of working, and also measure efficiency from an environmental perspective by answering questions such as how much energy or water has been used, and how these can be re-utilised to create virtuous production cycles? We are now also working on the afterlife of the tyre:

today 50 per cent of used tyres is transformed into energy as it contains a large component of organic materials, but our idea is also to recover significant quantities of other materials for reuse. In this same vein, our participation in motorsport competitions is fundamental as it enables us to hone more refined skills; indeed, this is a benchmark of sustainability for novel solutions that can be transferred to real life situations. This concept introduces new perspectives in the environmental field and by this, we do not mean recycling but more regeneration.

A great deal has changed in recent years. What is now different is our approach towards the design and construction of pneumatic tyres which are now considered not only a distinctive element of the vehicle but more something that is designed and develops in line with it.

Knowledge within the R&D sector has evolved: in addition to specific knowledge of physics and chemistry, we have vehicle dynamics and other skills from the fields of electronics and algorithms which are used to model performance characteristics. Today understanding the dynamics of a vehicle is a fundamental passage and from past experience, we have a series of instruments to produce rubber and increasingly 'tailor made' to be perfectly tuned to a particular type of vehicle and in line with the characteristics requested by automobile manufacturers. A series of avant-garde technologies such as virtual systems generation reduces the time needed in the design phase and maximises efficiency. Previously, before reaching the finished product, many steps were needed: the tyre was studied, it was then given to the automobile manufacturer to evaluate, recommendations were proposed, and the necessary modifications were made.

Today, this chain of actions does not exist: the manufacturer gives us the software and the vehicle model, and we proceed to design a definitive product using the simulators which are part of our R&D system. This also responds to the demands of today's market which require shorter development times than before: now we are able to achieve in one year results that were unthinkable previously. This is a technological leap that is the fruit of our long-term vision and of our penchant for innovation that always inspires our work.

A great contribution to innovation is made by our participation in sporting events such as the Formula 1 and Superbike events. New materials are put to the test for the public in the competition sector, with Formula 1 *in primis*, but the same is valid for the world of motorbikes or rally racing. This cross-fertilization of technologies brings important benefits for the 'real' market and *virtualisation*, and simulators are the 'children' of this project. The importance of our presence in competitive events is seen through experimentation of new materials in extreme conditions, but also the study of their geometries and forms to be adapted for more 'common-day' situations. Not surprisingly, we backed the move to change Formula 1 tyres from 13 to 18 inches bringing them much closer to everyday reality. This is our way of 'reading' the market: if we are a sole supplier and produce tyres to meet the requirements of different sporting teams and racing pilots with different driving styles, then even more reason to apply this versatility to the everyday market by constructing the 'perfect fit' for original equipment for high-range automobiles (the already cited homologations and markings), but also tyres for mid-range segments which we call the Synergic range.

There is another challenge that we have started to face for some time which is the 'sensorification' of data, another fundamental element in the evolutionary process of knowledge needed to tackle scenarios which are already on the horizon. Our Cyber Tyre project aims at producing a pneumatic tyre with the customary characteristics of performance, grip and safety but which is also capable of transmitting data and information. How does one drive a car today? The person behind the wheel has a certain more physical perception of what is happening and therefore corrects steering, acceleration and braking in function of the visual stimuli perceived. With the arrival of self-driving cars, these physical perceptions will no longer exist. Self-driving cars function with a series of data which they elaborate and then they implement a complex strategy allowing the vehicle to move and avoid any obstacles. Whoever is able to produce and elaborate these data successfully will have a competitive lead in the market. The true finishing line is to widen those competencies related to the world of electronics and the capacity to elaborate performance in terms of algorithms. An example would clarify this: when dealing with aquaplaning—when the car skids on wet surfaces—the tread used to be incised directly onto the tyre by highly-skilled and artistic workers known in the trade as *sgorbiatori* (from the Italian to scribble). This prototype was then taken to the test track in Vizzola Ticino near Varese and it was tried out on wet surfaces and only on the basis of this experimentation was the tyre further developed and modified. Today, virtualisation allows us to shorten the development phase through mathematical calculations and simulations which are now done through modelling and no longer through direct field work. This is why the Cyber Tyre initiative is an ambitious

one: in our case the finishing line is a tyre which, due to sensors incorporated within the structure, can 'advise' us when we are about to enter an area susceptible to aquaplaning. We are working on this project in collaboration with McLaren which launched in 2021 Artura, the first supercar with an electronic control system integrated with data from a last-generation tyre. This means that the vehicle's electronic control systems recognises the tyre and its specific characteristics and evolves its response based on the information received. For example: an ABS braking system today does not recognise if a car is fitted with a winter or summer tyre: the control system therefore must operate by calculating an average which gives a good but not excellent performance. In the case that the tyre can 'dialogue' with the vehicle then the electronic control system knows what it is dealing with and therefore can propose the best possible solution.

If this is the future to be expected then we can proudly say that Pirelli is on the front line. I spoke of the velocity of innovation in materials and product development, but I also confirm that the same is true for our production processes which is another competitive factor that differentiates us from our main contenders. The classical examples is the creation of the MIRS™, but I also point out that with Next MIRS, in less than twenty years we have already reached the next generation of robotic factories. We should keep in mind that this all started from a fundamental concept: simplification and miniaturisation of processes for greater flexibility, with software to manage and control the production of different types of tyres, modulating the quantities and reducing wastage, thus giving lower costs and increased productivity. We have seen that the results of our main competitors in this area have not always been similar to ours. There is an explanation for this: the competitive advantage of Pirelli was and still is its high level of integration between the production, industrial and quality areas. Perfect alignment between these areas is the main competitive factor that has taken us to where we are today. I like to define ourselves as being *commandos*, rapid and decisive while others have mobilized the might of entire armies but with slower operational times.

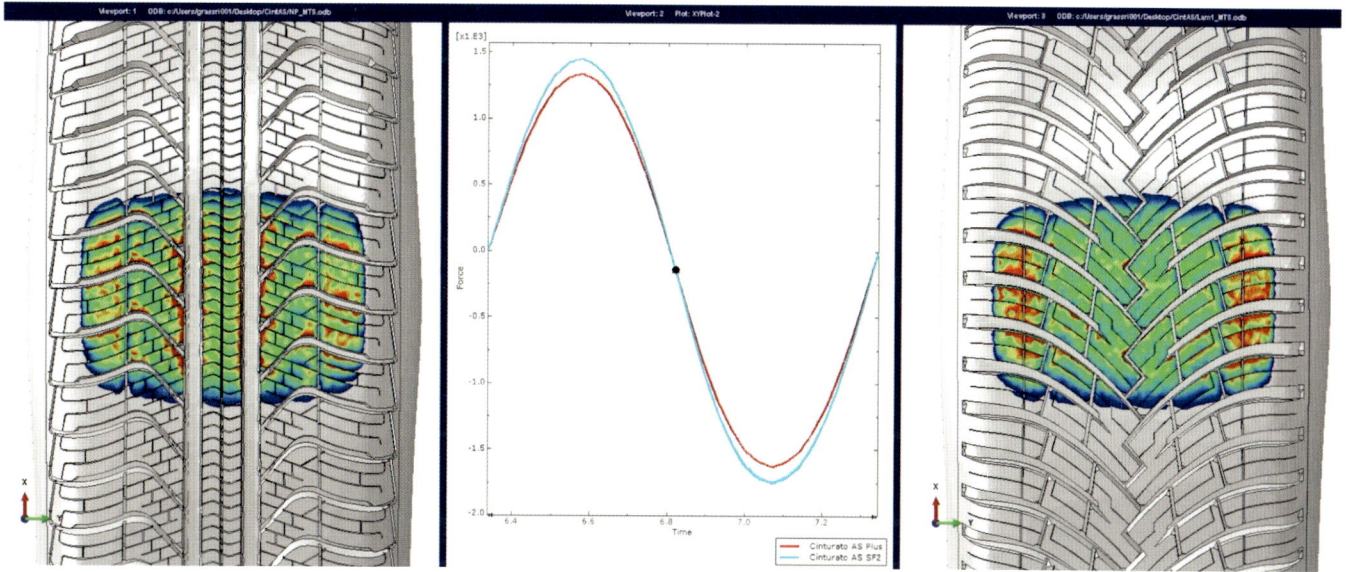

Excerpt from a presentation by the Pirelli Research & Development Department: 'Tyre Performance Comparison (Old Product SX vs New Product DX)'

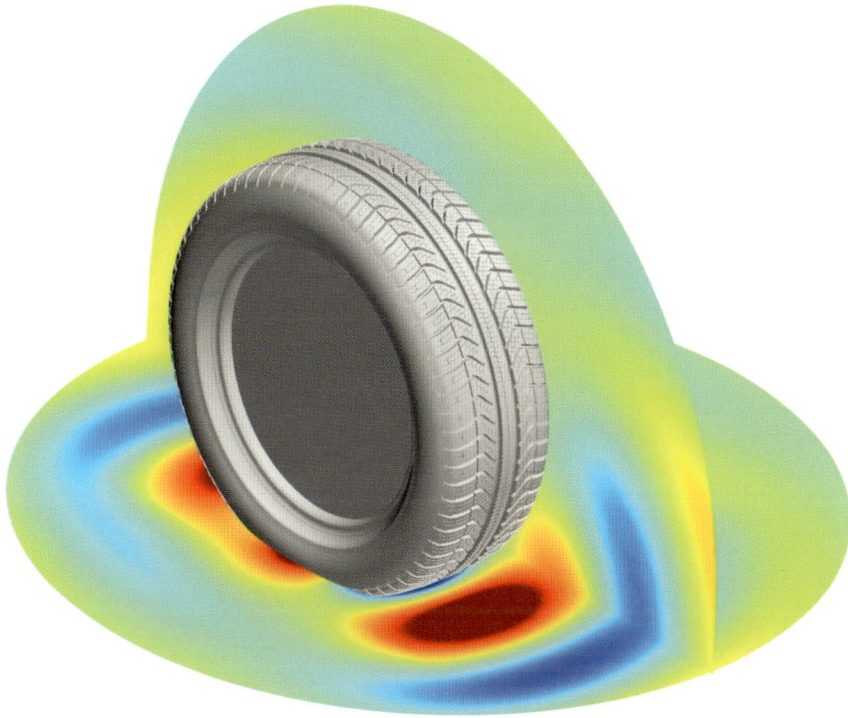

Excerpt from a presentation by the Pirelli Research & Development Department: 'Tyre noise emission'

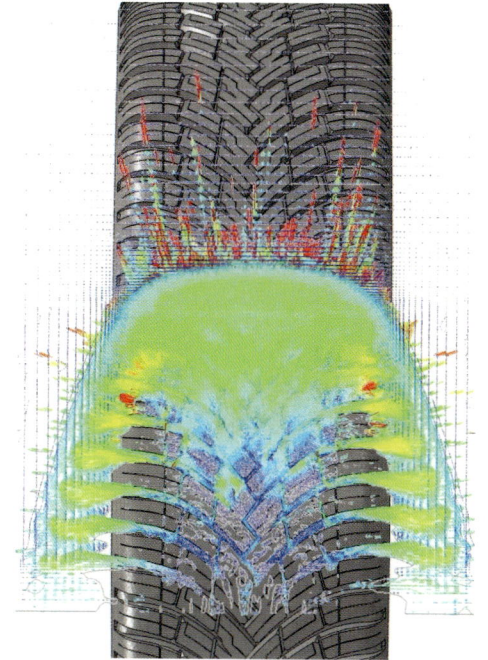

Excerpt from a presentation by the Pirelli Research & Development Department: 'Hydroplaning'

POWER IS NOTHING WITHOUT CONTROL.

Young & Rubicam, Ronaldo in the advertisement for the Pirelli P3000 tyre, 1998, photo Ken Griffiths

The P3000 Energy. Excellent grip, drivability and a reduction in rolling resistance to improve fuel consumption. All this at no extra cost means you can do the saving while Ronaldo does the scoring.

As I said before, it is the passion in our work at Pirelli that makes Pirelli so great. This is tangible when walking through the factories or in the Pirelli R&D world. To see a Pirelli tyre mounted on a fine car is gratifying also from an identity point of view for those who have worked towards that objective. Thus, the Pirelli identity is the result of an investment on human capital, which has given fruitful returns: first and foremost a sense of pride and belonging and then, a distinctive process that drives each of us to give our best to the Company.

For me, this sense of pride was evident four years ago when we decided to return to produce for the sailing sector and to reclaim our heritage by participating in the *Maratona delle Dolomiti* which for cyclists is equivalent to the New York Marathon for runners. Not only because I am an amateur cyclist and love that sport but also because this signified a return to our origins, to those times when Pirelli signed up Alfredo Binda to create a *Gran Premio* for cycling from nothing and which became an unmissable date in the national sporting calendar for many years. Making tyres for bicycles—and in our case high-range bicycles—is not as simple as before: it requires leading-edge innovation and avant-garde technological solutions. The bicycle tyre is as complex as a vehicle tyre with a fundamental difference, that everything is miniaturised. Every single component—

from the beads, bands, carcass, sidewalls and tread—must be perfectly integrated and fully functional. It is a world in which experimentation plays a bigger role than one might expect, where detail is of the greatest importance to create competitive products destined for consumers that demand the best that technology can offer and—for their passion and understanding—are similar to the client segment that drives supercars. This return to the past with a modern outlook and dusting off our ancient DNA to project ourselves into the future will have its base in the factory in Bollate, which has been designated to host this new initiative under the sign of innovation. Today, we are present in the bicycle market using external suppliers, but in the meantime we are preparing our own resources by focusing on the development of materials. I can proudly say that we are ready to start: Bollate will become a 'pole for sailing' with its own sophisticated and advanced machinery to guarantee the finest range of products entirely 'Made in Milan' for a highly-discerning market. This is a challenge that I feel comfortable to take on as although its origins date far back, it has a clear direction and well-defined objectives. This project encompasses the characteristics of a company that has left a deep mark in the economic scenario of the country, but also a company with an outlook projected into the future.

In three words: pure Pirelli spirit.

THE 'BEAUTIFUL FACTORY' WHERE MUSIC AND WORK MINGLE

The concept of 'beauty', understood not as a merely aesthetic ideal, but as a profound human and intellectual value, is a genuine company asset for Pirelli.
Bringing art and culture into the factory is an element of conjunction between two only apparently distant worlds. It is from this perspective that the projects of the Centro Culturale Pirelli first, and Fondazione Pirelli later, come to life, projects capable of transforming the locations of 'know how' into spaces of aggregation and exploitation of creative capacity in all its forms. And so, in the factories and offices, great literature echoes, the music of Salvatore Accardo resounds, the architectural revolutions of Renzo Piano take shape and great contemporary art finds its space.

*Design by Renzo Piano
for the future Pirelli
Industrial Pole in
Settimo Torinese
© RPBW - Renzo Piano
Building Workshop
Architects, 2007*

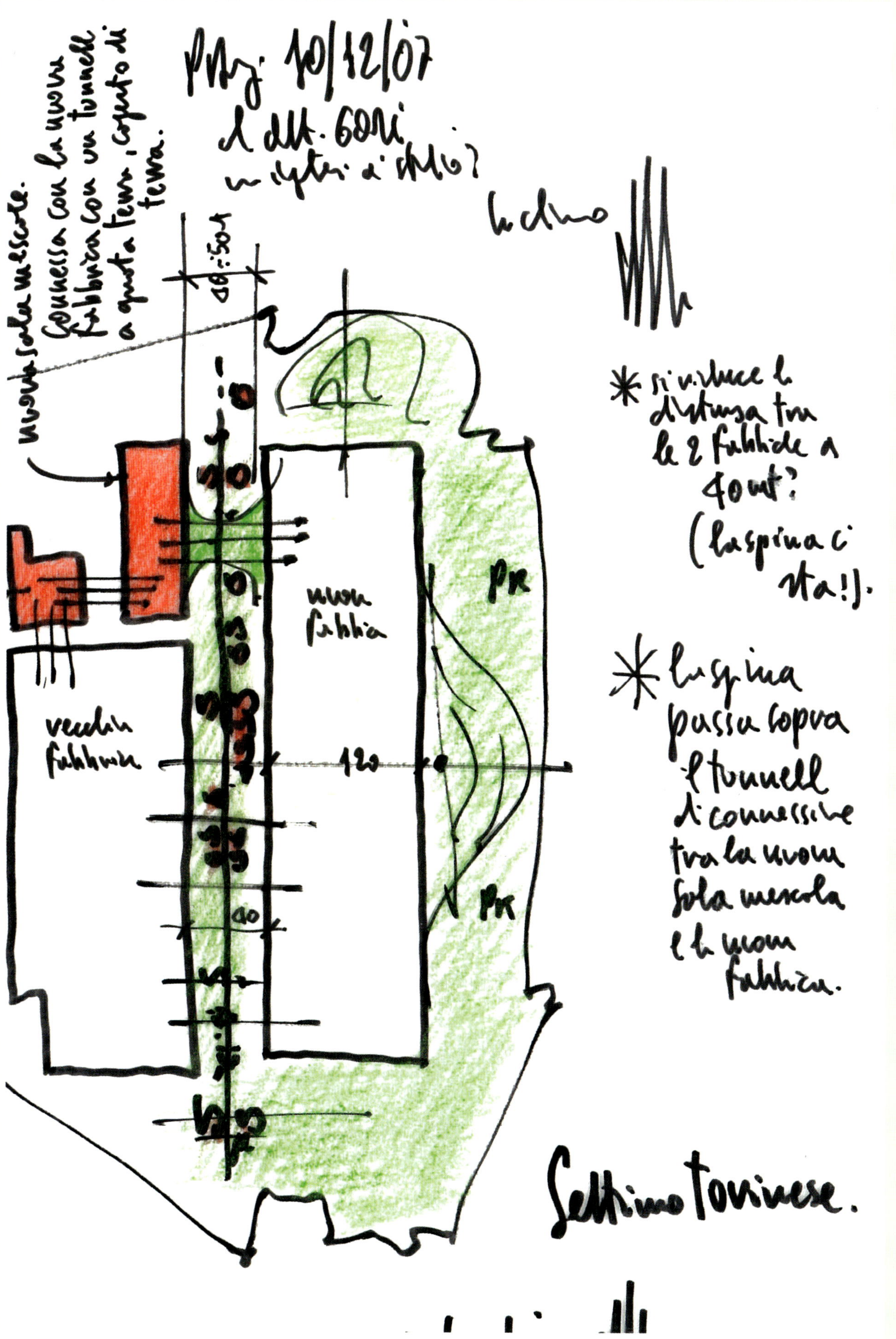

A Human-Scale Project
Renzo Piano, Architect, Chairman and Founding Partner of RPBW

Architecture alone cannot change the world. Yet, it can interpret its transformations: it builds them, makes them visible, makes them become an inhabited space. In my case, this has been true on a number of occasions, due to luck, or simply because an architect finds himself in the right place at the right time. This happened with the Centre National d'Art et de Culture Georges Pompidou in Paris, when in the 1970s Richard Rogers and I found ourselves interpreting a major transformation that was to happen in the realm of culture. The idea of building a factory, although cultural, in the noble centre of Paris, was a slap in the face for the sacredness of the idea of museum. Someone had to take up the challenge of making places of culture more accessible and, if this had to happen through a heresy, as the Beaubourg was to be, then we might as well be the ones to do it. All this happened to me several more times.
In 1989, the Berlin Wall fell and I found myself, definitely not changing the world, but in some way trying to interpret it, to record and give physical form to this process under way. It also happened to me with the realm of university and then of justice, with the Paris Courthouse, a building located north of the city in the new urban landscape of 'Grand Paris'. A major public craft that symbolises the aspiration of a state to improve justice, and that serves above all the purpose to connect the *banlieue* together with the heart of the city.
These are all projects that are in some way the materialisation of a change. The same mechanism was also triggered in Settimo

Torinese with the Pirelli factory. In this case too the building is nothing but the making of a transformation that was inevitably and naturally bound to happen. It was a matter of connecting up two factories, one that had been there for a long time, with another new one and of building a functional pole for the workers, for the office staff, for research, and for meetings. After some initial assumptions came the idea of creating a four hundred metres long linear element, at the centre between the two factories, in order for it to function as a structure of union, to make the two volumes become one whole. The project gradually developed along this line through the very close collaboration with Marco Tronchetti Provera, the people running the factory, the engineers and technicians because, as always, whenever a job works there is a team of people behind it who function, and this means 'teamwork'. All this brought to the 'Spina' came about, a building that carries within itself a fundamental element that we immediately all sensed, architects and client: the idea of beauty. Beauty is a word that has rather fallen into disuse, or is at times used in a romantic way. When speaking of it you almost feel a slight sense of shame. Yet, beauty, when not cosmetic, when not superficial, is an extraordinary value. And beauty also goes through the four hundred cherry trees that run along the side of the 'Spina', it goes through a space made of light, and of continuity. A walk four hundred metres long, a kind of journey, through spaces devoted to many functions: people having

lunch, relaxing, working, meeting. These elements are part of a form of beauty that is also human and intellectual and that itself becomes an instrument to create a beloved place where people can feel good.
The real change that happened in this factory is not conveyed solely by the architecture, but by the quest for innovation, to create a sense of pride and of belonging to an organisation that makes products developed through a lengthy work on research and quality. A place where this feeling finds its own expression.

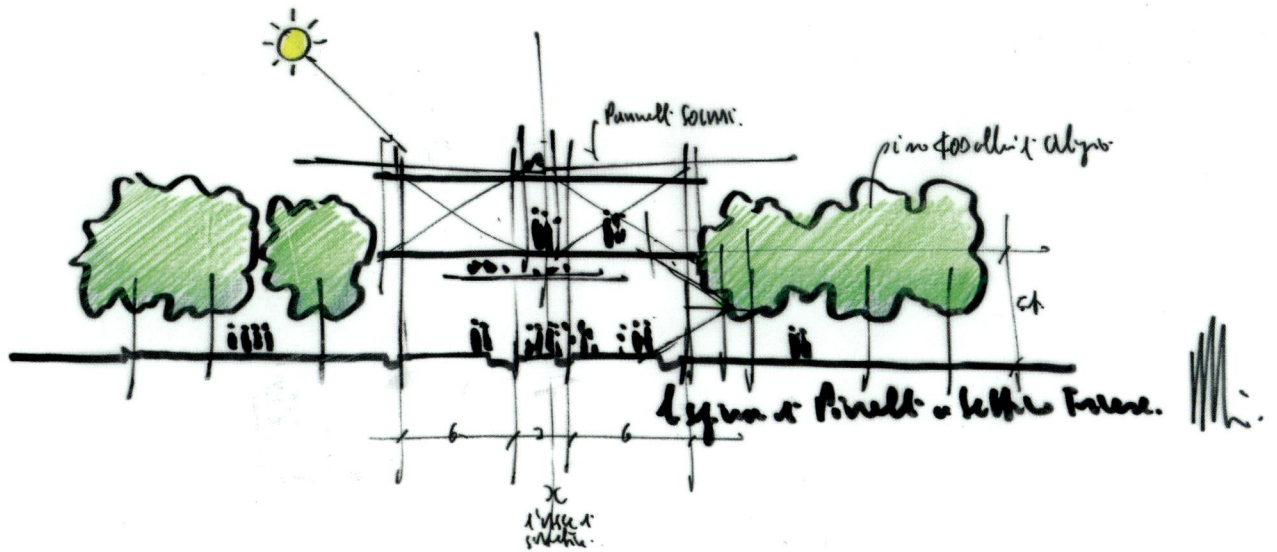

Marco Tronchetti Provera visiting the worksite of the Pirelli Industrial Pole in Settimo Torinese, 2010

Construction work on the
Pirelli Industrial Pole in
Settimo Torinese, 2010,
photo Carlo Furgeri Gilbert

The lit-up offices
of the 'Spina',
2014, photo Enrico Cano

Nighttime view of the 'Spina' flanked by cherry trees, 2014, photo Enrico Cano

Nighttime view of the 'Spina', 2014, photo Enrico Cano

The canteen room
in the 'Spina', 2016,
photo Carlo Furgeri Gilbert

Production Rhythm for String Orchestra

Salvatore Accardo, Maestro

My relationship with Pirelli dates way back in time. It was 1971 when, aged just thirty, I was called upon to take part in the VI Festival Musicale organised at the Centro Culturale Pirelli. In the main Auditorium at the Pirellone in Piazza Duca d'Aosta in Milan, together with pianist Lodovico Lessona, I performed a programme that included music by Petrassi, Webern, Ravel, Mozart and Beethoven. A complete overview of the violin, from the classical to the contemporary age. Many of the spectators in the hall were the company employees themselves.

In the same years Maurizio Pollini, Luigi Nono, Claudio Abbado and I also held concerts in factories, as an exercise in democracy: music must be heard by everyone, it cannot and must not be a privilege. We believed then and I am still convinced today that listening to great music must become a part of life, of a life well spent.

In 2012, after the foundation in 1996 of the Italian Chamber Orchestra composed of students and former students of the Accademia Walter Stauffer in Cremona, my bond with Pirelli was renewed and reinforced. Immediately, with Marco Tronchetti Provera, Antonio Calabrò and the Fondazione Pirelli, I decided to open up the orchestra rehearsals to the company's employees and their relatives.

This time, however, it was another headquarters, the one designed by Vittorio Gregotti in Milan Bicocca, created inside the factory's former cooling tower. I remember that, while we were rehearsing, we often happened to meet the attentive and curious gazes of the employees, to perceive 'listening' faces. And we understood that this flow of energy and emotions could have a powerful meaning of intercultural exchange between them and us, without the need for words. And then, also thanks to this silent dialogue, came the shockwave, the idea of composing and presenting to the public *Il Canto della fabbrica*, a new musical piece that could tell of the contemporary factory. A challenge and an opportunity, both at the same time. A composition that would take up the long tradition that there is between music and production sites, that would bring it up-to-date, but above all that could bring the audience closer to the world of production. A project of aggregation, in which the people that work in the factory every day also had to take part.

My wife, Laura Gorna, first violinist of the orchestra, and I immediately chose Francesco Fiore as composer, also on account of his in-depth knowledge, as an instrumentalist, of the violin. Together we visited the Pirelli factory in Settimo Torinese, one of the company's most technologically advanced plants. People, robots, sophisticated hi-tech machines and raw materials treated with innovative techniques.

An interweaving of rhythms and sounds that, in *Il Canto della fabbrica*, is found particularly in the fugue, which has a special rhythm, a rhythm that passes from one instrument to the next. The repetition of a

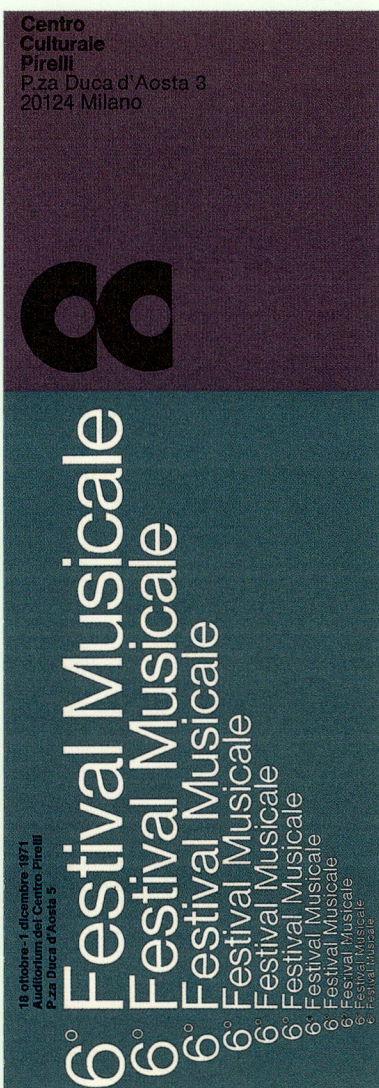

Centro
Culturale
Pirelli
P.za Duca d'Aosta 3
20124 Milano

*Poster for the 6th Music
Festival at the Centro
Culturale Pirelli*

theme, a number of beats later, according to an identical form, but in another tonality. When we played this fugue with the orchestra for the first time, it was truly exciting: the robots in the factory in Settimo Torinese immediately came to mind. The beginning of the *Canto* is also powerfully evocative; it immediately makes one think of something that comes from underground and gradually takes shape and is developed. The idea that lies at the basis is birth, creation from nothing, everything that originates from nothing, like the rubber that comes about from the materials taking shape and then leading to the finished product. A music that is born from below, which, a little at a time, all the other instruments bring to life, to symbolise the individual parts that, all together, lead to the creation of rubber. But the profound meaning of the piece lies mainly in the dichotomy between the orchestra's part and that of the violin. While the orchestral part, with its severity and rigidly structured counterpoint, represents the world of modern, digital production machines, which inexorably act at the heart of the factory, the part entrusted to the violin, on the other hand, uses a language that is at times capricious, virtuosic, meditative and unpredictable, capable of guiding the entire path of the piece towards an ideal synthesis, as though it were human thought. Bringing this piece to a conclusion was a long and laborious process: we spent a year rehearsing, experimenting with sounds and harmonies.
The following step once again came

naturally: making *Il Canto della fabbrica* live precisely there where it was born, in front of an audience also comprising workers and technicians from the Settimo Torinese plant and their families. And this time too, from the audience present at the concert, we felt a wave of emotion arrive that overwhelmed us and touched us deeply. And this is satisfaction and the greatest result.

Detail of the score for
Il Canto della fabbrica,
2017, photo Ippistudio

*Salvatore Accardo
at the Pirelli
Headquarters
in Milan Bicocca,
2017, photo Ippistudio*

Il Canto della fabbrica *performed in front of a Milanese audience at the Piccolo Teatro Studio Melato, 2017, photo Ippistudio*

The Italian Chamber Orchestra conducted by maestro Salvatore Accardo and with first violin Laura Gorna prepares to perform Il Canto della fabbrica *at the Pirelli Industrial Pole in Settimo Torinese, 2017, photo Ippistudio*

TRANS
MATIO

SFOR—
NS

Yesterday's inheritance
influences what awaits the world
of tomorrow: the integration
between man and machine, the
combination worker/workplace,
citizen/urban landscape,
the attention devoted to
sustainability.

Juan Carlos De Martin

-

**FULL PROFESSOR
OF I.T. ENGINEERING
AT THE POLITECNICO DI TORINO**

THE HUMAN GOVERNANCE OF MACHINES

It is impossible to think of a better future without a strong awareness of the past, also in the field of manufacturing. The traditional world of the factory has dissolved; we are heading towards structures that integrate products and services, with increasing shares of intangible assets (data, bits, pixels). We will live a hybrid time, continually updated, learning new cultures of integration between the human person and digital machines. And sensitivity will increase towards all issues of the environmental sustainability of industry. A challenge that will be above all cultural, cognitive, moral.

*Riccardo Manzi,
illustration of the article
'Automazione e piccola
industria' by Paul
B. Wishart, published in
the* Rivista Pirelli,
issue 3, 1957

t is impossible to think about the future without a strong awareness of the past. This is valid in general and is also valid in the specific case of manufacturing: in order to talk about its future, it is essential to be aware of what has happened in the last fifty years. A good point of departure is what some people attempted to argue, eloquently, in 1987. In that year Stephen S. Cohen and John Zysman, two brilliant lecturers at the University of California, Berkeley, one of the best in the world, published a book entitled: *Manufacturing Matters: The Myth of the Post-Industrial Economy* (New York).

In that historical moment it was a very courageous book and in part—despite the enormous changes that have taken place in the meantime—it still remains so today, thirty-five years later.

In 1987 and for around twenty years, the cultural, media, economic and political climate—first in the United States and then in the other industrialised countries—was fascinated by the idea of a post-industrial society.

The trend, at least with the public opinion, was launched in 1973 by the renowned US sociologist Daniel Bell with his famous book *The Coming of Post-Industrial Society: A Venture in Social Forecasting* (New York). Then, in the years that followed, more and more people urged that the twentieth century of the big factories, of the masses and workers, of Taylorism, of assembly lines, of physical objects produced in large numbers, should be considered to be closed early.

The future presents itself as intangible, like information, the word 'society' is increasingly often combined with the word 'knowledge', and in the collective imagination steel has found itself being progressively replaced with silicon or, even better, with bodiless bits.

Just as from agriculture we move to industry—as is said, professing a kind of historical determinism—now, from industry, it is natural that we will move to services.

At the same time—and perhaps this is not simply a temporal coincidence—Postmodernism, as argued by Jean-François Lyotard in 1979 with a famous book, invites us to renounce all metanarration, that is, to file away all the metaphysical narrations that have accompanied—supporting, analysing, criticising—the industrial revolution ever since its origins, namely the Enlightenment, idealism and Marxism. From this philosophical perspective, it no longer makes sense to talk of progress, and even less of truth; even the project is a doubtful concept. According to Lyotard, postmodernity has begun. And postmodernity must be light, flexible, or rather, liquid—not heavy and bulky like industrial modernity.

So, the disappearance of the factories is welcome, also—and perhaps above all—in the cities that had found their *raison d'être* in the factories.

Indeed, since the end of the 1960s an increasing number of companies—exploiting considerable improvements in communication technologies and in transports— began to move their factories to countries where labour costs were lower and, not uncommonly, environmental and trade union regulations were more permissive. This is the phenomenon of so-called 'offshoring', which goes way beyond the previous tendency to build production plants close to the main markets of reference.

In 1987 Zysman and Cohen expressly positioned themselves against all this. Against the sociologists of post-industrial society, against the postmodernist mentality and also against those players in the production system who, ignoring the long-term consequences, were moving production capacity elsewhere due to short-term economic motivations.

The two Californian lecturers invited public opinion, and particularly politics, to change direction quickly, offering two main lines of argument.

The first was that an economy based entirely on services would be absolutely unable to sustain such a large and wealthy country as the United States of America. The United States enjoyed (and still enjoys) the 'exorbitant privilege' that derives from coining the currency of reference at world level, the Dollar, but it could not (and cannot) afford not to also export many goods with high value added. With the numbers at their disposal, Zysman and Cohen stated that it would not be sustainable.

The second line of argument, perhaps even more important than the first, was that manufacturing is not only closely tied to many advanced services, but also to the very capacity to innovate. In contrast with certain academic views which make innovation depend solely on explicit

A sound and advanced economy must be a polyphonic economy

knowledge, knowing how to produce, especially in the key sectors, is crucial to continue to innovate. Losing production capacity, therefore, sooner or later leads to the loss of technological leadership, with all the consequences of this.

Despite the favourable criticism and even the prizes awarded to their book, Zysman and Cohen have remained unheeded by US policy.

Rather, the collapse of the Soviet Union, the 1994 NAFTA treaty and the industrial take-off of China (which was

admitted into the World Trade Organization in 2001) powerfully reinforced the phenomenon of offshoring, provoking a huge transfer of production capacity from West to East.

Thirty-five years after that book, and almost as many since the beginning of the phenomenon that we call 'globalisation', the United States and Europe have now understood that unregulated offshoring has been a mistake of historic proportions, a mistake made even more evident by the COVID-19 pandemic.

We are not referring solely to the social consequences, or, first and foremost, the loss of millions of jobs in industry, generally decently remunerated and safeguarded, with the consequent profound discontent on the part of many electors. We are also referring to the fact that in some sectors, even crucial ones such as microelectronics, the West's production capacity is insufficient. The major profits made possible by offshoring are now paid for at a high price by entire countries, due to production structures with limitations that not only damage the economy as a whole but also make the USA and Europe geopolitically fragile— or in any case less strong than they could have been.

After a blunder that lasted around thirty years, therefore, manufacturing is returning to being important in the minds of many people, starting with the political decision-makers, as in Italy, which—despite an approximately 20 per cent decrease in its manufacturing capacity from the 2008 crisis onwards—today still remains the second European industrialised country and one of the main ones in the world.

Therefore, having moved beyond the premature filing away of the twentieth century, in the twenty-first century we are rediscovering that a sound and advanced economy must be a polyphonic economy, made of agriculture, manufacturing and services, where the three components do not move deterministically from one to the other, but coexist, interacting with each other, and are transformed together following the technological changes and changing social requirements.

Manufacturing, in particular, will continue its technological evolution by focusing strongly on digital, moving on from Industry 4.0 to the more recent Industry 5.0, where the emphasis moves from the connection between machines, now taken as read (even if, as history teaches us, in reality it will take decades to change exhaustively), first of all to the inclusion of workers in the dialogue between machines, and secondly, but no less importantly, to the respecting, by the entire industrial sector, of social needs, first and foremost those of the environment.

As regards the production process as such, the experts and the research among operators delineate a future of manufacturing that is very far removed from journalistic simplifications or from those of some intellectuals. We are not being awaited, for example, by the complete automation of manufacturing, as was feared back in the 1960s and as has been periodically taken as imminent from then to today. The future, rather, will be *hybrid*, that is, we will see a combined presence—variable according to the context— of machines and human beings, where both will change, as will the methods of communication and interaction between them. Moreover, these changes will require a periodic updating of the training of workers, not only to master the technological evolutions, but also to have the means to make the coexistence between man and machine better.

We can expect that the production process will also be hybrid from the point of view of production technologies, which will see the coexistence of both additive and subtractive processes—in view of the strong and weak points of both. The same applies to materials, which will see the combined presence of metals and composites.

As regards the workers, in addition to the already mentioned need to make sure training keeps in step with technological and production changes, in industrial countries with a low birth-rate, such as Italy, Germany and Japan, even more attention will be paid to the consequences of workers' aging. The development of appropriate technologies and adequate working environments and processes could not only soften the impact of age on productivity, but even take positive aspects from it, such as new ways to exploit the *savoir faire* of those who, due to their age, have more and better knowledge.

Another aspect that the pandemic has powerfully highlighted is that of the health system. Having left behind the illusion that the pandemic would last just a few months, or a year at most, and considering that the systemic causes of the passage of coronavirus Sars-CoV-2 to the human species are still unfortunately all active (deforestation, intensive farming, high housing densities, globalisation of transport and so forth), it will be in the interests of the production sector, as well as of the whole of society, to re-imagine working processes and spaces in expectation of possible new epidemic phenomena.

Finally, moving on to society, another decisive challenge for the manufacturing of the future is climatic and environmental sustainability. With the ever more incontestable evidence of the damage inflicted on the planet by mining activities, by the use of fossil fuels, by the release into the environment of huge quantities of man-made items that end up, directly or indirectly, in rivers, in seas, in the earth and even in living organisms, the entire production system, with manufacturing in the forefront, will be called upon to radically rethink its activities.

It will be a major cultural and cognitive, as well as technical, political and economic challenge. A challenge that, however, we are able to face and that we therefore *must* face, to also continue over the decades and the centuries to produce—with true, deep, systemic respect for the planet— those goods that make human beings' lives safer and more comfortable.

*Riccardo Manzi,
illustration of the article
'Le macchine "pesanti"' by
M.V. Wilkes, published in
the* Rivista Pirelli,
issue 3, 1957

Ermete Realacci
PRESIDENT OF FONDAZIONE SYMBOLA
-

Father Enzo Fortunato
**EDITOR-IN-CHIEF OF SAN FRANCESCO PATRONO D'ITALIA MAGAZINE
AND SPOKESPERSONS FOR THE ASSISI MANIFESTO**

CORPORATE VALUES FOR SUSTAINABILITY

The cornerstone of the future lies in the green economy, in line with the cultural and social sensitivities that are widespread above all among young people and according to the indications of Agenda 2030 and the EU's choices for the Next Generation. Strategies associated with a better use of resources, with in-depth research into the 'paradigm shift' that affects production, distribution and consumption, and with responsible scientific and economic appraisals. The Assisi Manifesto for a just and 'circular' economy and the studies of *GreenItaly* indicate the paths to follow. Beyond the GDP, towards the value of beauty.

previous pages
*Detail of the extraction
of latex from the bark
of a rubber tree,
Xapuri, Brazil, 1997*

n Italy sustainability and the green economy, which is its economic and productive heart, rhyme with beauty, innovation and culture. They have ancient roots and are a key for the future.

In order to promote them there is a need for general reference points, such as Agenda 2030, approved by the UN, after lengthy work, on 25 September 2015 with the relative seventeen SDGs—Sustainable Development Goals, structured into 169 targets to be reached by 2030. We need technologies, resources, international agreements, precise analyses and scientific and economic evaluations. But we also need a mobilising vision. Because, as the Assisi Manifesto, promoted by the Fondazione Symbola and by the Sacro Convento, states, courageously facing the trials we have before us, starting with the climate crisis, 'is not only necessary but also offers a major opportunity to bring our economy and our society to a more human scale and for this reason more capable of a future'. This is a challenge of enormous scope requiring the contribution of the best technological, institutional, political, social, and cultural energies. The contribution of all the economic and production worlds, and above all the participation of citizens. The role of the encyclical *Laudato si'* by Pope Francis has been and is important in this direction.

Europe already seemed to have recognised the stakes before the pandemic and reinforced its choices in order to restart the economy with Next Generation EU, as well as with a large part of the Community Budget 2021–27, concentrating resources in three main directions: social cohesion and health, green transition and combating the climate crisis, and digital and innovation. A number of times president Ursula von der Leyen herself has indicated 37 per cent as the minimum share of resources of the Recovery Plan that must be earmarked for tackling the climate crisis. For Italy this amounts to at least €80 billion. For Europe it is not only a choice associated with good intentions or a response to the alarms coming from science and the prompting of the 'Greta generation', but the redefinition of its own mission in the economy and in the world. And the European Union, before others, has set itself the goal of eliminating net greenhouse gas emissions by 2050. This is a target that must be pursued without leaving anyone behind, without leaving anyone alone. There is much to do, but, fortunately, our country is not starting from scratch.

As *GreenItaly*, the report prepared by the Fondazione Symbola and Unioncamere, has demonstrated for over ten years now, an important part of the Italian economy has been focused on green issues for a long time now. There were over 432 thousand Italian industrial and service companies that invested in green products and technologies in the five-year period 2015–19. In practice, almost one in three: 31.2 per cent of the entire non-agricultural business sector. And this figure has grown compared to the previous five-year period, when there were 345 thousand companies (24 per cent of the total). What predominate in these investments are improvements in energy efficiency and the recourse to renewable sources, together with the cutting of water consumption and waste production; these are followed by the reduction in polluting substances and the increase in the use of secondary raw materials.

These are the companies that export most, innovate most and produce the most jobs. 'Cohesive' companies appear stronger and oriented towards sustainability; in 2020 these increased by 37 per cent according to the *Coesione è competizione* [*Cohesion Is Competition*] report drafted by Symbola with Unioncamere and Intesa Sanpaolo: these are the companies that have the best relations with workers, the community, territories and subcontractors.

More than in the policies put in place, it is in the productive anthropology, in the shared culture, in the

'The real journey of discovery does not consist in looking for new landscapes, but in having new eyes'

'moral of the lathe'—well known at Pirelli—that the key to the results achieved in so many crucial sectors of our manufacturing is to be sought. This is the case of the circular economy, which is crucial for sustainability, thanks to which, even if it is necessary to do more, Italy is responding to the lack of raw materials with innovation and efficiency, with the use of that great source of renewable, non-polluting energy that is human intelligence. Italy, as Eurostat tells us, is the European country with the highest percentage of recycling out of total waste: 79 per cent, double the European average (only 39 per cent) and much more than all the other major countries of the continent (France is at 56 per cent, the United Kingdom 50 per cent, Germany 43 per cent). Overall, replacement with secondary raw materials in the Italian economy means a saving equal to 23 million equivalent tons of oil and to 63 million tons of CO_2. These

are values equivalent to 14.6 per cent of the internal demand for energy and to 14.8 per cent of our greenhouse emissions.

It is from our many talents that we can start in order to come to grips with age-old evils: not only the public debt, but also social and territorial inequalities, the black economy and illegality, an often suffocating bureaucracy and the uncertainty that generates fear and resentment. Because, as the Assisi Manifesto states, 'there is nothing wrong in Italy that cannot be corrected with what is right in Italy'.

For Marcel Proust 'the real journey of discovery does not consist in looking for new landscapes, but in having new eyes'. If we attempted to look with new eyes at our country, the roots of what we are and above all of what we can become, we would be spoiled for choice. The interweaving of and the positive contamination between beauty, quality, innovation and the strength of communities emerge like limestone under the soil in many periods of our history. We are thinking of the powerful passage in the Sienese Constituto 1309–10 in which it is stated that those who govern must have most at heart 'the beauty of the city, to cause joy and delight to visitors, for the honour, prosperity and growth of the city and its citizens'. A fantastic synthesis of good economics, soft power, identity and the strength of a community. Practically the screenplay for the fresco of *Good Government* by Ambrogio Lorenzetti, painted a few decades later. And a fantastic programme for our future. Again in Siena, in the first half of the fifteenth century, a great Franciscan preacher, Saint Bernardino, in his prayers in Piazza del Campo, also communicated his thesis on the market to all the people. He had already challenged gambling and usury head-on. His idea was that it was not permissible to live from a private income if you were able to do business, because in that way talents were taken away from the community. Such subjects are very close to the passage in

Laudato si' in which Pope Francis criticises the toxic finance that risks suffocating the real economy. Such topics cost Saint Bernardino a trial by the Holy Inquisition, which he won. However, above all, Saint Bernardino described summarily and effectively the characteristics that make the entrepreneur's activity positive for the community: efficiency, responsibility, laboriousness, the courage of enterprise. It would take many centuries for the social responsibility of business to be developed. But Italy is here. There is a thread that leads to the best part of our economy and our society. Voltaire found it hard to grasp this, when he asked 'why, amid so many upheavals, internecine wars, conspiracies, crimes and follies, have there been so many men who have cultivated the useful arts and the pleasant arts in Italy?' A basically similar question was asked two centuries later by the economist John Kenneth Galbraith. Attempting an answer to the question, after an ungenerous analysis, he concluded:

Italy, starting from a disastrous situation after the war, has become one of the principal economic powers. In order to explain this miracle, nobody can point to the superiority of Italian science and engineering, nor to the efficiency of its administrative and political direction. The real reason is that Italy has incorporated into its products an essential component of culture, and the cities such as Milan, Parma, Florence, Siena, Venice, Rome, Naples and Palermo, while having very poor infrastructure, display in their standard of living a huge amount of beauty. Much more than the economic index GDP, in the future the aesthetic level will become increasingly decisive in indicating the progress of society.

A partial answer, because those years also saw the Nobel Prize for Chemistry awarded to Giulio Natta and the most intense part of the adventure of Adriano Olivetti, in which the humanistic tension of enterprise, the drive towards technological innovation and the attention devoted to

An important part of the Italian economy has been focused on green issues for a long time now

the community, to workers, to culture, were indissolubly connected. This experience has all too often been considered exemplary yet isolated; instead it is the tip of the iceberg of a way of being in the world, of conceiving one's mission, consisting precisely of an important part of Italian enterprises and territories. The possible hinterland of a challenge on sustainability and the green economy. We are, therefore, if we wish to be, capable of fulfilling an important role, in Europe, in the open challenge to combat the climate crisis and to build 'a safer, more civil, kinder world', as the Assisi Manifesto again states.

A great US film director, who was born in Sicily, Frank Capra, stated powerfully: 'The amateurs play for fun when the weather is nice, the professionals play to win in the midst of the storm'. The Italy that is not waiting for nice weather can be the protagonist of an economy and a society that are more on a human scale.

Signage at the Pirelli
rubber plantation
in Java, 1922

The slow, precise gesture
of making an incision
into a rubber tree,
Indonesia, 2018,
photo Alessandro Scotti

Paola Dubini

-

**PROFESSOR OF MANAGEMENT
AT THE UNIVERSITÀ BOCCONI IN MILAN**

INDUSTRIAL SITES AS CULTURAL HERITAGE

The collective imagination of the urban landscape is focused on workplaces. And it moves from the traditional factories to the company headquarters, to the research centres, to structures where production and services meet. An evolving landscape. From the Pirelli Skyscraper designed by Gio Ponti to the industrial poles such as Settimo Torinese, designed by Renzo Piano, to the upgrading of an entire district of Milan, the Bicocca (project by Vittorio Gregotti), as a space for high-tech work and university training. History, also through architecture, is mixed with the future.

When we talk of cultural heritage and the city, people's thoughts and visions typically take two directions: churches, historic centres and institutions on one hand and the ability to attract tourists on the other. We look 'backwards' with the eyes of the art historian and 'forwards' from the perspective of the economy of services. All in all, we reflect little on the fact that our past is our present. And even when history calls upon us to reflect on 'its' present—museum houses or museums and archaeological sites—we struggle and easily revert into a merely aesthetic contemplation. Therefore, we inevitably cannot transfer the wealth of imagery that our cultural heritage may arouse to visitors in a renewed and contemporary form.

Indeed, within the debate on heritage and the city, the actions and efforts by many within our civil society, education, and culture to make use of our cultural heritage as a source of knowledge and research cannot be forgotten, since heritage has to go hand in hand with local communities surrounding us.

A central point of this highly structured construct is the awareness that monuments are nothing but stones when not filled with meaning, that heritage has a material and a non-material component, and that its meaning is not created by osmosis but by relations, through an enduring work of mediation and building of shared knowledge and respect.

Nevertheless, thoughts on cultural heritage and identity are often rather general. Reference to Article 9 of our Constitution—in my view, one of the most specific and important—might be interpreted as too formal and might sound rhetorical.

If we do not consider how amazed a pilgrim might have been when standing before a cathedral at the time when it was built, we might not be able to properly rate heritage in our present. So, the risk that heritage runs in the eyes of many is of being considered 'other' with respect to people's lives, an 'otherness' that is often awkward, in a historical, physical and economic sense. In short, we have lost a little impetus in building images around the density of communication and identity of the physical locations and the buildings that belong to our landscape and our history. The evidence of this is the abuse of the adjective 'beautiful' associated with culture and art, all the more clashing since we see an increasing number of abuses of and damages to a fragile territory. Things are not much better with contemporary artistic and cultural expressions. In the last two decades we have witnessed a debate centred around so-called 'creative cities', on the one hand painted as places in which operators in sectors with a high intensity of innovation are concentrated with good mobility, educational infrastructures and hybrid spaces of aggregation that attract talents, while on the other as centres that create social inequality and commodification.

The point of departure of the debate is often concerning political choices at local level following massive processes of industrial delocalisation during the last two decades of the twentieth century. Urban regeneration projects, involving rather large although circumscribed urban areas of medium to large size cities, generally include emblematic buildings that have the function of constructing new imaginary worlds, underlining the exceptional nature of the project, attracting resources and attention for a period of time long enough to allow the achievement of the overall project and the mobilisation of an adequate variety of interlocutors.

The need to reuse spaces, combat population decrease and transform the local economy is common to all the main western cities.

The presence of large decommissioned spaces has led to the activation of public-private partnerships involving

international groups and real estate companies.
A number of architectural studios active internationally
are important actors in the success of creative cities
and the construction and evolution of imaginary urban
worlds. They are the home to the 'archistars', who, within
projects for the upgrading of districts and cities, design
an iconic building for cultural purposes which becomes
the symbol of the whole project: a theatre, a museum or
a library.

The need to reuse spaces is common to all the main western cities

Their contribution is fundamental and instrumental to
market the local territory, trigger cultural tourism and
cause a change of attitude towards districts previously
characterised by social tensions and by limited
attractiveness, which then become interesting, desirable
and a source of discoveries once revamped. Besides
anointing the 'archistars', these buildings also become
icons for the city, since they become the mark of change
for residents, the instrument of 'city branding' for the

administration, and a reason for a visit for tourists.
Supporters of this model of development highlight the
importance of this creative, cosmopolitan, educated
class, at the same time producing and consuming
contemporary symbols, and the agent of transformation
and urban regeneration. Nevertheless, the economic
impact of these projects on the territory where they
are introduced is hard to estimate. The large amounts
of both private and public resources needed inevitably
generate issues on investments as well as maintenance.
Furthermore, creative cities compete with each other to
attract talents, tourists and capital of a predominantly
financial and property-related nature.
Critics of this model of development bitterly disapprove
of the processes of gentrification that favour some
sectors, social groups and venues to the detriment of
others, increasing socio-economic inequalities.
As regards their agglomerative effects, these projects
are focused on consumption more than on cultural
production and often bring about unsatisfactory results
in terms of social capital created, redistribution of
wealth, opportunities of expression and participation by
large sections of the population. The limited number of
'archistars' capable of supporting and carrying out these
projects mostly generates aesthetic homogenisation at
global level, placing the authenticity of the locations
under scrutiny. Then, since these buildings house
museums, theatres or libraries, this raises questions
associated with the 'instrumentalization' of culture,
made subject to economic interests instead of being
included within a civic horizon that is sustainable from
a socio-economic point of view.
Paradoxically, the imagery built around the creative
cities has not brought about an alliance between arts
and technology. Those creative cities in which culture
is an instrument of economic growth have made way for
an imaginary world built around 'smart' cities, in which

technology enables solutions to be developed that are oriented towards a more efficient use of resources. In the meantime, various communities of cultural operators have developed gradually more critical attitudes towards urban development policies, suggesting that the authentic creative urban class is made of cultural entrepreneurs that are socially and culturally active, but economically fragile, because their role is not acknowledged and adequately remunerated by the community. Apart from a few exceptions, creative work, like cultural work, is low-profile, seen as not being very useful or else a leisure activity, rather than a profession. This vicious circle, which also involves the contemporary world as well as the past has a dangerous consequence: in the absence of adequate remuneration, jobs in the cultural and creative sphere are destined solely for those who can afford long periods of insecurity from the psychological and economic points of view. Yet, if those who work in culture are not representative of the society of their time, the gap between cultural and real worlds is difficult to fill up. Contemporary imagery might be perceived as extraneous to most people, since large sections of the population are cut off from scratch. The growing awareness of the possible distorting effects of urban upgrading projects on a social level, the reduction of the resources available after the 2008 financial crisis as well as the gradual dissemination of the principles associated with the U.N. Agenda 2030, have led to creative cities and their iconic buildings are being looked at from a perspective of sustainability. In the meantime, local cultural policies, alongside 'culture-driven' economic development on the one hand and the promotion of artistic excellence on the other, aim at pursuing the democratisation of culture and, in more recent times, a cultural democracy characterised by the possibility that different communities have the opportunity for expression and cultural participation.

The road is obviously very long and the trajectory is non-linear; nevertheless, a gradual change of perspective is occurring: communities, and not only buildings create the imaginary world of those venues.
So far, we addressed iconic public buildings of the present and the past and their use in the development of collective imagination. In reality, the urban landscape is also profoundly marked by the presence of iconic private buildings, particularly those owned by companies. The transformation into creative cities is characterised by many strongly validating elements having an architectural as well as a commercial nature in view of the dominance of large and leading brands and in the conservation of the industrial (or mercantile) purpose and its icons, it is possible to identify the *genius loci* of many cities or territories, characterised by the presence not only of specific industrial concentrations, but also of specific entrepreneurial families and corporate cultures. Unlike many monuments, which become part of a landscape to which we are accustomed to and yet we struggle to regard as our own, the imagery built by companies through workplaces has at least one important point of contact: those who work there. When we think of the relationship between companies, iconic buildings and urban centres, three situations come to mind: industrial archaeology, business centres, and factories.
If 'words are important', defining archaeology as a workplace where nothing is produced anymore is risky in itself. Companies are not only places of economic production, but also of the construction of important imagery, especially if they are large, especially if they involve—as it often happens—people of different classes and professional skills and increasingly of different geographical origins. Nevertheless, the imaginary world of the 'culture of doing' is difficult to build and even more to preserve. When in a given location 'this is

*View of the square outside
Palazzo Reale from the
terraces of the Duomo in
Milan, 1965*

previous pages
*The former cooling tower
of the Pirelli factory in
Milan Bicocca, today an
integral part of the Pirelli
Headquarters designed by
Vittorio Gregotti, 2016,
photo Eleonora Salvatti*

following pages
*The cooling tower of the
Pirelli factory in Milan
Bicocca, 1958*

not happening anymore', maintaining memory is truly complicated. If we think of Crespi d'Adda on the one hand and the rather close Bertini hydroelectric plant on the other, the contrast is clear. Crespi d'Adda is an industrial village built in the late nineteenth century to house the workers at a textile factory that is the economic, geographical, social linchpin of the town. The workers' houses were built around the factory with orchards and gardens together with the dwellings of the executives, a school, a church, a cemetery, a hospital, a theatre, and a sporting ground. The plant was active for approximately one hundred years. The town is still there,

a sense of pride and belonging. Both venues are evocative and fascinating and speak of noteworthy courage and entrepreneurial vision, albeit in different ways.

Of course, workspaces that are no longer operational are hard to manage and maintain, also because their original purpose was to be instrumental to the production of goods, the generation of income and the creation of productive work. They often are very large spaces, not always successfully designed from the architectural point of view. It is hard to design a workplace that has both a high quality and low cost, flexible and practical,

Companies are not only places of economic production, but also of the construction of important imagery

a UNESCO heritage site, the houses are lived in, but the factory is closed and abandoned. The town has lost its soul—or so it seems to me—despite its landscape and architectural integrity and definite charm. The closing of the factory has turned the *genius loci* upside down. The case of the Bertini plant, built in almost the same years and still operational, is very different. Some of it has been turned into a museum and is the destination of educational and tourist visits. It is also a place where people work subject to its own discipline and develop

adjustable to the changes in industrial processes and be pleasant for those who work there. Therefore, it is not surprising that in projects of urban upgrading it often makes much more sense levelling them to the ground, or refurbish them, thinking of a radically different use: places of aggregation, sporting grounds, congress centres, university campuses or residential areas. Furthermore, these are often buildings that when being lived in, produced external negativities, polluted the air, the water, the ground, the silence and were experienced as grounds of conflict or as a necessary evil. Once their production function ended, they were perhaps abandoned for many years and experienced problems of reclamation, urban and social decay... Cultivating memory is not an easy exercise and imaginary worlds easily overlap.

The matter changes when we think about business centres and corporate headquarters, by definition prestigious buildings and therefore designed with care, with commemorative and promotional ambitions and with a clearer, more explicit idea of making a clear-cut mark on the territory. Business centres are instruments of communication for external stakeholders.

In this case, a great deal of attention is devoted to the aesthetic, functional and symbolic components of the buildings, and they are instruments of a rich communication, on a number of levels, the expression of a company culture, of a history but also of a present and a promise of future. The architectures of business centres speak to us about the way businesses project themselves into the future: the choice of materials, the shapes, the organisation of the internal spaces make visible the idea that a company wants to convey of itself. Also, the physical location in a given urban space plays its role: the history, the circumstances, the prospects of urban development and the features of the infrastructures are also key to it all.

Since business centres have an explicit communicative function, their architecture is often vertical, visible and impactful. The industry they belong to is also an important factor. In manufacturing companies, business centres are prestigious sites where staff members and central functions are concentrated; yet, the heart of the manufacturing processing is elsewhere. In service companies, in the commercial centres of multinationals and in cultural businesses, planning and often production functions coexist with offices. Business

buildings are often suggestive of a staple industry, as in the case of Milan with the publishing industry. Their widespread presence is rare, as is the case of architecture and design in Milan. Because of their nature, different people may be found in business centres, since they are both prestigious and working venues and are therefore somewhat permeable.

For many people, they are the mark of power, ambitions and exchange.

Then, factories, places of progress, innovation developed over the course of time materials, processes and products. Factories are still often thought of only as places where items are produced, even though those who work there spend a significant part of their adult life. Unlike other buildings, factories generally exhibit little, due to safety and security issues. They are part of a very specific present made of discipline and restrictions, but also of relationships, expectations and ambitions. They speak primarily to their in-house stakeholders, without too much attention, while those who work there inhabit the factory and generally know it well and have developed habits, built relationships and a sense of belonging, although made of conflicting feelings.

I know I am writing something well-known—the futurists, for instance, had already thought of it—yet a factory has rhythms, sounds, noises, smells, substance, characteristics and specific volumes that govern people's behaviour and bring about an economic and productive outcome. It sounds unbelievable and yet places that have such an important and rich meaning for those who attend them and so fascinating in their own way because they are contemporary, after all warm the hearts of those outside their premises very little. When it comes to communication and building imaginary worlds, they are rather low-profile.

The story of the factory is a tough one.

Therefore, what the past and present iconic places

of culture and the iconic business buildings have in common might be the construction of visible and material imaginary worlds on those sites, while inside those buildings one finds an immaterial component. These are imaginary worlds that display a stratified

The iconic building celebrates the company's DNA, the element of departure of the value creation process

asset value, the ambition to make an income and future impacts, but also their everyday content which gradually settles to form a shared meaning. We are used to see the first two, while discovering the third is harder, unless one belongs to that community, and they are associated with the pride of belonging and of the work done well,

since many products made well originate from work done well also when they are mass-produced.

It is difficult to describe work is well done. Companies, factories and cultural heritage have the same risk of rejection. I am not an expert, yet to date the one intellectually honest and convincing voice in praise of pride for work as an intrinsic value, notwithstanding the objectives of maximisation of efficiency, is Primo Levi.[1] In all his books, work done well is either the leading or supporting actor. Also when carried out in the violent and oppressive environment of a concentration camp, work done well has the power of redemption and helps the keeping of human dignity. What strikes me is the fact that Levi is capable of looking at the quality of work notwithstanding the nature of the profession. Work done well incorporates specifications which becomes part of it and transcends them, like in a race. Work includes the use of one's mind and hands. Without his work as a chemist, he himself would not have survived in Auschwitz. In *The Monkey's Wrench*, Levi writes:

[…] loving your work […] represents the best, most concrete approximation to happiness on earth […] but love, or conversely, hatred of work is an inner, original heritage, which depends greatly on the story of the individual and less than is believed on the productive structures within which the work is done.[2]

Pirelli is one of those companies on the Italian landscape that explicitly reflected the longest on the relationship among iconic business buildings, the city, the construction of imaginary worlds around labour and 'well made' products. I will mention—not in an exhaustive list—some elements that offered me cues when consulting the many materials collected by the Fondazione Pirelli and gradually made available in various forms. This documentation is a key for us to

The Pirelli Skyscraper,
1973, photo Fotoind

interpret various clusters of people inside and outside the company and the material and non-material component of its heritage in order to build powerful worlds, yet filled with irony and poetical imagery. The Pirelli Skyscraper—'il Pirellone'—is a highly symbolic building from a countless perspectives.

The 'grattacielo' complied with the all Milanese custom whereby the statue of the 'Madonnina' must be 'the tallest' in the city, and yet for many years it was the tallest building. Gio Ponti—the architect who designed it—said that the Pirelli skyscraper anticipated the idea of a lowland city in which tall buildings mark its

'A kind of mechanical cathedral, without a grain of dust, which sings its immobile basso continuo hymn'

In Milan the Pirelli Skyscraper, beside its undeniable beauty, or perhaps because of it, is a big persona. [...] It should bring to us tourists in their coaches through their ritual 'tour de la ville'. Once on top of it, the view is wonderful, like when on the mountains, the steep crests stack up before us one behind the other, taller and taller, and finally, up there, apparently unattainable, the momentous rock rises up against the sky. One of the few happy surges upwards of this adorable and horrendous city.[3]

Inaugurated on April 4, 1960 on a decommissioned and bombed industrial site, the 'grattacielo' stands beside the Central Station. Impossible to miss it and not to acknowledge in its iconic and symbolic role the rebirth of both the city and the company.

contemporary skyline. It is an ambitious building for an ambitious company; as Carlo De Carli writes 'In this building [...] one sees the change from a local sphere to a plane that involves the modern architecture of the entire world'[4]. The 'grattacielo' communicates with the community of planners and designers, politicians, the industrial world and the citizens. Its top storeys host the offices while the first ten levels are filled with third parties' shops and offices. Alongside the massive effort to promote rubber and its multiple uses, the skyscraper becomes the symbol of innovation, far-sightedness and wellbeing. It is not only the building that has a strong symbolic power, but also its interiors, with walls and floors covered in rubber and Pirelli linoleum and with a strong stylistic identity provided by the furnishings, all designed *ad hoc*. The operation was successful, I would

say, considering that still today, despite the change of owners, the skyscraper is known to the Milanese as 'il Pirellone'.

Despite the contribution by many actors to its conception and construction, the 'archistar' of reference here is Gio Ponti, who so defined its symbolic value:

We entrusted this work, writing of it at the beginning of its conception, to those principles that, before and after Pirelli, have inspired and still inspire our work in its truest expression: the principles of formal unity, of the finished form, of essentiality, of representativeness and, finally, of 'illusiveness'. Through this latter, we look at architecture that after fulfilling and even completing its original function takes on a quasi reality of appearance and art beyond the material reality.[5]

The Pirellone is to all intents and purposes a headquarters, a building that speaks of faith, progress and power to its many external stakeholders. However, at the same time, it also speaks of the productive soul of the building. Its story is told in an almost futurist way by Dino Buzzati, as though it were a factory, seen from the basement floors, the places known only to those who work there and yet can be visited:

Central heating and air conditioning plant, hydraulic power unit, telephone exchange, central refrigeration plant. [...] I simply advise going to see it (there is a guided visit on Wednesdays). These are very beautiful landscapes, impressively clean, as though they had been created this morning. Boilers, reservoirs and autoclaves like immense chalk hippos, bundles, tangles, floodgates, canopies and volutes of snow-white pipes sorted with solemn and mathematical rhythms sounding like Bach's music. Lines of swollen machines, pointed machines, rotating machines, in classical ballet poses dotted with scarlet cranks. A kind

of mechanical cathedral, without a grain of dust, which sings its immobile basso continuo hymn. The rustle of the rotors, the hums, the ticking of the clock, the lowing of the air conditioning, mysterious clicks, bells, roars, and borborygmi.[6]

At the time of its inauguration, the skyscraper hosted 1200 employees of both Pirelli and its subsidiaries. Although the skyscraper was conceived and built as an icon and soon became a landmark of Milan, I believe it would have been difficult to imagine such a strong evocative power without the construction of a non-material imaginary world 'around' the brand, made of photo reportages in the offices, the telephone exchanges and the meeting rooms. These were all pieces of evidence about the nature of clerical work which complemented factory work. After that, the *Piccole storie del Grattacielo* [Little Stories of the Skyscraper], which describe, half-seriously and half-facetiously—as we would say today—a community that acknowledges its members 'across' according to their social status,

based on the floor, office staff, managers, engineers, top executives come and go from the lift, and some say hallo to each other. They all belong to that small vertical city, the famous small city and are also quite proud to be citizens of this famous skyscraper.[7]

When it comes to the factory, a similar endeavour points to the opposite direction. The venues that speak to those who work in the company become almost by contrast the explicit object for the construction of imagery by the outsiders. Pirelli is an industrial company and has an industrial culture. Its roots and its results come from applications in many sectors different from rubber. The heart of Pirelli is factory work. Long before the construction of imagery and the building of 'il Pirellone',

In the new headquarters, the cooling tower so reinterpreted, recalls the company's DNA, its roots and is an element of identity and history for the whole district

the place of its success was the factory, and the company's reputation and image come from an industrial nature and are associated with the product. Rubber is the heart of Pirelli products.

The *Rivista Pirelli* places the company and its products—exhibited with pride as the result of a sound economic and technical culture—at the centre.

This organisation produces a huge number of different products [...]. It employs the largest variety of machines and tools. It develops scientific laboratories that nurture progress. Therefore, lots of opportunities to contribute to the most notable evolution of modern life! Yet, if in this magazine we are sometimes to raise ourselves even higher, we will do so knowing that every contribution to mechanised civilisation must be framed within the highest cultural and social values of life.[8]

Within the group, the pole at Settimo Torinese is the most advanced and efficient, both from the point of view of processes and products, allowing the economically sustainable production of even very small batches of tyres. Indeed, top performing tyres within the Pirelli range are manufactured at Settimo.
The central site of the top-performing factory, where research and development are as one with production, has been entrusted to Renzo Piano's architectural talent. The iconic building celebrates the company's DNA, the element of departure of the value creation process. Stakeholders from outside are also called upon 'to see' what those people who do not work in the factory do not normally see.
I am reluctant to believe that this endeavour of building imagery for those who are outside the company does not also involve those who work in it: Pirelli acknowledges that quality comes from and is produced in an innovative piece of architecture.

*View of the Bicocca area
in Milan from above, 2018*

As in the case of business inside the skyscraper, yet with an opposite approach, the *Rivista Pirelli* takes up the story of the labour community not only made of entrepreneurial dynasties, but also of 'dynasties of corporate lance-corporals', making visible the business culture of groups of workers who are normally invisible, stories of identity and sense of belonging that are highly important for staff inside the factory, unknown to those who are outside it, but equally relevant to build what we call enterprise-based culture and its imaginary world.

Nobody would have guessed that father-to-son rotations among workers would have made possible to write a chapter of the history of industry that an intellectual would title: 'Du côté de chez les ouvriers'. Indeed, that is what happened. Amid rubber and payslips, engagements and booms, undersea cables and weddings, births and deaths in the smoke of the factory, some dynasties came into being. [...] The lance-corporal dynasty of industry is rich and complicated. Grandchildren play around his feet and the connection of continuity branches out with daughters-in-law, sons-in-law, mothers- and fathers-in-law. There are no young cadets who go into exile or waste a wealth with famous singers. [...] These are rich and juicy stories of grandfathers, children and grandchildren who have passed through the same gate of the same factory, and have sunk their roots there. It is the factory Bible.[9]

The third instance when venues, corporate history and its culture were marked by architecture was the transfer of the headquarters from 'il Pirellone' to 'La Bicocca'. When the Pirelli Skyscraper was sold to the Regional Government of Lombardy in 1978, the headquarters moved onto the land of the factory that had been rebuilt after the Second World War bombing, which were part of a major real estate project: building of the 'Bicocca University', the 'Teatro degli Arcimboldi', the exhibition

centre 'HangarBicocca', residential and corporate buildings.

Where there used to be a factory, now there is a district and by all means, not a small one, its life changing from daylight to night time and through the several infrastructures created in sequence inevitably the memory of the factory and the outer suburbs were annihilated in the configuration of the urban layout. According to Vittorio Gregotti's project for the new Headquarters, the cooling tower which belonged to the thermoelectric plant built by Pirelli in 1950 to guarantee the continuity of its production, was to be incorporated into the prestigious building.

In the new headquarters, the Cooling Tower so reinterpreted, recalls the company's DNA, its roots and is an element of identity and history for the whole district, exactly like 'La Bicocca degli Arcimboldi'. The Fondazione Pirelli has, among others, the task of preserving both Pirelli's corporate and district history.

NOTES

1   M. Belpoliti, *Primo Levi di fronte e di profile*, Milan, 2015.

2   P. Levi, *The Monkey's Wrench*, New York, 1986, pp. 79–80.

3   D. Buzzati, 'Piccole storie del Grattacielo', in *Pirelli. Rivista d'informazione e di tecnica*, IX, 9, 1970, p. 30.

4   C. De Carli, 'La nuova sede Pirelli', in *Pirelli. Rivista d'informazione e di tecnica*, III, 3, 1955, p. 25.

5   G. Ponti, 'Perpetuità di un edificio', in *Pirelli. Rivista d'informazione e di tecnica*, IX, 9, 1970, p. 28.

6   Buzzati, 'Piccole storie del Grattacielo', cit., p. 32.

7   *Ibid.*, p. 30.

8   A. Pirelli, 'Questa nostra rivista', in *Pirelli. Rivista d'informazione e di tecnica*, I, 1, 1948, p. 8.

9   A. Cavallari, 'Dinastie operaie alla Bicocca', in *Pirelli. Rivista d'informazione e di tecnica*, V, 3, 1952, p. 37.

RESE

A photo report by Carlo Furgeri Gilbert *inside* the tyre. A transformation that, starting from the essential raw materials, passes through new technologies to arrive at a finished product that is increasingly secure, sustainable and innovative.

ARCH

The Amazing Face of Raw Materials and High–Tech Simulators

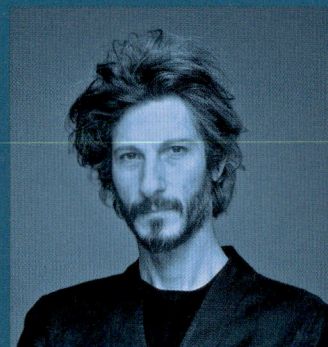

by Carlo Furgeri Gilbert

PHOTOGRAPHER AND DIRECTOR

O utside, only sound. Machinery working away. Busy workers running back and forth with prototypes, technical sheets, trials, results, printouts. The enormous doors covered in blue sound-absorbent cones are opened. We enter and then the door closes behind us. Inside, the silence is absolute. It is an anechoic chamber; a magical place where the noise of the outside world remains outside. This is where the sound of the pneumatic tyre is measured. There, alone at the centre of the room and without any sign of the customary automotive paraphernalia, a tyre is about to take its place on stage to deliver a monologue (or at least this is my interpretation). In utter silence and surrounded by high-precision microphones, the tyre starts to rotate. A barely perceptible sound, but this is what makes the difference on the road and the task in hand is to reduce this to a minimum.

But how can we draw that sound visually? How can this experience be told? Perhaps in these cases words are more useful. But how can this be done with photography?

For me, photography is an act of comprehension. It means to understand the world. Not in some technical or encyclopaedic acceptation but more from an emotive perspective (indeed, aren't emotions the only thing that unites us?). For me, a photograph becomes powerful and important when it depicts something beyond mere *documentation*. What is shown is a universal concept or sentiment which the individual is able to understand and comprehend, irrespective of any technical understanding of the represented object.

I observe products and materials. I investigate their weave, colours, and forms. I perceive their odours. And then suddenly all this is transformed and becomes something else; it becomes a tale, a sound, a painting, sculpture, city or persons. It becomes a world that embraces thousands of hours of toil of workers, engineers, scientists, labourers, farm workers, and encompasses the vision of all those who have created that very product or material. It is through photography that we are able to represent that world.

Photography cannot be objective because it is a personal perspective which is only one of countless possible visions. If we reflect closely on its origins, photography is a product of the Industrial Age. It first appeared with the advent of industry and technological and scientific progress that allowed for its development. Thus, photography evolves with the growth of industry and at the same time it documents its progress. The history of industry and of photography follow parallel pathways. If we take photography and industry and we analyse their evolutionary journeys, we can identify many similarities. In order to exist, both need *vision*.

The need to be visionary in the sense of 'seeing beyond'. But this seeing beyond or thinking out of the box, leads us to another fundamental concept.

Innovation.

There can be no innovation without vision.

To innovate means to look for new possibilities, it means to have a vision of one's own project which is open to the world. I believe that thinking out of the box means to make use of a series of processes and materials created specifically for other fields but then applied to suit our own needs.

The exact same process occurs with photography. A fashion photograph is never only about fashion; it tells something about our society, a specific moment in our history and of our customs. Similarly, so-called industrial photography is not only the mere reproduction of processes or products of a certain brand but the interpretation of expectations and projects conveying a passion and aspiration to improve.

Photographic languages have continually evolved, transformed and have been contaminated in time. If initially the stylistic canons of fashion photography, or even reportage or industrial photography were well-delineated within technological contexts, thus limiting their use to predetermined environments, today photography has been 'liberated'. Technical limitations no longer exist. The advent of digital technology and the coexistence with the analogical has allocated photography an immense space for its creative experimentation. But always with the understanding of having a 'vision'. Before, photography required technical preparation. There were certain basic techniques that had to be followed, if not the photograph would never become a reality. Today, with digital technology and with the recent growth of internet and social media, these steps are no longer required. Technical limitations are easily overcome. Today, many are able to create a technically fine photograph but perhaps mediocre in its linguistic declination. Today, good commercial photography can be attained by many. User-friendly instruments and the immediate dissemination of the image through the web have created a previously unknown abundance of images. This era of photographic abundance, however, has brought about totally unexpected results: while this abundance helps us relive our experiences, the sheer volume of photographs and the platform on which they are visible make them easy to forget. Indeed, often these photographs are conceived and produced to be used and consumed with a mere scroll or a *like*. Immediately after, they are swallowed up in the profound abyss of the world wide web.

Click, share, scroll. By scrolling in an infinite flux, the images become ephemeral and—for the greater part— forgotten and never to be seen again; rarely are they remembered.

In this scenario, the role of the photographer takes on great responsibility. Memory must be created but not in the sense of something that has already been, but more something that is 'memorable' and 'rememberable'. This task involves analysing, interpreting and comprehending to create a personal re-elaboration of the photographed reality which is fundamental in the creation of images that can remain and create memory. The memory of an enterprise is fundamental not only to comprehend its past and define its present, but as it also represents a fundamental base on which to construct its future.

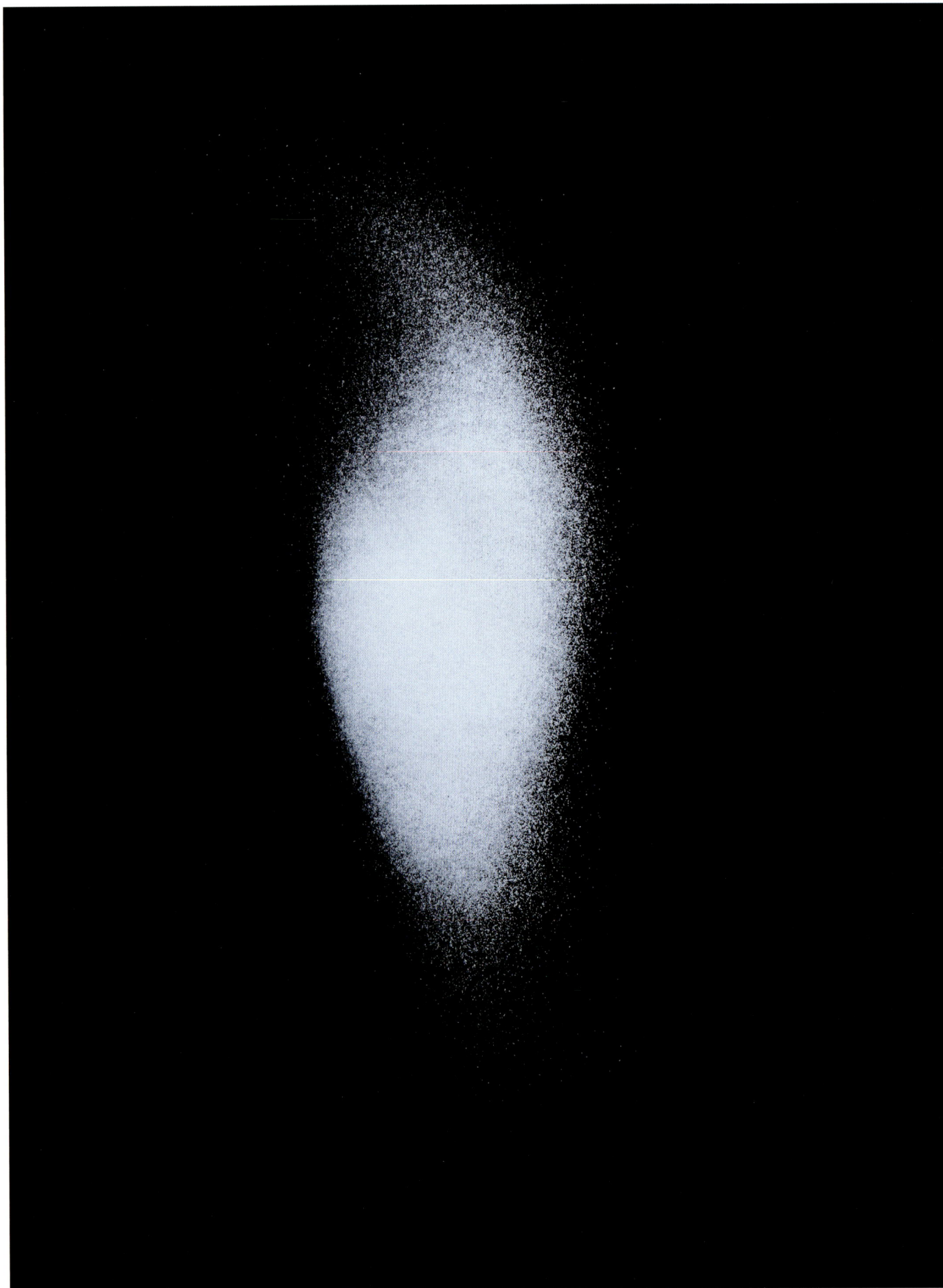

Silica from rice husks

Carbon black from pyrolysis of end-of-life tyres

Accelerant
in powder form

Sulphur
in powder form

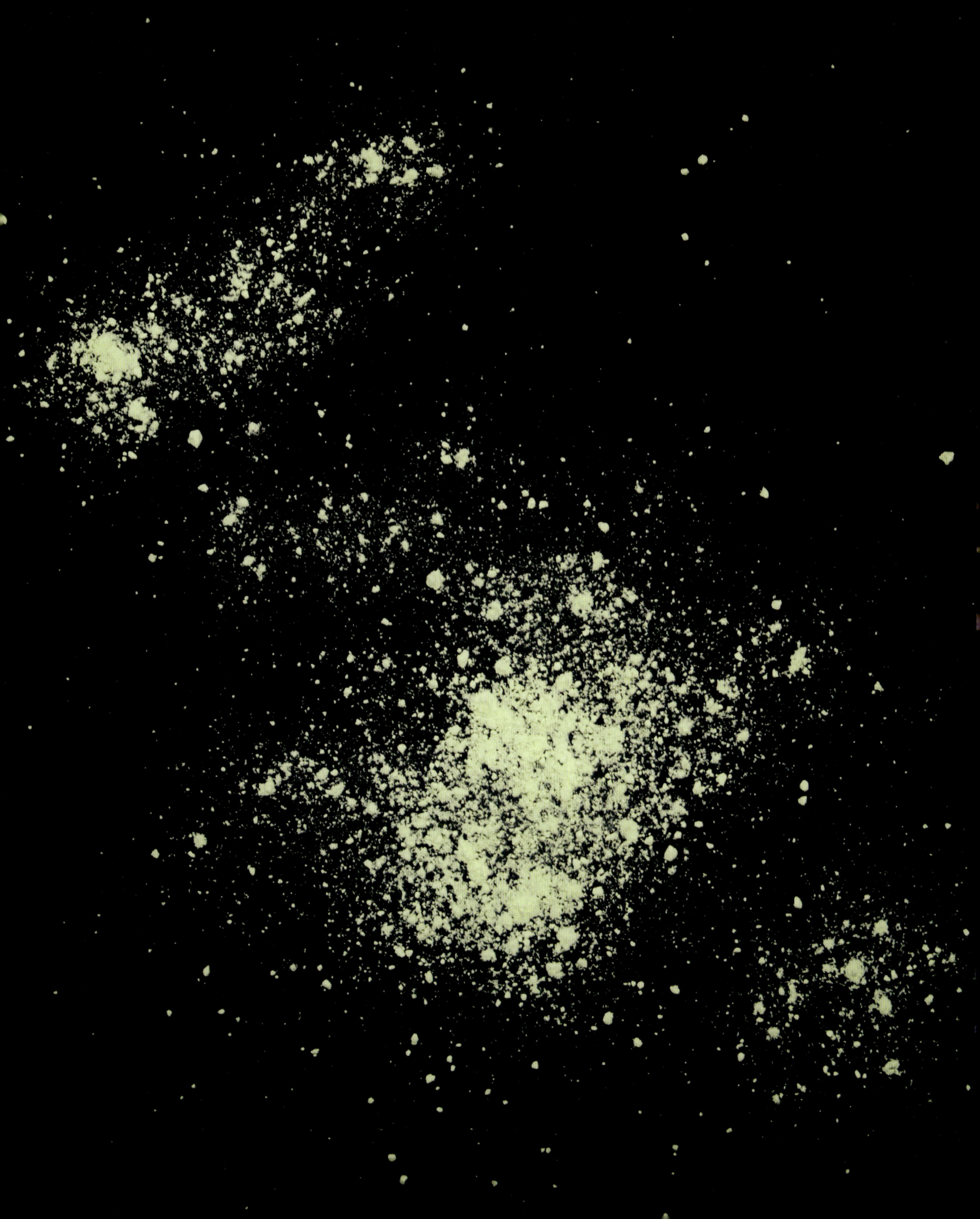

*Vegetable oil
from soy seeds*

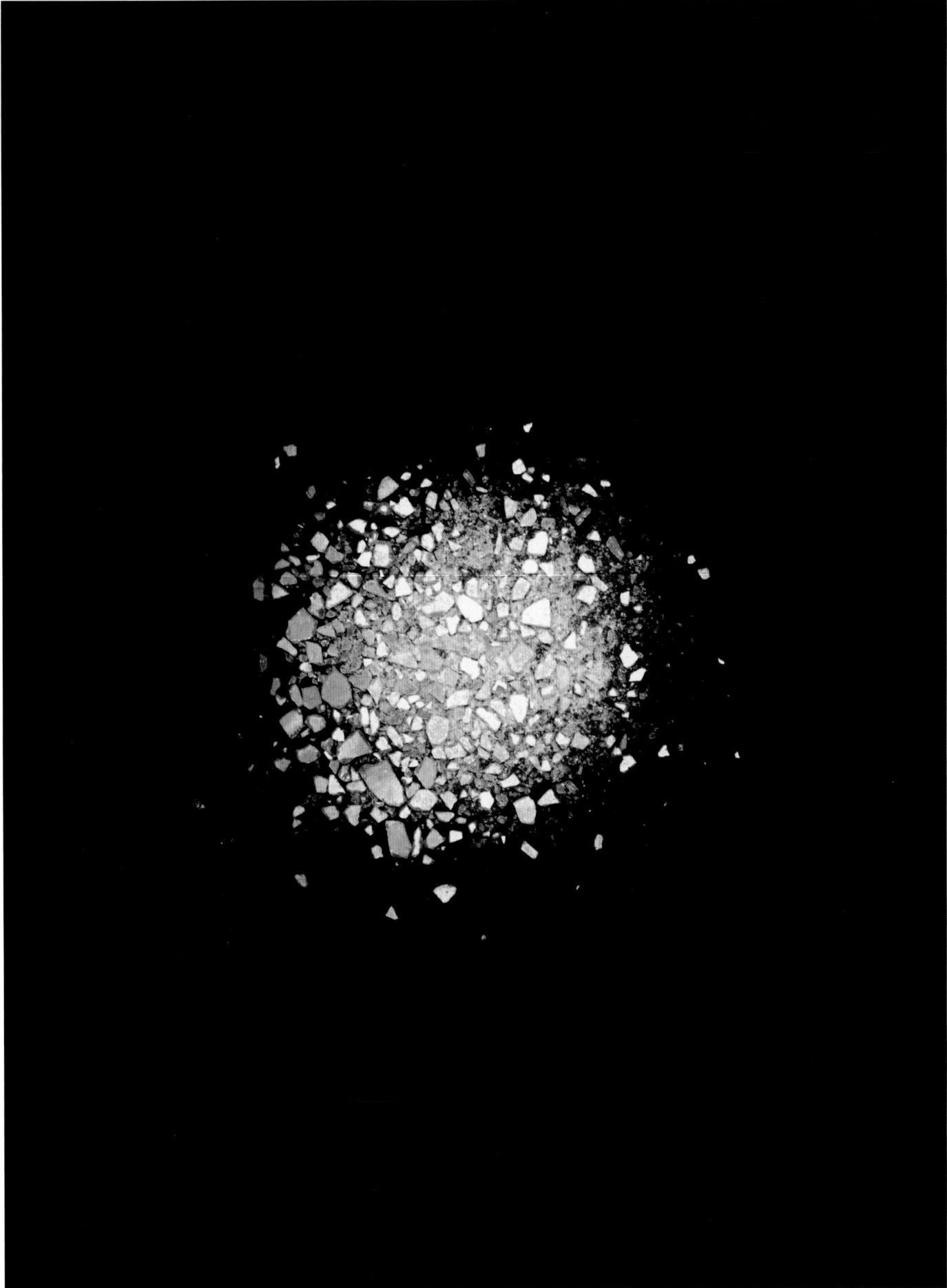

Plasticiser of
vegetable origin

Lignin

*Styrene-butadiene
synthetic rubber
extended with oil*

*Natural rubber after
passage through the
blender*

*Rice husk, precursor
to the production
of silica*

Sheets of natural
rubber

String made
of recycled PET

Powder from
end-of-life tyres

previous pages
*Control room of
the static driving
simulator. The tester
is about to take his
seat in the car to
begin the tests*

*Control room of
the static driving
simulator*

following pages
*The tester busy
driving the static
simulator*

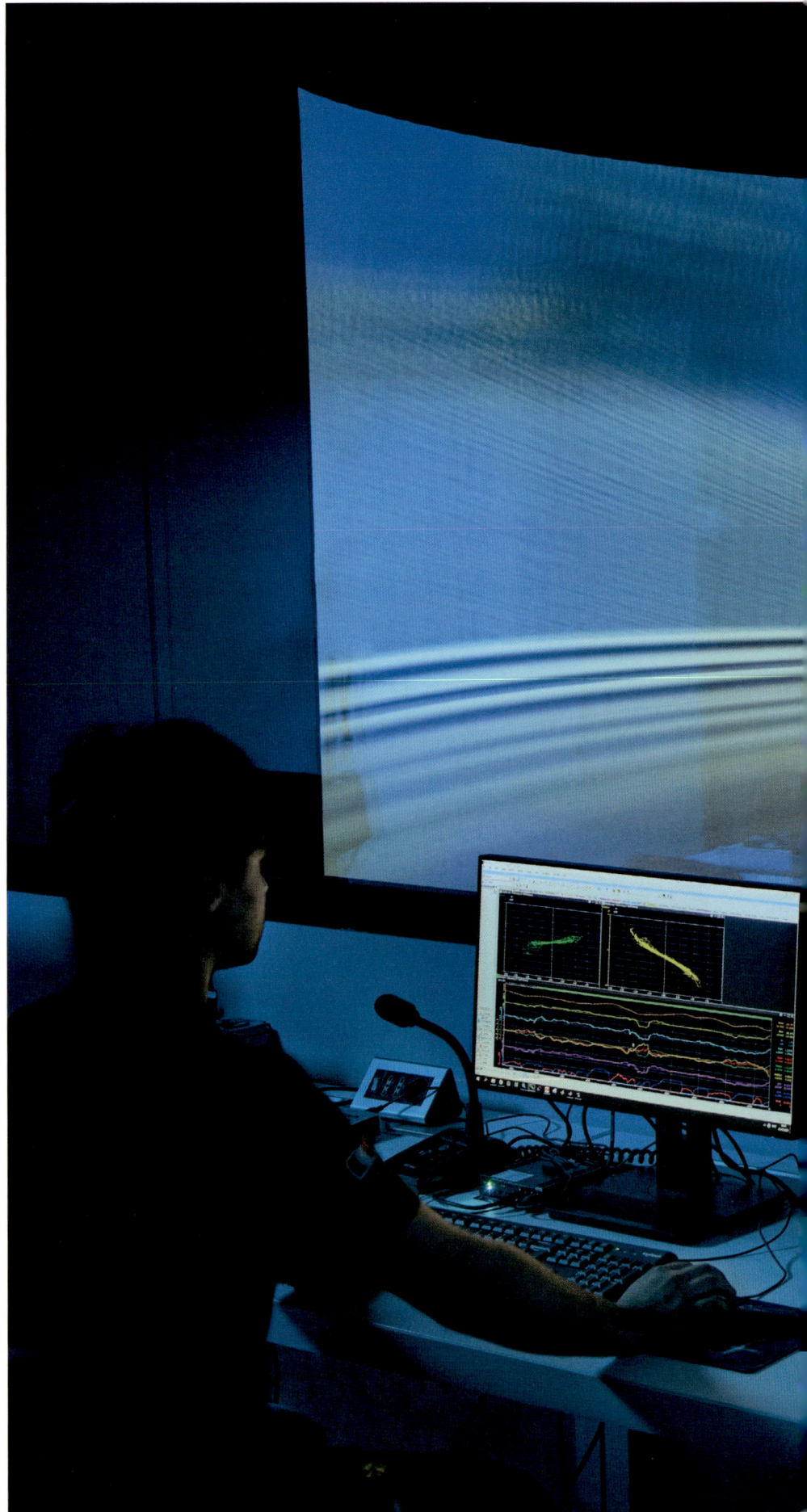

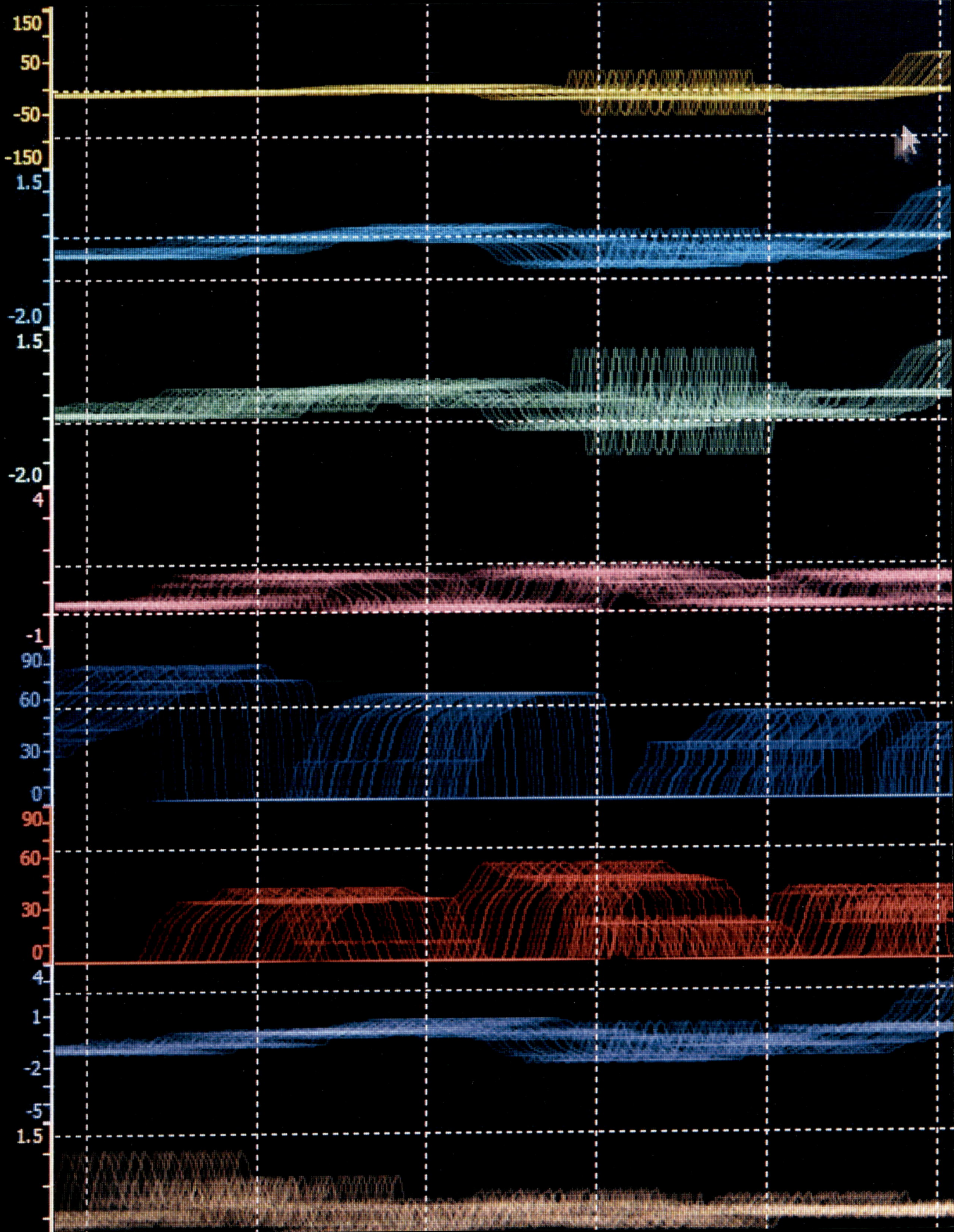

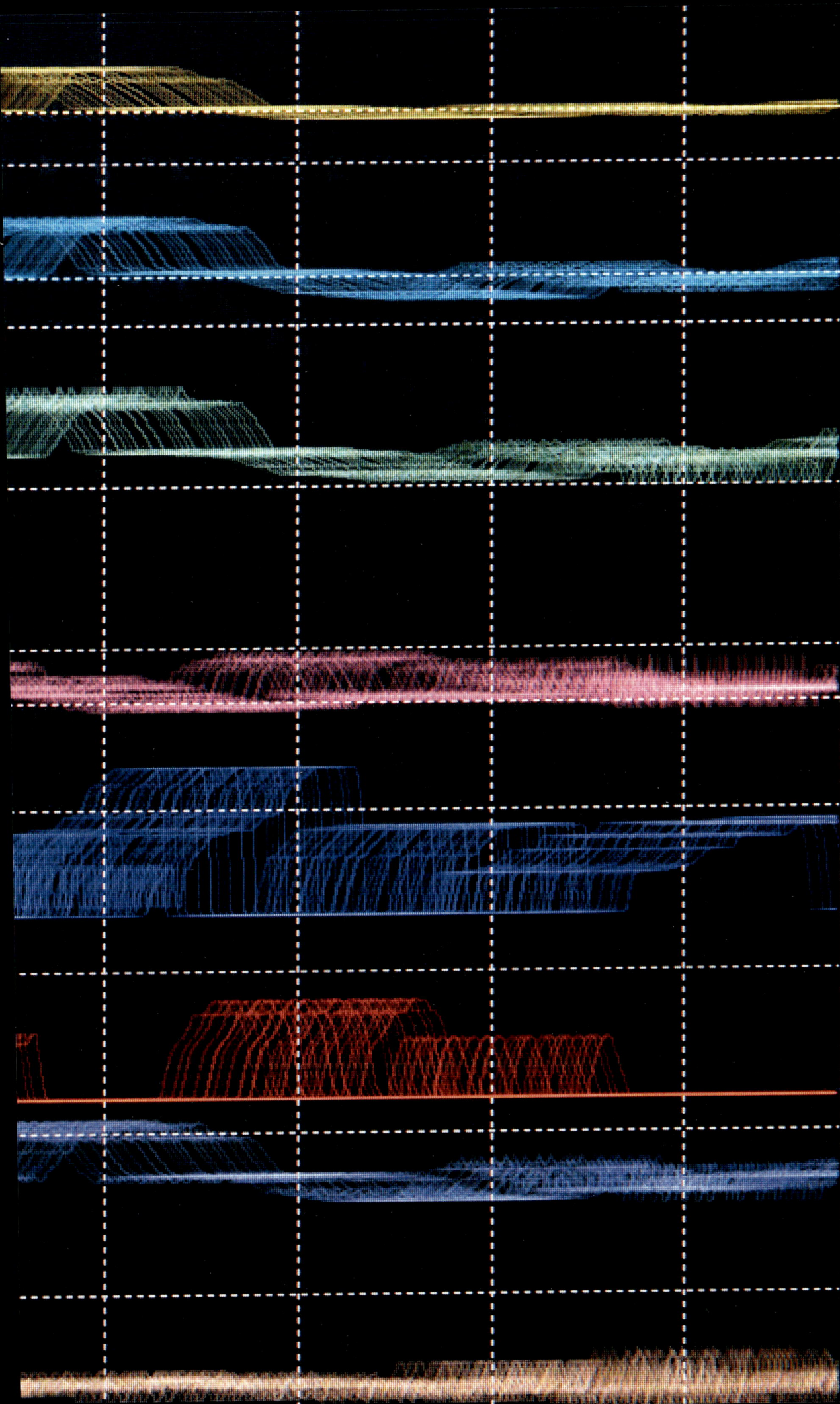

Ste
-0.00000

A
-0.0

Psip
-0.00039865

Pitc
0.00000

Peda
0.48.333

Brake

Rol
-0.00000

chassis_accelerations_vertical
-0.00000

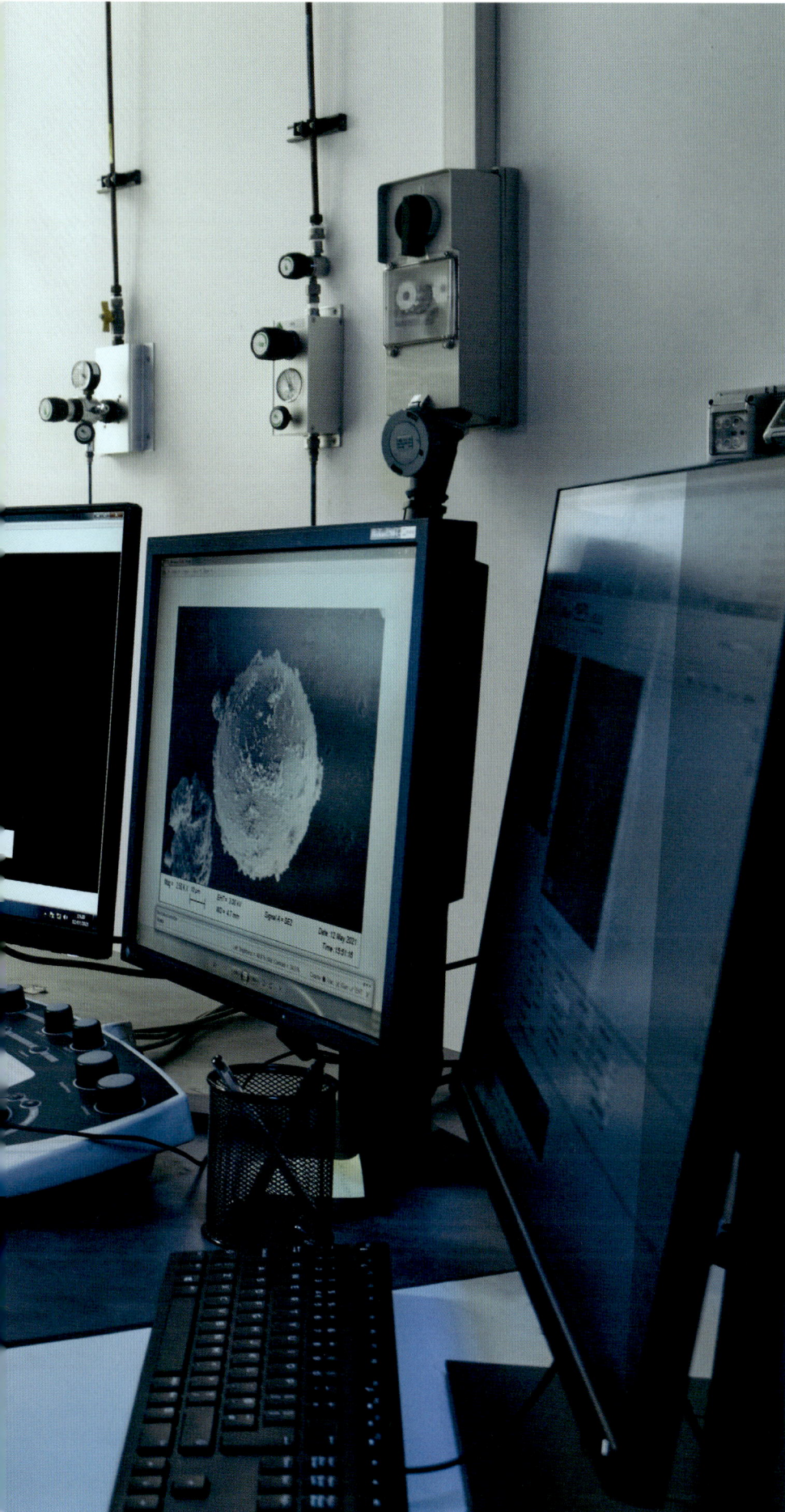

previous pages
*Detail of the
measurements
of dynamic
performance of the
tyres on flat belt
acquired using the
test bench*

*Electron microscope
for the morphological
characterisation of
materials*

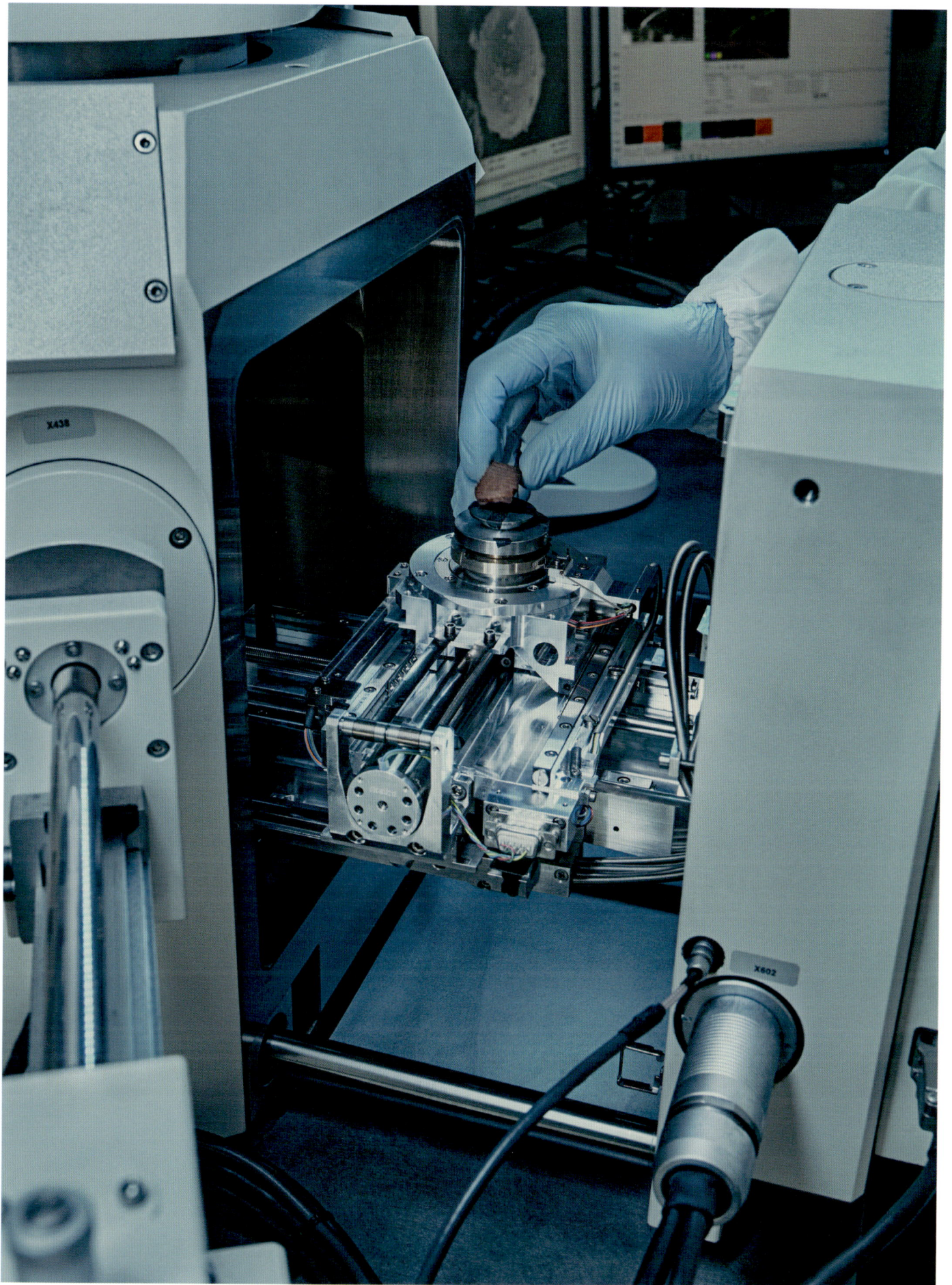

The view camera
that measures the
area and pressure
of contact of the tyre
subjected to vertical
load

Detail of the room
with a sample
from the electronic
microscope for
the morphological
characterisation
of materials

Detail of the view camera that measures the area and pressure of contact of the tyre subjected to vertical load

following pages
Detail of the measurements of dynamic performance of the tyres on flat belt acquired using the test bench

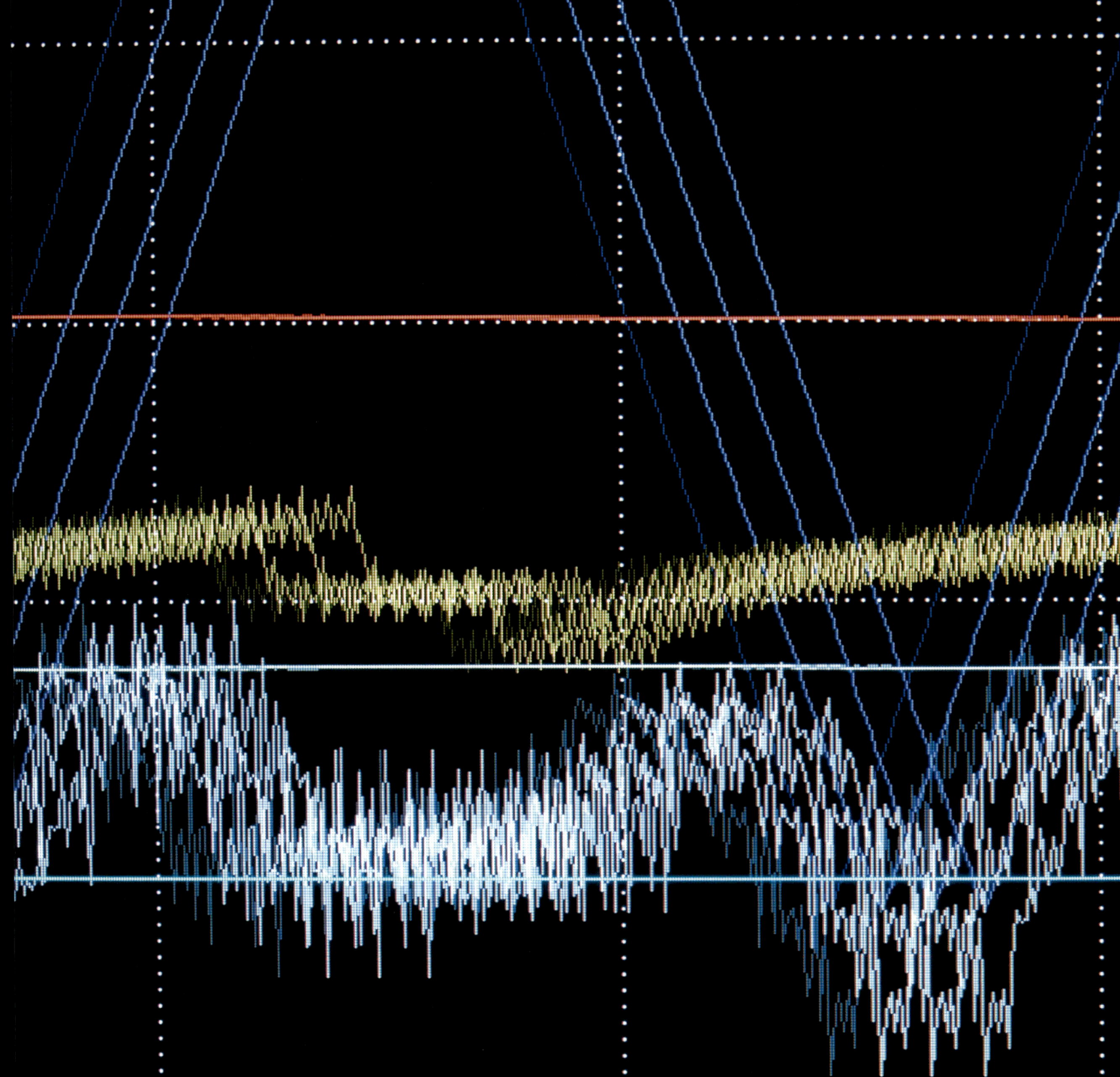

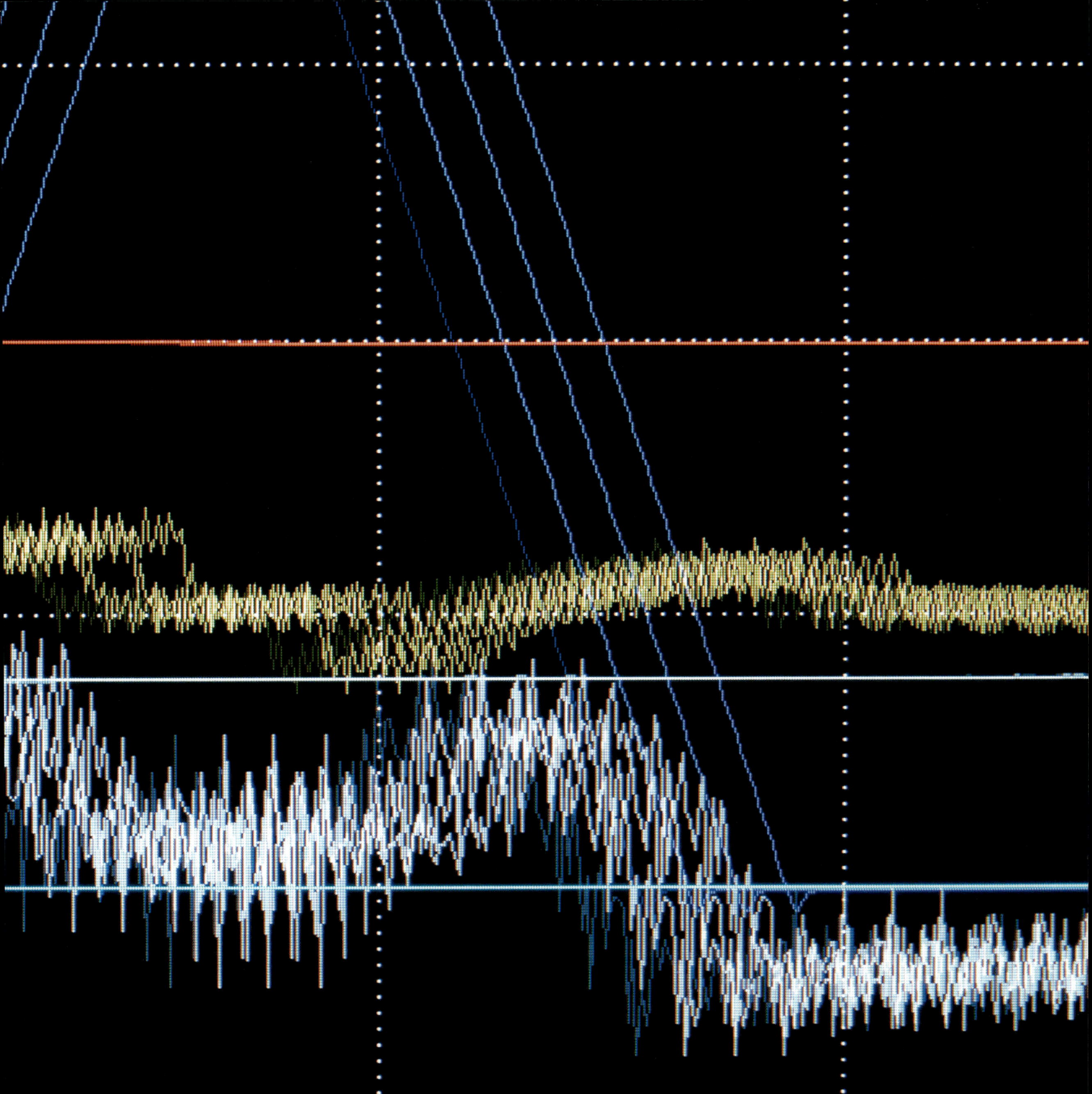

The Grosch
Machine, an
instrument for
measuring the
resistance to
abrasion and friction
of compounds

*Detail of the
specimen subjected
to testing in the
Grosch Machine,
an instrument
for measuring
the resistance to
abrasion and friction
of compounds*

following pages
*Control room of the
bench for measuring
the tyre's rolling
resistance*

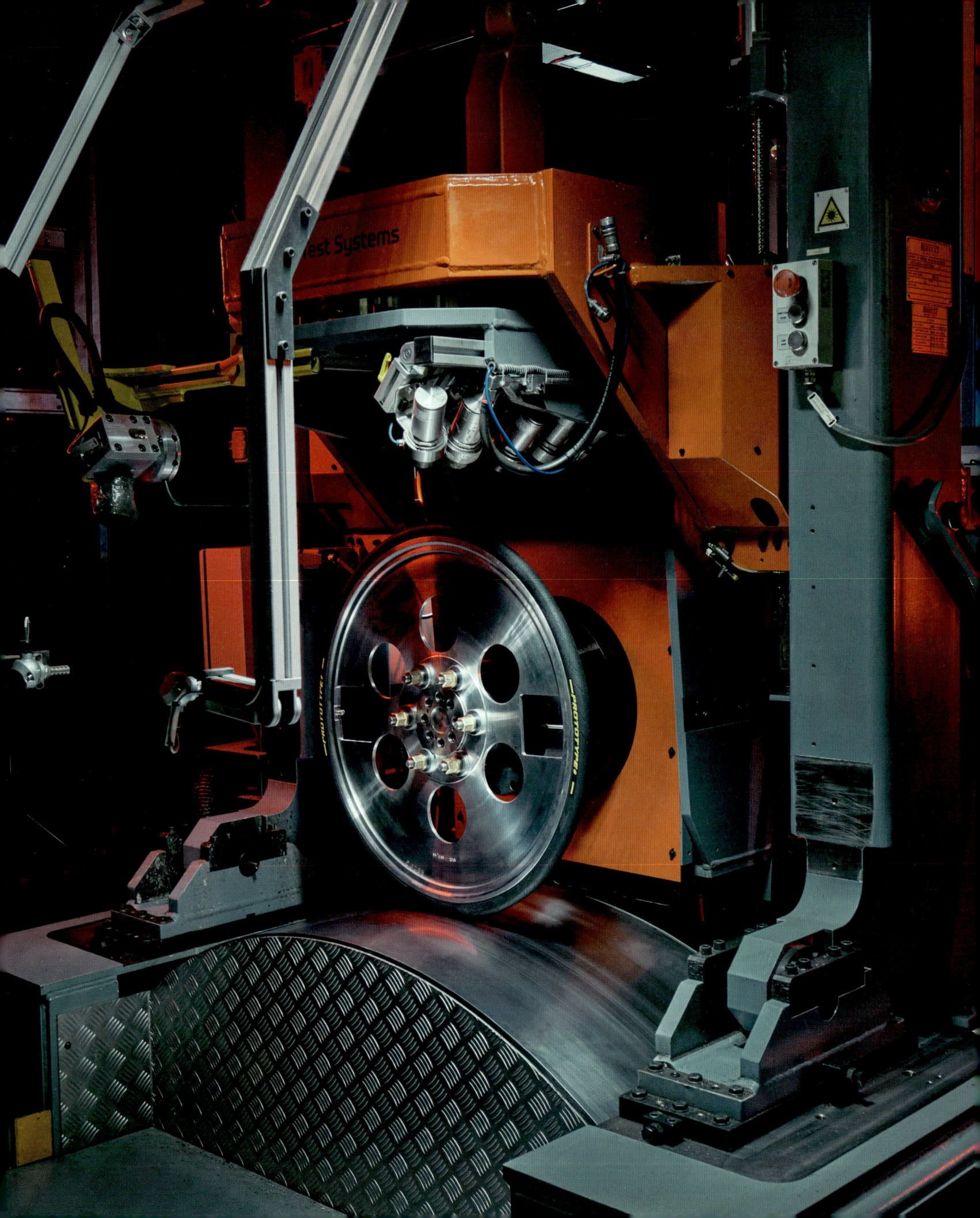

Detail of positioning
of the sample in the
chamber inside the
instrumentation
for studying the
mechanical-dynamic
properties of
compounds

Detail of the test on superbike motorcycle tyre on the tyre test bench on flat belt for measuring the forces and moments (F&M test) produced by the tyre in the different combinations of conditions of use

*Control room of the
tyre test bench on flat
belt for measuring
the forces and
moments (F&M test)
produced by the tyre
under the multiple
conditions of use*

following pages
*Control room of the
tyre test bench to
verify the integrity
of the tyre at high
speed*

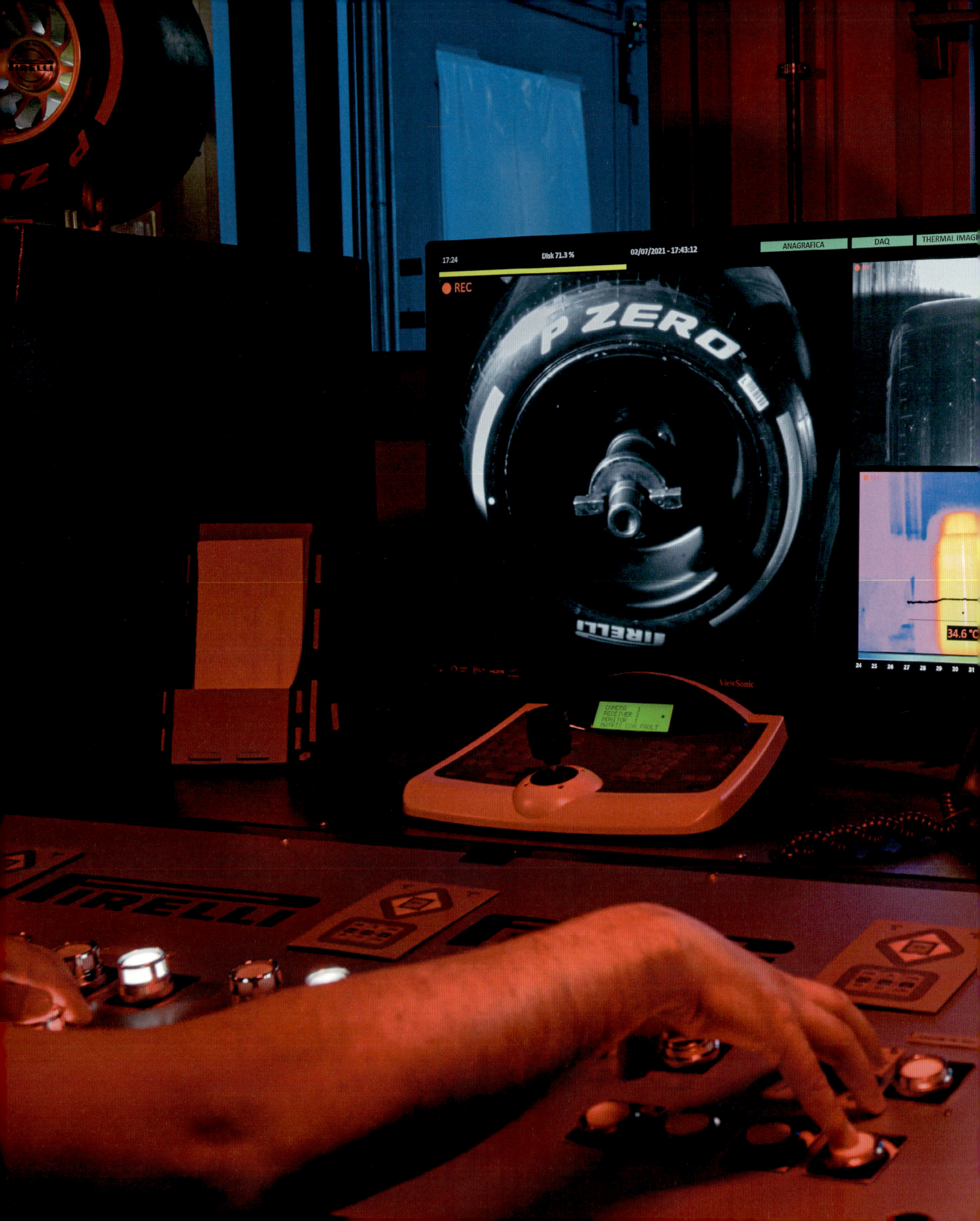

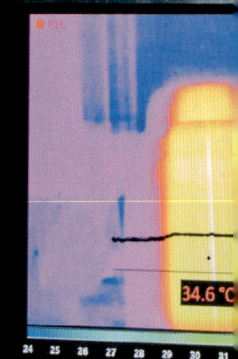

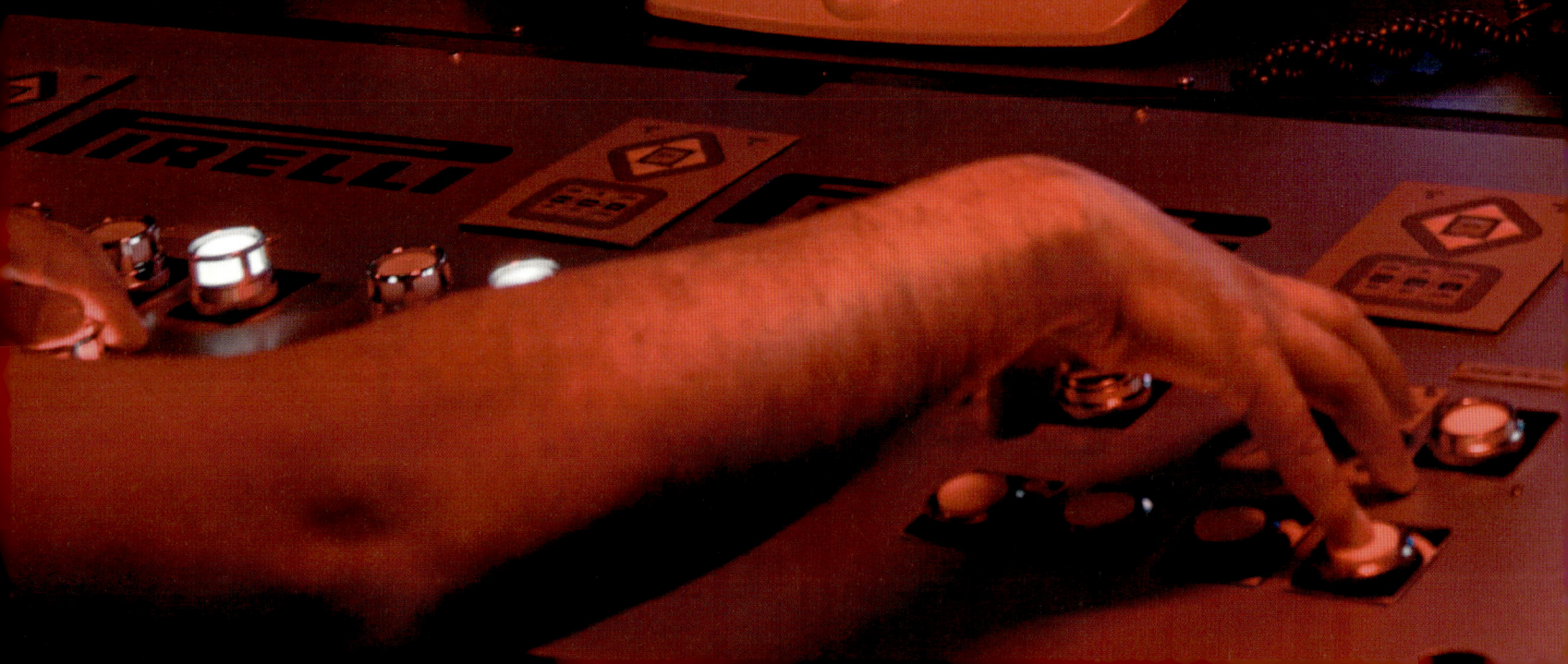

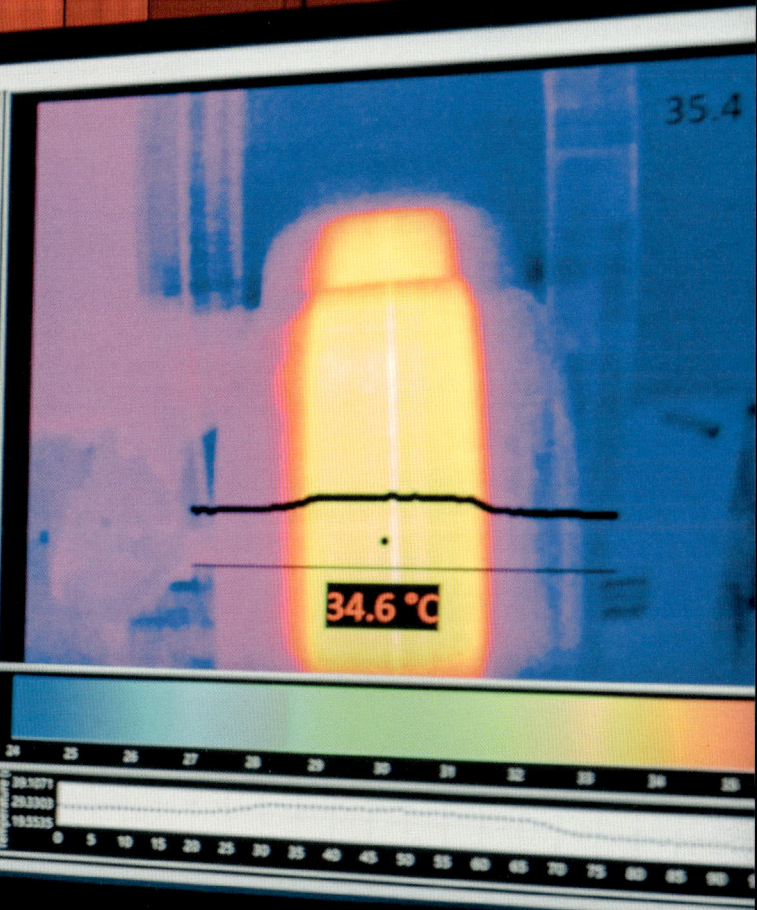

Detail of the buttons
of the control room
of the tyre test
bench to verify the
integrity of the tyre
at high speed

Detail of the buttons
of the control room
of the tyre test bench
at high speed to
verify the integrity
of the tyre subjected
to the maximum
severity of use

*Detail of the
semi-anechoic
chamber for
measuring noise
(sound pressure
level) emitted
by the tyre roll*

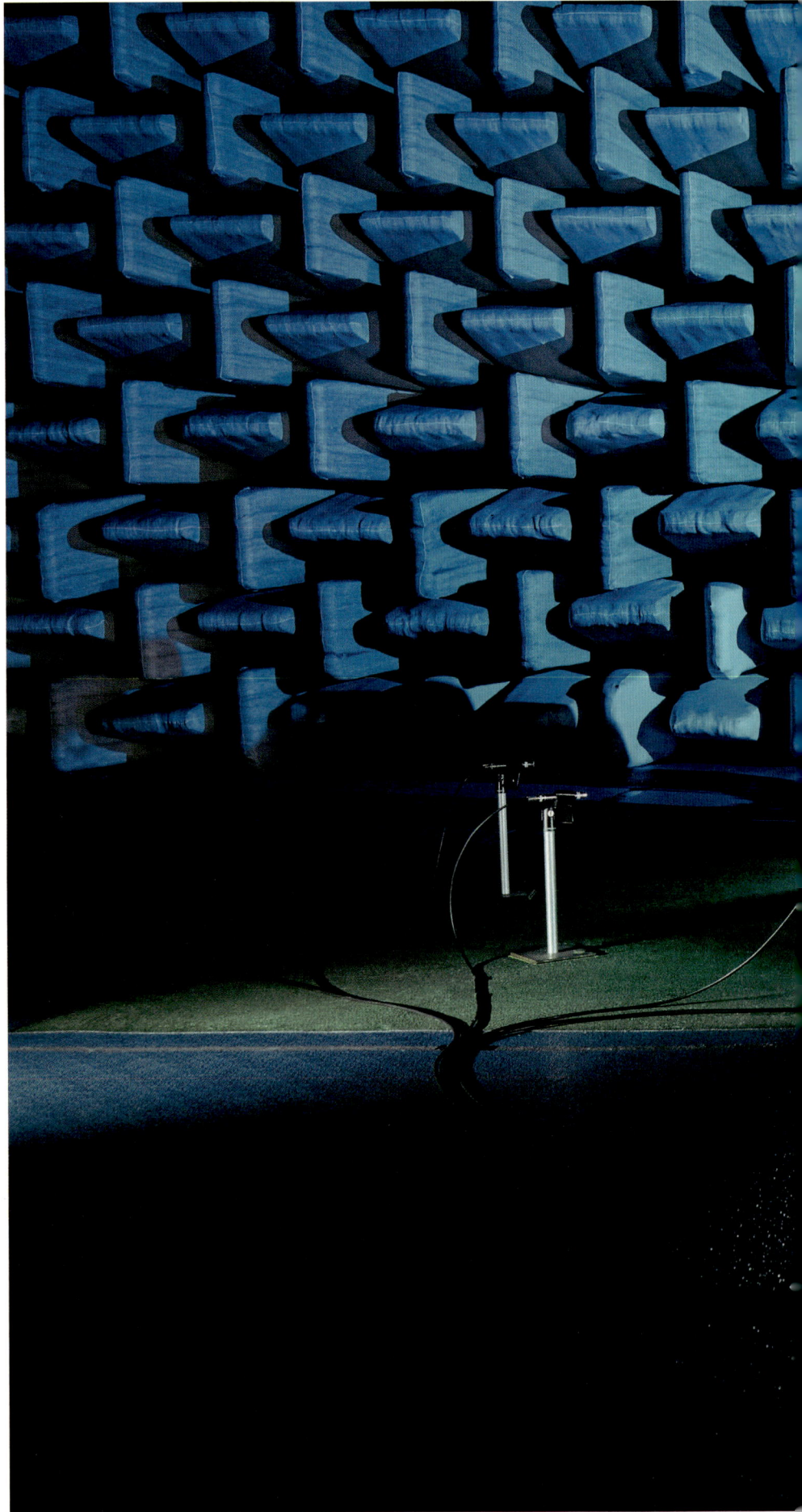

Fondazione Pirelli

Showcasing the Work, between Memory and Future

'Adess ghe capissaremm on quaicoss: andemm a guardagh denter'

'Adess ghe capissaremm on quaicoss: guardagh andemm denter' ('Now we'll understand something about it, we'll look inside it') is one of the quotations that welcome visitors at the entrance to the Fondazione Pirelli. The phrase, recalling one of the mottos of Engineer Luigi Emanueli, is a reference to the industrial concreteness and the attitude towards research that have characterised the culture of the group since its beginnings, and to the double nature of the company, a multinational that is strongly rooted in the Milanese territory.

The Pirelli identity has in fact always been characterised by a polytechnic enterprise culture capable of combining art, production, beauty, technology and innovation. The Fondazione Pirelli is in the forefront in supporting the company's cultural initiatives; it was created in 2008 due to the awareness that safeguarding its historical and contemporary heritage is of value for the company and its stakeholders. Confirming the importance that the Pirelli Archive has for the community, the Municipal

Authority's Archive Department proclaimed its historical interest back in 1972, placing it under its own tutelage.

The principal goal of the Foundation, which has its base in Fabbricato 134 (today the Stella Bianca Building) at the Pirelli Headquarters in Milan Bicocca, is therefore to preserve, value and promote this rich heritage: over 3.5 kilometres of documents testifying to the history of the company from its foundation in 1872 to the present day. Documents produced and received by the various company functions during 150 years of activity, with a large section devoted to advertising and visual communication, illustrating and offering evidence of the long tradition and the recognised avant-garde role of Pirelli in these areas. The photographic collection, the sketches and printed plans and the audio-visuals collection all belong to this section. The photographic collection includes more than 700,000 negatives on plate and on film, prints, slides, the subjects of which are shots of factories, products, exhibitions and fairs, automobile, motorcycle and cycle races, fashion features to be used to illustrate the company magazines and product catalogues or to realise the Pirelli advertising campaigns. Among the authors are great names of photography such as Aldo Ballo, Gabriele Basilico, Arno Hammacher, Annie Leibovitz, Ugo Mulas, Federico Patellani, Fulvio Roiter and Albert Watson and well-known agencies such as Farabola and Publifoto. The sketches and original drawings collection contains hundreds of sketches, drawings and printed plans realised by famous illustrators, graphic designers and advertising agencies from the first decade of the twentieth century to today. Among the best known: Renzo Bassi, Gerard Forster, Robert François, Tomás Gonda, Lora Lamm, Riccardo Manzi, Alessandro Mendini, Bruno Munari and Bob Noorda and international agencies such as Young & Rubicam and Armando Testa. The numerous works commissioned by Pirelli from artists of the calibre of Fulvio Bianconi, Renzo Biasion and Renato Guttuso, among others, to illustrate the *Rivista Pirelli*, also belong to this fund. The audio-visuals fund contains hundreds of clips on film and magnetic tape datable from 1912 to the present day. From the films of Luca Comerio to documentaries such as *La fabbrica sospesa*, commissioned by Pirelli in 1985 from director Silvio Soldini, from the cinema adverts and editions of Carosello on TV by the masters of Italian animation such as Roberto Gavioli and the brothers Nino and Toni Pagot, to the TV ads from the 1990s and 2000s, with art directors such as Derek Forsyth and famous endorsers such as athlete Carl Lewis, actress Sharon Stone and footballer Ronaldo. The Pirelli Archive also includes the complete collections of the company periodicals *Pirelli. Rivista d'informazione e di tecnica*, *Vado e torno*, *Pi vendere*, *Fatti e Notizie*, *Paginas Pirelli*, *Noticias Pirelli* and *Pirelli World*, among others.

The Foundation also conserves the private archives of the Pirelli family, including the papers of Alberto and Leopoldo Pirelli. The Alberto Pirelli Archive provides evidence of his activities in service of the country as a diplomat and finance and international economics expert and his roles inside important organisations, national and international, such as the International Chamber of Commerce, Assonime and the ISPI. Leopoldo Pirelli's papers, on the other hand, concern his activity as president of the group, starting from 1965, and offer evidence of crucial events in the history of the company, such as the Pirelli Commission for the reform of the Confindustria Statute.

The collections of architectural and urbanistic interest, such as the documents of the Bicocca Project, with evidence of the various phases of transformation of the area, the personal files of the company's employees, papers of a business bookkeeping and administrative

To preserve, value and promote this rich heritage: over 3.5 kilometres of documents testifying to the history of the company from its foundation in 1872 to the present day

nature, such as the group's Annual Reports, are all included in the Pirelli Archive; in recent years this has been enriched by the contributions of major international authors such as Emmanuel Carrère, Javier Cercas, Hans Magnus Enzensberger, Luciano Floridi, Adam Greenfield, Lisa Halliday, Hanif Kureishi, William Least Heat-Moon, Javier Marías, Guillermo Martínez, Tom McCarthy and John Joseph 'J.R.' Moehringer. The archive also conserves technical documentation relating to the planning and development of products and machinery: original designs-prints, studies on treads, specific test techniques, approval documents, price lists and catalogues. This is an asset that makes it possible to reproduce tyres that are historically and philologically correct, identical in appearance to those originally fitted, though adopting the materials, technologies and quality and safety standards of current tyres: this is sensitive research, finding a balance between respect for the original product and production standard 5.0.

The Technical-Scientific Library is also of considerable interest; it was created by the company for its researchers and engineers and became part of the Foundation's assets in 2010. Over 16,000 volumes on the technology of rubber and cables from the nineteenth century to the present day, foreign technical magazines, of which the Foundation holds the only copies present in Italy, such as the English *India Rubber Journal*, the oldest magazine in the world on the rubber industry, founded in 1888, and the American *India Rubber World*, published in New York between 1889 and 1954.

This is an asset that is not only technological but also cultural, which well reflects the vision of founder Giovanni Battista Pirelli: 'This industry, is technically among the most complex and among the least known and studied. It is full of curious details, for which there is no guide outside of the experience and recipes that the few technicians devoted to it gradually put together for their own use.' (1881).

The showcasing of this precious heritage passes through the planning of exhibitions, publications, guided visits, conferences on the history of the business and its work, the management of the company libraries in Bicocca and Bollate, and, in the educational field, the creative and training paths aimed at schools and institutes of various orders and levels, as well as constant work on reconditioning, restoring, cataloguing and digitising the documents produced by the company during its activities.

The Foundation also invests constantly in the expansion of projects and instruments of cultural dissemination in the digital sphere. The *fondazionepirelli.org* website allows the remote use of the Historical Archive online, access to virtual tours such as *Fondazione Pirelli Experience*, which enables the spaces of the Fondazione Pirelli to be explored, interaction with a chatbot, software endowed with artificial intelligence, podcasts to be listened to and *Stories from the World of Pirelli* to be read. Furthermore, exhibitions, publications and studies on the archive and the libraries are available through hubs connected to the Foundation's website.

The Pirelli corporate culture has always been characterised by a strong drive towards innovation in all the fields of knowledge, and the publicising of this is one of the Foundation's key objectives, a constant commitment in combining memory and future.

1872

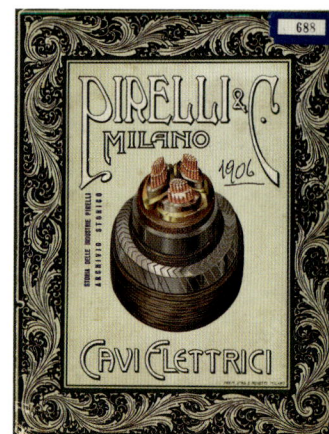

1875   **1877**   **1886**

1872 On 28 January the limited partnership G.B. Pirelli & C. is established in Milan by twenty-three-year-old engineer Giovanni Battista Pirelli to manufacture elastic rubber items. On 29 March the land for construction of the factory is purchased in the zone called 'dei Corpi Santi' outside Porta Nuova.

1873 In June the factory in Via Ponte Seveso begins operating. The plant employs forty workers in the production of technical rubber items, under the management of Antoine-Aimé Goulard. The first drive belts are manufactured.

1874 Giovanni Battista Pirelli takes up the role of production manager following Goulard's dismissal. Young Emilio Calcagni, son of the master builder who had directed the construction work for the plant, becomes manager of the technical items department. Rubber production is extended to 'various items for railways, ropes, valves, carpets, rubberised textiles'.

1875 The production of rubber erasers begins.

1877 François Casassa, an expert in the production of 'haberdashery items and fine articles for surgery', joins the company. The business name for the partnership changes to Giovanni Battista Pirelli, François Casassa & C.; it will return to being Pirelli & C. in 1883, with Casassa as technician manager until his death in 1886. Production is extended to include haberdashery and surgical articles, hot water bottles, toys, raincoats and balls for games.

1879 The production of electrical conductors and insulated telegraph wires is launched, in addition to the processing of gutta-percha.

1880 First splitting of the company into three departments: manufacture of technical items; consumer items; electrical wiring. Production of the first bath caps, gloves and rubber floors begins.

1883 The company's production is extended to elastic thread. At the opening of the season at La Scala, for the first time the theatre is illuminated electrically by 2450 incandescence lamps powered by Pirelli cables.

1886 Pirelli & C. is awarded an order for the manufacture and laying of twelve undersea telegraphic cables by the Telegraph Administration of the King's Government to connect the mainland with the minor islands.

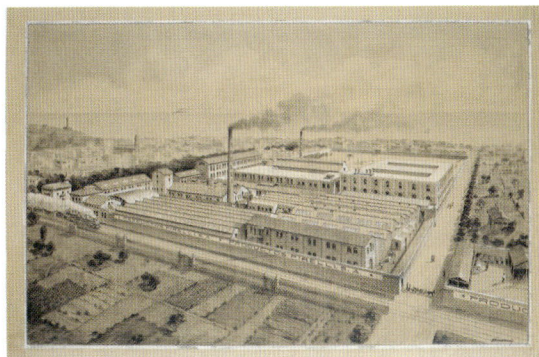

19 02

1889   1890   1902

To honour the contract, in La Spezia Pirelli lays the foundations of a factory entirely devoted to the production of undersea telegraphic cables, while at the English production sites in Sunderland work begins on the construction of a special cable-laying ship. Emanuele Jona, a graduate from the Politecnico di Torino, is recruited as head of the Electrical Office and the Technical Office for Undersea Cables and Electrical Applications, created to deal with the increasing complexity of the types of conductors manufactured.

1887 The cable-laying ship *Città di Milano* is launched. Using the English ship *Seine*, Pirelli also lays the Massaua-Assab-Perim telegraphic cable in the Red Sea. Engineer Leopoldo Emanueli joins the company and will specialise in the field of underground cables.

1888 Once the laying of the Italy-minor islands telegraphic cables is completed, Pirelli is awarded a new contract by the Spanish government for the laying under sea of a cable between Jávea, on the Iberian mainland, and Ibiza.

1889 • The production of rubber soles and heels begins.

1890 • A further plot of 6,428 square metres beyond the Sevesetto is added to the plant in Via Ponte Seveso: this is the so-called area of 'La

Brusada', where the manufacture begins of 'pneumatiche' [tyres] for velocipedes, destined to replace the solid rubber rings used until that time. Among the first models, the Stella and the Tipo Milano from 1894, followed in 1901 by the Ercole, specially devised for automobiles, and in 1904 by the Semelle with leather tread.

1894 Pirelli & C. takes over the insolvent Società per la fabbricazione degli oggetti in caucciù, guttaperca e affini di Narni [Company for the manufacture of rubber, gutta-percha objects and similar in Narni], converting it to manufacture linoleum and naming it Società del linoleum, established in 1898.

1895 The production of underground cables for the distribution of electric lighting in the major inhabited centres is launched: among the first international orders are cables to be used for lighting in Berlin.

1901 Production of tyres for cars with the patent for Ercole begins. Some patents concerning the main weak points of the first tyres also date back to this period: the attachment to the rim, the perforability and lacerability of the tyre itself, the problem of skidding.

1902 • The first foreign factory of the group, to be used to produce electrical conductors and various rubber items, is built in Spain, in Vilanova i la Geltrú, near Barcelona.

1904

1907   **1913**   **1916**

1904 The shareholders' meeting appoints two managers in addition to the founder: his two sons Piero and Alberto, who will take up the position from 1 January 1905.

1906 Since it is impossible to further expand the plant in Milan city, in August a plot of 115 hectares in the locality of Bicocca, between the municipalities of Niguarda and Greco Milanese, is acquired from Count Sormani's family. The work on the construction of the new factory begins in 1907. Pirelli participates in the Universal Exposition in Milan.

1907 This is the year of the Peking-Paris, considered the first international racing competition in the history of the automobile. Prince Scipione Borghese wins in an Itala fitted with Pirelli tyres.

1908 The 'P lunga' [Long P] is created; it is still the group's logotype today.

1909 The affiliate Pirelli Ltd is founded in London, with the aim of handling the sale of all the group's products throughout the British Empire. In the first Giro d'Italia cycle race, thirty riders out of fifty who finish have Pirelli & C. tyres fitted. The plant in Bicocca gradually begins operating. The production of rubberised fabrics for aircraft is developed.

1910 The daily newspaper *Il Mattino*, with the title 'Another Victory for the Pirelli Company in Milan', gives the news that 'The Pirelli company of Milan, which has already made so many appearances in all the sporting competitions, has been appointed exclusive supplier to the Royal House of Her Majesty the Queen Mother, to the House of His Royal Highness the Duke of Aosta and to the House of His Royal Highness the Count of Turin. In addition, all military commands adopt Pirelli tyres for their cycling battalions, as do all the trucks of the King's Army'.

1911 Pirelli participates in the establishing of the Compañía Ítalo-Argentina de Electricidad.

1912 During the Dodecanese War the ship *Città di Milano* cuts seven undersea cables of the Ottoman Empire in the Aegean Sea.

1913 The Société Française Pirelli is established in Paris, with commercial aims and also to participate in major sporting events: the first Grand Prix de France is won by Georges Boillot in a Peugeot with Pirelli tyres. In England, from the association with General Electric, Pirelli General Cable Work Ltd is established, with a factory in Southampton.

1915 From the very beginning of the war there are many military orders: the production of tyres for aircraft is launched. The labour force at the company is predominantly female.

Museo della Bicocca - La Sala della Gomma Elastica

19 22

1920   **1922**

1916 A factory is built in Vercurago, near Lecco, devoted to the production of chemical ingredients for the processing of rubber. The plant in La Spezia suffers huge damage due to the destruction of a number of wagons of the Italian Royal Navy loaded with explosive materials that were standing in the proximity.

1917 The first non-European affiliate is Pirelli S.A. Platense, which succeeds the Buenos Aires branch and which from 1920 will directly undertake the construction of electrical conductors, gradually extending production to other rubber items. In Spain tyres for cars begin to be built. For the enlargement of the Bicocca plant another plot of ground is acquired that includes the fifteenth-century Villa Bicocca degli Arcimboldi.

1919 The ship *Città di Milano* is wrecked off Filicudi, with twenty-six victims including head electrician engineer Emanuele Jona. He is succeeded by Luigi Emanueli, while the ship is replaced by a German cable-laying ship received as a war debt, which is rechristened *Città di Milano II*. In this same year two plantations of rubber trees are acquired in Java and Singapore.

1920 The Compagnie Internationale Pirelli is established in Brussels, bringing together all the group's foreign companies in its portfolio. In Milan the Società Italiana Pirelli is created, with all the national industrial and commercial organisations being transferred to it. The partnership Pirelli & C., which controls both new holding companies, retains the functions of a financial corporation. From a convention between Pirelli & C. and the Istituto autonomo case popolari [Autonomous Institute for Social Housing], the Borgo Pirelli is created. A part of the dwellings will be allocated to employees of the company.

1921 Serious industrial crises all over the world: at Pirelli the number of workers drops from 9520 to 4580; investments in the renovation of installations and the introduction of radical innovations in the production of telecommunications cables increase from 25 to 48 million lire, with the development of the quaded structure. Pirelli promotes the establishment of the Società Italiana Reti Telefoniche Interurbane, SIRTI.

1922 The partnership limited by shares Pirelli & C. is quoted on the Milan Stock Exchange. There are major celebrations to mark the fiftieth anniversary of the company; among the initiatives: the inauguration of the Museum of Rubber of Pirelli Industries in the Sala del Camino in the Bicocca degli Arcimboldi. The Cord tyre is launched for cars, in which the 'square' woven fabric is replaced with 'cord' without weaving.

19
24

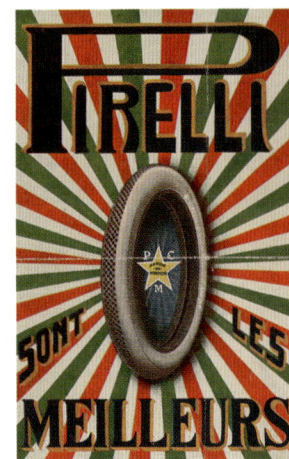

1925 **1927** **1930**

1924 The first fluid oil-filled cable devised by Luigi Emanueli for the transportation of energy is successfully tested in the electrical substation of Brugherio: 1,000,000 volts is surpassed with this technology. Neumáticos Nacional Pirelli, with factory in Manresa, is founded in Spain. The Cord Superflex low-pressure tyre, more comfortable and flexible, is placed on the market.

1925 5,150 kilometres of transatlantic undersea telegraphic cable are laid for Italcable: the line links Italy directly with the two Americas. Gastone Brilli Peri wins the Italian Grand Prix in Monza in an Alfa Romeo with Pirelli tyres and wins the World Championship.

1926 132,000-volt fluid oil-filled cables are installed between New York and Chicago: the first in the world at such a voltage. The Società Italiana Pirelli is quoted on the Milan Stock Exchange.

1927 Stella Bianca, a tyre with reinforced tread using trapezoidal block to avoid rips at high speed, is placed on sale: it will be the most popular between the 1930s and 1940s. On 20 June King Vittorio Emanuele III visits the factory in Bicocca: photographer and director Luca Comerio makes a film to commemorate this.

1928 In Burton-on-Trent Pirelli Ltd builds a factory to manufacture tyres for vehicles and rubber footwear in Great Britain, thus avoiding the 33 per cent customs charge on imported rubber products that the UK government had imposed from 1927.

1929 With the issue of a 4,000,000 dollar bond loan, Pirelli joins the official listing of the New York Stock Exchange. Its industrial presence is expanded in Brazil, with a factory making insulated conductors and electrical and telecommunications cables. On 23 July, Prince of Wales Edward Windsor visits the new English tyre factory in Burton-on-Trent.

1930 Industrial plant in France: with the business name Industrie du Caoutchouc Souple, Pirelli manufactures tyres for vehicles, pipes and various other products.

1931 Launch, with excellent results, of a new type of giant tyre, the Sigillo Verde.

1932 Giovanni Battista Pirelli passes away on 20 October. Piero becomes president, Alberto vice president, but both retain the position of managing directors.

1941

1933

1933 — Agreement with Dunlop and United States Rubber for the joint exploitation of a number of patents for the processing of latex. The production of foam rubber begins. In the Mille Miglia first, second and third places are won by Alfa Romeo drivers using Pirelli tyres. At the Italian Grand Prix in Monza the winner is also an Alfa-Pirelli, and Pirelli also wins the International Motorcycle Trophy.

1935 — From an idea by Giuseppe Vigorelli, sales director for tyres for Lombardy and a passionate cyclist, the velodrome named after him is opened in Milan. A new procedure for the manufacture of carbon black specially adapted for use in the rubber industry is patented.

1936 — The 'grand ring', the first Pirelli 230,000-volt fluid oil-filled cable line in the world, begins operating around Paris. The Belgian SACIC, producers of various rubber items, is taken over and reorganised.

1937 — On 8 October the Institute for the Study of Synthetic Rubber is established by the Institute for Industrial Reconstruction (IRI) and the Società Italiana Pirelli. The laboratories are run by Giulio Natta. In the field of textile materials, the replacement of cotton with rayon is also studied.

1938 — In Basel in Switzerland, Pirelli Holding S.A. is established, with president and managing director Alberto Pirelli and vice president the Swiss banker Alfred Sarasin; the new company takes over the Belgian Compagnie Internationale Pirelli in the financial control of the foreign group. The Società tessili artificiali [Artificial Textile Company] is established, with a factory in Pizzighettone, for the progressive replacement of cotton with rayon in the production of tyres. Gino Bartali wins the Tour de France on a Legnano bicycle with Pirelli tyres.

1939 — Two plants are built, in Ferrara and Terni, in a partnership with IRI (the company is SAIGS), to produce synthetic rubber, as in the pilot plant in Bicocca managed by Giulio Natta. In Brazil, production in the factory in Capuava is extended to include tyres. At the height of the Civil War in Spain, the factory in Vilanova i la Geltrú is completely destroyed by the Republican occupying forces.

1941 — The holding company in Basel makes formal commitments with British and US governments in order that the foreign companies of the group are not the object of hostile measures. The Swiss banker Albert Nussbaumer is named president of the holding.

1942

1944 **1947** **1948** **1949**

1942 In accordance with the provisions of the new Civil Code, the Società Italiana Pirelli takes the name Pirelli spa.

1943 On 8 September, the cable-laying ship *Città di Milano II* is sunk by its crew to prevent it from being captured by the Germans. The machinery in the process of being installed at the synthetic rubber plant is moved to Germany by the Wehrmacht. The factory in Via Ponte Seveso in Milan is bombed.

1944 The technical and industrial management of all the factories of the group is entrusted to engineer Luigi Emanueli.

1945 By order of the Allied Military Government, Pirelli, along with all the other major businesses in Northern Italy, is made subject to the commissariat system: the company's general manager Cesare Merzagora is named commissioner and engineer Luigi Rossari of the Central Cable Department deputy commissioner. Merzagora's role proves decisive in representing the interests of the industry in the delicate phase of recovery. In 1946 Merzagora will also be appointed board member of IRI and subsequently minister and then senator under the De Gasperi government.

1946 Piero and Alberto Pirelli return to running the company. Albert Nussbaumer is confirmed as head of the holding, alongside a general manager in the person of Vittorio Rostagno. The Motor scooter tyre for this new class of vehicles is presented at the International Exposition of Cycles and Motorcycles. The Fondazione Piero e Alberto Pirelli is established with the aim of ensuring the economic improvement of workers.

1947 The introduction of many new working processes and technological modernisation take production, in quantity terms, back to average pre-war levels. Pirelli, FIAT, Edison and Montecatini found the CISE (Information Centre for Studies and Experiences) and earmark sizeable sums to finance its research. In Milan the activities of the Pirelli Cultural Centre begin. Piero and Giovanni Pirelli become active members of the Piccolo Teatro in Milan.

1948 The publication of *Pirelli. Rivista d'informazione e tecnica* begins; founded by Giuseppe Luraghi, its editor-in-chief is Leonardo Sinisgalli, who is also responsible for all the company's advertising campaigns.

1949 Success of the Pirelli Motor scooter, the small tyre capable of withstanding the exceptional wear and tear due to the high rotation speed of the mini-wheels. Franco Nacci rides

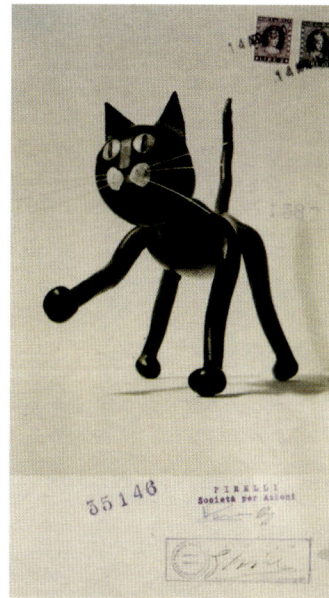

1951

1954

19 56

from Palermo to the Arctic Circle and back in a Fiat 500C with Pirelli tyres with daily stages of 400 kilometres. The first edition begins of the Gran Premio Pirelli, a cycling championship—conceived by Alfred Binda—devoted to up-and-coming young cyclists. The GPP will take place annually until 1957.

1950 Coaxial cables for the new intercity telephone network and for television communication are commissioned by the Italian Post Office Ministry; new installations are activated for the application of synthetic resins as an insulating material in the manufacture of electrical conductors. Publication of *Fatti e Notizie*, the house organ for all the Italian workers of the group begins.

1951 On conclusion of the studies begun in 1949, a new type of tyre for motorcars is patented, characterised by a belt of radial fabric between the carcass and the tread; placed on the market in 1953 with the name Cinturato, it marks the debut of Pirelli's radial technology. In the same year the production of tyres in a joint venture with United States Rubber begins in Argentina.

1953 A new type of cable insulated with polyethylene for the transatlantic connection between North Africa and Brazil is supplied by Pirelli. The production of cables begins in Canada. Pirelli tyres win eight Formula 1 Grand Prix

with Ferrari and Maserati: Alberto Ascari is World Champion for the second time

1954 Pirelli Holding in Basel changes its business name to Société Internationale Pirelli without changing its statutory aims. The Azienda Meccanica is established in Milan, manufacturing machinery both for the group and for export, and a rubber plantation is acquired in Brazil, after the definitive sale of those in Indonesia. The Scimmietta Zizì, a foam rubber toy monkey designed, together with the Gatto Meo cat, by Bruno Munari for Pigomma, wins the design prize at the first edition of the Compasso d'Oro.

1955 The activities of the old undersea cable factory in La Spezia cease: production moves to the new one in Arco Felice, in Campania. In collaboration with the US firm Anaconda, Conductores Eléctricos SA is established in Mexico and sells its own products under the name of Anaconda Pirelli.

1956 Piero Pirelli passes away on 7 August. Alberto takes on the role of president of the company, leaving that of managing director; he is supported by his son Leopoldo and by engineer Luigi Emanueli as vice presidents. Pirelli suspends the production of racing tyres, while the construction begins of the skyscraper in Piazza Duca d'Aosta in Milan.

19 58

1960   1961   1962

1958 The first particle accelerator to be used in Italy begins operation at the cable research laboratory. The Istituto Piero Pirelli, a training centre for the company's future employees, is inaugurated in Milan Bicocca.

1959 Pirelli France is established, while the first plant for the production of metal cord for tyres begins operating in Figline Valdarno. The plastic jerrycan for transporting liquid designed by Roberto Menghi for the Azienda Monza, a company in the Pirelli group, is exhibited at the MoMA in New York.

1960 The new business complex of the group, the Centro Pirelli, is inaugurated in Milan in the skyscraper designed by Gio Ponti. In Greece Pirelli Hellas is opened, with a factory in Patrasso. In Turkey Türk Pirelli Laştikleri is established, with its production centre in İzmit.

1961 The abandonment of work in the various articles sector begins due to the limited technical content. In the Pirelli pavilion at the International Exposition of work in Turin the large mosaic *La ricerca scientifica* is displayed, realised from a design by painter Renato Guttuso. Successful sales of the N+R tyre (nylon + rayon). The 120-channel telephone cable between Sicily and Sardinia is laid, the first in the world equipped to carry 120 simultaneous telephone communications.

1962 The monthly magazine *Vado e torno*, dedicated to the road haulage world and produced by the Pirelli publicity office, comes out in the newspaper kiosks. The new Sempione - Spalla di Sicurezza tyre is marketed (with rounded tread edge, without a sharp edge, so as to broaden the surface that adheres to the ground).

1963 Pirelli acquires Veith-Gummiwerke in Germany, which changes its name to Veith Pirelli AG. Activities begin at the plant in Settimo Torinese, firstly for the production of inner tubes and then for the original Cinturato tyres, for motorbike tyres in Villafranca Tirrena and for plastic cables in Giovinazzo.

1964 Pirelli UK Tyres Ltd publishes the first Calendar, an international icon and a tribute to photography and to great photographers such as Annie Leibovitz, who also designs the 2000 and 2016 editions. Again in the UK, production of high-voltage cables doubles with the coming into operation of the new factory in Eastleigh.

1965 Alberto Pirelli, who retires at the age of eighty-three, is given the role of honorary president. He is succeeded by his son Leopoldo in the position of executive president. Undersea cable for the transmission of direct current energy at 220kV between Sardinia, Corsica and the Continent is laid; the

il Cinturato ha vinto
i rally
più importanti
del mondo

CINTURATO
CN54
PIRELLI

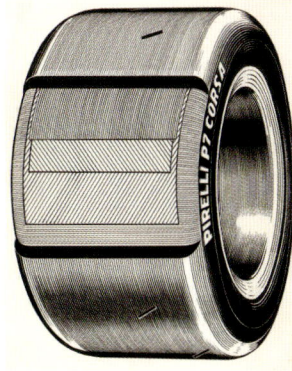

19 76

1968

1972

1974

Corsica-Continent line is 100 kilometres long and has a depth of over 400 metres: it is the first of its kind in the world.

1967 A five-year agreement of scientific collaboration is signed between Pirelli spa and the Committee for Science and Technology of the Council of Ministers of the USSR.

1968 In Carlisle, in the United Kingdom, production begins at a factory solely for radial tyres; the factory in Argentina is enlarged to deal with the vast development of motor transport and increasing international competition.

1969 The Italian 'hot autumn': the prolonged trade union unrest and the soaring increases in labour costs mean that the balance sheet of Pirelli spa closes with a loss and no dividends are distributed. A new test track for tyres is inaugurated in Vizzola Ticino. Seven 138,000-volt undersea cables are laid between Long Island and Connecticut in the USA: the longest and most important underwater connection in the world.

1971 Alberto Pirelli passes away on 19 October. With an agreement between Dunlop and Pirelli the industrial activities of the two groups are integrated, and each has shares in the other; the responsibility for the

Dunlop-Pirelli Union is entrusted to a joint committee, while Pirelli spa becomes a financial corporation and its activities are concentrated in Industrie Pirelli spa, with 49 per cent control by Dunlop.

1972 The Cinturato with a metal belt is created. The Fiat 124 Spider-Pirelli wins the first European Rally title. High oil prices and the crisis of the car industry also have heavy repercussions in the rubber sector. The materials contained in the Pirelli Archive are declared of historical interest by the Government Archive and Bibliographical Department.

1973 Giovanni Pirelli dies on 3 April following a road accident in which his brother Leopoldo is also seriously injured.

1974 Optic fibres are studies in the laboratories of Bicocca to improve the transmission of telephone cables. The P7, which came about as a competition tyre for the Lancia Stratos thanks to the insight of engineer Mario Mezzanotte, is the first super low-profile high-performance tyre. The Pirelli Motovelo group is established for the study and production of motorbike tyres.

1976 Four new factories for the production of cables and tyres are inaugurated in Brazil.

19 77

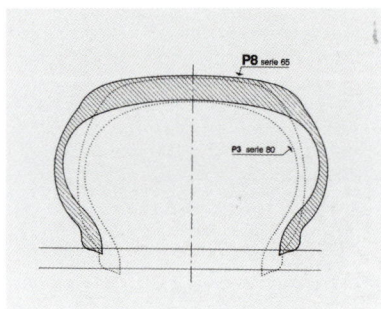

1980   **1983**   **1985**

1977 The first experimental connection with optic fibre telephone cable is set up, one kilometre long, for CSELT, the studies centre of STET; a 1,100,000-volt system is installed for ENEL in Suvereto, an experimental station. The Pirelli Cables Australia factory is inaugurated in Sydney.

1978 The Pirelli Tower is sold to the Lombardy Regional Government, which will move there in 1982. Significant quantities of machinery for rubber tyres and components are supplied to Soviet factories, while a memorandum of understanding is signed with Algeria for the construction of a tyre factory.

1980 The P8 is perfected, a radial tyre for cars characterised by low resistance to rolling, and consequent reduced fuel consumption. In the cable sector, Pirelli acquires the French company Treficable and a majority share in the Sicable company of the Ivory Coast.

1981 The first fibre-optic telephone line on the national network is installed between Padua and Mestre. Meanwhile, the Dunlop-Pirelli Union is dissolved. Equipping the English constructor Toleman with its radial P7s, Pirelli returns to Formula 1 after twenty-five years of absence: this commitment will last until 1991 with the supply of tyres to teams such as Brabham, Lotus and Benetton.

1982 Through the company Fibre Ottiche Sud, in a joint venture with SIRTI, Pirelli launches the Italian production of optic fibres in Battipaglia, immediately followed by many other foreign subsidiaries. With the joint participation of Pirelli spa and Société Internationale Pirelli, Pirelli Société Générale is established in Basel with the task of coordinating the management of all the affiliates of the group on a worldwide basis.

1983 Pirelli is the first to create a radial for motorcycles: the MP7, devised for the new generations of bikes, able to exceed 240 kilometres per hour.

1984 The second generation of super low-profiles: P600 and P700.

1985 To equip the Lancia Delta S4 rally car, Pirelli designs the P Zero Corsa super-tyre. In Turkey the company Celikord is established to produce metal cord.

1986 The acquisitions continue: the German Metzeler in motorbike tyres, the French Filergie in cables and Standard Telephone Cable in underground cables for telecommunications. The Bicocca Project is launched for the conversion of the area where the Pirelli plant stands.

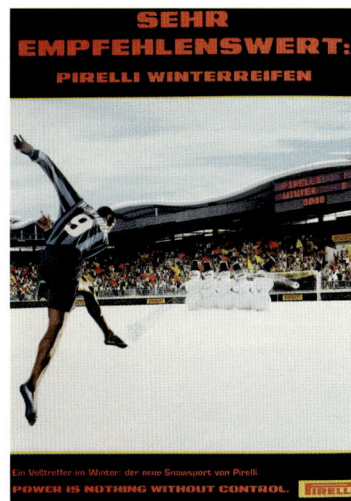

19 95

1994   **1995**

1987   The P Zero, the road version of the P Zero Corsa, is created.

1988   Through the acquisition of the US Armstrong Tires, the tyre sector focuses on establishing itself industrially in North America.

1989   All the group's stakes in the tyre sector are grouped together in the new company Pirelli Tyre Holding, quoted on the Amsterdam Stock Exchange.

1990   Pirelli Venezuela is formed. In September, Pirelli presents a proposal to Continental AG in Hanover to unify the respective tyre activities. Negotiations are protracted for over a year, until the eventual decision by Pirelli to withdraw the proposal.

1992   After a demanding restructuring programme also involving the transfer of non-strategic activities in the diversified products sector, under the guidance of Marco Tronchetti Provera the group begins and consolidates an international relaunch phase, with new technologies, new products and above all an opening up towards emerging markets such as the Far East and Africa.

1994   Pirelli launches the global communication campaign *Power is nothing without control*, destined to enter the history of advertising. The image of Olympic sprinter Carl Lewis on the starting blocks in red spike heels is iconic.

1995   In the tyre sector we witness the progressive worldwide diffusion of the Pirelli lines P Zero, ultra-low profile destined for the most prestigious top-of-the-range models, and P6000, the mass-consumption low-profile. A three-year agreement is signed with BellSouth on the basis of which Pirelli will supply its new optic amplifiers and wave multipliers. Corecom, a non-profit consortium having as its object 'research activity, on behalf of partners, in the photonics sector' is established. Pirelli and FC Internazionale sign a partnership agreement that takes the 'long P' brand onto the shirts of the Milanese football team. In 1997 a Brazilian striker named Luís Nazário de Lima, Ronaldo, arrives at Inter, and is chosen as the face of the 1998 tyre campaign devised by Young & Rubicam and realised by photographer Ken Griffiths. The image of the footballer in the position of the statue of Christ the Redeemer in Rio de Janeiro goes viral.

1996

Pirelli HangarBicocca

1996

2004

1996 Marco Tronchetti Provera succeeds Leopoldo Pirelli as president of Pirelli spa. Pirelli becomes a shareholder of Internazionale FC: the 'long P' logo appears on the shirts of the *nerazzurri*. The company participates in the formation of the Fondazione Pier Lombardo and the Teatro Franco Parenti.

1997 A new plant for the manufacture of optic fibres is inaugurated in Sorocaba, in Brazil: it is the largest in South America. In Bukit Indah, in Malaysia, a new factory of optic cables for telecommunications begins operating. The cables and systems sector strengthens its supremacy in energy with the acquisitions of Siemens' activities in nine countries. The Scorpion tyre is launched on the market.

1999 The acquisitions of Siemens' activities continue with Metal Manufacturers Ltd in Australia and Draka Holding in Holland and Finland. The acquisition is formalised of 47 per cent of the capital of the Egyptian Alexandria Tyre Co. The automated tyre production system MIRS™ is presented in Bicocca.

2000 The activities of BICC General in Europe, Asia and Africa also become part of the group, while underground optic systems are sold to Cisco and optical components to Corning.

2001 Pirelli invests part of the liquidity deriving from this operation into the entry—through Olimpia spa, the special-purpose vehicle established with Benetton, Banca Intesa and Unicredito—in the share capital of Telecom Italia, thus realising an asset swap targeting a strategic reinforcement. The launch takes place of EUFORI@: the first tyre created with the MIRS™ system and with new Run Flat technology.

2002 At the Milan Bicocca pilot plant, the futuristic CCM-Continuous Compound Mixing begins operations. At the same time Pirelli Labs, the centre of excellence for the development of new technologies in the fields of the photonics, optic fibres and the sciences of materials, are created in Milan. Pirelli Real Estate is quoted on the stock exchange.

2003 The process of streamlining the group's structure is completed with the establishing of Pirelli & C. spa.

2004 New projects in the field of broadband and photonics (Pirelli Broadband Solutions) and actions associated with the environment and renewable energy sources (Pirelli Ambiente Holding) also become part of the core business of the group. Pirelli becomes founding partner of HangarBicocca—one of the largest contemporary art spaces in

2011

2006

2008

2011

Europe. Today it is managed and financed entirely by Pirelli and has been renamed Pirelli HangarBicocca.

2005 The group sells its energy and telecommunications cables and systems businesses to Goldman Sachs. Pirelli inaugurates the first plant for the production of tyres in China, in the province of Shandong, in what will become the group's production pole in that country.

2006 In Slatina Pirelli opens its first plant for the production of tyres in Romania. At Pirelli HangarBicocca the solo exhibition by Marina Abramović is inaugurated.

2007 On 23 January Leopoldo Pirelli passes away in Portofino. During the year the company reinforces its presence in China, where, in addition to producing tyres for trucks, the production of tyres for cars is begun, and shares in Telecom Italia are sold.

2008 The expansion of the group's production continues. Pirelli and Russian Technology sign an agreement to give rise to a joint venture for the production of tyres in Russia. The Fondazione Pirelli is officially inaugurated in the Bicocca area in Milan to showcase the company's historical archive and develop its enterprise culture. The Nuovo Cinturato is launched, a tyre with low resistance to rolling.

2010 Pirelli refocuses on its core business of tyres, becoming a 'pure tyre company' after the sale of Pirelli Broadband Solutions and the separation of the real estate activities of Pirelli Real Estate from the group. The 2010 balance sheet, illustrated with the contribution of the NABA of Milan, becomes the first of a series of Annual Reports combining financial reporting with the narration of the values, worlds and history of the company, with contributions by artists, writers and intellectuals.

2011 Pirelli returns to Formula 1 as the exclusive supplier of all the teams. A first three-year agreement 2011–2013 is confirmed for the following three-year period and then subsequently extended. Shares in Pirelli & C. Ambiente spa and Pirelli & C. Eco Technology spa are sold. On 19 March, president of the Italian Republic Giorgio Napolitano visits the new industrial pole of Settimo Torinese. The central volume of the establishment devoted to Services, the so-called 'Spina', is designed by architect Renzo Piano.

2011– 2013 Pirelli and Russian Technologies announce the launch of two new production lines in the Russian factories of Voronež and Kirov.

2012

2015

2017

2012   A new factory is inaugurated in Silao, Mexico, the production centre of the group on the NAFTA market. In the same year the joint venture is announced between Pirelli and the Indonesian group Astra Otopart that will lead to the construction of a motorbike tyre plant in Southeast Asia. The Cinturato P7 Blue is created, a tyre characterised by low resistance to rolling, among the first to gain top marks for energy efficiency and safety. The show *Settimo, la fabbrica e il lavoro* [Settimo, the Factory and Work] is staged at the Piccolo Teatro in Milan, directed by Serena Sinigaglia, inspired by the testimonies of over thirty employees of the Pirelli plant in Settimo Torinese.

2014   Pirelli sells its steel cord activities to Bekaert, group leader in technologies of transformation and coating of steel cables.

2015   The historical shareholder Camfin, ChemChina and Lti, through Marco Polo Industrial, launch a takeover bid for Pirelli with a view to the delisting and reorganisation of the company. Pirelli participates in the Universal Exposition in Milan, the sponsor, among other things, of the symbolic *Tree of Life*.

2016   In April the opening is announced of a second factory inside the Puerto Interior industrial pole in Silao, in Mexico. The Pirelli Annual Report 2013 *Spinning the Wheel* is awarded the platinum medal in the edition of the competition organised by *Graphis*, a magazine that gathers together the best production in design at world level.

2017   In March, Pirelli brings to fruition, through the sale of the Industrial division, the path focusing on the production of consumer tyres. Pirelli returns to the stock exchange on 4 October transformed into a 'Pure Consumer Tyre company' focusing on tyres for cars, motorbikes and cycles, particularly in the 'High Value' segment at high technological level. In the month of September, in the packaging department of the industrial pole of Settimo Torinese, the Italian Chamber Orchestra conducted by maestro Salvatore Accardo performs *Il Canto della fabbrica*, a concert inspired by the sounds and rhythms of factory 4.0 before an audience of a thousand people, including the workers at the factory. Pirelli sponsors the Emirates New Zealand team, winners of the 35th America's Cup. The exhibition on Lucio Fontana is inaugurated at the Pirelli HangarBicocca.

PIRELLI 150 YEARS

20 22

2018 ●────────────────────────────────● **2022**

2018 ● The partnership with Luna Rossa Prada is agreed, with a view to the America's Cup 2021.

2019 Ninety years after the visit of the Prince of Wales to Burton-on-Trent, Prince Charles visits the English plant in Carlisle on the occasion of its fiftieth anniversary. At the Geneva Motor Show a new tyre is presented with the brand Elect, developed by Pirelli in collaboration with the main car companies to respond to the specific technological demand for electric and hybrid plug-in vehicles.

2020 In February, Pirelli receives EST Leader recognition from the FTSE4Good Index Series for its commitment in environmental, social and governance issues, positioning itself top in the Tyres and Consumer Goods sector with a rating of 4.6 points out of the maximum achievable total of 5. Together with the 4Good Index, Pirelli is also awarded gold within the sphere of the Sustainability Yearbook 2020 published by S&P Global, which has considered the sustainability profile of over 4,700 companies.

2021 Pirelli is the first company to produce tyres certified FSC: the P Zero model, which uses natural rubber and rayon certified FSC, is launched for the first time on the BMW X5 Plug-in Hybrid. Pirelli and the BMW Group also present a project associated with the sustainable natural rubber supply chain, in collaboration with BirdLife International, with the aim of contributing to the safeguarding of the ecosystem of the Indonesian forest of Hutan Harapan, on the island of Sumatra, and the life of the communities and animal species at risk of extinction that live there. Today the Pirelli group is among the main producers of high-end and performance tyres. The company has always been strongly committed to research and development, an area in which it invests around 6 per cent of proceeds from high-end sales annually, among the highest levels in the sector; this enables the company to constantly expand innovative and highly technological systems for the production of its tyres. In pursuing its objectives, Pirelli operates according to a sustainable management model inspired by the highest standards of responsibility to be recognised at international level. After the victory of the New Zealand team in the America's Cup 2021, the participation of Luna Rossa in the 2024 edition is announced.

2022 ● Pirelli celebrates the 150th anniversary of its Foundation.

AUTHORS' BIOGRAPHIES

Salvatore Accardo, violinist and orchestra conductor, made his public debut aged thirteen playing Paganini's *Capricci*; at fifteen he won the Geneva International Music Competition and then the 'Paganini Prize' International Violin Competition in Genoa.
His vast repertoire ranges from Baroque to contemporary music. Sciarrino, Donatoni, Piston, Piazzolla, Xenakis and Colasanti have all dedicated their works to him. He plays all over the world with leading orchestras and the most important conductors on the international scene, performing as a soloist and as an orchestra conductor. In 1986, together with Bruno Giuranna, Rocco Filippini and Franco Petracchi, he created the master courses at the Accademia Walter Stauffer in Cremona; in 1992 he founded the Quartetto Accardo; in 1996 he revived the Italian Chamber Orchestra, comprising the best students and former students of the Accademia Walter Stauffer, with which he engages in intense concert and recording activities. He teaches at the Accademia Walter Stauffer in Cremona and the Accademia Musicale Chigiana in Siena. He has made countless recordings for various labels. He has received many awards and honours and in 1982 president of the Italian Republic Sandro Pertini named him a Cavaliere di Gran Croce, the highest honour of the Italian Republic.
He plays a Guarneri del Gesù "Hart" violin from 1730.

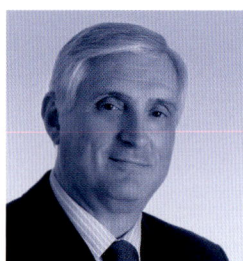

Enrico Albizzati
After gaining his diploma as a chemical expert, in 1967 he was recruited by the Milan Research Centre of Montedison, part of the group founded by Nobel prizewinner Giulio Natta. In 1972 he graduated in Biological Sciences. In 1995 he was appointed director of Basic Research at Montell Polyolefins; in 1996 he joined Pirelli Cavi e Sistemi as Research and Development manager and in 1999 moved to Pirelli Pneumatici as director of Research into Advanced Materials. In the two thousands he fulfilled important roles within the Pirelli group, including that of CEO of Pirelli Labs, and in scientific institutions such as the CNR and CORIMAV. He has published over 70 articles in international magazines and is the author of 197 initial patent applications in the fields of chemicals, cables and tyres, which have given rise to 1895 international patents. In 2015 he was awarded an honorary degree in Materials Sciences.

Bruno Arpaia was born in Ottaviano (Naples) in 1957 and lives in Milan. Graduated in Political Sciences, he is a journalist (he works with *la Repubblica*), editorial consultant and expert on and translator of Hispanic literatures. His novels, translated into eight languages and winners of numerous awards, include: *I forestieri*, 1990; *Il futuro in punta di piedi*, 1994; *Tempo perso*, 1997; *L'angelo della storia*, 2001; *Il passato davanti a noi*, 2006; *L'energia del vuoto*, 2011; *Prima della battaglia*, 2014. *Qualcosa, là fuori*, from 2016, takes place in an international setting modified by climate change. His most recent novel, *Il fantasma dei fatti*, appeared in 2020.
He is also the author of a book-conversation with Luis Sepúlveda entitled *Raccontare, resistere*, 2002, as well as of a book with Javier Cercas entitled *L'avventura di scrivere romanzi*, 2013. In 2007 he published an essay entitled *Per una sinistra reazionaria*, and in 2013, together with Pietro Greco, *La cultura si mangia!*, on the importance of cultural investments for economic development. In 2021 *Luis Sepúlveda. Il ribelle, il sognatore* appeared.

Maurizio Boiocchi, who gained his diploma in 1969 as an industrial mechanical expert at the Istituto Giorgi in Milan, the following year joined Technical Tyres Department at the Pirelli group, to then move on, in 1984, to the Product Department, where his career quickly progressed till he became head of Vehicles. Since the early two thousands he has been in the top management of the group in the Product and Research and Development sector. In 2014 he was awarded an honorary degree in Mechanical Engineering from the Milan Politecnico. Since 2018 he has been executive vice president & strategic advisor Technology and Innovation of Pirelli.

Antonio Calabrò
A journalist and writer, he is senior vice president Institutional Affairs and Culture of Pirelli and director of Fondazione Pirelli. President of Museimpresa and the Fondazione Assolombarda, he is vice president of the Unione Industriali of Turin and president of the Advisory Board of UniCredit Lombardy and board member of various institutions and foundations (Nomisma, Touring Club, Orchestra Verdi, LIUC University and so forth). He teaches at the Università Cattolica of Milan. He has worked at *L'Ora*, *Il Mondo* and *la Repubblica*, has been editorial director of the Il Sole 24 Ore group and has directed the ApCom agency and *La lettera finanziaria*. Among his most recent books: *Oltre la fragilità*, *L'impresa riformista*, *La morale del tornio* and *Orgoglio industriale*.

Claudio Colombo was born in Monza in 1957. A professional journalist, he has worked at *Corriere d'Informazione*, at *La Gazzetta dello Sport* and, for over thirty years, at *Corriere della Sera*, where he has been Editor-in-Chief of Sport, Lombardy news coverage and special correspondent. He has also been director of *Il Cittadino di Monza e Brianza*.

Juan Carlos De Martin, full professor of I.T. Engineering and co-director of the Centro Nexa su Internet & Società, since 2018 has been the rector's delegate for culture and communication at the Turin Politecnico. Since 2011 he has been an associate at the Berkman Klein Center for Internet & Society of Harvard University and since 2012 he has been a member of the Scientific Council of the Istituto Treccani. Between 2014 and 2018 he was a member of the Commission of Studies of the Presidency of the Chamber of Deputies that drafted the Declaration of Rights on the Internet. He is co-curator of the Technology Biennale and a member of the steering committee of the Democracy Biennale. He is the author of the book *Università futura. Tra democrazia e bit* and of over one hundred and twenty international scientific publications.

Paola Dubini is professor of Management at the Bocconi University in Milan, researcher at the ASK centre at the same university and visiting professor at the Scuola IMT in Lucca. Her research and professional interests concern the conditions of sustainability of cultural, private, public and non-profit organisations and territorial policies for culture from the perspective of sustainable development. Among her most recent publications: *"Con la cultura non si mangia" Falso!*, 2018, and with Aura Bertoni and Alberto Monti 'Participatory Event Platforms in the Urban Context: The Importance of Stakeholders' Meaning of "Participation"', in *Cultural Initiatives for Sustainable Development*, edited by Paola Demartini, Lucia Marchegiani, Michela Marchiori and Giovanni Schiuma, 2021.

Ernesto Ferrero, Turinese, has worked in the publishing industry for a long time and directed the Salone del Libro book fair in Turin from 1998 to 2016. Among his books, the novels *N.*, Strega prizewinner 2000; *L'anno dell'Indiano*, 2001; *Disegnare il vento*, 2011, Selezione Campiello prize; *Storia di Quirina, di una talpa e di un orto di montagna*, 2014; *Amarcord bianconero*, 2018; *Francesco e il Sultano*, 2019, together with the essays *Barbablù. Gilles de Rais e il tramonto del Medioevo*, 2004, *Primo Levi. La vita, le opere*, 2007, and *Napoleone in venti parole*, 2021. In 2002 he published *Lezioni napoleoniche*, and in 2005 the book of memoirs at publishers Einaudi *I migliori anni della nostra vita*. Translator of Flaubert, Céline and Perec, he is honorary president of the Centro internazionale di studi Primo Levi in Turin.

Father **Enzo Fortunato** (Northampton 1966), friar minor conventual, journalist and writer.
From 1997 to 2021 he was director of the Press Office of the Sacred Convent of Assisi and *San Francesco* magazine. In 2003 he devised the solidarity-based TV event on Rai1 *Con il cuore, nel nome di Francesco*.
Since 2011 he has been co-presenter of the programme *TG1 Dialogo*. On Rai Radio 1 he presents *In viaggio con Francesco*. In 2012 he received the Biagio Agnes international award for journalism.
He contributes to *Corriere della Sera*, Gruppo QN and *Huffington Post*. He has written: *Vado da Francesco* (2014), *Francesco il ribelle* (2018), *La tunica e la tonaca* (2020) and *Buongiorno brava gente* (2021). For Rai3, together with journalist Lucia Annunziata, he realised the report *Decimati*, on Christians in Iraq. He is the spokesperson, together with Ermete Realacci, of the Assisi Manifesto to Combat the Climate Crisis. He drafted the Assisi Charter with Beppe Giulietti, FNSI (National Federation of the Italian Press) president.
He has conducted a number of missions for humanitarian projects: Brazil, China, Colombia, Cuba, Egypt, Jordan, India, Iraq, Kenya, Mexico, Norway, Palestine, Peru, Russia, United States of America, Sri Lanka and Tibet, and on behalf of the U.N.

Carlo Furgeri Gilbert was born in London, grew up in Romagna and has lived in Milan for years now. After graduating in Architecture, he devoted his energies to photography and to directing documentaries, TV commercials and corporate videos. He has collaborated as a photographer with a number of publications, including *Rolling Stone*, *The Wall Street Journal* and *L'Officiel Art*. In 2008 at the Milan Triennale he created a digital multi-vision system for photographs as part of the collective *Un viaggio, ma...*; the same year, a project on the world of work in the Pirelli factories in Europe was brought together in the volume *Pirelli. Racconti di lavoro*. In 2009 the Milan Triennale hosted his solo exhibition *Working. Uomini, Macchine, Idee*. In 2018 he founded Studio Nicama, a collective of photographers and film directors, and, together with Marcello Pastonesi, he directed the documentary *L'altro spazio* produced by Someone and RAI Cinema and presented in Venice at the Architecture Biennale. In 2019, with Studio Nicama, he produced and directed *Playground Addiction*, a short film on sport and multiculturalism that received awards at international festivals such as FIPADOC in Biarritz and the Sport Governance Film Festival.

Giuseppe Lupo was born in Lucania (Atella 1963) and lives in Lombardy, where he teaches at the Catholic University in Milan. In 2018 he won the Viareggio prize with *Gli anni del nostro incanto*. He is the author of numerous other novels, including *L'americano di Celenne*, 2000, Berto prize, Mondello prize; *La carovana Zanardelli*, 2008, Grinzane prize for Mediterranean culture; *L'ultima sposa di Palmira*, 2011, Selezione Campiello prize, Vittorini prize; *Viaggiatori di nuvole*, 2013, Dessì prize; *L'albero di stanze*, 2015, Alassio-Centolibri prize, Frontino Montefeltro prize; *Breve storia del mio silenzio*, 2019; and *Il pioppo del Sempione*, 2021. He has published various essays on the culture of the twentieth century and industrial modernity, such as *La letteratura al tempo di Adriano Olivetti*, 2016; *Le fabbriche che costruirono l'Italia*, 2020; and *La Storia senza redenzione. Il racconto del Mezzogiorno lungo due secoli*, 2021. He contributes to the cultural pages of *Il Sole 24 Ore*.

Monica Maggioni, born in Milan in 1964, a graduate in foreign languages and literatures, is a journalist, writer and documentary-maker. After joining Rai in 1992, she worked in the editorial office at Euronews. After 11 September 2001 she worked on the Middle-Eastern reactions to the attack on the Twin Towers. In 2003 she was the only Italian journalist to follow the US Army in the Iraq War. In 2010 and 2011 she made two documentaries that were presented at the Venice Film Festival: *Ward 54* and *Out of Tehran*. From 2009 to 2013 she was central editor-in-chief of Specials on Tg1 and in 2013 she was asked to direct the Rai's all-news pole: Rai news24, Televideo and Rainews.it. She has received numerous awards and recognitions, including the Luigi Barzini Prize to a special correspondent. She is a board member of the ISPI and the European Council on Foreign Relations and a member of the Aspen Institute and the Trilateral Commission. She has collaborated with Italian and foreign newspapers and periodicals, and has written the following books: *Dentro la guerra*, 2005; *La fine della verità*, 2006; *Terrore mediatico*, 2015. From 2015 to 2018 she was president of the Rai. In 2019 she was awarded the honorary title Chevalier de la Légion d'Honneur. Between 2019 and 2020 she was managing director of Rai Com and since November 2021 she has been director of Tg1. She is a lecturer at the Università Cattolica del Sacro Cuore in Milan.

Ian McEwan's works have earned him worldwide critical acclaim. He won the Somerset Maugham Award in 1976 for his first collection of short stories *First Love, Last Rites*; the Whitbread Novel Award (1987) and the Prix Fémina étranger (1993) for *The Child in Time*; and Germany's Shakespeare Prize in 1999. He has been shortlisted for the Man Booker Prize for Fiction numerous times, winning the award for Amsterdam in 1998. His novel *Atonement* received the WH Smith Literary Award (2002), National Book Critics' Circle Fiction Award (2003), Los Angeles Times Prize for Fiction (2003), and the Santiago Prize for the European Novel (2004). *Atonement* was also made into an Oscar-winning film. In 2006, Ian McEwan won the James Tait Black Memorial Prize for his novel *Saturday* and his novel *On Chesil Beach* was named Galaxy Book of the Year at the 2008 British Book Awards where McEwan was also named Reader's Digest Author of the Year. *Solar* won The Bollinger Everyman Wodehouse Prize for Comic Fiction in 2010 and *Sweet Tooth* won the Paddy Power Political Fiction Book of the Year award in 2012. Ian McEwan was awarded a CBE in 2000. In 2014 he was awarded the Bodleian Medal. McEwan is published by Jonathan Cape in the UK and Nan A. Talese/Doubleday in the US.

Cristina Messa, a graduate in medicine and surgery with a specialisation in nuclear medicine, is a full professor of medical imaging.
She has worked at the IRCCS San Raffaele Hospital in Milan and the ASST San Gerardo in Monza. She has engaged in various periods of study in the United States and in England. She has published over 180 scientific works. From 2013 to 2019 she was rector of the Bicocca University of Milan, the first woman to be head of a Milanese athenaeum. Committed to the promotion of research and innovation as the strategic basis of institutional activity, during her mandate she devoted particular attention to the relations between university and territory at national and international level.
From 2011 to 2015 she was vice president of the Italian National Research Council (CNR) where, among other things, she worked to encourage the internationalisation of research, the diffusion of innovation and the competitive growth of the industrial system, promoting the activities and results of research.
Since 13 February 2021 she has been Minister for Universities and Research.

Pierangelo Misani, a graduate in Aeronautical Engineering, entered Pirelli in 1985 as junior tyre designer, joining the team that developed the first radial tires for road motorcycles. Between 1989 and 1991 he was head of the team that designed the innovative technology of the zero degree steel belt for motorbike tyres. After a period as head of the Pirelli factory in Breuberg, in 1996 he returned to Milan as Manufacturing Processes manager to develop innovative processes for the production of tyres for cars and motorbikes that were to be replicated in all the Pirelli factories throughout the world. Head of Basic Research and Technologies in 2000 and of MIRS™ Operations in 2002, in 2008 he returned to the Motorbike Business Unit in the capacity first as Research and Development and Manufacturing manager and then as chief operating officer, until, in 2017, he became manager of the Business Unit. Since 2019 he has been senior vice president Research & Development and since 2020 senior vice president Research & Development and Cyber.

Sir **Geoff Mulgan** is professor of Collective Intelligence, Public Policy and Social Innovation at University College London (UCL). He was previously CEO of Nesta, the UK's national endowment for science, technology and the arts (from 2011–19). From 1997–2004 Geoff had roles in UK government including director of the Government's Strategy Unit and head of policy in the Prime Minister's office. Geoff advises many foundations and governments around the world and has help set up a dozen organisations, including Action for Happiness and the Social Innovation Exchange. Past books include *Good and Bad Power* (Penguin) and *Big Mind: how collective intelligence can change our world* (Princeton UP).

Renzo Piano was born in Genoa in 1937. He graduated in 1964 at the Milan Politecnico and during university he worked in Franco Albini's studio. In 1970, in London, with Richard Rogers he founded the Piano & Rogers studio, in 1971 winning the competition for the realisation of the Centre Pompidou in Paris. From 1977 to 1981 he worked with engineer Peter Rice, creating the Atelier Piano & Rice, and in 1981 he established the Renzo Piano Building Workshop, which today is an office numbering 120 people with sites in Paris and Genoa. Among his main creations, apart from the Centre Pompidou: the Menil Collection in Houston, the Terminal of the Kansai International Airport in Osaka, the Fondation Beyeler in Basle, the Centre Culturel Jean-Marie Tjibaou in New Caledonia, Potsdamer Platz in Berlin, the Auditorium Parco della Musica in Rome, the Nasher Sculpture Center in Dallas, the California Academy of Sciences in San Francisco, The Shard in London, the extension to the Art Institute of Chicago, the Harvard Art Museums in Boston, the extension to the Morgan Library, the head office of the New York Times, the Whitney Museum of American Art and the new Campus for Columbia University in New York, the Cultural Centre of the Stavros Niarchos Foundation in Athens, the Centro Botín in Santander, the new Tribunal Judiciaire in Paris, the Academy Museum of Motion Pictures in Los Angeles and GES-2 in Moscow. In 1998 he received the Pritzker Architecture Prize, considered the Nobel prize for architecture. Among his other awards: the RIBA Royal Gold Medal in 1989, the Praemium Imperiale in Tokyo in 1995 and the Gold Medal of the American Institute of Architect in 2008. On 4 September 2013 he was named life senator by the president of the Italian Republic Giorgio Napolitano and in May 2014 he received an honorary degree from Columbia University in New York.

Ermete Realacci has run Legambiente, of which he is honorary president, ever since the organisation's early years. He is among the founders of the Kyoto Club. He has promoted and chairs Symbola. He has pursued many initiatives in defence of the environment and to encourage an idea of Italy understood as an inimitable interweaving of history, nature, culture, creativity and innovation. The circular economy, sustainability, beauty, the green economy, social cohesion and products made in Italy have long been the themes that have inspired his commitment. In the previous legislature he was president of the Chamber Commission for the Environment, Territory and Public Works. Together with Padre Enzo Fortunato, he is the spokesperson of the Manifesto of Assisi for an economy on a human scale.

Ferruccio Resta has been rector of the Milan Politecnico, the number one technical university in Italy and among the top twenty in Europe in the three areas of study and research: architecture, design and engineering, since 2017. He has been president of the Conference of Rectors of Italian Universities – CRUI since 2020. Born in 1968, he graduated in Mechanical Engineering at the Milan Politecnico, where in 2004 he became full professor of Mechanics Applied to Machines. He is a Commendatore della Repubblica Italiana, an honour conferred upon him by president Sergio Mattarella in 2018.

Guido Saracco
Born in Turin in 1965, since 2018 he has been rector of the Turin Politecnico. He graduated in Chemical Engineering at the same university in 1989, gaining his PhD in 1994. Full professor of industrial and technological chemistry since 2003, in 2011 he moved his professorship to the sector of the Chemical Bases of Technologies. He has founded and coordinated research laboratories (Environmental Catalysis, Hydrogen Systems Lab, Biosolar Lab, Graphene@PoliTo, etc.), promoting interdisciplinary collaborations there. He has coordinated over ten European and national research projects, participating in thirty or so collaborative projects. The author of over 600 publications, in 2017 he published his first book in the area of popular science for Zanichelli: *Chimica Verde 2.0*. Since 2015 he has been a corresponding member of the Accademia delle Scienze in Turin.

Marco Tronchetti Provera has been chief executive officer of Pirelli from 1992 and executive vice chairman from 20 October 2015.
Born in 1948, he graduated in Economics and Commerce in 1971 at the Bocconi University in Milan.
In the early 1970s he began to collaborate with the family's entrepreneurial activities, where in particular he developed those associated with the sea transport sector.
In 1986 he joined Pirelli; from 1996 to 2001 he was president of *Il Sole 24 Ore* and from 2001 to the 2005 board member of the Teatro alla Scala.
From 2001 to 2006 he occupied the position of president of Telecom Italia and from 2008 to 2017 that of vice president of Mediobanca – Banca di Credito Finanziaria. Until 2013 he occupied the position of president of Prelios.
He is currently also president of Marco Tronchetti Provera & C. and administrator of the RCS MediaGroup. He is honorary joint president for the Italian part of the Council for Relations between Italy and the United States and of the Italo-Russian Entrepreneurial Committee for Economic Cooperation and he is a member of the Italian Group of the Trilateral Commission.
He is on the General Council and the Advisory Board of Assolombarda as well as on the General Council of Confindustria, and is a member of the Board of the Bocconi University.

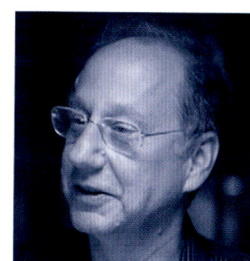

David Weinberger
Trained as a philosopher and with decades of work in the tech industry, David Weinberger, Ph.D., explores the effect of technology on ideas. He was for many years a senior researcher at Harvard's Berkman Klein Center for Internet & Society and recently was a writer-in-residence at a Google AI research group. His award-winning latest book, *Everyday Chaos* (HBR Press), explores how machine learning is changing our ideas about how the future happens. He also edits the open access *Strong Ideas* book series for MIT Press. He has been a co-director of the Harvard Library Innovation Lab, a journalism fellow at Harvard's Shorenstein Center, an adviser to presidential campaigns, and a Franklin Fellow at the U.S. State Department.

BIBLIOGRAPHY

A

Andreolli Elena, *L'innovazione tecnologica nell'industria del pneumatico: l'impatto del pneumatico Run-flat e dei nuovi sistemi produttivi*, degree thesis in Management Engineering, University of Brescia, academic year 2002–2003.
Arpaia Bruno, Greco Pietro, *La cultura si mangia!*, Parma, Guanda, 2013.
Azzarita Vittoria, Monti Stefano, 'La sottile linea rossa tra cultura e innovazione', in *Doppiozero*, www.doppiozero.com/materiali/che-fare/la-sottile-linea-rossa-tra-cultura-e-innovazione.

B

Barzini Luigi, *La metà del mondo vista da un'automobile. Da Pechino a Parigi in 60 giorni,* Milan, Hoepli, 1908.
Beccalli Falco Nani, Calabrò Antonio, *Il riscatto. L'Italia e l'industria internazionale*, Milan, Bocconi University-EGEA, 2012.
Bell Daniel, *The Coming of Post-Industrial Society: A Venture in Social Forecasting*, New York, Basic Books, 1973.
Bellavite Pellegrini Carlo, *Pirelli. Innovazione e passione 1872-2017*, Bologna, il Mulino, 2017.
Belpoliti Marco, *Primo Levi di fronte e di profilo*, Milan, Guanda, 2015.
Benjamin Walter, *Selected Writings*, 4 vols., Harvard University Press, 1996–2003.
Bentivogli Marco, *Contrordine compagni. Manuale di resistenza alla tecnofobia per la riscossa del lavoro e dell'Italia*, Milan, Rizzoli, 2019.
Bonazzi Mauro, 'Ulisse, l'esiliato che porta alla Bibbia', in *la Lettura*, literary supplement of the *Corriere della Sera*, 19 December 2021.
Braudel Fernand, *The Mediterranean and the Mediterranean world in the age of Philip 2*, New York, Harper & Row, 1976.
Buzzati Dino, 'Piccole storie del grattacielo', in *Pirelli. Rivista d'informazione e di tecnica*, XXIII, 9–10, 1970, pp. 30–33.

C

Il Canto della fabbrica, edited by Fondazione Pirelli, Milan, Mondadori, 2018.
Cavallari Alberto, 'Dinastie operaie alla Bicocca', in *Pirelli. Rivista d'informazione e di tecnica*, V, 3, 1952, pp. 36-38.
Censis, *Rapporto sulla situazione sociale del Paese 2021*, Milan, Franco Angeli, 2021.
Cohen Stephen S., Zysman John, *Manufacturing Matters: The Myth of the Post-Industrial Economy*, New York, Basic Books, 1987.
Chatwin Bruce, *In Patagonia*, London, Picador, 1979.

D

Darley Gillian, *Factory*, London, Reaktion, 2003; Italian translation *Fabbriche. Origine e sviluppo dell'architettura industriale*, Bologna, Pendragon, 2007.
De Carli Carlo, 'La nuova sede Pirelli', in *Pirelli. Rivista d'informazione e di tecnica*, VIII, 3, 1955, pp. 18-25.

F

Finocchiaro Giusella, Floridi Luciano, Pollicino Oreste, 'Intelligenza artificiale e norme', in *Il Sole 24 Ore*, 7 December 2021.
Fitoussi Jean-Paul, Stiglitz Joseph E., Durand Martine, *Measuring What Counts for Economic and Social Performance*, Paris, OECD, 2018.
Floridi Luciano, *Pensare l'infosfera. La filosofia come design concettuale*, Milan, Raffaello Cortina, 2020.
Fortis Marco, 'Il rimbalzo post pandemia dell'economia italiana è figlio anche di Industria 4.0', in *Il Sole 24 Ore*, 8 December 2021.

G

L'Italia e il sistema finanziario internazionale, 1919-1936, edited by Marcello De Cecco, Rome-Bari, Editori Laterza, 1993.
Gennarini Pier Emilio, 'Nel cervello di uno studente romantico il progetto di un'industria nuova', in *Pirelli. Rivista d'informazione e di tecnica*, II, 1, 1949, pp. 50-53.
Grasso Giorgio, *Presentati a Bicocca i nuovi laboratori R&S del Gruppo. Pirelli Labs: la sfida della ricerca*, in «Fatti e Notizie», 347, 2001.

H

Heidegger Martin, *Saggi e discorsi*, translated and edited by Gianni Vattimo, Milan, Mursia, 1954.
Horkheimer Max, Adorno Theodor W., *Dialectic of Enlightenment*, London, Allen Lane, 1973.

I

Iacci Paolo with Galimberti Umberto, *Dialogo sul lavoro e la felicità*, Milan, EGEA, 2021.
Irti Natalino, 'L'università vive nella continuità maestri-allievi', in *Il Sole 24 Ore*, 12 December 2021.

L

Leopoldo Pirelli. Valori e passioni di un uomo di impresa, Milan, Archinto, 2012.
Levi Primo, *La chiave a stella*, Turin, Einaudi, 2001.
Levi Primo, 'Lettera al direttore', in *La Chimica & l'Industria*, November 1947.

M

Magatti Mauro, 'Salto tecnologico e nuova coscienza digitale', in *Corriere della Sera*, 23 July 2021.
Maggi Maurizio, 'La mia rivoluzione l'ho fatta di gomma', in *Fatti e Notizie*, 343, 2000, p. 3.
Montale Eugenio, *Ossi di seppia*, Turin, Piero Gobetti Editore, 1925.

N

Natta Giulio, 'Le nuove grandi sintesi organiche', in *La Chimica & l'Industria*, 20, April 1938, pp. 187–198.

O

Olivetti Adriano, *Città dell'Uomo*, Milan, Edizioni di Comunità, 1960.

P

Pasquale Frank, *Le nuove leggi della robotica. Difendere la competenza umana nell'era dell'intelligenza artificiale*, Rome, Luiss University Press, 2021.
Pirelli. Racconti di lavoro, edited by Fondazione Pirelli, Milan, Mondadori, 2008.
Pirelli Alberto, *La Pirelli. Vita di un'azienda industriale*, Milan, unnumbered, 1946.
Pirelli Alberto, 'Questa nostra rivista', in *Pirelli. Rivista d'informazione e di tecnica*, I, 1, 1948, p. 8.
Pirelli Giovanni Battista, *Viaggio di istruzione all'estero. Diario 1870-1871*, edited by Francesca Polese, Venice, Marsilio, 2003.
Polese Francesca, *Alla ricerca di un'industria nuova. Il viaggio all'estero del giovane Pirelli e le origini di una grande impresa, 1870-1977*, Venice, Marsilio, 2004.
Ponti Gio, 'Perpetuità di un edificio', in *Pirelli. Rivista d'informazione e di tecnica*, XXIII, 9–10, 1970, p. 28.
Popper Karl R., *Conjectures and refutations: the growth of scientific knowledge*, New York, Routledge, 2002.
Progetto Bicocca, Milan, Electa, 1986.

Q

Qohélet o l'Ecclesiaste, edited by Guido Ceronetti, Turin, Einaudi, 1970.

R

Ratti Carlo, *Smart city, smart citizen*, Milan, EGEA, 2013.
Ravasi Gianfranco, *Qohelet. Il libro più originale e 'scandaloso' dell'Antico Testamento*, Cinisello Balsamo, San Paolo Edizioni, 2012.
Ross Alec, *The Industries of the Future*, New York, Simon & Schuster, 2016.

S

Sacco Pier Luigi, 'Innovazione: tecnologia e impegni sociali', in *Il Canto della fabbrica*, edited by Fondazione Pirelli, Milan, Mondadori, 2018.
Scaletta Salvatore, *L'innovazione industriale e gli impatti sulla performance. Il caso Pirelli tra Next Mirs e CVA*, degree thesis in Company Economics, LUISS Guido Carli, academic year 2017–2018.
Sereni Vittorio, 'Una P lunga cinquant'anni', in *Pirelli. Rivista d'informazione e di tecnica*, XI, 2, 1958, pp. 43–45.
Sinisgalli Leonardo, 'L'operaio e la macchina', in *Pirelli. Rivista d'informazione e di tecnica*, II, 2, 1949, p. 27.
Skyscraper Stories, edited by Fondazione Pirelli and by Alessandro Colombo, Venice, Marsilio, 2020.
Spagna Fabrizio, *L'industriale. La storia di Marco Tronchetti Provera*, Rome, Memori, 2005.

U

Umanesimo industriale. Antologia di pensieri, parole, immagini e innovazioni, edited by Fondazione Pirelli, Mondadori, 2019.

V

Veca Salvatore, 'Idee da cambiare', in *Città*, November 2021.
Vittorini Elio, *Il Politecnico*, Turin, Einaudi, 1975.

INDEX OF NAMES

A

Abbado, Claudio, 186
Abramović, Marina, 295
Academy of Science and Letters, 54
Accademia Walter Stauffer, 186,
Accardo, Salvatore, 141, 152, 176, 186, 190, 191, 296
Adorno, Theodor W., 29
Aegean Sea, 284
Aeneas, 30
Affondatore (ship), 57, 68
Africa, 72, 143, 289, 293, 294
Agenzia Centro, 126
Agnelli, 116, 135
Agrippa Menenius, 62
aircraft, 284
Air Force, 96
Albini, Franco, 24
Albizzati, Enrico, 143, 148, 162
Alexandria Tyre Co., 294
Alfa Romeo 20-30, 101
Alfa Romeo Giulietta Sprint, 119
Alfa Romeo P2, 93, 101
Alfa Romeo, 93, 101, 119, 286, 287
Algeria, 292
Allied Military Government, 116, 288
Allocchio, Stefano, 27
Alps, 71, 72
Amazon (company), 40, 42
Amazon (river), 78
Amazonia, 61, 76, 106
Ambrosini, Giuseppe, 19
America, 99, 108, 111, 197, 293
America's Cup, 148, 296, 297
Americas, 62, 95, 286
Amsterdam Stock Exchange, 293
Anaconda Pirelli, 289
Anchises, 30
Ancona, bay of, see gulf of Ancona
Ancona, gulf of, 57, 68
Andreoni, Arrigo, 143
Annual Report, 119, 296
Annuario (Yearbook) of Politecnico di Milano, 105
Ansaldo, 75
Arbasino, Alberto, 24
Arco Felice, 123, 289
Argentina, 27, 65, 96, 119, 142, 289, 291
Aristotle, 36, 37
Armstrong Tires, 293
Arpaia, Bruno, 140,
Artura, 172
Ascanius, 30
Ascari, Alberto, 100, 118, 289

Ascari, Antonio, 101
Assisi Manifesto, 201, 202, 203, 204
Assonime, 280
Aston Martin, 168
Astra Otopart, 296
Athens, 29
Atlantic, 101
Audi, 144, 156
Augé, Marc, 151
Auschwitz, 107, 215
Australia, 41, 294
Austria, 54, 99, 127
automobile(s), 7, 18, 22, 62, 72, 75, 76, 88, 101, 120, 156, 163, 171, 172, 279, 283, 284
autonomous drive cars, 148
Autonomous Institute for Social Housing (*Istituto autonomo case popolari*), 285
autonomous mobility, 15
Azienda Monza, 290

B

Bach, Johann Sebastian, 218
Baldini, Raffaello, 19
Balearic Islands, 61
Balestrini, Nanni, 24
Ballo, Aldo, 126, 279
balls for playing games, 71, 76
Banbury, 157
Banca Intesa, 294
Bangladesh, 43
Barcelona, 14, 76
Barilla, 116
Bartali, Gino, 287
Barzini, Luigi, 76, 88
Basic Books, 196
Basel, 287, 289, 292
Basilico, Gabriele, 279
Bassi, Renzo, 279
bath caps, 282
Bauman, Zygmunt, 151
Bayer, 107
Beaubourg, see Centre national d'art et de culture Georges Pompidou
Beccaris, Bava, 75
Beethoven, Ludwig van, 186
Bekaert, 296
Belgium, 57
Bell, Daniel, 196
Bellavite Pellegrini, Carlo, 28, 65, 143, 152
belts, 7, 27, 58, 68, 76, 168, 282

Bencini, Giuseppe, 144
Benetton, 140, 142, 292, 294
Benjamin, Walter, 29
Bergamo, 233
Berlin, 28, 107, 127, 143, 178, 283
Berlin Motor Show, 107
Bernardine, 203, 204
Berra Kramer, Teresa, 54, 58
Bertini, hydroelectric plant, 213
Bertoglio, Mario, 103
Bianchi (motorcycle), 77
Bianconi, Fulvio, 280
Biasion, Miki, 142
Biasion, Renzo, 280
BICC General, 294
Bicocca degli Arcimboldi, 221, 285
Bicocca, 13, 21, 23, 62, 64, 65, 75, 79, 101, 105, 108, 119, 124, 137, 140, 143, 144, 147, 148, 151, 152, 153, 156, 162, 163, 186, 190, 207, 211, 220, 221, 279, 281, 284, 285, 286, 287, 290, 291, 292, 294
Bicocca Project, 280, 292
Binda, Alfredo, 120, 175, 289
Binda, Ambrogio, 53
Biennale Tecnologica (Technology Biennale), 19
BirdLife International, 297
Bismarck, 68
Bloomsbury, group, 99
BMW Group, see BMW
BMW X5 Plug-In Hybrid, 287
BMW, 144, 156, 168, 297
Bobbio, Norberto, 3
Bocconi University, 61, 62, 95, 207
Bogatyr, 105
Boillot, Georges, 284
Boiocchi, Maurizio, 143, 147, 148, 156, 298
Bollate, 124, 185, 281
Bonamini, Domenico, 64, 98
Bonamore, Antonio, 72, 73
Bordino, Pietro, 101
Borghese, Scipione, 76, 88, 284
Borghi, 116
Borgo Pirelli, 285
Brabham, 140, 292
Brambilla, Franco, 123
Brazil, 27, 61, 107, 112, 119, 123, 143, 156, 171, 202, 286, 287, 289, 291, 293, 294
Braudel, Fernand, 30
Brecht, Bertolt, 21
Brescia, 23, 29, 54, 119
Breuberg, 147
Bridgestone, 127
Brilli Peri, Gastone, 286
Brioschi, Francesco, 53, 58
Brooklyn Law School, 29
Brugherio, 286
Bruni, Giuseppe, 105

Brussels, 144, 285
Buazzelli, Tino, 21
Buenos Aires, 76, 285
Bukit Indah, 294
Buna S, 105
Buna-Monowitz, 107
Burton-on-Trent, 102, 147, 286, 297
Buzzati, Dino, 218

C

Cabella, 54
cable(s), 7, 27, 28, 57, 60, 62, 65, 76, 96, 101, 102, 116, 123, 124, 140, 143, 144, 221, 281, 282, 283, 284, 285, 286, 290, 291, 292, 294, 295, 296
   coaxial cable, 289
   fluid oil-filled cable, 286
   telecommunications cable, 7, 285, 286, 292, 294, 295
   underground cable, 62, 76, 283, 292,
   undersea cable, 71, 72, 75, 76, 82, 221, 284, 289, 290, 291
   undersea telegraphic cable, 282, 283, 286
   telegraph cable, 72
cable-laying ship, 60, 61, 72, 79, 101, 283, 285, 288
Cadorna, 95
Caffè, Federico, 31
Cage, John, 118
Calabrò, Antonio, 20, 151, 186
Calcagni, Emilio, 65, 282
California, 151
Calvino, Italo, 151
Cam Spa (later Camfin), 127
Camfin, 296
Campari, Giuseppe, 101
Canada, 43, 289
Candiani, Giuseppe, 53
Canestrini, Giovanni, 19
Cantoni, Eugenio, 58
caoutchouc, 27, 57, 58, 81
Capra, Frank, 204
Capuava, 287
carbon black, 76, 107, 147, 151, 168, 171, 226, 287
Cardinale, Claudia, 118
Carducci, Giosuè, 72
Caretta, Renato, 144, 147
Carlisle, 123, 291, 297
Carosello, 119, 280
Carrère, Emmanuel, 151, 281
Casassa, François, 58, 59, 61, 71, 282
Casati, Gabrio, 53

Cassini, Gino, 108
Castellani, Arrigo, 119
Castiglioni, Achille, 24
Cattaneo, Carlo, 24, 65
caucciù, 57, 283
CCM (Continuous Compound Mixing), 147, 154, 162, 294
Cederna, Camilla, 119
Celikord, 292
Censis, 21
Centre for Information, Studies and Experiences (CISE), 119
Centre national d'art et de culture Georges Pompidou, Paris, 178
Centro Casa Severino, 29
Centro Culturale Pirelli, 118, 118, 176, 186, 187
Cercas, Javier, 151, 281
Cesura, Guido, 19
Chabod, Federico, 123
Chamber of Commerce, 61, 101, 102, 105, 280
Chatwin, Bruce, 3, 29
ChemChina, 148, 296
Chicago, 286
Chiesa, Eugenio, 99
China, 27, 143, 148, 151, 157, 197, 295
Cisco, 147, 294
Città di Milano II, 285, 288
Città di Milano, 61,72, 79, 82, 283, 284, 285
Cohen, Stephen S., 196, 197
College of Engineers of Milan, 26, 134
Colombo, Claudio, 116
Colombo, Giuseppe, 54, 57, 58, 68, 72, 81
Comerio, Luca, 69, 75, 280, 286
Como, 53
Como, Lake, 53, 68
Compagnie Internationale Pirelli, 285, 287
Compañía italo-argentina de electricidad, 96, 284
Compasso d'Oro, 289
Conductores Electricos SA, 289
Confindustria (Italian Confederation of Industry), 62, 124, 135, 280
Congo, 107
Connecticut, 291
Consortium for Research into Advanced Materials (Consorzio per la ricerca sui materiali avanzati, CORIMAV), 151, 162, 163
Construction company of major roads in Munich, 107
Conti, Ettore, 99
Continental AG, 293
Continental, 107, 127, 143, 156,
Copenhagen, 41
Corfu, 95
Corning, 147, 294
Corriere della Sera, 62, 95, 148
Corvaja, Salvatore, 68, 69

Creative Commons, 47
Credito italiano, 62
Cremona, 186
Crespi d'Adda, 213
CRISPR, 46, 49
Croce, Bendetto, 123
CSELT (STET Study Centre), 292
CVA (prototype), 148
Cyber Tyre, 7, 18, 19, 28, 148, 154, 157, 172
Cycling Grand Prix (Gran Premio Pirelli), 120, 289

D

D'Amelio, Mariano, 99
Dalmatia, 72
Dardanelles, 61
Darley, Gillian, 13
Darwin, Charles, 36
De Carli, Carlo, 216, 221
De Gasperi (government), 95, 288
De Gasperi, Alcide, 116
De Luna, Giovanni, 102
De Martin, Juan Carlos, 194
Del Grande, Ernesto, 84
Department of Automatics and IT, Turin Politecnico, 148
Department of IT, Science and Engineering, University of Bologna, 148
Depretis, Agostino, 72
design, 6, 28, 96, 111, 129, 163, 171, 214
Digital Services Act, 29
Dodecanese, 284
Dogali, 72
Dow Jones, 102, 112
Draka Holding, 294
Dropbox, 47
Dubini, Emanuele, 123
Dubini, Paola, 207
Dudovich, Marcello, 96, 97
Dunlop-Pirelli Union, group, 124, 291, 292
Dunlop, 124, 127, 135, 140, 287
Durand, Martine, 26
Düsseldorf, 162

E

Eastleigh, 96, 123, 290
Eco, Umberto, 24
Edison, company, 62, 72, 119, 288
Edison, Thomas, 61
Edward VII, Prince of Wales, 102, 286
Egypt, 123
Einaudi, Luigi, 65, 95, 108
elastic thread, 58, 76, 282
Elect, 297
electric car(s), 7, 28, 143
electrical conductors, 76, 282, 283, 289
electrical wiring, 72, 282
Emanueli, Leopoldo, 79, 289
Emanueli, Luigi, 27, 79, 105, 119, 123, 129, 279, 285, 288, 289
Emilia, 23
Emirates New Zealand, 148, 296
Empress Elisabeth of Austria, 53
Empress Maria Theresa of Austria, 53
ENEL, 23, 292
England, see also Great Britain and United Kingdom, 54, 58, 60, 61, 72, 79, 95, 99, 102, 135, 284
ENI, 23, 151
Enzensberger, Hans Magnus, 151, 281
Eritrea, 72
ESG (Environmental, Social and Governance), 43
Ethiopia, 102
EU, see European Union, 202
Europe, 7, 17, 18, 21, 23, 24, 27, 28, 29, 61, 62, 71, 91, 92, 95, 99, 101, 102, 108, 110, 111, 112,116, 127, 147, 156, 197, 202, 204, 294, 295
European Coal and Steel Community (ECSC), 24
European Common Market (ECM), 24
European Union, 202
Eurostat, 203
Expo, 70, 72

F

F1, see Formula 1
Falck, 116
Fangio, Juan Manuel, 119
Farabola, 279
Farina, Nino, 118
Fatti e Notizie, 120, 152, 169, 280
FC Internazionale, 293

Fellini, Franco (Giovanni Pirelli), 123
Fergusson, 71
Ferrara, 105, 107, 108, 287
Ferrari 375, 118
Ferrari 500, 101
Ferrari F40, 140
Ferrari, 100, 120, 168, 289
Ferrari, Enzo, 119
Ferrero, Ernesto, 53
FIAT, 62, 75, 76, 101, 119, 120, 121, 288, 289, 291
Fiat 124 Spider-Pirelli, 291
Fiat 500, 120
Fiat 500C, 289
Fiat 525SS, 101
Fiat 600, 121
Fiat 804, 101
Fiat 8V, 119
fibre-optic, 282, 292
Fibre Ottiche Sud, 292
Fiera Campionaria di Milano, 105, 111
Figline Valdarno, 123, 290
Filergie, 127, 292
Filicudi, 79, 84, 285
Finland, 294
Firestone, 127, 135
First World War, 62, 96, 101, 102, 107, 110, 112
Fitoussi, Jean-Paul, 26
Florence, 95, 204
Floridi, Luciano, 29, 281
foam rubber, 287, 289
Foer, Franklin, 151
Fondazione Pier Lombardo, 294
Fondazione Piero e Alberto Pirelli, 288
Fondazione Pirelli, 6, 7, 20, 83, 119, 152, 153, 176, 186, 215, 221, 278, 279, 281, 295
Fondazione Silvio Tronchetti Provera, 21, 151, 163
Fondazione Symbola, 201, 202
Fondazione Umberto Veronesi, 21
Fontana, Lucio, 296
Ford, Henry, 46
Ford, Model T, 46, 48
Formula 1, 28, 101, 119, 120, 140, 141, 148, 157, 169, 171, 289, 292, 295
Formula 1 Grand Prix, 289
Formula 2, 140
Forster, Gerard, 279
Forsyth, Derek, 280
Fortunato, Enzo, 201
France, 68, 203, 284, 287, 290
François, Robert, 279
Franz Joseph I of Austria, 53
FSC, Forest Stewardship Council, 171, 297
FTSE4Good Index Series, 297
Fuà, Giorgio, 31
Furgeri Gilbert, Carlo, 149, 169, 181, 185, 222, 224

G

G.B. Pirelli & C., 56, 68, 71, 282
G7 Ministerial Conference on the Global Information Society, 144
Gadda, Carlo Emilio, 151
Galbraith, John Kenneth, 204
Galilei, Galileo, 21, 24, 29, 36
Galimberti, Umberto, 30
gaskets, 58
Gatto Meo, 289
Gavioli, Roberto, 280
Gemina, 127
General Association of Mutual Aid for Milanese Workers, 53
General Electric, 79
Geneva Motor Show, 148, 297
Genoa, 23, 76
Genovesi, Antonio, 31
Germany, 24, 27, 54, 57, 68, 72, 81, 99, 101, 105, 107, 108, 123, 127,147, 170, 198, 203, 288, 290
Gfeller, Raymond, 126
Ghello, Monte, 95
Gim, 127
Giovanni Battista Pirelli, François Casassa & C., 58, 61, 71, 282
Giovanni, Pirelli, 288, 291
Giovinazzo, 290
Giro d'Italia cycle race, 76
Global Compact, 151
gloves, 282
Gobetti, Norman, 319,
Goldman Sachs, 295
Gonda, Tomás, 141, 279
Goodyear, 57, 58, 71, 127, 135
Gorla, 108
Gorna, Laura, 186, 191
Goulard, Antoine-Aimé, 58, 71, 282
Gran Premio di Galoppo (horse race), 101
Gran Premio Pirelli, 120
Grand Paris, 178
Grand Prix de France, 284
Grant, Duncan, 99
Graphis, 296
Grasso, Giorgio, 143, 148
Great Britain, 27, 101, 109, 147, 286
Greco Milanese, 79, 284
Greece, 72, 120, 123, 290
Greenfield, Adam, 151, 281
Gregotti Associati International, 137
Gregotti, Vittorio, 6, 186, 207, 211, 221
Griffiths, Ken, 174, 293
Gross Domestic Product (GDP), 26, 102, 120, 201, 204

Gruppo 63, 24
Guangdong, 43
Guglielmi, Angelo, 24
gutta-percha, 60, 61, 75, 282, 283
Guttuso, Renato, 123, 151, 280, 290
Gyulai, Ferenc, 53

H

haberdashery items and fine articles for surgery, 74, 282
Halliday, Lisa, 151, 281
Hammacher, Arno, 117, 279
HangarBicocca, 6, 152, 153, 221, 294, 295, 296
Hanover, 127
Harvard, 43
Heidegger, Martin, 30
Historical archive of the Milan Chamber of Commerce, 105
Hoffmann, Fritz, 107
Homer, 29
Horkheimer, Max, 29
hot water bottles, 71
House of Lords, 95, 96
Hungary, 99
Hutan Harapan, 297

I

Ibiza, 72, 283
Il Politecnico, 24
India Rubber Journal, 281
India Rubber World, 281
Indonesia, 27, 43, 205, 289, 296, 297
Industriale, 71
Industrie du Caoutchouc Souple, 286
Industrie Pirelli S.P.A, 291
Innocenti, 120
Institute for Industrial Reconstruction (IRI), 95, 123, 287
Institute for the Study of Synthetic Rubber (Istituto per lo studio della gomma sintetica), 105, 113
International Chamber of Commerce, 101, 280
International Exposition of Cycles and Motorcycles, 288
International Exposition of Work, Turin, 290

International Motorcycle Trophy, 287
Intesa Sanpaolo, 202
Inventions Show, 107
Irkutsk, 88
Irti, Natalino, 29
ISO 26000, 151
ISPI, 102, 280
Istat, 26
Istria, 72
Itala 61,
Itala, 8, 62, 78, 88, 101, 284
Italcable, 286
Italy, 7, 13, 17, 19, 22, 23, 24, 26, 27, 28, 29, 53, 54, 57, 58, 61, 67, 68, 71, 72, 75, 79, 81, 83, 88, 89, 92, 95, 96, 99, 101, 102, 105, 107, 108, 116, 119, 120, 123, 124, 127, 128, 135, 143, 156, 197, 198, 201, 202, 203, 204, 281, 283, 286, 288, 290
Italian Army, 65
Italian Chamber Orchestra, 141, 152, 186, 191, 296
Italian Committee for Customs Tariffs and Trade Treaties, 95
Italian Grand Prix, 101, 286, 287
Italian Institute for Historical Studies (Istituto italiano per gli studi storici), 123
Italian Motorcycling Championship, 77
Italian Railways, 57
Italian Royal Navy, 285
Ivrea, 22
İzmit, 290

J

Japan, 127, 198
Java, 79, 111, 205, 285
Jávea, 283
jerrycan, 126, 290
John XXIII, Pope, 24
Joint Labs, 163
Jona, Emanuele, 72, 73, 79, 84, 105, 283, 285
Jerusalem, 29

K

Keynes, John Maynard, 99
Kiefer, Anselm, 153
Kirov, 295

Kraków, 107
Kramer (prize), 68, 71
Kramer, Berra, 54, 58
Kureishi, Hanif, 281

L

L'Espresso, 144
La Chimica & l'Industria, 107
La Spezia, 65, 283, 285, 289
La Spezia, San Bartolomeo plant, 72
Lamborghini, 168
Lambretta, 120
Lamm, Lora, 279
Lancia Aurelia B20, 119
Lancia Delta, 142
Lancia Delta S4, 140, 292
Lancia Lambda, 101
Lancia Stratos, 291
Land & Water, 97
Latin America, see also South America, 127
Lazio, 68, 122
Le Figaro, 75
Le Matin, 78
Le Temps, 95
Least Heat-Moon, William, 281
Lecco, 53, 101, 285
Leeuwenhoek, Antony van, 36
Legnano (brand), 287
Leibovitz, Annie, 144, 145, 279, 290
Leonardo da Vinci, 53
Lesbos (island), 36
Lessona, Lodovico, 186
Levi, Primo, 107, 108, 215
Lewis, Carl, 144, 145, 160, 280, 293
linoleum, 75, 123, 216, 283
Lisbon, 144
Lissa, 57, 68
Lombardy, 24, 53, 287
Lombardy Regional Government, 124, 221, 292
Lombardini, Siro, 31
London, 43,79, 95, 96, 102, 284
Long Island, 291
Long P, (small P, roof-shaped P, elongated P), 89, 96, 11, 152, 284, 293, 294
Lorenzetti, Ambrogio, 203
Lotus, 140, 292
Lti, 296
Luftwaffe, 107
Luna Rossa Prada, 148, 297
Luna Rossa, 297

Lupo, Giuseppe, 68
Luraghi, Giuseppe, 119, 151, 288
Lyotard, Jean-François, 196

M

Maastricht (Treaty), 143
Madrid, 72
Maffeis, Carlo, 77,
Magatti, Mauro, 29
Magenta, 53
Maggi, Maurizio, 144
Maggioni, Monica, 92
Magistretti, Vico, 24
Maglione, Luigi, 108
Malaysia, 294
Malerba, Gian Emilio, 77
Manresa, 286
Mantua, 53
Manzi, Riccardo, 195, 199, 279
Maratona delle Dolomiti, 175
Marco Polo Industrial, 296
Mari, Enzo, 24
Marías, Javier, 151, 281
Marinetti, Filippo Tommaso, 75
Martínez, Guillermo, 281
Marzotto, 116
Maserati, 120, 289
Massachusetts Institute of Technology
Microphotonics Center, 148
Massaua-Assab-Perim, 283
Matteotti, Giacomo, 102
Maximoff, Alexander, 105
Mazzini, Giuseppe, 53, 54
McCarthy, Tom, 281
McEwan, Ian, 34
McLaren, 168, 172
McQuade, Walter, 120
Mediobanca, 127
Mediterranean, 36, 41, 72, 101
Mendini, Alessandro, 24, 279
Menghi, Roberto, 126, 290
Mentana, 54
Mercedes, 144, 156, 168
Merloni, 116
Merzagora, Cesare, 95, 116, 288
Messa, Maria Cristina, 8,
Mestre, 143, 292
Metal Manufacturers Ltd, 294
metal belt, 291
Metzeler, 127, 292

Mexico, 27, 148, 150, 157, 289
Mezzanotte, Mario, 140, 291
Michelin, 124, 127, 135, 147
Milan Consortium for the Research and
Development of Optical Switching (CoreCom), 144
Milan Stock Exchange, 285
Milan Bicocca, 137,148,186, 190, 211, 279, 290, 294
Milan-Turin (train line), 53
Milan, 11, 13, 21, 22, 23, 24, 26, 27, 29, 43, 53, 54,
57, 58, 61, 62, 63, 64, 65, 68, 69, 70, 71, 72, 73, 75,
83, 83, 96, 104, 105, 107, 108, 111, 120, 124, 127, 128,
134, 135, 144, 147, 153, 175, 186, 204, 207, 211, 214,
216, 218, 220, 221, 282, 284, 285, 287, 288, 289, 290,
294, 295, 296
    Bovisa, 13
    Brusada, 72, 283
    Central Station, 53, 120, 127, 216
    Duomo, 211
    Fatebenefratelli, 53
    Galleria, 53
    Niguarda, 79, 284
    Palazzo Marino, 53
    Palazzo Reale, 211
    Piazza del Duomo, 53
    Piazza della Scala, 53
    Piazza Duca d'Aosta, 117
    Porta Nuova, 68, 282
    Porta Venezia, 53
    San Vittore, 53
    San Siro stadium, 101
    Via Fabio Filzi, 58
    Via Ponte Seveso, 7, 27, 69, 71, 72, 76, 282, 283,
    288
    Viale Abruzzi, 93
    Viale Sarca, 143, 147
Mille Miglia road race, 119
MIRS™ (Modular Integrated Robotized System),
147, 154, 157, 162, 169, 172, 294
Misani, Pierangelo, 168
Modigliani, Franco, 31,
Moehringer, John Joseph "J.R.", 151, 281
MoMA, Museum of Modern Art of New York, 290
Montale, Eugenio, 19, 119, 151
Montecatini, 24, 119, 120, 288
Montedison, 162
Montemurro, 22
Monti, 119
Monza, 79, 101
Monza Grand Prix, 286, 287
Monza racing circuit, 93, 101
Moplen, 123
Moratti, 119
Morchio, Giuseppe, 162
Moro, Aldo, 24
Moscow, 105
motorbike(s), 7, 127, 171, 290, 291, 292, 296

Motor Show, Fiera Campionaria, Milan,105
Mozart, Wolfgang Amadeus, 186
Mulas, Ugo, 279
Mulgan, Geoff, 39
Munari, Bruno, 24, 126, 278, 289
Munich, 57, 107, 127
Museum of Modern Art of New York, see MoMA
Museum of Rubber of Pirelli Industries, 285
Mussolini, Benito, 95, 102, 108

N

NABA, 295
Nacci, Franco, 288
NAFTA, 197, 288
Naples, 123,153, 204
Napoleon III, 53, 68
Napoleon, Bonaparte, 54
Napoleoni, Claudio, 31
Napolitano, Giorgio, 295
Narni, 75, 283
National Liberation Committee for Northern Italy,
95
National Exposition, 71
Natta, Giulio, 24,105, 107, 108, 113, 123, 162, 204,
287
Navy, 57, 68, 96, 285
Nazzaro, Felice, 101
Nera, river, 75
Nervi, Pier Luigi, 120
Netherlands, the, 42
Neumáticos National Pirelli, 286
New York, 62, 76, 89, 120, 196, 221, 281, 290
New York Marathon, 175
New York Stock Exchange, 102, 112, 286
New Zealand, team, 148, 296
Next MIRS, 147, 152, 154, 157, 169, 172
Niagara, 76
Nobel, prize, 6, 21, 24, 31, 105, 113, 119, 123, 162, 204
Nono, Luigi, 186
Noorda, Bob, 279
Nuremberg, 57
Noticias Pirelli, 280
Nussbaumer, Albert, 287, 288
Nuvolari, Tazio, 93, 101

O

Olivetti (company), 116, 151
Olivetti, Adriano, 17, 22, 23, 26, 204
OM Superba, 101
Oscar Masi, prize, 148
Ovadia, Moni, 152

P

Paginas Pirelli, 280
Pagot, Nino and Toni, 280
Palandri, Fabio, 65
Palaeolithic, 46
Palermo, 204, 289
Palestro, 53
Paolini, Marco, 152
Paris, 14, 57, 58, 71, 75, 79, 99, 101, 178, 284, 287
Paris Courthouse, 178
Paris Commune, 57
Paris Peace Conference, 99
Parisi, Giorgio, 21
Parma, 152, 204
Pasquale, Frank, 29
Patellani, Federico, 279
patent(s), 28, 58, 76, 105, 107, 108, 126, 129, 144, 147, 148, 156, 283, 287, 289
Patrasso, 290
Pavia, 53, 54, 68, 102
Pax System, 147
Peking to Paris (motor race), 7, 27, 62, 76, 88, 284
Peschiera, 53
Pesenti, 119
Petrassi, Goffredo, 186
Petrograd, 95
Peugeot, 284
Pi vendere, 280
Piaggio, 120
Piano, Renzo, 6, 27, 124, 147, 149, 176, 177, 178, 179, 207, 219, 295
Piccolo Teatro, 21, 191, 288, 296
Piccolo Teatro Studio Melato, 191
Piedmont, 17,18, 19, 24
Pigomma, 126, 289
Pirelli World, 146, 280
Pinelli, Ettore, 84
Pirelli & C. Ambiente Spa, 295
Pirelli & C. Eco Technology Spa, 295

Pirelli & C. Spa., 294
Pirelli & C., 56, 58, 61, 68, 127, 285
Pirelli Ambiente Holding, 294
Pirelli Annual Report, 296
Pirelli APAC R&D Open Innovation Center, 150
Pirelli Broadband Solutions, 294, 295
Pirelli Cables Australia, 292
Pirelli Calendar (*The Cal*), 120, 151,
Pirelli Casassa & C., 71
Pirelli Cavi, 162, 298
Pirelli Commission, 135
Pirelli France, 290
Pirelli General Cable Work Ltd, 79, 284
Pirelli HangarBicocca, 152, 153, 295, 296
Pirelli Hellas, 290
Pirelli Holding S.A., 287, 289
Pirelli Labs, 147, 152, 294
Pirelli Ltd, 79, 284, 286
Pirelli Motovelo, 124, 291
Pirelli Photonic Unit, 143
Pirelli Real Estate, 294, 295
Pirelli S.A. Platense, 285
Pirelli skyscraper, 23, 115, 117, 120, 124, 125, 127, 131, 207, 216, 218, 221, 289, 290
Pirelli S.P.A., 288, 291, 292, 294
Pirelli Société Générale, 292
Pirelli tyres, 7, 62, 63, 76, 77, 78, 88, 97, 103, 118, 120, 141, 142, 145, 170, 284, 286, 287, 289
Pirelli Tyre Holding, 127, 293
Pirelli UK Tyres Ltd, 290
Pirelli Venezuela, 293
Pirelli, Alberto, 61, 65, 78, 81, 82, 91, 92, 93, 95, 96, 99, 101, 102, 105, 106, 108, 109, 111, 116, 123, 129, 80, 287, 288, 290, 291
Pirelli, Cecilia, 127
Pirelli, family, 108
Pirelli, Giovanni Battista, 7, 11, 13, 26, 27, 53, 54, 55, 58, 61, 64, 65, 67, 68, 71, 72, 75,76, 79, 81, 92, 102, 281, 282, 286
Pirelli, Giovanni, 288, 291
Pirelli, Leopoldo, 26, 72, 109, 123, 124, 125, 127, 132, 134, 137, 139, 143, 280, 283, 289, 290, 274, 295
Pirelli, Piero, 112,123, 289, 290
Pirelli, Santino, 53
Pirelli. Rivista d'informazione e di tecnica, 119, 221, 280
Pirellone (Pirelli skyscraper), 120, 131, 132, 186, 216, 218, 221
Pizzighettone, 79, 123, 287
plantations, 65, 79, 105, 111, 123, 285
plug-in hybrid vehicles, 297
Politecnico di Milano, 7, 12, 13, 21, 27, 55, 105, 163
Politecnico di Torino, 16, 17, 18, 19, 105, 283
Pollini, Maurizio, 186
Pirelli Industrial Pole, Settimo Torinese, 141, 149, 177, 179, 180, 181, 191

Ponti, Gio, 6, 23, 24, 120, 131, 207, 216, 218, 290
Pope Francis, 26, 202, 204
Popper, Karl, 30
Porsche, 144, 168
Portofino, 295
Premium, technology, 147, 156,
Prestige, 147
Prince Charles, 297
Progetto Italia, 152
Proust, Marcel, 203
Prussia, 54, 57
Ptolemy, 36, 37
Publifoto, 125, 132, 179, 279
Puerto Interior di Silao, 296
Pure Tyre Company, 139, 148, 295

Q

Quasimodo, Salvatore, 19, 119, 151

R

Radetzky, Johann Joseph Franz Karl, 53
raincoats, 27, 58, 68, 74, 76, 282
rally, 28, 140, 142, 171, 291, 292
Rally Argentina, 142
Ravel, Maurice, 94, 157
rayon, 107, 287, 290, 297
Realacci, Ermete, 201
Red Sea, 61, 72, 283
Regio Istituto Tecnico Superiore, Milan (now Politecnico di Milano), 13, 53, 68
Kingdom of Italy, 54
United Kingdom, 101, 119, 123, 124, 143, 203, 291
Reparations Commission of the Peace Conference, 99
Federal Republic of Germany, 123
Roman Republic, 54
synthetic resins, 289
Resta, Ferruccio, 12
EST recognition, 297
Rio de Janeiro, 171
Riva, 54
Riva, Rosa, 53
River Amazon, 78
Rivista mensile del Touring, 76, 77

Rivista Pirelli, see *Pirelli. Rivista d'informazione e di tecnica*
Rogers, Richard, 178
Roiter, Fulvio, 279
Rome, 54, 92, 95, 105, 147, 204
Roma, Villa Ada, 95
Romania, 27
Rome (United States), 147
Ronaldo, 144, 171, 174, 280, 293
Roowy, Stanley Charles, 62, 63
Rossari, Luigi, 123, 288
Rovereto, 79, 95, 123
rubber, 7, 11, 13, 26, 27, 57, 58, 61, 62, 67, 68, 70, 71, 72, 74, 75, 76, 79, 81, 96, 105, 106, 107, 108, 111,113, 123, 124, 127, 151, 156, 157, 168, 171, 187, 202, 205, 216, 218, 219,221, 235, 239, 281, 282, 283, 284, 285, 286, 287, 288, 289, 291, 292, 297
    BUNA synthetic rubber, 105,107
    eraser rubber, 71, 282
    sustainable natural rubber, 297
    synthetic rubber, 105, 107, 118, 113, 123, 235, 287, 288
rubber items, 11, 68, 282, 283, 285, 287
Ruhr, 107
Run Flat, run-flat, 147, 294
Russell Group, 151
Russia, 27, 54, 57, 65, 105, 107, 148, 295
Russian Technologies, 295

S

Saatchi and Saatchi Compton, 170
SACIC, 287
Sacro Convento di San Francesco, Assisi, 202
Salandra, Antonio, 99
Saldini, 54
Salmoiraghi, 54
Sandbach, 123
Sanguineti, Edoardo, 24
Santa Marta Technical Institute, 54
Sap, software, 143
Saracco, Guido, 16
Sarasin, Alfred, 287
Sardinia, 53, 72, 290
Savoy, dynasty, 53
Savoia, Umberto di, 92
Scaletta, Salvatore, 151, 152
Sciascia, Leonardo, 151
Scimmietta Zizì, 126, 289
Schumacher, Michael, 142
SDGs - Sustainable Development Goals, 202

Second World War, 15, 19, 82, 89, 113, 120, 123, 128, 221
Seine, 283
Semelle (tyre), 76, 283
Sereni, Vittorio, 22, 62, 76, 89
Serra, Pietro, 127
Sesto San Giovanni, 108
Settimo Torinese, 18, 27, 117, 123, 124, 141, 147, 149, 152, 157, 177, 179, 180, 181, 186, 187, 191, 207, 219, 290, 295, 296
Sevesetto, 58, 71, 82, 283
Sforni, Davide, 58
Shandong, 151, 295
Shanghai, 43
Sicable (company), Ivory Coast, 292
Sicily, 72, 204, 290
Siemens, 41, 294
Siemens-Martin (furnaces), 54
Siena, 203, 204
Siena, Piazza del Campo, 203
Silao, 296
Silicon Valley, 151
Silverstone, 101, 109
Singapore, 79, 285
Sinigaglia, Serena, 296
Sinisgalli, Leonardo, 19, 22, 23, 119, 151, 288
Slack, 47
Slatina, 295
Società Anonima Cooperativa di Consumo, 63
Società del linoleum (linoleum company), 75, 283
Società italiana per la produzione della gomma sintetica (Italian company for the production of synthetic rubber), 123
Società Italiana Pirelli, 143, 144, 145
Società italiana reti telefoniche interurbane – SIRTI (Italian long-distance telephone network company), 285, 292
Società per la fabbricazione degli oggetti in caucciù, guttaperca e affini (Company for the manufacture of objects in rubber, gutta-percha and similar materials), 283
Società Tessili Artificiali (Artificial Textile Company), 287
Société Française Pirelli, 79, 284
Société Internationale Pirelli, 127, 289, 292
Society for Encouragement of Arts and Crafts, 57
Soldini, Silvio, 280
Government Archive Department, 291
Sormani, Count, 79, 284
Sormani, Maria, 61
Sorocaba, 294
Sottocornola, Giovanni, 75
Sottsass, Ettore, 24
Southampton, 76, 96, 284
Soviet Union, 28, 105, 123, 197
Spain, 62, 65, 76, 101, 119, 123, 283, 285, 286, 287

Spagna, Fabrizio, 140
Spina, 27, 147, 149, 178, 179, 182, 184, 185, 295
Sraffa, Piero, 31
St. Louis, 76
Standard Telephone Cable, 292
steel cord, 296
State University of Milano, 21
Stigler, Augusto, 53
Stiglitz, Joseph, 26
Stuttgart, 57
Stock Exchange, 26, 294, 296
Stone, Sharon, 144, 280
Strehler, Giorgio, 21
Stringher, Bonaldo, 99
South America, 28, 79, 96, 101, 119, 123, 294
Sumatra, 297
Sunderland, 283
superbike, 171, 268
Supreme Economic Council, 99
Suvereto, 292
Sweden, 156, 162
Switzerland, 57, 68, 287
Sydney, 292
Sylos Labini, Paolo, 31
Synergic, 172

T

TAAS (Tyre As A Service), 157
carpets, 71, 76, 282
Teatro alla Scala (La Scala), 53, 61, 72, 282
Teatro degli Arcimboldi, 221
Teatro Franco Parenti, 294
technical items, 72, 282
Tecnocity, 152
Telecom Italia, 147, 148, 294, 295
Telecom, 28, 152
telegraph wires, 58, 71, 282,
Telemachus, 30
Terni, 108, 287
Terzi, Aleardo, 76, 77
rubberised fabrics, 71, 284
Testa, Armando, 155, 280
Textile Show, Rome, 105
The Architectural Forum, 120
The Foreign Service Journal, 102
Tipolitografia Angelo Restelli, 83
Tivoli, 79
Todeschini, Pietro, 103
Todt, Fritz 107
Toleman, 292

Turin-Milan-Genoa ("industrial triangle"), 23
Turin, 17, 18, 29, 53, 72, 75, 107, 148, 194, 290
Total Production Manufacturing, 143
Toulouse-Lautrec, Henri de, 96
Tour de France, 76, 287
Tovaglia, Pino, 119, 121
toys, 27, 123, 282
Treaty of Rome, 24
Tree of Life, 296
Treficable, 292
Trentino, 68
Trojan War, 16
Tronchetti Provera, Marco, 7, 139, 140, 143, 144, 147, 148, 162
Tronchetti Provera, Silvio, 127, 178, 180, 186, 293, 294
TSM, 19
tube(s), 7, 22, 27, 57, 58, 68, 76, 163, 290
Turati, Filippo, 62, 75
Turkey, 27, 120, 123, 290, 292
Türk Pirelli Laştikleri, 290
tyre(s)
 Aerflex, 105
 BUNA, 107
 BS3, 120
 Cinturato, 115, 119, 121, 124, 129, 141, 289-291
 Cinturato CN54, 126
 Cord, 285
 Cyclin, 256
 Dragon, 144
 Elect, 297
 Ercole, 283
 EUFORI@, 294
 Moto, 288
 Motor scooter, 120, 288
 MP7, 292
 N+R, 290
 Neroferrato, 76
 Nuovo Cinturato, 295
 P Zero, 140, 292, 293, 297
 P Zero Corsa, 293
 P Zero System, 143
 P200 Chrono, 143
 P3000, 171, 174
 P3000 Energy, 171
 P5000 Vizzola, 143
 P600, 292
 P6000, 143, 156, 160, 293
 P6000 Powergy, 171
 P7, 140, 291, 292
 P7 Blue, 296
 P7 Corsa Montecarlo, 141
 P700, 292
 P8, 292
 pneumatico da bicicletta, 76
 Powergy, 171
 radial, 124, 129, 140, 289, 292
 Rolle, 121
 Scorpion, 294
 Sempione, 290
 Sigillo Verde, 286
 Stella, 72, 283, 101
 Stella Bianca, 101, 103, 286
 Super Ribassato
 Superflex Cord, 101, 103, 286
 Tipo Milano, 72, 283
tyres for velocipedes, see also tyre(s), 11, 72, 75, 105, 283

U

Ubaldi, Umberto, 98
Uber, 43
Ulysses, 29, 30
Umbria, 75
UNESCO, 213
Ungaretti, Giuseppe, 19, 151
Unicredit, 294
Unioncamere, 202
United States Rubber, 289
United Nations (UN), 151
United States of America, 7, 99, 101, 102, 196, 197, 287, 289
Universal Exposition, Milan, 96, 284, 286
Università Cattolica di Milano, 29, 299
Università degli Studi Milano-Bicocca, 163
University of California, Berkeley, 196
University of Brescia, 29
University of Pavia, 54, 68
University of Trento, 29
University College, London,
Upper Silesia, 107
US Chamber of Commerce, 102
USA, see United States of America
USSR, 24, 291

V

Vado e torno, 118, 120, 280, 290
valves, 7, 27, 58, 71, 282
Valentino Grand Prix, 118
Vanzetti, 102
Varenna, 53, 68
Varese, 172
Vatican, 108
Veca, Salvatore, 29
vehicle(s), 15, 18, 19, 76, 107, 120, 140, 157, 163, 168, 171, 172, 175, 286, 288, 294, 297
Veith Pirelli AG, 290
Veith-Gummiwerke, 123, 290
velocipede(s), 11, 72, 75, 76, 105, 283
velodrome, 287
Venice, 65, 143, 204
Venosta, Giuseppe, 65
Vercurago, 65, 79, 98, 101, 282
Verga, Giovanni, 19, 71
World, 6, 146, 151, 164, 165, 280
Zeitschrift des Vereines Deutscher Ingenieure, 107
Vergani, Orio, 19
Versailles, 99
Versalis, 151
Vespa, 120
Vienna Polytechnic, 29
Vigorelli, Giuseppe, 135
Vilanova i la Geltrù, 76, 283, 287
Villafranca (armistice), 53
Villafranca Tirrena, 123, 290
Visconti di Modrone, Raimondo, 58
Visconti, Ermes, 58
Visconti, Luchino, 23
Vittorini, Elio, 24
Victor Emmanuel II, 95, 108
Vittorio Emmanuel III, 286
Vizzola Ticino, 172, 291
Voltaire, François-Marie Arouet, known as, 204
von der Leyen, Ursula, 202
Voronež, 295

W

Wall Street, 65, 101, 102, 112
watering can, 126
Watson, Albert, 279
Weber, Max, 40
Webern, Anton, 186
Weinberger, David, 45
Wehrmacht, 108, 288
Windsor, Edward, 286
World Championship (Cycling), 120
World Championship (motor racing), 101, 286
World Trade Organisation, 197

X

Xapuri, 202

Y

Yanzhou, 151
Young & Rubicam, 145, 146, 160, 174, 279, 293

Z

Zanussi, 116
Ziegler, Karl, 123
Zoom, 40
Zucchi, Onorato, 58
Zysman, John, 196, 197

FONDAZIONE PIRELLI

FONDAZIONE PIRELLI

ACKNOWLEDGEMENTS

Our special thanks go to the Pirelli
Research & Development Department

Marco Arimondi
Simone Barzaghi
Damiano Leonardo Belluzzo
Mauro Callipo
Paola Caracino
Guido Carlo Carosio
Giancarlo Casarin
Alessandro Marciano
Dario Marrafuschi
Paolo Massimino
Michele Modugno
Francesco Parazzoli
Alessandro Pinto
Tino Redaelli
Andrea Ronchi
Alberto Rustici
Marco Sbrosi
Samuel Soldati
Diego Speziari
Ugo Tartaglino
Davide Turco
Andrea Vergani

We also wish to thank

Francesca Bianchi
Alex Calcatelli
Giuseppe Festinese
Laura Gorna
Monica Lancini
Roberto Pacilio
Denise Petriccione
Maria Paola Romeo
Chiara Stangalino
Simon Turner

THINKING AHEAD
PIRELLI: 150 YEARS OF INDUSTRY, INNOVATION AND CULTURE
EDITED BY FONDAZIONE PIRELLI

Graphic design and layout
Leftloft

Editing
Maria Giulia Montessori
Elisabetta Righes

Copy-editing
Anna Albano

Translations
Paolo Maria Noseda
Leslie A. Ray (Language Consulting
Congressi – Milan)

© 2022 Pirelli & C. S.p.A.
© 2022 Fondazione Pirelli
© 2022 Marsilio Editori® S.p.A.

First edition May 2022
ISBN 978-88-297-1623-4
www.marsilioeditori.it

Available through ARTBOOK | D.A.P.
75 Broad Street, Suite 630
New York, NY 10004
www.artbook.com

Cover
Control room of the static driving
simulator. The tester is about to take
his seat in the car to begin the tests,
2021, photo Carlo Furgeri Gilbert

Images
© 2022 Pirelli & C. S.p.A.
© Federico Caputo / Alamy Stock
Photo (p. 38)
© Luca D'Agostino (pp. 140, 298)
© Eleonora Ferretti (pp. 201, 300)
© Renato Guttuso, by Siae 2022
(p. 290)
© Carlo Furgeri Gilbert (pp. 149,
166–167, 181, 185, 226–229, 231–235,
237–253, 255–259, 261–269, 271–277)
© Stefano Goldberg (p. 179)
© Kheng Ho Toh / Alamy Stock Photo
(p. 44)
© Annalena McAfee (pp. 34, 301)
© Lorenzo Palmieri (p. 153)
© Vitalij Sova / Alamy Stock Photo
(p. 35)

The images reproduced, unless
otherwise stated, come from the
Archivio Storico Pirelli preserved
in the Fondazione Pirelli.

Colour reproduction
Studio Pointer S.r.l.,
Mogliano Veneto (Treviso)

Printing
Grafiche Zanini S.r.l.,
Anzola dell'Emilia (Bologna)

for
Marsilio Editori® S.p.A.
in Venezia